Deciphering IP Law and Its Conflict and Complementarity with Competition Law

This book introduces a general theory of intellectual property (IP) law, highlighting its importance and relevance in addressing complex IP issues in the digital economy, which often intersect with competition law.

The book argues for the need for a unified theory of IP to elevate it as a discipline in its own right, while recognizing the diversity and nuance of IP laws. It explores how such a theory can address the challenges posed by the knowledge economy, the platform economy, the data-driven economy, and generative AI. The book views IP as a market regulatory mechanism designed to remedy market failures in public goods by providing sufficient protection to incentivize human creation and its operation and sharing across societies. It also emphasizes the need for competition law when IP oversteps its legitimate boundaries and becomes the source of other market failures. The study critically examines the TRIPS Agreement and many established stereotypes of IP theories and regimes. It offers a global perspective with a special focus on Asian considerations.

The title will be essential reading for scholars, students, practitioners, and policymakers interested in regulatory reform and the evolving landscape of intellectual property law and its interaction with competition law in the digital age.

Kung-Chung Liu is a professor of law at Renmin University of China and Singapore Management University. He is also an adjunct chair professor at Shandong University, China. His research focuses on IP law, competition law, and telecommunication and broadcast law with a geographic emphasis on Asia.

Deciphering IP Law and Its Conflict and Complementarity with Competition Law

Global Norms Against Asian Context

Kung-Chung Liu

Routledge
Taylor & Francis Group
LONDON AND NEW YORK

This publication was supported by the fund for building world-class universities (disciplines) of Renmin University of China.

First published in English 2025
by Routledge
4 Park Square, Milton Park, Abingdon, Oxon OX14 4RN

and by Routledge
605 Third Avenue, New York, NY 10158

Routledge is an imprint of the Taylor & Francis Group, an informa business

British Library Cataloguing-in-Publication Data
A catalogue record for this book is available from the British Library

ISBN: 978-1-032-97853-6 (hbk)
ISBN: 978-1-032-98255-7 (pbk)
ISBN: 978-1-003-59776-6 (ebk)

DOI: 10.4324/9781003597766

Typeset in Times New Roman
by Apex CoVantage, LLC

Contents

Preface

I have worked on and around the theme of the present volume in the last two decades. I am convinced and therefore argue that a general theory of intellectual property (IP) law is indispensable for IP to be a stand-alone discipline and guide us through tumultuous IP issues of knowledge economy, platform economy, data-driven economy, generative AI, and whatnot. It also has the merits of streamlining IP, making it more accessible to laymen, liberating it from disconnected silos for IP professionals, and it can dissolve many conflicts between IP and competition into complementarity. However, it is a humbling endeavor as IP laws are so diverse and driven and shaped by many conflicting interests. Any general theory risks overgeneralizing and neglecting some fine nuances.

Looking back, it was the bestseller by Joseph Stiglitz *Making Globalization Work* (2006 Penguin) I read in the winter of 2008 when visiting Queen Mary University at the invitation of the British Academy that opened my eyes for me. Its relentless criticism against the TRIPS Agreement has got me thinking that we as IP specialists might be so wrong about IP norms and emboldened me to think critically and globally and at the same time factor in national differences. Therefore, the present book is written with universal concerns, not limited to any one specific area of IP or any particular jurisdiction. However, it is with a bit more emphasis on Asian features and considerations that contrast with other norm-setting economies.

I have toiled and struggled to finish the book for more than two years.

> The composition of this book has been for the author a long struggle of escape . . . a struggle of escape from habitual modes of thought and expression. The ideas which are here expressed so laboriously are extremely simple and should be obvious. The difficulty lies, not in the new ideas, but in escaping from the old ones.
>
> John Maynard Keynes,
> *The General Theory of Employment, Interest, and Money*

However, all good work must come to an end, especially when macular degeneration set in which was followed by excruciating pain caused by dengue fever caused.

If, in all likelihood, the book ends up being yet another failed attempt to holistically grasp the mansion of IP, my efforts should be all the reason more for latecomers to keep trying.

Here I'd like to thankfully acknowledge the following institutions and persons for the completion of this monograph: Remin University's book project with Routledge has pushed me through all obstacles, after almost a five-year delay. YPH School of Law, Singapore Management University generously granted me a six-month sabbatical leave to start the actual writing of the book. Max Planck Institute for Innovation and Competition, my alma mater, has always opened its doors to me, my quests, and inquisitions during my writing. IPKM at the Maastricht University has facilitated my many returns to MPI among other numerous supports.

Professors David Llewelyn, Reto Hilty, Mark Findley (IP for the future!), Heinz Goddar, Christopher Heath, Loy Weeloon, Masabumi Suzuki, Yoshiyuki Tamura, Lim Heng Gee, Byungil Kim, Robert Merges ("what author isn't biased"), Anselm Sanders, Annete Kur, Ansgar Ohly, Matthias Leistner, Lin Xiuqin, Liu Yinliang, Yang Ming, Cui Guobin, Yu Xiang, Li Yahong, Jyh-An Lee, Haochen Sun, Su-Hua Lee, Hsiao-Fen Hsu, Wei Lizhou, Li Yanbing, He Tianxiang, Zhang Haoran, Liu Jianchen, Jakkrit Kuanpoth, Ichiro Nakayama, and Titus Levi have graciously lent me illuminating inspirations. Justices Richard Arnold (the UK), Prathiba Singh (India), Sutatip Yuthayotin (Thailand), and He Jun (the PRC) have provided me with their writing and/or decisions. Dr. Lu Tian, Prashant Reddy, Zhang Weiyu, Li Rui, Marco Mazzeschi, Wang Bin, Xin-Yi Lin, and especially Dr. Zhao Xinyang are thanked for their various help, so is Dr. Robert Tian for reminding me of the importance of epiphany.

Given the fast-changing nature of IP laws and regimes covered, this book will only refer to the latest terms, nomenclatures, and numbering (such as articles or sections) to maintain updates and consistency and avoid confusion. For example, the Taiwan IP Court was set up in 2008 and renamed as Taiwan IP and Commercial Court with expanded mandates in July 2021. Taiwan IP and Commercial Court will then be used throughout the book. All online materials have been checked as of July 2024 and their access dates will therefore not be individually indicated in the footnotes.

The book is dedicated to the late

Professor Liu Chuntian (1949–2023)
Renmin University of China—a great mind of his time!

Part I

A General Theory of IP, IP Code, Market Competition, and Competition Law

1 The Prelude

1. The Merchant of Venice: A Metaphor for the Conflict Between the Exercise of IP and Competition Law

The famous play "The Merchant of Venice" by William Shakespeare written in the 16th century is about a Christian merchant in Venice Antonio defaulted on a large loan provided by a Jewish moneylender, Shylock. The loan was made under the condition that if Antonio was unable to repay it at the specified date, Shylock may take a pound of Antonio's flesh "Nearest his heart." Shylock adamantly refused any compensation and insisted on one pound of flesh. Portia, disguised as a man, honored the contract but played on specific performance and challenged that the contract allowed Shylock to remove only the *flesh* but not the blood of Antonio. Thus, if Shylock were to shed one drop of Antonio's blood, his lands and goods are confiscated under Venetian laws. She also warned Shylock that he must cut precisely one pound of flesh, nor less nor more: "if the scale do turn, But in the estimation of a hair, Thou diest and all thy goods are confiscate."[1]

This is a story about how much one should be allowed to hold on to one's contract without making it inhumanly cruel and unmerciful. It is at the same time also an inspiration of how wise people can defeat draconian contracts from within the contract.

In the commercial realities of our times, there are many similar dilemmas reoccurring, not only in the name of tangible property ("To have the due and forfeit of my bond") but also intangible property, such as IP. IP is one of the key elements of market competition in more developed economies, especially since the advent of a knowledge economy. The exercise of IP intersects with proliferating competition law that aims at keeping market competition free and fair, which leads to repeated disputes and conflicts. We are constantly being tormented by the question of whether we should honor IP-related contracts and tolerate the exercise of IPRs at all costs, or whether we should find ways to avoid or mitigate injustice resulting

1 Shakespeare, W. (1952). The Merchant of Venice (act IV). In Harrison, G.B. (Ed.), *Shakespeare the Complete Works* (pp. 606, 607). Harcourt, Brace & World.

DOI: 10.4324/9781003597766-2

from those contracts and IP exercises. The following cases and disputes exemplify these conundrums.

2. In the Realm of Trademark

To many people's surprise, trademark rights intersect with competition law in a variety of ways, ranging from the trademarkable subject matters, protectable functions of a trademark, use of others' trademarks in advertisement, the contracting out of limitations to trademark rights, and the exhaustion of trademark rights. The additional point of contention where brand owners impede the business of second-hand dealers of their used goods will be separately treated in Chapter 11, as it has other dimensions.

2.1. Trademarkable Signs? LEGO Trying to Trademark Once Patented Objects

LEGO, the famous interlocking toy bricks, was invented by Hilary Page in 1939 and granted several UK patents for the technical feature of being "manufactured to an exacting degree of precision. When two pieces are engaged, they must fit firmly, yet be easily disassembled," without the intervention of parents of toy-playing children. Those patents covered a brick (LEGO brick) which possessed the infra dimensions and circular studs:[2]

Long after the patents have expired and LEGO bricks attained market recognition, its owner filed in 1996 an application for a community trademark with EUIPO, inter alia, to be applied to "games and playthings" goods in Class 28 of the Nice Agreement concerning the International Classification of Goods and Services.

The trademark in respect of which registration was sought is the red three-dimensional sign:

It is evident that the shape of the LEGO brick has become distinctive as a result of market popularity and wide use, and it is therefore a sign capable of distinguishing its products from other similar products from other sources. However, can trademark law be used to protect technical solutions or functional characteristics of a product, which is the reserved turf for patent protection? May undertakings use trademark law to "perpetuate, indefinitely, exclusive rights relating to technical solutions?" More specifically, is the shape of the LEGO brick necessary to obtain a technical result ("they must fit firmly yet be easily disassembled"). If so, can it still be registered as a trademark?[3]

2 See https://en.wikipedia.org/wiki/Lego

3 OHIM decided that the shape of the LEGO brick had acquired distinctive character in the European Union and did not consist exclusively of the shape of goods which is necessary to obtain a technical result and registered it as trademark in 1999. An invalidation application was filed against that mark, arguing that its registration was contrary to the absolute grounds for refusal. By decision of July 30, 2004, the Cancellation Division declared the mark invalid. The decision was upheld by the Grand Board of Appeal of OHIM, the General Court and CJEU (C-48/09 September 14, 2010).

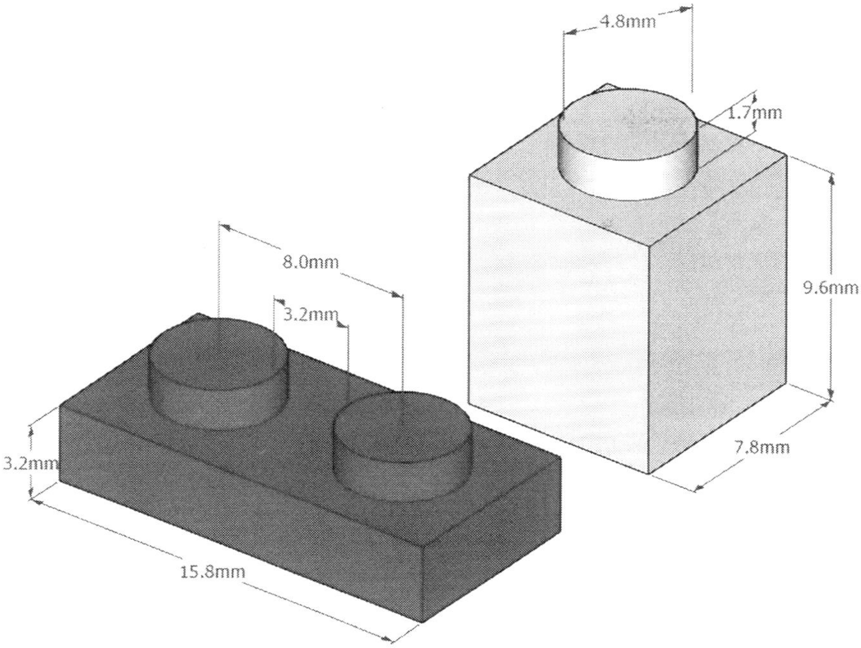

Figure 1.1 Two LEGO pieces showing they must fit firmly yet be easily disassembled.

Figure 1.2 A LEGO piece.

2.2. *Protectable Functions of a Trademark: Investment Function of Mitsubishi?*

One of the major differences that trademark has vis-à-vis patent and copyright is that while the latter two are themselves the reason for their legal protection and have relatively fixed scope of protection, the scope of trademark protection depends on what functions it actually possesses as a result of commercial use of it and is not fixed, which can grow or shrink.[4]

In the US, the Ninth Circuit subscribed to a theory that confined a trademark's protection to source identification function to favor a free and competitive economy:

> The rule rests upon the traditionally accepted premise that the only legally relevant function of a trademark is to impart information as to the source or sponsorship of the product. . . . The courts, however, have generally confined legal protection to the trademark's source identification function for reasons grounded in the public policy favouring a free, competitive economy.[5]

In contrast, the CJEU in the Mitsubishi case recognizes the investment function of a trademark which renders trademark holders the right to first put the concerned goods on the market in the EEA (the initial marketing right).[6] CJEU considers that the owner of a trademark is entitled to oppose a third party, who removed all the signs identical to that mark and affixed other signs on products, without its consent, with a view to importing them or trading them in the EEA where they have never yet been marketed. Consequently, Mitsubishi was deprived of controlling the initial marketing of said goods in the EEA and was unable to retain customers by the quality of its goods. This affects the functions of investment and advertising of the mark.

How shall we then decide what functions a trademark actually has?

2.3. *Use of Others' Trademarks in Advertisement*

2.3.1. *"Sorry Sony!" Comparative Advertisement*

Comparative advertisement is an advertisement in which the advertiser compares their products and services with those of others. It has strong eye-catching effects. In Taiwan in the 1980s, the then-new market entrant Proton TV promoted a provocative ad with a slogan "Sorry Sony!" followed by a list of comparisons between the two. This is of course annoying for Sony. However, can Sony stop this by resorting to its trademark rights, alleging the likelihood of dilution of its reputation by blurring consumers' immediate association with/linkage to Sony?

2.3.2. *Google's Keyword Advertisement*

Search engines, led by Google, started its business as a provider of free search services. With the accumulated searches comes invaluable big data for Google to

4 Kur, A., Bomhard, V. & Albrecht, F. (2020). *MarkenG·UMV—Markengesetz Verordnung über die Unionsmarke* (3. Auflage, p. 118). C.H. Beck.

5 *Smith v. Chanel, Inc.*, 402 F.2d 566 (1968).

6 CJEU C 129/17 ((Second Chamber) decided on 25 July 2018).

use for free. Search engines then deploy the Keyword Suggestion Tool actively to suggest advertisers "buy" and "use" certain keywords indicated by big data as the popularly sought words. The tool further optimizes such use. As it often happens, certain keywords are also well-known marks of others. Can search engines conduct keyword ad business without any consideration of the fact that these keywords are someone else's well-known trademarks? Can search engines treat them as free as any meaningless digital bites (only machine-readable) for everyone, including advertisers and Google to use? Can search engines argue in defense of trademark infringement that they have not "used" the searched trademark in the course of trade? But the competitors of the trademark owners, and therefore no trademark infringement?[7]

2.4. Contracting Out Limitations on Trademark Rights: Branded Lift Manufacturers Refused to Sell Spare Parts

In Singapore, third-party lift maintenance contractors faced difficulties obtaining spare parts of different lift brands from the original lift manufacturers, making it impossible for them to compete in tenders for lift maintenance called by town councils, where multiple brands of lifts are installed in each Housing and Development Board (HDB) estate.

Complaints were filed with the Competition and Consumer Commission of Singapore (CCCS), whose investigations into the matter revealed restrictive trade practices that could have amounted to refusals by a dominant or sole supplier to supply essential products that cannot be otherwise obtained. Which were potentially in breach of the no abuse of dominance prohibition of the SG Competition Act (section 47). Three suppliers of particular brands of lift spare parts provided commitments to the CCCS to supply these products to third-party maintenance contractors in Singapore at FRAND rates to enable the latter to more effectively compete for lift maintenance contracts. This also allowed town councils to call for a single tender for lift maintenance services that covered a range of different lift brands, rather than having to contract with multiple parties representing different lift brands.

However, the commitments made were qualified by the following conditions: The purchaser undertakes not to reverse engineer or otherwise modify the purchased lift spare parts; the purchaser acknowledges that suppliers hold various proprietary trademarks, service marks, certification marks, logos, and other images, none of which may be used by the purchaser in any way without the written permission of the supplier, even if such uses would otherwise be considered legally permissible or fair use.[8]

7 For the actual court case and decision in Taiwan see Liu, K.-C. (2022). *IP Laws and Regimes in Major Asian Economies—Combing Through Thousand Threads of IP to Peace in Asia* (pp. 61–65). Routledge.

8 CCCS Investigates Restrictive Industry Practices in the Supply of Lift Spare Parts in HDB Estates (July 14, 2016), at: https://www.cccs.gov.sg/media-and-consultation/newsroom/media-releases/

Questions arise, as the purchaser of the spare parts is the lawful property right owner of these products and should be entitled to use them as they see fit, in particular, reverse engineering, the humanly most natural thing to do for anyone who comes in contact with technical matters. Isn't the commitment not to reverse engineer the spare parts too restrictive to be legally binding even if it is under the aegis of CCCS? In addition, under such a contractual restriction, the purchaser would not be able to make referential use of the brand names/marks of the lift spare parts that he has acquired when advertising his lift maintenance services without the written permission of the lift spare parts supplier, even it is permissible under Singapore's trademark laws.[9] Should such a contractual restriction that carves out limitations on trademark rights be allowed? Even at the expense of hampered competition on the secondary market, or lessened competition on the primary market, as third-party lift maintenance contractors being prevented from uplifting itself from maintaining lifts to manufacturing lifts?

2.5. *The Exhaustion of Trademark Rights*

2.5.1. *Parallel-Import of Genuine Products as They Are*

Owners of well-known trademarks would understandably try to maximize their profits by prohibiting intra-brand competition via parallel import of their genuine products into the markets where they have an exclusive agent. The interests of the exclusive agent in the respective national market would lie in banning any free-riding of their branding efforts and parallel importers being the primary suspect. The interests of parallel importers (traders) lie in the free import and advertising of the parallel-imported products as they are. Most importantly, the interests of consumers demand both price and quality competition of their preference. Do or should trademark owners enjoy a right to import? Does such a right prevail over consumers' interests? How to balance these conflicting/competing interests?

2.5.2. *Debranding and Rebranding of Parallel-Imported Genuine Products*

Some parallel importers undertake to debrand, modify, and rebrand (by putting their own logo on the goods) parallel-imported products out of their business

investigation-of-lift-spare-parts-industry-em-services. It is therefore not entirely correct to state that "The CCCS has not intervened in any IP case thus far," as asserted by Ng-Loy, W. (2021). *Law of Intellectual Property of Singapore* (3rd ed.), 2.4.6. Sweet & Maxwell.

9 Section 28(1)(c) of Singapore's Trade Marks Act provides that a person does not infringe a registered trade mark when "(c) he uses the trade mark to indicate the intended purpose of goods (in particular as accessories or spare parts) or services, and such use is in accordance with honest practices in industrial or commercial matters." For criticism of CCCS's decision see Ong, B. (2019). FRAND as a legal concept at the intersection between competition law and intellectual property law–The road ahead for Singapore? In Liu, K.-C. & Hilty, R. (Eds.), *SEPs, SSOs and FRAND—Asian and Global Perspectives on Fostering Innovation in Interconnectivity* (pp. 301–328). Routledge.

considerations. This is what happened when some European companies acquired from a company within the Mitsubishi group, outside the EEA, Mitsubishi forklift trucks. They then removed from those trucks all the signs, identification plates and serial numbers of the Mitsubishi marks (debranding), made the necessary modifications to comply with EU standards, and finally put on their own signs (rebranding). Once done, those trucks are imported and marketed both within and outside the EEA. Can the owner of the trademark Mitsubishi oppose such debranding and rebranding by a third party who has legitimately parallel imported these forklift trucks in the EEA?

3. In the Realm of Geographic Indication

Famous geographic indications (GIs) have certain appeals that not only attract purchases but also transaction premiers. Owners of cherished GIs guard zealously against any freeride. Following the Paris Convention, Articles 22 and 23 of the TRIPS Agreement also provide protection to GIs. What's striking about the TRIPS Agreement is that it provides absolute protection to GIs for wine and spirits, even where the true origin of the goods is indicated or the GI is used in translation or accompanied by expressions such as "kind," "type," "style," "imitation," or the like, and there is no likelihood of confusion.[10] One wonders if the TRIPS Agreement overstepped its legitimate boundary by offering such absolute protection to wine and spirits, and why wine and spirits alone.

In Italy, the Ferrari winery has become a legend whose founder, Giulio Ferrari, dreamed of creating sparkling wine in Trentino (an autonomous province in Italy's far north, renowned for its mountains, such as the Dolomites, which are part of the Alps) capable of competing with the best French Champagnes. He allegedly has painstakingly followed all the techniques of making Champagnes.[11] What if it decided, knowing that to call his sparkling wine "Champagne-styled" is prohibited by Article 23(1) of the TRIPS Agreement, to label on the bottles that it was "inspired by Champagne?" Would they be infringing the GI of the Champagne region?[12]

10 Article 23(1) (Additional Protection for Geographical Indications for Wines and Spirits) of the TRIPS Agreement provides: Each Member shall provide the legal means for interested parties to prevent use of a geographical indication identifying wines for wines not originating in the place indicated by the geographical indication in question or identifying spirits for spirits not originating in the place indicated by the geographical indication in question, even where the true origin of the goods is indicated or the geographical indication is used in translation or accompanied by expressions such as "kind," "type," "style," "imitation" or the like.

11 See Cantine Ferrari. (2023). *Retrospective of Passion*, at: https://www.ferraritrento.com/en/history

12 Italy enacted in 2003 legislation that targets "Italian sounding" products that falsely claim to be Italian. Recently, the Italian industry minister resorted to this law to criticize the calling of Alfa Romeo's first fully electric vehicle made in Poland "Milano," the iconic northern Italian city as misleading consumers. See Italy government chides Stellantis over Polish-made Alfa Romeo 'Milano' Reuters 12 April 2024, at: https://www.reuters.com/business/autos-transportation/

4. In the Realm of Copyright

4.1. Microsoft Refused to Help Compatibility With the De Facto Standard Software

There was a period when software companies competed to dominate the personal computer operating system market. Soon Microsoft (MS) won dominance with its MS-DOS in the mid-1980s, later the Windows line of operating systems, the Microsoft 365, etc. Sun Microsystems, which supplies, in particular, servers and server operating systems, created the Java programming language and the Solaris operating system among others. Sun, like other developers of operating systems, needed interface information from MS in a timely fashion in order to be accepted by the market (network effect, as no one will buy any product that is not compatible with the dominant MS) and made such a request but was rejected by from MS.[13]

Is MS's refusal to license one of its most vocal antagonists for interoperability legally sound as a normal (non) exercise of its copyright? Or it should be incumbent on MS to be concerned about the social costs caused by its refusal, and obliged to help its competitors under FRAND-compliant terms and conditions, as every competitor needs to do its reverse engineering on MS' operating system to be compatible with MS?[14]

---

italy-government-chides-stellantis-over-polish-made-alfa-romeo-milano-2024-04-11. The episode highlights how GI can be misused.

13 Sun wrote to MS on September 15, 1998: We believe it is in the industry's best interest that applications written to execute on Solaris be able to seamlessly communicate via COM and/or Active Directory (technologies defining the data structure and services that provide organization, management, and security of accounts and resources in a MS network) with the Windows operating systems and/or with Windows-based software. MS should include a reference implementation and such other information as is necessary to insure, without reverse engineering, that COM objects and the complete set of Active Directory technologies will run in full compatible fashion on Solaris. We think it necessary that such information be provided for the full range of COM objects as well as for the full set of Active Directory technologies currently on the market. It is necessary that such information be provided in a timely manner and on a continuing basis for COM objects and Active Directory technologies which are to be released to the market in the future. On October 6, 1998, MS wrote back to Sun and refused its request. Cited from Judgement of the EU Court of First Instance (Grand Chamber) Case T-201/04 (September 17, 2007).

14 Sun filed a complaint against MS with the EC in 1998. In 2003, the EC ordered MS to offer both a version of Windows without Windows Media Player and the information necessary for competing networking software to interact fully with Windows desktops and servers. The decision was upheld by the EU Court of First Instance Case T-201/04. MS announced that it will demand 0.4% of the revenue in patent-licensing royalties, only from commercial vendors of interoperable software and promised not to seek patent royalties from individual open-source developers. The interoperability information alone is available for a one-time fee of €10,000, see https://en.wikipedia.org/wiki/Microsoft_Corp._v._Commission

4.2. JASRAC Blanket Licensed Music Copyrights

For the ease of management collecting societies world over issue the so-called blanket license that allows the licensees to use the entire repertoire irrespective of whether they make such use. In Japan, the collecting society JASRAC adopted such a mechanism and calculated copyright royalty on an across-the-board price rather than based on actual use. However, new emerging collecting societies felt this practice of restricting market competition would be preferred by users over their "use-as-you-go" approach. A complaint was filed with the JFTC.[15]

Does the exercise of copyright need to take into account its effects on market competition? And why?

4.3. RecordTV Streamed MediaCorp's Over-the-Air Broadcast

The rise of the internet and its ubiquity have switched many of the traditional over-the-air broadcasting to online streaming. In the US, Aereo provides a system to its fee-paying subscribers which consists of thousands of small antennas and other equipment housed in a centralized warehouse. A server tunes an antenna, which is dedicated to the use of one subscriber alone, to the broadcast carrying the selected show. A transcoder translates the signals received by the antenna into data that can be transmitted over the Internet. A server saves the data in a subscriber-specific folder on Aereo's hard drive and begins streaming the show to the subscriber's screen once several seconds of programming have been saved. The streaming continues, a few seconds behind the over-the-air broadcast, until the subscriber has received the entire show.

RecordTV in Singapore provided complimentary recording services to users who had pre-registered with them on their website. Subscribers of this online service were able to request certain MediaCorp's free-to-air TV programs to be recorded by RecordTV for their later viewing. Once a request is received from a subscriber, RecordTV's internet DVR ("iDVR") system identifies the relevant program and makes a copy of it at the time of its broadcast. Thereafter, the recorded program is stored on RecordTV's online servers for a period of 15 days, during which time the subscriber (end-user) can log on to RecordTV's website, gain access to the requested recording and view it at his leisure. After 15 days, the recorded program is deleted by the plaintiff.

15 On February 27, 2009, the JFTC ruled against JASRAC's blanket licensing practice, finding it effectively preventing other collecting societies from entering the market, bordering private monopolization. The decision was though overturned by the Appeal Board of the JFTC on June 12, 2012, yet confirmed on appeal by the Tokyo High Court (decided on November 1, 2013) and the Supreme Court (Third Petty Bench decided on April 28, 2015, Minshu Vol. 69, No. 3, p. 518). For analysis see Ando, K. (2019). Blanket licenses of music copyrights for broadcasting were found to be private monopolization in Japan. In Liu, K-C. (Ed.), *Annotated Leading Copyright Cases in Major Asian Jurisdictions* (pp. 136–152). City University of HK Press.

While the US Supreme Court found Aereo's service copyright infringing and Aereo filed for bankruptcy as a result,[16] the Court of Appeal in Singapore overturned the High Court's decision favoring Mediacorp[17] and determined that RecordTV did not infringe Mediacorp's rights to duplicate or publicly communicate its programs, nor did it authorize its users to do so,[18] and RecordTV's founder was subsequently named Young Global Leader by the World Economic Forum.[19] Which one of the two approaches is more conducive to the introduction of new business models enabled by new technologies and therefore new competition? And is this worthy of consideration when determining the legitimate boundary of exercise of one's copyright?

4.4. *Google Made Every Book Searchable Online*

In an ambitious effort to make every book searchable online, Google scanned the full text of books and magazines and stored it in its digital database, through the Google Books Partner Program with publishers and authors, and through the Library Project with Google's library partners. The Google Books initiative has the potential to offer unprecedented access to human knowledge and promote the democratization of knowledge.

However, copyright could stand in Google's way. Did Google need copyright holders' permission to engage in the scanning and display of snippets of their books, which is technologically feasible and socially desirable? What damages did authors suffer as a result of Google's act?[20] Why should authors care about democratizing knowledge?

4.5. *Goole Copied 11,500 Lines From Oracle's Software*

Oracle owns copyright in Java SE, a computer platform that uses the popular Java programming language developed by Sun. In 2005, Google acquired Android and sought to build a new Android software platform for mobile devices. To allow

16 The US Supreme Court found in a six to three decision that Aereo's service violated copyright law, see *American Broadcasting Cos., Inc. v. Aereo, Inc.*, 573 U.S. 431 (2014). On November 21, 2014, Aereo filed for bankruptcy and was later purchased by the DVR company TiVo for $1 million in March 2015. See https://en.wikipedia.org/wiki/American_Broadcasting_Cos.,_Inc._v._Aereo,_Inc.

17 *RecordTV Pte Ltd v. MediaCorp TV Singapore Pte Ltd* (2010 2 SLR 152).

18 *RecordTV Pte Ltd v. MediaCorp TV Singapore Pte Ltd* (2011) 1 SLR 830.

19 See Wikipedia: InstantTV, at: https://en.wikipedia.org/wiki/InstantTV.

20 In the US, the Authors Guild and Association of American Publishers separately sued Google in 2005 for copyright infringement. After legal back and forth for ten years, the Second Circuit Court of Appeals ruled unanimously on October 16, 2015, that Google's library book scanning project is protected by fair use and does not constitute copyright infringement. In April 2017, *Wired* reported that there were only a few Google employees working on the project, and new books were still being scanned, but at a significantly lower rate. It commented that the decade-long legal battle had caused Google to lose its ambition. See Rosenberg, S. (2017). How Google book search got lost. *WIRED*, at: https://www.wired.com/2017/04/how-google-book-search-got-lost/

the millions of programmers familiar with the Java programming language to work with its new platform, Google first sought license from Oracle, and after being rejected, copied roughly 11,500 lines of code from the Java SE program, virtually all the declaring code needed to call up hundreds of different tasks. Those 11,500 lines, however, are only 0.4% of the entire Application Programming Interface (API) at issue,[21] which consists of 2.86 million total lines. Oracle sued Google for copyright infringement and Google resorted to transformative fair use defense.

Here copyrighted software becomes an indispensable element of market competition. Can Oracle be allowed to refuse to license to its competitor Google? Do we only have a zero-sum choice between either free fair use (0) or copyright infringement (100)? Or can we opt for a middle ground, such as fared use via compulsory license? Which way is fairer?

4.6. Google and OpenAI Use Others' Works to Develop Generative AI

The genesis of generative AI can at least be traced back to IBM's Watson, a computer system introduced in about 2011 and capable of answering questions posed in natural language (unstructured data, which takes up 80% of data). ROSS began in 2014 at the University of Toronto as a student-built entrant in a cognitive-computing competition staged by IBM to develop applications for its Watson computer—then famous for having won Jeopardy! ROSS was touted as the robot lawyer of the future! Denton, the biggest law firm on earth, made ROSS one of its earliest investments, NextLaw Labs. However, Ross was shut down on January 31, 2021, as a lawsuit against it by Thomson Reuters. However, the company vows to continue its legal battle, using insurance funds to pay its litigation costs. "The company will continue as a going concern so that the facts at the heart of this lawsuit are brought to light and so that Westlaw's tactics—using litigation as a weapon and stifling competition—do not succeed," the statement said.[22]

Then came the ChatGPT developed by OpenAI and more importantly with the financial support of the deep-pocked Microsoft. Google launched its version of generative AI product: Gemini. Generative AI companies need to train their chatbots by feeding millions of existent works, often without asking for a copyright license. These companies later become competitors of copyright holders of those works and are poised to make huge profits at the costs of the latter. Following other similar lawsuits,[23] The New York Times sued OpenAI and Microsoft for copyright infringement on December 26, 2023. The suit does not include an exact monetary demand. But the NYT says the defendants should be held responsible for "billions of dollars in statutory and actual damages" related to the "unlawful copying and

21 An API allows programmers to call upon prewritten computing tasks for use in their own programs.

22 See Ambrogi, B. (2020). Legal research company ROSS to shut down under pressure of Thomson Reuters' lawsuit. *LawSites*, at: https://www.lawnext.com/2020/12/legal-research-company-ross-to-shut-down-under-pressure-of-thomson-reuters-lawsuit.html

23 For example, a class-action lawsuit was filed against OpenAI and against Meta respectively in July 2023, see https://www.nytimes.com/2023/07/10/arts/sarah-silverman-lawsuit-openai-meta.html

use of The Times's uniquely valuable works." It also calls for the companies to destroy any chatbot models and training data that use copyrighted material from The Times.[24]

Is using copyrighted material to train machines or for machine learning purposes an act of use of work in the traditional sense, as it is non-consumptive, not for human enjoyment, and therefore copyright infringement? Or is it covered by transformative fair use defense?

4.7. Dallas Buyers Club Sent "Pay Up or Else" Warning Letters

Copyrighted works are often being used by numerous individual users around the globe, in addition to commercial users. Copyright holders are sometimes tempted to sue individual users, either to make an example out of them to deter others, or even extract quick and sometimes handsome damages from them, often with the help of statutory damages or criminal punishment. This can be a very controversial tactic.

In the US, from 2003 to 2008 RIAA expanded its legal assault to target internet users and has filed, settled, or threatened legal actions against at least 30,000 individuals. However, suing music fans has proven to be an ineffective response to P2P file-sharing and bad publicity too.[25] RIAA announced in 2008 that it would stop suing consumers directly.[26]

The RIAA's practice of targeting individual online users was followed by Dallas Buyers Club LLC (DBCL) and Voltage Pictures which in 2014 sent out a large number of letters of demand to suspected infringers in the US, UK,[27] and Australia to pressure people to "pay up or else."[28] In a parallel effort, in 2015 DBCL sent out 500 warning letters in Singapore, asking for a written offer of damages and costs within three days of receiving the letter.[29]

Obviously, this practice of opportunistic exercise of copyright, commonly called speculative invoicing, is coercing and therefore hurting netizens, especially so in countries where statutory damages are foreseen, and courts have no discretion not to apply them to minor cases and not to issue injunctive relief. Should legislature

24 See The Times Sues OpenAI and Microsoft over A.I. use of copyrighted work. *New York Times*, at: https://www.nytimes.com/2023/12/27/business/media/new-york-times-open-ai-microsoft-lawsuit.html

25 See Electronic Frontier Foundation (EFF). (2008). *RIAA v. The People: Five Years Later*, at: https://www.eff.org/wp/riaa-v-people-five-years-later

26 See Paine, A. (2008). RIAA stops suing individuals over file-sharing. *Hollywood Reporter*, at: https://www.hollywoodreporter.com/business/business-news/riaa-stops-suing-individuals-file-124702

27 See Ong, C. (2016). *Dallas Buyers Club Case: Some Things to Know If You Have Illegally Downloaded the Movie*, at: https://www.straitstimes.com/singapore/dallas-buyers-club-case-some-things-to-know-if-you-have-illegally-downloaded-the-movie

28 See Liu, K.-C. (2017). Individual licensing models and the role of internet platform providers. In Liu, K.-C. & Hilty, R. (Eds.), *Remuneration of Copyright Owners—Regulatory Challenges of New Business Models* (pp. 231–232). Springer.

29 id.—*Regulatory Challenges of New Business Models* (pp. 231–232). Springer.

be called upon to endow courts with discretionary power so that they can impose conditions to address concerns about opportunistic exercise of copyright, such as any letters to be sent by the rights holders must be vetted by the court first?

4.8. Dmitri Shostakovich Objected to "Political Use" of His Works

Probably the most telling story of how a moral right overshoots is when around 1948 Dmitri Shostakovich, who has been persecuted by Soviet Union Russia for formalism and has his works banned, along with other composers objected to the unchanged use of their music by "The Iron Curtain," an American anti-communist spy movie. The objection was based on the allegation that the use was "political use." The plight of Shostakovich under the totalitarian Soviet Union deserves sympathy. However, this is nevertheless far-fetched. In the US, the case was of no avail, as his works were not protected and belonged to the public domain. However, in France, courts found such use damaged the moral right of Shostakovich, therefore banned the screening of the film and awarded Shostakovich compensation.[30]

The over-protection of moral rights can hamper the commercialization of works that require astronomic financial investment and therefore also market competition. Do we need to factor this in when deciding the scope of or enforcing moral rights?

5. In the Realm of Patent

In addition to blunt refusal to supply patent lists, suing OEM suppliers for patent infringement, rather than OEM brand owners,[31] suing buyers of competing and allegedly infringing products, rather than suing the manufacturer of the products,[32] patentees are astonishingly ingenious in scheming up all kinds of contractual agreements to safeguard their interests, entrench their market position, and leverage against their current licensees who are or are quickly becoming their potential rivals. Some strategic acts include the imposition of no-challenge of patent validity clause, requiring exclusive assign-back or grant-back of subsequent patents, restricting the right of the purchaser of products, patented or not, in their resale, bundling non-SEPs with SEPs, or requiring licensees to provide detailed "list of manufacturing equipment, suppliers, dates of installing and testing" and "sales

30 Liu, K.-C. (2017). Individual licensing models and the role of internet platform providers. In Liu, K.-C., & Hilty, R. (Eds.), *Remuneration of Copyright Owners—Regulatory Challenges of New Business Models* (pp. 1). Springer.

31 For example, Qualcomm had sued FoxComm for patent infringement, rather than Apple for whom FoxComm manufactured iPhones under OEM arrangement. If ever infringing, it should be Apple, and Qualcomm should go after Apple directly.

32 For example, Intel had sued Taiwanese PC manufacturers which deployed CPUs that allegedly infringed on Intel's IPR and supplied by Intel's competitor, Advanced Micro Devices (AMD), rather than suing AMD and clearing the IP dispute from its roots, it was an intimidating tactic applied on parties with weaker market power.

report in writing" (breaking down in countries, product specifications, buyers, and trademarks used) 30 days after the end of each quarter.

In the following, only several classic cases will be reported.

5.1. Philips et al.'s Patent Pool With One Royalty Formula

In the early 1990s when Philips, Sony, and Taiyo Yuden were leading the introduction of CDs to replace cassettes, they established the standards for CD-Rs and pooled their patents for CD-Rs together, jointly licensed the pooled patents, and held a worldwide absolute monopoly power in the licensing market for CD-R patents, as CD-R became a de facto standard. Philips was designated as the sole contact for licensing the pooled patents with only one royalty formula: 3% of the net sales price but not lower than ¥10.

The retail price of a CD-R disc at the time the said licensing agreements were entered into was approximately ¥ 300 (× 3% = ¥ 10). However, the price for a CD-R disc dropped to around US $2.55 in 1997, to US $0.44 in 2000, and further to US $0.2 in 2006.[33] Philips et al. refused to accommodate repeated requests from licensees to lower the minimum royalty to reflect the falling prices of CD-Rs. ¥ 10 presented unbearable burdens and could be likened to asking a pound of Antonio's flesh for CD-R manufacturers. Are then the patentees obliged to renegotiate the terms and conditions of their licensing agreement in the face of falling prices and declining CD-R manufacturing business in Taiwan? What remedy can patent law offer? What remedy can competition law provide?

5.2. Qualcomm Insisted on License and No Sale: "No License, No Chips"

Qualcomm is the world's number one in terms of patent portfolio for mobile communication. Qualcomm is also the world's number one in engineering a host of license arrangements.[34] Although as far as OEM mobile phone manufacturers supplying brand names such as Apple are concerned, all they want from Qualcomm is to buy its chips, which incorporate all of Qualcomm's SEPs, and assemble them onto the smartphones they make. They are least interested in getting licenses to work with the technology of the SEPs. Qualcomm maintains a "no license, no chips" policy, asking OEM mobile phone manufacturers to sign a patent package

33 Liu, K.-C. (2010). The Taiwanese "Philips" CD-R cases: Abuses of a monopolistic position, cartel, and compulsory patent licensing. In Heath, C., & Sanders, A. (Eds.), *Landmark Intellectual Property Cases and Their Legacy* (pp. 83–104). Aspen Publisher.

34 One such "licensing" practice for Qualcomm is that it has consistently refused to license its SEPs to competing chip designers, such as Intel and MediaTek, although it has made FRAND licensing commitments to SSOs. Such a refusal eliminated the possibility of a FRAND rate with Qualcomm being negotiated by its competitors, who are best placed to do so because they know the technology and are immune from a threatened chipset supply disruption.

licensing agreement with its licensing subsidiary, or there will be no supply of chips.[35]

Is this patent license agreement a harmless exercise of patent rights of SEP patentees? Or is it overstepping the legal boundary of such an exercise after factoring in the market dominance of Qualcomm and the unavoidability of SEPs?

5.3. Licensing of Bundled Patents

With the building up of patent portfolios that could encompass thousands of patents, which is common among ICT giants, such as Qualcomm, Huawei, and Interdigital, bundled licensing of patents (portfolio licensing or package licensing) becomes popular practice. The patent portfolios are licensed in a package and the licensees can only either take the whole package or leave it. This is similar to the blanket license of copyright.

From the perspectives of patentees, licensing of individual patents based on individual licensing negotiation is simply not feasible; bundled licensing has the advantage of ease of portfolio management and the guarantee of comprehensive coverage for the licensees which does not come at extra costs to patent licensees. However, patent license seekers might see bundled licensing very differently, as they worry that they would be required to pay for patents that they have no actual use for.

The legal controversies related to bundled licensing of patents can be exacerbated if the bundling involves SEPs and non-SEPs, as SEPs are very difficult, if not impossible, to bypass and therefore could elevate their patentees into the market-dominant position.[36] How shall we then treat bundled licensing of patents? As a normal and even welcome exercise of patents? Or abusive exercise of patents? Or to see "coercive package licensing" therein and address it as a ground for applying for compulsory license (Section 84(7)(c) of the Indian Patent Act)?

5.4. Bringing Patent Suits

Bringing Patent Suits is probably the most natural way of exercising one's patent. Still, they can be used strategically as the following examples show.

35 The Northern District of California found Qualcomm's practice violated Section 2 of the Sherman Act, which was overruled completely by the 9th Federal Circuit Court (Federal *Trade Commission v. Qualcomm Incorporated*, 19–16122 (9th Cir. 11 Aug. 2020). See https://cdn.ca9.uscourts.gov/datastore/opinions/2020/08/11/19-16122.pdf

36 For discussion of these issues see Liu, K.-C. (2020). As a matter of standard for Asia and beyond? In Liu, K.-C., & Hilty, R. (Eds.), *SEPs, SSOs and FRAND—Asian and Global Perspectives on Fostering Innovation in Interconnectivity* (pp. 4, 19–20). Routledge.

5.4.1. *Patent Trolls Use Patent Litigation as a Business Model*[37]

Speculative invoicing in the copyright area (Subsection 4.7) has a patent cousin. Particularly in the ICT field, patent litigation can become a business model in and of itself, when there are so many patents to litigate, the litigation system favors the losing party that does not ask him to pay the legal fees of the winning party, and there is criminal punishment for patent infringement: business entities first buy in bulk patents and then sue others over patent infringement, not with the goal of determining the right or wrong of the matter, which is too costly and time-consuming, but with the goal of "smash-and-grab" to quickly settle out of court. They bet that the accused would pay settlement fees that are lower than the litigation costs. Such patent holders no longer make the efforts to invest in R&D, manufacture, product marketing, and reinvestment, and use regime/rights strategically as a monetizer, and therefore are called patent assertion entities, or even patent trolls.[38]

Actually, trolls are not limited to the patent realm. Rather, they are also active in other IP areas, particularly in trademark (hoarding and squatting trademarks for the sole purpose of suing others to bring in damages) and copyright. The term "IP trolls" can be appropriately coined to describe trolls in all IP fields.

We then need to ask ourselves are trolls posing a serious challenge to the rationale of the patent (IP) regime, are trolls the symptom or the disease, what are the systemic problems of the patent (IP) system that give rise to trolls, and what are the patent (IP)-internal and patent (IP)-external remedies that can deal with trolls. What if instead of aggregating, complimentary patents are strategically sold to trolls? How real is the vice of this "patent privateering?" What shall we do about it?[39]

5.4.2. *The Patentee Plaintiff Sued but Paid the Defendant (Reverse Payment)*

The US is a global leader in encouraging generic drug companies to seamlessly come into the market when protection terms for patented drugs expire. The 1984 Drug Price Competition and Patent Term Restoration Act, aka Hatch-Waxman Act (HWA) provide the Abbreviated New Drug Application (ANDA) process for generic drug companies, which however requires them to make one of the four certifications regarding the listed patents (registered in the Orange Book) to acquire new drug approval from the Food and Drug Administration (FDA), namely (I) that

37 Borrowing from Robert Merges' phrase, see Merges, R. (2022). *American Patent Law—A Business and Economic History* (p. 418). Cambridge University Press.

38 Patent trolls are worse than non-practicing entities (NPEs) which do not implement their patents themselves, due to specialization, such as universities and their professors.

39 Lemley, M., and Melamed, D. (2013). Missing the forest for the trolls. *Columbia Law Review, 113*, 2117. They suggest three possible forms of antitrust limits: (I) Agreement to sell or disperse patents that seem likely to create or exacerbate the double marginalization problem could be challenged under both Sections 1 and 2 of the Sherman Act and Section 7 of the Clayton Act (substantial lessening of competition). (II) Antitrust agencies can condition merger or other consent decree settlements on an agreement not to engage in privateering. (III) The law might be revised to require disclosure of privateering agreements so that sham transactions can be detected and deterred.

such patent information has not been filed, (II) that such patent has expired, (III) of the date on which such patent will expire, or (IV) that such patent is invalid or will not be infringed by the manufacture, use, or sale of the new drug for which the application is submitted.[40]

The first generic company to successfully challenge the patents of the innovative company will be rewarded a 180-day exclusive right to sell the generic drugs, if it has made the Paragraph IV certification and its application satisfies all legal requirement.[41] However, generic companies, after making Paragraph IV certification, shall inform the patentee who has 45 days to decide whether to bring patent infringement suit against the generic company. If no patent infringement suit was filed, the FDA will issue approval for the new drug if it satisfies all legal requirements. Patented drug companies then developed a "pay-for-delay" litigation strategy. It first brings a patent infringement suit against the applicant but settles out of court through paying the applicant or other arrangements. In return, the applicant drops the Paragraph IV certification or delays its launch of the new drug. Different from the usual patent infringement case where the plaintiff sues the defendant with the goal of having the defendant pay damages, here the patentee plaintiff sues the defendant only to later pay the defendant to settle the case and delay the new generic drug. Therefore, it is commonly known as reverse payment patent settlement.

With the US exporting its HWA to its trading partners, reverse payment agreement proliferates. For example, in the PRC, the IP Court of the Supreme People's Court in a case involving AstraZeneca (patented drug company) suing a Chinese generic drug company over drug patents but later withdrew its appeal through settlement with the defendant, reminds courts to exercise certain level of review to see if there is any violation of the Anti-monopoly Law (AML) when facing agreements between parties that have the appearance of "reverse payment for patented drugs" (where rightsholders of patented drugs promised the applicants of generic drugs direct or indirect interest compensation, including reducing the latter's disadvantage, in return the latter promised not to challenge the validity of patents at issue or delay entering into the relevant market of the patented drugs).[42] However, the court continues to articulate that due to the strong professional knowledge and high complexity involved in the determination of AML violation courts should conduct only preliminary review in non-AML cases where parties withdrew their cases or appeal; if the preliminary review shows that the settlement agreement or the agreement in question is suspicious of violating AML, courts shall take corresponding measures according to law, including allowing the withdrawal of case or appeal, or disallowing the withdrawal and continuing the trial, referring the case to competition authority. The decision assessed that this type of (reverse payment) agreement

40 21 U.S.C. §355(j)(2)(A)(vii).

41 21 U.S.C. §355(j)(5)(B)(iv).

42 IP Court of the SPC ZuiGaoFaZhiMinZhong No. 388 civil ruling (on procedural issues rather than a decision on substantive issues) (decided on December 17, 2021).

is slightly unusual, often more secretive and could lead to exclusion or restraining of competition and possible violation of AML.

5.5. *Patentee Applying for Injunctive Relief*

5.5.1. Does Patent's Exclusivity Automatically Include Injunction?

The world over, patents are treated as exclusive rights that enjoy the strongest exclusivity among all IPs. Yet, the intensity of patent exclusivity varies from country to country. In Germany, such exclusivity historically includes automatic injunction, until recently. The US has followed suit until the 2006 e-Bay case, which signals a paradigm shift since. The online platform eBay is popular for buying and selling countless products but was once held up by MerckExchange, whose patent covers eBay's "Buy it Now" function—over 30% of the company's business. MerckExchange prevailed in a 2003 Virginia jury trial, which ordered eBay to pay nearly $30 million in damages. Following the verdict, MercExchange sought an injunction to prevent eBay's continued use of its patent, which if granted would paralyze or cripple eBay's business.[43]

How shall we design the exclusive right for patents? Should courts turn a blind eye to the plight of the defendant and grant injunctive relief according to the exclusivity of a patent right? Or courts could exercise discretionary power and not grant injunctive relief?

5.5.2. Does SEP Patentee's FRAND Commitment Automatically Exclude Injunction?

The two leading smartphone companies, Apple as world number one and Samsung as world number two were embroidered in design patent fights around 2011 throughout the world. US Samsung applied with the USITC to stop the import of Korean Apple smartphones which allegedly infringed upon Samsung's design patents. However, Samsung made FRAND commitment to an SSO that it will issue a license to any willing license-seeker on FRAND term.[44] Is a SEP patentee prevented from applying for injunctive relief after making the FRAND commitment to an SSO?

43 *eBay Inc. v. MerckExchange LLC*, 547 U.S. 388 (2006).

44 The USITC ruled in June 2013 that the import of some older iPhones and iPads should be banned according to Section 337 because Korea Apple infringed a patent of US Samsung. The Obama administration overturned this ruling against on August 3, 2013, the first such veto in more than 25 years. In a letter explaining the veto (USTR Letter Vetoing ITC-794 Exclusion Order), the then US Trade Representative Michael Froman said he "strongly shares" concerns raised by the USDOJ and USPTO that ITC product bans should rarely be allowed in cases involving SEPs.

In the US, there has been a change of mind on these issues. In 2013 USDOJ and USPTO promulgated a joint "Policy Statement on Remedies for Standards-Essential Patents Subject to Voluntary F/RAND Commitments." It stated that:

> In some circumstances, the remedy of an injunction or exclusion order may be inconsistent with the public interest. This concern is particularly acute in cases where an exclusion order based on a F/RAND-encumbered patent appears to be incompatible with the terms of a patent holder's existing F/RAND licensing commitment to an SDO.

"For SEP, which is subject to FRAND licensing agreement, no injunction should be available."[45]

However, since November 2017, the then Assistant Attorney General of DOJ Makan Delrahim moved the DOJ in a direction that allows SEP owners more freedom to use the exclusionary potential of those patents. The DOJ also has redirected its focus toward the conduct of licensees and the SSOs. In December 2018, Delrahim took another step and withdrew the DOJ's assent to the more balanced 2013 joint "Policy Statement on Remedies for Standards-Essential Patents Subject to Voluntary F/RAND Commitments."[46]

Which one of the US positions is more appropriate for the world to follow?

This leads us to question whether these agreements, as part of the exercise of patent rights by patented drug companies, harm consumers, unreasonably restrain market competition, constitute abuse of patent rights and should therefore be regulated and stemmed by antitrust law.[47]

45 USDOJ and USPTO. (2013). *Policy Statement on Remedies for Standards-Essential Patents Subject to Voluntary F/RAND Commitments* (p. 5), at: https://www.justice.gov/atr/page/file/1118381/download.

46 USDOJ and USPTO. (2013). *Policy Statement on Remedies for Standards-Essential Patents Subject to Voluntary F/RAND Commitments* (p. 5), at: https://www.justice.gov/atr/page/file/1118381/download

47 In the *Federal Trade Commission v. Actavis, Inc., et al.* case, the respondent Solvay Pharmaceuticals obtained a patent for its approved drug AndroGel. Subsequently, respondents Actavis and Paddock filed applications for generic drugs modeled after AndroGel and certified under Paragraph IV that Solvay's patent was invalid and that their drugs did not infringe on it. Solvay sued Actavis and Paddock, claiming patent infringement. The FDA eventually approved Actavis' generic product but instead of bringing its drug to market, Actavis entered into a "reverse payment" settlement agreement with Solvay, agreeing not to bring its generic to market for a specified number of years and agreeing to promote AndroGel to doctors in exchange for millions of dollars. The FTC filed suit, alleging violation of Section 5 of the FTCA, and sought a presumptively illegal rule for reverse payment arrangement. The District Court dismissed the complaint. The Eleventh Circuit affirmed the complaint's dismissal and concluded that as long as the anticompetitive effects of a settlement fall within the scope of the patent's exclusionary potential, the settlement is immune from antitrust attack. However, the US Supreme Court overruled and favored the rule of reason approach: "the FTC should have been given the opportunity to prove its antitrust claim." The Court "declines to hold that reverse payment settlement agreements are presumptively unlawful. Courts reviewing such agreements should proceed by applying the 'rule of reason,' rather than under a 'quick look' approach." 570 US138 (2013).

6. In the Realm of Designs

6.1. Daimler Benz Sued Spare Parts Manufacturer Depo

The car industry is a billion-dollar-generating business and a key industry in major economies across the globe. It is also a very mature one, with branded car manufacturers leading spare parts producers who support the former as their satellites. Automobiles, having generally a life cycle of about twenty years, rely on repair and maintenance service that again relies on spare parts. Other independent spare parts manufacturers see the business opportunity and come uninvited to challenge the eco-system.

In Taiwan there are no internationally well-known branded car manufacturers, it has a thriving auto spare parts industry after years of hard work on catching up. However, it is now facing insurmountable IP barriers from the designs of original car brand owners. The spare parts they manufacture must fit the original cars whose brand owners often have registered designs for protection. However, original car brand owners refuse to license Taiwanese spare parts manufacturers as they compete against them and undercut their profits. Taiwan does not yet recognize the "must match or repair exception" to infringement of design rights—a specialized doctrine applicable to component parts of complex products for which a market exists (for more, see Section 5 of Chapter 5). Daimler Benz recently sued in Taiwan, a Taiwanese spare parts manufacturer, Depo, for infringement of their designs in car lights. The TIPCC found Daimler not obliged to issue licenses for its designs on car lights, and Depo therefore violated Daimler's design rights thereon. The TIPCC ordered Depo to award Daimler NTS30 million damages, and to cease to directly and indirectly manufacture, offer to sell, use, or import for the aforementioned purposes or have others to manufacture, offer to sell, use, or import for the aforementioned purposes infringing products, to demolish infringing products, including semi-finished products, the mold and equipment that are dedicated to producing the infringing products.[48]

Is there a way to break the gridlock that would create multiple wins: Daimler gets reasonable remuneration, the spare parts industry conducts legitimate business, consumers pay reasonable prices for repairing and maintaining their cars, and resources such as cars get used to their maximum utilities for a sustainable economy?

6.2. Fashion Designs

Copying in the fashion industry has been around since there has been a modern fashion industry. While some perceive this as natural as weather and live with it,

48 TIPCC 2017 Min-Zhuan-Su-Zi 34 (decided on August 16, 2019). The decision on infringement and other measures is upheld by the appeal instance of the TIPCC (2019 Min-Zhuan-Shang-Zi 43 (decided on July 14, 2022) and the Supreme Court 2023 Tai-Shang-Zi 9 (decided on October 4, 2023)).

some are determined to fight fashion piracy. In the US, a fashion industry organization, the Fashion Originators' Guild, created in the 1930s a system of design registries, secret shoppers, and red cards that aimed to police and punish those who copied and sold registered dress designs. Would this kind of effort help the fashion industry? Will it have anti-competitive concerns? What is the proper boundary of exercising one's registered design rights?

7. In the Realm of Trade Secret Protection

7.1. Google Used Dedicated Algorithms in Addition to Generic Ones

Having big data at its disposal, Google ventured into comparison shopping services which allow consumers to search for products on online shopping websites and compare prices between different vendors. Google's general search service has a global market share of 80.47% (desktop) and 94.87% (mobile) as of 2017, clearly a market dominance. Google deployed algorithms to search, rank, and display search results, which have enabled it to dominate online search. These algorithms include the PageRank algorithm and at least two kinds of dedicated algorithms that identify and drastically demote competing comparison-shopping services in Google's general search results.[49]

Should the authorities and courts audit Google's algorithms? Can Google hide its algorithms behind the cloak of trade secret protection? Moreover, is Google entirely unrestrained in choosing its ways of providing "free" services? Is there anything wrong for Google to favor its own services, given that Google enjoys market dominance?[50]

7.2. Making Every SEP License Agreement a Trade Secret?

As a standardized licensing practice, SEP patentee licensors will ask their licensees not to disclose the terms and conditions, especially licensing rates. The current situation is that every licensing rate is kept confidential, and no one could assert that they have actually read any license rates for any SEP. If that is the case,

49 The EC opened an investigation in November 2010 against Google, targeting Google's systematic favorable treatment of its own comparison shopping product in its general search results pages, artificial diverting traffic from rival comparison shopping services and hindering their ability to compete on the market. In March 2015, the EC issued a Statement of Objections to Google alleging Google has abused its dominant position. The EC imposed a fine of Euro 2.42 billion on Google in 2017. EC Case AT.39740—Google Search (Shopping).

50 Social media app TikTok successfully attracts some 170 million users in the US alone. Citing national security concerns, the US Congress passed a bill, signed into law by President Biden on April 24, 2024, which requires TikTok to find a non-Chinese buyer, within nine months, or a year if the president gives it an extension. If it doesn't, US app stores and web hosting services are banned from working with it—essentially a ban. TikTok's success hinges on its (recommendation) algorithm, which helps surface tailored content to its users. Subjecting its algorithms to auditing would be a more proportional measure than the drastic move in dispute.

neither judges nor arbitrators would be in the position to know or judge whether any specific licensing rate is indeed FRAND, and if any licensee is being treated discriminatorily. The licensing practice of SEP patentees is shielding itself from any meaningful oversight that serves to implement SEPs efficiently and equitably. It then begs the question shall we continue to allow the SEP licensor to keep licensing rates in the dark?

7.3. Relentless Micron as Mincer for Its Former Employees?

Resorting to trade secret protection is a delicate thing to do, especially when criminal punishment, cross-border economic espionage, and geopolitical drama are involved. It can easily backfire and ridicule the plaintiff.

For eight years or so, such an episode unfolds before our eyes, against the backdrop of the de-risking policy across the Atlantic that employs all instruments to achieve enhanced supply chain resilience and independence of China. Microelectronics Corporation (UMC), headquartered in Taiwan, had signed a technical cooperation agreement in January 2016 with Fujian Jinhua, a PRC-based and state-owned company, to develop a DRAM-related manufacturing process, according to which Jinhua promised to provide US $300 million to purchase R&D equipment, pay UMC US $400 million, co-own the R&D results with UMC, and have the entire technology transferred for mass production of DRAM. The agreement was approved by the Investment Commission, Ministry of Economic Affairs, shortly before the change of government power, which adopted a hostile position towards the PRC. UMC set up a "New Business Development Centre" to execute the technical cooperation agreement, which was headed by Chen Zheng-Kun. Chen left Micron Taiwan as a board director and joined UMC a month later as Senior Vice President.

Micron filed trade secret misappropriation complaint cases in Taiwan and the US. Micron alleges that UMC and Jinhua conspired to induce former Micron Memory Taiwan Co., Ltd. ("MMT") employees to misappropriate electronic and paper files containing Micron trade secrets from MMT and to deliver those trade secrets to UMC, that UMC then recruited various MMT personnel with access to Micron trade secrets, that two MMT employees, prior to resigning from MMT and beginning employment with UMC, took Micron trade secrets from MMT and that UMC incorporated Micron's trade secrets into technologies that it transferred and/or plans to transfer to Jinhua to enable Jinhua to mass produce advanced DRAM products as early as 2018.

In the US, a federal grand jury indicted on September 27, 2018, Jinhua, UMC, and three individuals, charging them with crimes related to a conspiracy to steal, convey, and possess stolen trade secrets of Micron for the benefit of a company controlled by the PRC government. However, two years later, the DOJ announced on October 28, 2020, that UMC pleaded guilty to one count of criminal trade secret theft (but not economic espionage) and agreed to pay a US $60 million fine. The other criminal charges and a parallel civil suit brought by the DOJ on behalf of the

US against UMC were all dismissed. However, the DOJ vowed to continue "the criminal prosecution of Fujian Jinhua and the three individual defendants."

In Taiwan, the case was tried by the Taichung District Court, which conducted all thirteen court sessions *in camera* proceedings. In December 2020 the court sentenced Defendant Mr. He (former employee of MMT) to five and a half years in prison for economic espionage with the intention of using the trade secret in Mainland China, a fine of TWD five million, and confiscation of the illicit gain of TWD 5,413,910; Defendant Mr. Wang (former employee of MMT) to four and a half years in prison, a fine of TWD four million, and confiscation of the illicit gain of TWD 1,527,812 for the same crime. It further sentenced Defendant Mr. Rong (employee of UMC) to six and a half years in prison, a fine of TWD six million, and confiscation of illicit gain of TWD 1,610,952 for the same crime, and UMC to pay a TWD 100 million fine in total for its three employees, namely for Mr. He TWD 30 million, for Mr. Wang TWD 50 million, and for Mr. Rong TWD 40 million.[51] Surprisingly Micron after winning the criminal case, announced a global settlement with UMC on November 25, 2021. UMC would make a one-time payment of an undisclosed amount to Micron. "UMC and Micron look forward to engaging in mutual business cooperation opportunities."[52]

On appeal, the TIPCC revoked in January 2022 the decision and found the two defendants who were former employees of MMT guilty of only domestic trade secret misappropriation, not economic espionage, and reduced the imprisonment to one year for Mr. He and six months for Mr. Wang and a fine of TWD one million for both, and with probation of four and two years respectively. The defendant Mr. Rong was acquitted and UMC's fine was reduced to TWD 20 million with two-year probation.[53] However, the public prosecutor insisted on appealing the case. The Supreme Court revoked the decision and remanded it back to the TIPCC in August 2022 for further trial to correct what has been decided in violation of the law.

On December 23, 2023, Micron reached a global settlement with Jinhua. This resolution follows complications stemming from the May 2023 Chinese government's restrictions on Micron's chip use in critical infrastructure due to cybersecurity concerns, impacting a substantial portion of sales connected to Chinese clients.[54] In February 2024, Fujian Jinhua was cleared by US District Judge Maxine

51 For more see Liu, K.-C. (2021), The criminal punishment for trade secret theft and economic espionage in Taiwan. In Liu, K.-C., & Hilty, R. (Eds.), *Trade Secret Protection—Asia at a Crossroads* (pp. 217–224). Kluwer.

52 See https://investors.micron.com/news-releases/news-release-details/micron-and-umc-announce-global-settlement.

53 TIPCC 2020 Xing-Zhi-Shan-Chong-Su-Zi No.4 (criminal decision decided on January 27, 2022).

54 See Wu, D. (2023). Micron settles IP theft lawsuit amid push to repair Beijing ties. *Bloomberg Law*, at: https://news.bloomberglaw.com/ip-law/micron-settles-ip-theft-lawsuit-amid-push-to-repair-beijing-ties

Chesney in San Francisco of allegations that it stole Micron's trade secrets.[55] When the guns of the battle have silenced, the criminal retrial case is still pending before TIPCC, on whose decision hinges the fate of the three individual defendants who have done nothing more than change jobs.

The case leads us to reflect on a whole range of issues, such as the many side-effects of criminal punishment of trade secret misappropriation, especially for cross-border cases. Employees could be trapped for years, even minced once and for all under current geopolitical tension among rival economies.

8. After Services

Since the early 1990s, companies from "automobiles, white goods, industrial machinery, and information technology" in North America, Western Europe, and Japan have "sold so many units over the years that their aftermarkets have become four to five times larger than the original equipment businesses."[56] As a result, they started to value after-service markets for their products.

To tap into the much bigger and lucrative after-service markets, IP holders routinely apply tactics to maximize their profits, such as imposing contractual duties on buyers of their products that there will be no after-service if the buyers do not buy exclusively from them spare parts or complementary materials (such as paper or ink cartridge for printers, etc.). Another such common tactic is to contractually disallow temporary reproduction of software for the purpose of repairing software-operated devices (e.g. software-driven key).

What are we to do as legal owners of the products we bought from IP holders? Will breaking the contractual prohibition of temporary reproduction of software for the purpose of repairing amount to copyright/patent infringement?[57] Leaving consumer protection issues aside, do we have the right to repair to counterbalance IP rights? Do third-party manufacturers of spare parts have the right to compete for the after-service market?

55 See Singh, K. (2024). Chinese firm Fujian Jinhua cleared of US allegations that it stole trade secrets. *Reuters*, at: https://www.reuters.com/technology/chinese-firm-fujian-jinhua-cleared-us-allegations-that-it-stole-trade-secrets-2024-02-28/

56 Cohen, M., Agrawal, N., & Agrawal, V. (2006). *Winning in the Aftermarket*, at: https://hbr.org/2006/05/winning-in-the-aftermarket

57 In the US, Lexmark, a large manufacturer of laser and inkjet printers, had argued in one of its "sprawling" copyright law cases that Justice Scalia thought would have the potential to go on as long as *Jarndyce v. Jarndyce* (Bleak House by Charles Dickens), that the defendant's replacing of its microchips that enforces the agreement with buyers that they "use the cartridge only once and return it only to Lexmark for manufacturing or recycling" violated copyright law (unauthorized reproduction of its microchips) and the DMCA (circumventing its technical protection mechanism). However, the Court of Appeals of the Sixth Circuit ruled against Lexmark, affirming that replacing the microchips is not in violation of copyright. *Lexmark International, Inc. v. Static Control Components, Inc.*, 697 F.3d 387 (6th Cir. 2012).

9. After IP Expires

IPRs are termed and will expire. What does the expiration of IP actually mean for the competitors of IP-holders? Can they then place on the market slavish copies of the once IP-protected products or apply to register the same trademark on the next day its trademark right expires?[58] Or will there be any issue of unfair competition?[59] Does IP licensees' duty to pay royalty stop the moment IP expires, despite contractual agreements that outlive the patent term? Or parties are allowed to continue to pay/receive royalties even after the licensed patent expires?

In the US, there is one recent case that dealt with such an arrangement: Marvel agreed to purchase Kimble's patent for the gadget "Web Blaster for Spiderman" in exchange for a lump sum (about a half-million dollars) and a 3% running royalty on Marvel's future sales of the products. The parties set no end date for royalties, apparently contemplating that they would continue for as long as customers wanted to buy the product. The US Supreme Court adopts the categorical principle that all patent-related benefits must end when the patent term expires.[60] Is such a rigid rule the right approach? Why cannot the parties agree otherwise?

10. Non-IP-Infringing but Unfair Practice

In addition to IP infringement that is to be handled by IP laws, there are many non-IP-infringing but unfair practices that could only be helped by unfair competition law. For example, comparative advertising might use others' trademarks in a manner that is not trademark right infringing but yet annoying at least to trademark owners. Article 6(2) of the German Unfair Competition Prevention Act comprehensively regulates this issue,[61] which would lead to the question of whether this

58 *TrafFix Devices, Inc. v. Marketing Displays, Inc.*, 532 U.S. 23(2001). In the LEGO case mentioned, the CJEU ruled that: The position of an undertaking which has developed a technical solution cannot be protected, with regard to competitors placing on the market slavish copies of the product shape incorporating exactly the same solution, by conferring a monopoly on that undertaking through registering as a trademark the three-dimensional sign consisting of that shape, but can, where appropriate, be examined in the light of rules on unfair competition. CJEU C-48/09 (decided on September 14, 2010), Paragraph 61

59 In this regard, German Unfair Competition Prevention Act provides some answer: Unfairness is deemed to have occurred where a person: (3) offers goods or services that are replicas of goods or services of a competitor if he a) causes avoidable deception of the purchaser regarding their commercial origin; b) unreasonably exploits or impairs the assessment of the replicated goods or services; or c) dishonestly obtained the knowledge or documents needed for the replicas (Article 4(3)).

60 *Kimble v. Marvel Entertainment*, 135 S. Ct. 2401 (2015).

61 It stipulates: (2) Unfairness shall have occurred where a person conducting comparative advertising uses a comparison that 1. does not relate to goods or services meeting the same needs or intended for the same purpose; 2. does not objectively relate to one or more material, relevant, verifiable and representative features of the goods concerned, or to the price of those goods or services; 3. leads, in the course of trade, to a risk of confusion between the advertiser and a competitor or between the goods or services offered or the distinguishing marks used by them; 4. takes unfair advantage of or impairs the reputation of a distinguishing mark used by a competitor; 5. discredits or denigrates the goods, services, activities, or personal or business circumstances of a competitor; or 6. presents

amounts to over-protecting brand owners at the cost of market competition, not to mention freedom of commercial speech. In contrast, the US has no specific provisions on this issue.

In a case close to a comparative advertisement from the US in the1960s, a certain Smith advertised a fragrance called "Second Chance" and stated in ads that his perfumes "duplicate 100% perfect the exact scent of the world's finest and most expensive perfumes and colognes at prices that will zoom sales to volumes you have never before experienced!" Smith used inciting ads that a "Blindfold Test" be used "on skeptical prospects," challenging them to detect any difference between a well-known fragrance and Smith's duplicate. One suggested challenge was, "We dare you to try to detect any difference between Chanel #5 (25.00) and the 2nd Chance $7.00." The US Court of Appeals Ninth Circuit held that such advertising may not be enjoined under either the Lanham Act (Trademark Act) or the common law of unfair competition, so long as it did not contain misrepresentations or create a reasonable likelihood that purchasers would be confused as to the source, identity, or sponsorship of the advertiser's product.[62]

However, isn't Smith taking a free ride on or unfair advantage of Chanel's goodwill by mentioning its trademark as a steppingstone or springboard for marketing Smith's product? More importantly, are we to follow the US's approach or Germany's model of a detailed regulation in the unfair competition law in dealing with comparative advertisement?

goods or services as imitations or replicas of goods or services which are sold under a protected distinguishing mark.

62 402 F.2d 562 (1968).

2 IP as Market Regulation to Enrich the Public Domain

1. In Search of a General Theory of IP

1.1. A General Theory Consisted of Legal Principles

In order to solve all the questions reported in Chapter 1 in a more coherent fashion, we need a general theory of IP. Of course, we must first start from what a general theory of law is about. A general theory of law is a systemic effort to understand law from its constituting legal principles and to make law a legitimizing force. It aims at directing people's behavior through a coherent set of rules. Legal principles are direction-pointing typologies, not rigid doctrines, therefore open to case differences.

Legal principles come from the observation of historical experiences, comparative law study, reasoning, and normative postulation. Some legal principles are of absolute value, such as human life, dignity or conscience, equality, etc. which are not subject to questioning, qualification, or change. Some legal principles are formulae that need to be applied pursuant to changing conditions and understandings, such as proportionality, cost and benefit analysis, efficiency, etc.

Why is a general theory of law important? It is important because it will provide or ensure coherent and systemic application of law, creating thus trust in law and a sense of justice. Sometimes, the law itself is not coherent and systemic. Then a general theory of law is even imperative, as it will summarize, streamline, and reconceptualize legal principles and eventually rectify defective laws, and achieve predictability (coherent and systemic application) and justice at the end of the day.

Unfortunately, there is a lack of an easily apprehensible general theory of IP law. IP remains arcane and the expensive toy of elite professionals. The TRIPS Agreement offers little help. Article 1(2) provides a bucket, not a general theory, of IP: "For the purposes of this Agreement, the term 'intellectual property' refers to all categories of intellectual property that are the subject of Sections 1 through 7 of Part II." Accordingly, GIs, IC layout designs, trade secrets, and test data submitted for drug approval are all IP. But are they really?

Without its own general theory, IP cannot be a stand-alone discipline. Without the guidance of a general theory, IP can be easily alienated from its original rationales and why it is needed and justified in the first place. Currently, the three

DOI: 10.4324/9781003597766-3

major areas of IP, cultural IP (copyright and neighboring rights), commercial IP (trademarks), and technical IP (patent and its likes) stand in isolation, seen vertically as unrelated silos or horizontally as separated fields.[1] Only with the help of a general theory could people perceive holistically that they share the same DNA and many interconnecting common themes, although on appearance they might look starkly. A general theory of IP could provide easily understandable access to IP laws, reduce the complexity of IP laws, decipher the labyrinth created by interest groups and lobbyists, and democratize IP laws to become laws for people on the streets.[2]

To build a general theory of IP, the next section will first go back to the origins of IP and then propose an analytical framework of a general theory of IP.

1.2. Going Back to the Origins of IP

1.2.1. IP Laws in the UK

A. PATENT LAW

The first statutory patent system is generally regarded to be the Venetian Patent Statute of 1474. As Venetians emigrated, they sought similar patent protection in their new homes. This led to the diffusion of patent systems to other countries. The UK was the first major European power to adopt patent law, namely in the Statute of Monopolies 1624.[3] The law first abolished all monopolies granted by King James I, which were used as his personal favor and harmed the trade and industries (Section 1).[4] The Statute then makes an exception for letter patents which were intended to strengthen England's economy by making it self-sufficient and promoting new industries. It was an act of economic policy to catch up with France and

1 "[S]uch is the degree of specialization that the various subfields of intellectual property—patent, copyright, and trademark—are seen as separate fields," quoted from Balganesh, S. (2022). The genius of common-law intellectual property. *The Journal of Legal Studies, 50*, S102.

2 In this context it is worth pointing out that the Copyright Act of Singapore as the worst example in terms of easy access as it has 541 sections in total (v. 67 Articles of China's Copyright Law), making it probably the least understandable copyright act on earth.

3 It has the full title as "An Act concerning Monopolies and Dispensations with Penal Law and the Forfeitures thereof."

4 Section 1 of the Statute of monopolies stipulated:

> [A]ll Monopolies, and all Commissions, Grants, Licences, Charters and Letters Patents heretofore made or granted, or hereafter to be made or granted, to any Person or Persons, Bodies Politick or Corporate whatsoever, of or for the sole Buying, Selling, Making, Working or Using of any Thing within this Realm, or the Dominion of Wales . . . or of any other Monopolies, or of Power, Liberty or Faculty, to dispense with any others, or to give Licence or Toleration to do, use or exercise any Thing against the Tenor or Purport of any Law or Statute . . . are altogether contrary to the Laws of this Realm, and so are and shall be utterly void and of none Effect, and in no wise to be put in Use or Execution.

Holland, the objectives of which were the encouragement of industry, employment, and growth, rather than justice to the inventor.[5]

The protection term of 14 years is twice as long as the required term for an apprentice to finish their professional training and was considered sufficient for inventors to recoup their investment and gain profit.[6] From its inception, the legislators were very conscious of the danger that patents might be abused to the detriment of society, especially by raising prices of commodities or generally inconvenient. Therefore, they foresaw the limitation on patent rights the moment they recognized them. The protected manufacturers were not to be "contrary to the law nor mischievous to the state by raising prices of commodities at home, or hurt of trade, or generally inconvenient."[7]

The Statute was the crucial legal foundation upon which the First Industrial Revolution could emerge from and flourish in the United Kingdom.[8]

B. COPYRIGHT LAW

The first copying industry in the UK was run by stationers (publishers) and their guild the Stationers' Company, which got a charter in 1556 from Queen Mary to help her suppress religious heterodoxy. This charter enabled the company to set up a licensing system that required lawfully printed books to be entered and only company members had the right to make an entry. However, the parliament finally refused to renew the licensing system in 1694.

The stationers managed to secure legislation in 1709 to provide them with definite substantive rights and effective procedures to enforce those rights.[9] This is

5 Llewelyn, D., & Aplin, T. (2023). *Intellectual Property: Patents, Copyright, Trade Marks and Allied Rights*, 3–005. Sweet & Maxwell.

6 Merges, R. (2022). *American Patent Law—A Business and Economic History* (p. 48). Cambridge University Press. According to https://en.wikipedia.org/wiki/Apprenticeships_in_the_United_Kingdom "In 1563, the Statute of Artificers and Apprentices was passed to regulate and protect the apprenticeship system, forbidding anyone from practising a trade or craft without first serving a 7-year period as an apprentice to a master."

7 Section 6 of the Statute of Monopolies provided:

> Section 1 shall not extend to any letters patents (b) and grants of privilege for the term of fourteen years or under, hereafter to be made, of the sole working or making of any manner of new manufactures within this realm (c) to the true and first inventor (d) and of such manufactures, which others at the time of making such letters patents and grants shall not use(e), so as also they be not contrary to the law nor mischievous to the state by raising prices of commodities at home, or hurt of trade, or generally inconvenient: the same fourteen years to be accounted from the date of the first letters patents or grant of such privilege hereafter to be made, but that the same shall be of such force as they should be if this act had never been made, and of none other (g).

8 Llewelyn, D., & Aplin, T. (2023). *Intellectual Property: Patents, Copyright, Trade Marks and Allied Rights*, 3–005. Sweet & Maxwell.

9 Llewelyn, D., & Aplin, T. (2023). *Intellectual Property: Patents, Copyright, Trade Marks and Allied Rights*, 10–001 et seq. Sweet & Maxwell.

the Statute of Anne, which has eleven articles in total.[10] The full title of the Act was "An Act for the Encouragement of Learning, by Vesting the Copies of Printed Books in the Authors or Purchasers of such Copies, during the Times therein mentioned." The right granted was the right to copy; to have sole control over the printing and reprinting of books, with no provision to benefit the owner of this right after the sale. This right would automatically be given to the author as soon as the book was published.[11]

Despite being driven by the self-interest of the stationers, the Statute's title still reveals the ultimate understanding of copyright not as an end in itself but a means to achieve the higher goal of encouraging learning.[12] The UK legislature was conscious of keeping the right balance and carefully designed. It provides renewable protection terms, rather than a one-off period. It also allows the bouncing back of copyright to authors after the expiration of fourteen years, if they are then living, and for another term of fourteen years (Article XI).[13] More pertinent to the theme of this book is the Act's price control mechanism against "too high and unreasonable" prices,[14] which shows the Act was keenly aware of the danger that exclusive rights would be abused and needed to be reined in.

10 According to https://en.wikipedia.org/wiki/Statute_of_Anne:

> Prior to the statute's enactment in 1710, copying restrictions were authorized by the Licensing of the Press Act 1662. These restrictions were enforced by the Stationers' Company, a guild of printers given the exclusive power to print—and the responsibility to censor—literary works.

11 Article II of the Statute of Anne stipulated:

> the author of any book already printed, who hath not transferred to any other the copy of such book, share thereof, or the bookseller, printer, or other person, who hath or have purchased or acquired the copy of any book or books, in order to print or reprint the same, shall have the sole right and liberty of printing such book.

12 Article I of the Statute of Anne indicates the purpose of the legislation:

> Whereas Printers, Booksellers, and other Persons, have of late frequently taken the Liberty of Printing, Reprinting, and Publishing, or causing to be Printed, Reprinted, and Published Books, and other Writings, without the Consent of the Authors or Proprietors of such Books and Writings, to their very great Detriment, and too often to the Ruin of them and their Families: For Preventing therefore such Practices for the future, and for the Encouragement of Learned to Compose and Write useful Books.

13 This exclusive right's length was dependent on when the book had been published. If it was published after April 10, 1710, the length of copyright was 14 years; if published before that date, then 21 years (Article II).

14 Article IV of the Statute of Anne stipulated:

> That if any bookseller, printer shall set a price upon, or sell, or expose to sale, any book at such <u>a price or rate</u> as shall be conceived by any person or persons to be <u>too high and unreasonable</u>; it shall and may be lawful for any person, to make complaint thereof to the lord archbishop of Canterbury, the lord chancellor, or lord keeper of the great seal of Great Britain, the lord bishop of London, the lord chief justice of the court of Queen's Bench, the lord chief justice of the court of Common Pleas, the lord chief baron of the court of Exchequer, the vice chancellors of the two universities; the lord president of the sessions, the lord chief justice general, the lord chief baron of the

1.2.2. IP Laws in the US

In the early American economy, there were "ample reserves of open land together with a general labor shortage" which contributed to the inventive spirit of the young country, and its rapid mechanization and industrialization.[15] This explains why the US is the first country to embrace an IP regime in its constitution.[16] Article I, Section 8, Clause 8 of the US Constitution of 1789 empowers Congress to enact federal laws "To promote the progress of science and useful arts, by securing for limited times to authors and inventors the exclusive right to their respective writings and discoveries." It also has clear purpose orientation, seeing IP not as an end in and of itself, but a means to achieving another higher purpose, namely, the promotion of science and useful arts.

The US Congress legislated the Patent Act in 1790, followed by milestone legislations in 1793, 1836 (birth of the examination system), and 1870.[17] The 1790 Act is aptly entitled "An Act to promote the progress of useful Arts." It set the patent term also at fourteen years, with explicit reference to the training time for two apprentices.[18]

> The American patent system was designed to be different from existing institutions in the world . . . patents for new inventions were not monopolies . . . instead of deprecating patentees as monopolists, policymakers and the courts regarded them as benefactors. . . . Social welfare coincided with the individual welfare of patentees.[19]

The US enacted the Copyright Act in 1790 (seven sections in total), shortly after the enactment of the Patent Act, which traces its lineage back to the British Statute

Exchequer, the rector of the college of Edinburgh; shall and have hereby full power and authority to send for, summon, or call before him such bookseller, printer and to examine and enquire of the reason of the dearness and inhauncement (enhancement) of the price or value of such book by him so sold or exposed to sale; and if . . . the price of such book or books is inhaunced, or any wise too high or unreasonable, . . . have hereby full power and to reform and redress the same, and to limit and settle the price of every such printed book, according to the best of their judgments, and as to them shall seem just and reasonable; and in case of alteration of the rate or price from what was set or demanded by such bookseller, printers, to award and order such bookseller, printer, to pay all the costs and charges that the person so complaining shall be put unto, by reason of such complaint, and of the causing such rate or price to be so limited and settled; all which shall be done.

15 Merges, R. (2022). *American Patent Law—A Business and Economic History* (p. 48). Cambridge University Press.

16 Khan, Z. (2020). *Inventing Ideas—Patents, Prizes, and the Knowledge Economy* (p. 34). Cambridge University Press.

17 Merges, R. (2022). *American Patent Law—A Business and Economic History* (p. 39). Cambridge University Press.

18 Merges, R. (2022). *American Patent Law—A Business and Economic History* (p. 49). Cambridge University Press.

19 Khan, Z. (2020). *Inventing Ideas—Patents, Prizes, and the Knowledge Economy* (p. 34). Cambridge University Press.

of Anne with the same goal of "encouragement of learning."[20] However, the US Copyright Act did not install control mechanisms for enhanced prices as a result of exclusive copyright.

1.2.3. Other Utilitarian Approach to IP Regimes

Many countries follow similar Zeitgeist in the design of their IP regimes. IP regimes were tasked to achieve practical national goals, rather than something revered as an absolute natural right for the sole sake of protecting the IP rights holders. Switzerland, Netherlands, and India are renowned examples for tailor-making their respective patent law a utilitarian success.

A. SWITZERLAND

At the turn of the eighteenth century, Switzerland enacted its first patent law of 1801. Article 1 of that law allowed a citizen of the Republic who invented, improved, or introduced from abroad a new essential industry and practiced it in the country, to apply for a patent, which was protected for up to seven years. This law was abolished with the fall of the Helvetic Republic in 1803.[21] It was up to individual Cantons to legislate on patents.

This state of affairs continued as the Swiss "excelled in a narrow range of industries producing artisanal items that typically were not patentable."[22] It lasted until the adoption of a federal patent law on November 15, 1888, after examining the American experience of technologically driven economic growth.[23] However, the protection was limited to inventions represented by mechanical models applicable to the industry.[24] The 1907 patent amendment eliminated the mechanical model requirement and extended the protection to chemical processes after pressure from Germany, the biggest market for Swiss chemical products.[25] However, it protected only chemical processes and not chemical products or substances themselves. Furthermore, the new law excluded the protection of all chemical processes related

20 The US Copyright Act has been updated several times, including, notably, the Copyright Act of 1976 and the Sonny Bono Copyright Term Extension Act of 1998.

21 Ritter, D. (2004). Switzerland's patent law history. Fordham intellectual Property. *Media and Entertainment Law Journal*, *14*, 472, at: https://ir.lawnet.fordham.edu/iplj/vol14/iss2/3.

22 Khan, Z. (2020). *Inventing Ideas—Patents, Prizes, and the Knowledge Economy* (p. 61). Cambridge University Press.

23 Khan, Z. (2020). *Inventing Ideas—Patents, Prizes, and the Knowledge Economy* (p. 63). Cambridge University Press.

24 Ritter, D. (2004). Switzerland's patent law history. Fordham intellectual property. *Media and Entertainment Law Journal*, *14*, 464.

25 Ritter, D. (2004). Switzerland's patent law history. Fordham intellectual property. *Media and Entertainment Law Journal*, *14*, 464.

to the fabrication of products, whether chemically or not, for human or animal nutrition.[26]

In summary, Switzerland set up its patent regime in ways that suited its national developmental needs. The patent regime, among other things, has made Switzerland the champion of the patent world, filing the most patent applications per capita to the EPO in 2022 (9,008 patents, up 5.9% from 2021).[27] Switzerland ranks number one in 2023 for the 13th consecutive year according to the WIPO Global Innovation Index.[28]

B. THE NETHERLANDS

Although a patent system existed in the Netherlands as part of French law before, the 1817 Patents Act was the first patent act approved in the Netherlands. However, the act did not benefit the Dutch industry and was repealed in 1869 under the behest of patent abolitionists: "The Netherlands was not concerned about offering incentives for discoveries by domestic investors, because foreigners completely dominated its patent rosters both before and after their reforms."[29]

Only when the Dutch industry had managed to catch by making meaningful use of the "free to copy" period, was the Patent Act reintroduced in 1912.[30] The Nederland not only ranks number two in patent applications per capita (6,806 patents, up 3.5% from 2021) to the EPO in 2022 but also ranks number seven in 2023 according to the WIPO Global Innovation Index.[31]

C. INDIA

Indian Patents and Designs Act of 1911 was imposed on India, like many formal European colonies, by the United Kingdom, for the purpose of protecting British products, rather than the encouragement of Indian Indigenous invention: After India gained its independence in 1947, the foreigner-favoring patent laws stunted the development of the Indian pharmaceutical industry and forced independent India to import even basic medicines at unaffordable prices. Consequently, since

26 Ritter, D. (2004). Switzerland's patent law history. Fordham intellectual property. *Media and Entertainment Law Journal, 14*, 480.

27 See https://report-archive.epo.org/about-us/annual-reports-statistics/statistics/2022/statistics/patent-applications.html#tab2.

28 See https://www.wipo.int/edocs/pubdocs/en/wipo-pub-2000-2023-en-main-report-global-innovation-index-2023-16th-edition.pdf.

29 Khan, Z. (2020). *Inventing Ideas—Patents, Prizes, and the Knowledge Economy* (p. 61). Cambridge University Press.

30 See https://en.wikipedia.org/wiki/Patent_law_in_the_Netherlands.

31 See https://www.wipo.int/edocs/pubdocs/en/wipo-pub-2000-2023-en-main-report-global-innovation-index-2023-16th-edition.pdf.

1949, the Indian government constituted several high-powered committees often headed by eminent judges to review the existing patent laws.[32]

In 1957 the Indian Government commissioned retired Supreme Court justice N. Rajagopala Ayyangar to draft a Report on the Revision of the Patent Law. The Report was driven by the conviction that "It would not be an exaggeration to say that the industrial progress of a country is considerably stimulated or retarded by its patent system according as to whether the system is suited to it or not."[33] It concluded that:

> the Indian Patent system has failed in its main purpose, namely, to stimulate invention among Indians and to encourage the development and exploitation of new inventions for industrial purposes in the country so as to secure the benefits thereof to the largest section of the public,[34]

as foreigners held more than 90% of India's valid patents on January 1, 1958, and only a very small proportion of which were actively worked in India.[35]

The report reached the conclusion that "the chemical and pharmaceutical industry of this country would be advanced and the tempo of research in that field would be promoted if . . . permitting only process claims were adopted."[36] It suggested that "no patents should be granted for claims for articles of food and medicine as such but that processes for producing them should be patentable."[37]

This suggestion, among others, was integrated into the Patents Act 1970, effective on 20 April 1972. Thereafter, India had ceased to protect chemical products. This left open a window period of at least 30 years for the Indian generic pharma industry to catch up by freely reverse engineering drugs patented in foreign countries, before it resolved to join the WTO in 1994 and to again protect chemical products, including drugs.[38] Now, the Indian generic industry has become the pharmacy of the world, which also propels India to the ranks of new drug developers.

32 Racherla, U.S. (2019). Historical evolution of India's patent regime and its impact on innovation in the Indian pharmaceutical industry. In Liu, K.-C., & Racherla, U. (Eds.), *Innovation, Economic Development and IPR in China and India—A Study of Six Economic Sectors* (pp. 275–298). Springer.

33 Ayyangar, N. R. (1959). *Report on the Revision of Patent Laws* (p. 11). Government of India.

34 Ayyangar, N. R. (1959). *Report on the Revision of Patent Laws* (p. 13). Government of India.

35 Ayyangar, N. R. (1959). *Report on the Revision of Patent Laws* (p. 14). Government of India.

36 Ayyangar, N. R. (1959). *Report on the Revision of Patent Laws* (p. 35). Government of India.

37 Ayyangar, N. R. (1959). *Report on the Revision of Patent Laws* (p. 39). Government of India.

38 See Racherla, U. (2019). Historical evolution of India's patent regime and its impact on innovation in the Indian pharmaceutical industry. In Liu, K.-C., & Racherla, U. (Eds.), *Innovation, Economic Development and IPR in China and India—A Study of Six Economic Sectors* (pp. 281–298). Springer.

1.3. Analytical Framework

Here I propose an analytical framework that sees IP as a form of market regulation and looks both inside and outside of IP for its redemption.

1.3.1. IP as a Form of Market Regulation[39]

The market is the virtual and actual platform for competition to take place. Why do governments regulate the market in the first place? It has to do with the various needs to control for multiple reasons (see Subsection 3.1 of Capter 4). Prior to the emergence of IP, perfect competition envisioned by Adam Smith in his "Wealth of Nations" reigned. There had been free market entry and exit, and competition by imitation.[40] However, given the public goods nature of new creation, namely non-rivalrous[41] and non-excludable (at least with high costs of excluding, such as lighthouse guiding passing vessels universally) and no cost of usage, new creation risks being not paid for, over-used, under invested and sub-optimally supplied. There was no market mechanism in place to recuperate the investment in IP. Put differently, this was a serious market failure.

To address this market failure, through a deliberate government intervention, IP was created as private rights that restrict the usage of IP-protected goods to people who have paid royalties to rightsholders. That way, incentives for substitutive innovation and competition will be created. Of course, the restriction of using new creation will also lead to certain economic deficiencies or insufficiencies. However, IP is only there for a limited period and the inefficiencies of exclusive power will be offset by increased innovation, competition by substitution, and the expanded public domain. in the end, the economy and human society progress at a much faster pace.

Therefore, it is evident that IP is a means to a higher end, not an end in itself. IP is not an absolute natural right as advocated by some continental European traditionalists in the last three centuries. IP is a sector-specific market regulation[42] that addresses market failure, enhances, and enriches, not encloses or hollows

39 Yoshiyuki Tamura suggests a similar perspective that "intellectual property rights are nothing more than 'governmental regulation of actions'", Tamura, Y. (2023). "Intellectual Property" as a metaphor: A recommendation for an understanding as "Governmental Regulation of Actions." *GRUR International, 73*, 285–286.

40 Drexl, J. (Ed.). (2008). *Research Handbook on Intellectual Property and Competition Law* (p. 45). Edward Elgar.

41 In a famous letter of 1813, Thomas Jefferson compared the spread of ideas to the way people light one candle from another: "He who receives an idea from me, receives instruction himself without lessening mine; as he who lites his taper at mine, receives light without darkening me." See https://www.nybooks.com/articles/2011/11/24/jeffersons-taper-national-digital-library.

42 For Robert Merges, patent law is also a specialized regulatory system, and patents can be regulated without triggering a constitutional obligation to compensate patent owners under the constitution's "taking" principle, see Merges, R. (2022). *American Patent Law—A Business and Economic History* (pp. 22–23). Cambridge University Press, footnote 44.

out, the public domain by encouraging new creation and its actual use through commercialization.[43]

The general theory of IP that this book is exploring is about a set of coherent principles explaining why we have IP in the first place, and how best IP can fulfill its rationale of incentivizing new human creations, the use of those creations to benefit human conditions and enrich the public domain. In that effort, we can look IP-internally and externally for guidance,[44] so that the exercise of IP will not lead to yet another market failure caused by the overprotection of IP.

1.3.2. Looking for IP Internal and External Guidance

IP-internal guidance can be likened as following the common law approach to contract, namely, not to fix contracts afterwards, but to honor contracts at all costs. Even by so doing, one can rely on the terms of the contract in question to defeat the contract (contract-internal approach, e.g. specific performance), the tactic employed by Portia of The Merchant of Venice, and to avoid any ultimate injustice.

IP-external guidance can derive from good morals, public order, public policy (such as helping those who are in a systematically weaker position), and specifically for the present book, competition law.

The traditional and normative view on the relationship between IP and competition law was that IP was an "exception" to competition law which applied only where IP was used to constrain competition outside the scope of the exclusive right,[45] or there was "conflict" between IP and competition law.[46] However, the

43 Britian and America empowered authors since the 19th century because they enriched the public domain, not because they were owners of their works, see Baldwin, P. (2014). *The Copyright War–Three Centuries of Trans-Atlantic Battle* (p. 11). Princeton University Press.

44 Similarly, Ng-Loy talks about "Regulation of anti-competitive behaviors on the part of IP proprietors may come from within and outside of the IP regime." Ng-Loy, W. (2021). *Law of Intellectual Property of Singapore* (3rd. ed.), [2.4.2] et al. Sweet & Maxwell.

45 Competition laws of Japan, Korea, Taiwan, and the PRC basically follow this approach. See Subsection 3.5.2 of Chapter 3.

46 Specifically, Herbert J. Hovenkamp sees antitrust/patent conflicts and proposes principles for resolving them, which include:

> 1. Pre-issuance conduct involving patents is generally not addressable under the antitrust laws, 2. A practice that is expressly authorized by the Patent Act cannot be the basis of an antitrust claim, 3. -issuance practices that are not authorized by the Patent Act should be evaluated under ordinary antitrust Rules, 4. Active production under a patent license can indicate that a restraint is "ancillary," justifying rule of reason treatment, Innovation affecting conduct falls within the domain of antitrust just as much as patent law, with the important limitation that antitrust applies only to innovation affecting conduct that is also anticompetitive, 6. The range of "agreements" covered by the antitrust laws is broader than the range of "licenses" authorized by the Patent Act, and 7. A court generally need not determine patent validity or infringement in order to assess the antitrust legality of a settlement or other license agreement,
>
> Hovenkamp, H. (2015). Antitrust and the Patent System: A Reexamination. *Ohio State Law Journal, 76*, 515–517, at: https://scholarship.law.upenn.edu/faculty_scholarship/1820

dominant theory has evolved and now perceives a complementary relationship between IP and competition law, with both sharing the common goal of promoting innovation and enhancing consumer welfare while balancing the interests of IP holders on the one hand and the public interest,[47] competition in particular, on the other.[48]

However, different jurisdictions interpret and apply this complementary relationship differently when assessing the legality of various specific IP agreements, as each has its unique assessment of competitive effects.

This volume sees the complementary relationship in that IP is there to provide sufficient incentives for new creation and its sharing, while competition law is there to stem overprotection of IP which leads to market inefficiency and failure. To be sure, however, there is no telling in advance and in general what constitutes sufficient incentives and overprotection. The decision must and can only be made on a case-by-case basis. And it is exactly this constant calibration work that makes the process dynamic and therefore responsive to changing conditions and environments, rendering humans irreplaceable by AI.

2. Proposing a Three-Step Exchange General Theory of IP

This section proposes a three-step exchange theory of IP.

2.1. Recycling the Notorious Three-Step

I recycle the "three-step" part of the highly controversial "three-step test" as the principle of setting limitations and exceptions to IPRs. Article 9(2) Berne

---

However, these principles are self-axioms for deciding which one of the two conflicting laws is applicable, which can be better decided if we see complementarity between patent law, or generally IP, and competition law.

47 Drexl, J. (2008). Is there a "more economic approach" to intellectual property and competition law? Drexl, J. (Ed.), *Research Handbook on Intellectual Property and Competition Law* (pp. 27, 35). Edward Elgar. The EC Guidelines on the application of Article 101 of the Treaty on the Functioning of the European Union to technology transfer agreements (2014/C 89/03) follow similar thinking:

> Indeed, both bodies of law share the same basic objective of promoting consumer welfare and an efficient allocation of resources. Innovation constitutes an essential and dynamic component of an open and competitive market economy. Intellectual property rights promote dynamic competition by encouraging undertakings to invest in developing new or improved products and processes. So does competition by putting pressure on undertakings to innovate. Therefore, both intellectual property rights and competition are necessary to promote innovation and ensure a competitive exploitation thereof.
>
> Paragraph 7

48 Some suggested that the complementarity theory can be further replaced by an integrated innovation-economic concept of IP protection and competition, see Podszun, R. (2010). *Lizenzverweigerung-Ernstfall im Verhältnis von Kartell-und Immaterialgüterrecht, in Jahrbuch Kartell-und Wettbewerbsrecht* (p. 75), P. Matousek, E. Müller, and T. Thanner (Hrgb.). NWV.

Convention introduces the three-step test as a guide for exception/limitation to the reproduction right under copyright law:

> It shall be a matter for legislation in the countries of the Union to permit the reproduction of such works in certain special cases, provided that such reproduction does not conflict with a normal exploitation of the work and does not unreasonably prejudice the legitimate interests of the author.[49]

The TRIPS Agreement expands the test to become the overarching principle for setting exceptions and limitations to all IPs.[50]

The three-step test is closely followed by both common law and civil law jurisdictions,[51] with the exception of the US copyright jurisdiction. The three-step test can be interpreted to be so suffocating that any free fair use of IP-protected creation would not be possible. The Japanese provision on the transfer of ownership of copies made in accordance with the provisions of limitations on reproduction rights is one case in point.[52] As this volume advocates for a more liberal, holistic, and proportionality-spirited understanding of the three-step test (see Subsection 5.2 of Chapter 4), I will reinforce that advocacy here by paraphrasing the "Three-Step" to form a general three-step-exchange exchange (between the public domain and the private sphere of IPRs) theory of IP. Under that theory, the life cycle of IP will

49 See also Article 10(1) Berne Convention:

> It shall be permissible to make quotations from a work . . ., provided that their making is compatible with fair practice, and their extent does not exceed that justified by the purpose, including quotations from newspaper articles and periodicals in the form of press summaries.

50 Articles 13, 17, 26, and 30 of the TRIPS Agreement.

51 For example, in the copyright realm, fair dealing under common law jurisdictions typified by the UK is strictly enumerated and lists exhaustive exceptions. So is copyright law of civil law jurisdictions. German Copyright Act provides a good example: Articles 44a (Temporary acts of reproduction), 44b (Text data mining), 45 (Administration of justice and public security), 45a (Persons with disabilities), 45b (Persons with visual impairment or reading disability), 45c (Authorized entities; remuneration; authorization to issue statutory instruments), 45d (Use permitted by law and contractually authorized use), 46 (Collections for religious use), 47 (School broadcasts), 48 (Public speeches), 49 (Newspaper articles and broadcast commentaries), 50 (Reporting on current events, 51 (Quotations), 51a (Caricature, parody and pastiche), 52 (Communication to public), and 53 (Reproduction for private and other personal uses).

52 Article 47, Japanese Copyright Act provides:

> Works permitted to be reproduced pursuant to the provisions of Article 31, item (i), Article 32, Article 33, paragraph 1 including the cases where applied mutatis mutandis pursuant to paragraph 4 of the same Article, Article 33–2 (1), Article 34(1), Article 35(1), Article 36(1), Article 37 (1) or (2), Article 39(1), Article 40(1) or (2), Article 41, 42, 42–2, 46, or 47 (excluding, however, in cases involving the provisions of Article 31, item i, Article 35(1), Article 36(1) or Article 42, reproductions of cinematographic works (including, in the case of works reproduced in cinematographic works, reproductions of such cinematographic works; the same shall apply below in this Article) may be offered to the public by transferring ownership of the reproductions made pursuant to these provisions.

be dissected in three conceptual steps of the mutual enrichment between the public domain and private sphere of IPRs. The three steps are:

Step 1 (granting IP): allowing privatization of some parts of the public domain to provide incentives for new creation and its sharing.
Step 2 (using IP): Requiring IP holders to benefit the public through various ways, including disclosure and allowing limitations and exceptions.
Step 3 (terminating IP): Requiring IPRs to flow back to the public domain upon expiration of the protection term to enrich it for everyone to enjoy and use for free.[53]

2.2. *Step 1: Granting IP*

The first step to kick off the IP life cycle is to privatize some contents of the public domain in the form of exclusive rights or at least rights to remuneration (not to exclude but entitled to remuneration) or "liability rights" to incentivize new creations and their usage. However, those that are indispensable for later creation may not be privatized at all, such as ideas, law of nature, generic terms, business methods,[54] software as such (not patentable)[55] and cultural commons.

The granting of IP has three basic avenues, patent rights for technical creation, copyright rights for cultural creation, and trademark rights for commercial creation of source-identifying indicators. Over time, there have been other creations that did not, or initially did not (such as computer software) fit into the three avenues. The sui generis IP laws were therefore enacted to grant stand-alone rights, such as design rights and plant variety rights. However, some sui generis IP has later proven to be hard even for courts to understand.[56] Some became of no use. The IC-layout design right might be one example in point (see Subsection 4.1.1 of Chapter 4).

53 R. Merges is of similar opinion when he states:

> The apprentice analogy, in other words, contained both a property element and a post-property-expiration element of free movement. It explains not just the patent term but also the importance of populating the public domain with useful economic assets after that term is over.
>
> Merges, R. (2022). *American Patent Law—A Business and Economic History* (p. 50). Cambridge University Press

54 Menell, P., & Meurer, M. (2009). *Nonpatentability of Business Methods: Legal and Economic Analysis*, at: https://ssrn.com/abstract=1482022.

55 Commuter programs can be protected by copyright law as literary works. However, commuter programs are not patentable under Article 52(2)(c) and (3), European Patent Convention.

56 For example, in the PRC, the sui generis right for IC-layout designs "does not work well in judicial practice, which is due to courts confusion about its entitlement mode." See Jianchen, L. (2023). From exclusivity to getting paid: The evolution of the entitlement mode for IC layout designs (in Chinese). *Peking University Law Journal*, *35*, 1368.

2.2.1. Exclusive Rights or Rights to Remuneration

In deciding the scope of privatization, namely whether to prefer exclusive rights over rights to remuneration or vice versa and the respective reach of the two rights, we should factor in the characteristics of the to-be-protected objects and the needs of their creators. Then to weigh the costs and benefits of under-protection against those of overprotection.

Under the protection of IP in the form of remuneration rights, could not provide the necessary incentives. Overprotection of IP in the form of strong exclusive rights leads to monopolization and efficiency loss, in terms not only of static inefficiency but also reduced dissemination and use of knowledge, follow-on research and innovation.

The most decisive factor in this context would probably be whether the users are difficult to locate, the usage is hard to detect, and the enforcement costs are therefore high. If the answer is yes, as this is the typical case for our pre-interconnected world, then exclusive rights should be preferred; as they can best ensure that every caught user and usage pay (prior consent of IP holders will be given only upon users' payment) or get punished for not paying (statutory or punitive damages). If, however, the answer is no, then rights to remuneration should be favored, as it will stimulate usage and actual payment for usage, a win-win for users and IP creators.

In the current online environment where users are registered and paying in their real names, anonymity is no more or highly limited, and every online usage is traceable, the rights to remuneration for IP creators could be favored.

2.2.2. Protection Terms

In the granting of patents states need to consider the fact that technology advances at a fast speed, therefore protection terms for patented technology should be shorter. Yet they need to equip patents with stronger exclusivity (in fact the strongest) to compensate for the shorter protection term so that patentees could recuperate investments made and reap the expected profits.

In the granting of trademark rights, states have to take into consideration that such source identifiers normally tend to have a shorter life span than natural persons due to fierce market competition.[57] Therefore, the protection term for trademarks should be commensurate with the life span of businesses that use those marks and therefore shorter.[58] However, trademark rights should be

57 According to https://www.granitefirm.com/blog/us/2023/05/23/lifespan-of-companies, 62% of American companies have an average life span of less than five years, small- and medium-sized companies less than seven years.

58 Article 18 of the TRIPS Agreement foresees a seven-year protection term for trademarks: "Initial registration, and each renewal of registration, of a trademark shall be for a term of no less than seven years. The registration of a trademark shall be renewable indefinitely."

renewable, even indefinitely, to reflect the protection needs of business entities which manage to survive market competition. States also need to decide whether to examine or not to examine applications of trademark registration, and further decide whether examination should include absolute and relative grounds for refusal to register or be limited to relative grounds for refusal to register.

Designed products tend to have a shorter shelf life, therefore the protection term for designs (whether design patent, sui generis rights) should be even shorter. Then the necessity of examination can be an issue. Take the EU for example, people can choose between not registering designs (unregistered designs) and enjoying three-year protection without examination and enjoying five-year protection for registered designs that need to undergo examination. Registered designs are renewable up to a maximum of 25 years to reflect the protection needs of longer-enduring designed products.

In granting or recognizing copyright, states must decide which level of threshold (originality) works must reach, it being understood that a low threshold consisting of the combination of minimum personality and self-creation (not copying others) is the global trend. States must weigh in the fact that authors of artistic, literature and scientific works usually live long after the creation of their works and works are daily bread for everyone, decide a much longer protection term for works (life of the authors plus fifty or seventy years), and significantly weaken exclusivity (in fact the weakest!).

2.3. Step 2: Using IP

The rigidity of exclusive IPRs can sometimes be very strong and the protection terms of IPRs are rather long. Waiting for IP to flow back to the public domain could be too distant for too many. To prevent IP from enslaving the world as absolute monopolies in a protracted fashion, IP holders in their status as private rightsholders are obliged to benefit the public through various mechanisms to facilitate the use of the protected subject matters during the protection terms of their IPRs.

Therefore, the second step of the IP life cycle is for rightsholders to disclose, use or authorize the use of the protected subject matters. Only then can IPRs deliver their promise of inspiring others, stimulating new creations and sharing through commercialization. These obligations of IP rightsholders have thus far not been systemically theorized and recognized. To that extent, Step 2 deserves more attention.

These obligations expected of IP holders should include sufficient disclosure of, working or licensing of, allowing free fair use and fared compulsory and statutory use of the protected subject matters. For an uninterrupted presentation of the three-step exchange theory in this subsection, a detailed discussion of these obligations during Step 2 can only be referred to subsections 5.7–5.11 of Capter 3.

2.4. Step 3: Terminating IP

2.4.1. After the Protection Term Expires

IP is not conventional property (houses, factories, farms, etc.) and cannot be protected perpetually,[59] as this would lead to the weakening and even depletion of the public domain. Therefore, IP can only be interim taking away of some parts and eventually giving back with new additions to the public domain. Therefore, the term of protection must be limited for the public domain to be enriched upon expiration of the protection. IP-protected subject matters must flow back to the public domain and become new components of our human common legacy.

The US Supreme Court in *Brulotte v. Thys Co.*[60] required categorically that when a patent expires, the licensee will be exempted from continuing to pay for royalty. The apex Court reaffirmed its position in *Kimble v. Marvel Entertainment*.[61] The majority opinion by Justice Elena Kagan explained how the US patent system reflects a congressional "balance between fostering innovation and ensuring public access to discoveries." Consequently, once the statutory term of the patent monopoly ends, "the right to make or use the article, free from all restriction, passes to the public." The patentee cannot continue to receive royalties for sales after his patent expires; so doing conflicts with patent law's policy of establishing a "post expiration . . . public domain."[62] It also stated that Congress, not the courts, gets to make a different patent policy.

Yet parties can still find ways around to achieve the same end of paying the inventor. To start, a licensee can contractually defer payments for pre-expiration use of a patent into the post-expiration period. For example, a licensee could agree to pay the licensor a sum equal to 10% of sales during the 20-year patent term but to amortize that amount over 40 years. That arrangement would at least bring down early outlays. Post-expiration royalties are allowable so long as they are tied to a non-patent right, such as trade secrets. Business arrangements other than

59 IP is treated more favorably than conventional property. One example is that it is not taxed. California assesses annual property taxes at 1% of the sales price, and takes your house, at least its cash value, once every century! In addition, conventional property is no longer absolute and only possessed on society's premises and insofar as private ownership is compatible with broader social objectives. See Baldwin, P. (2014). *The Copyright War—Three Centuries of Trans-Atlantic Battle* (p. 4). Princeton University Press.

60 379 U.S. 29 (1964).

61 *Kimble v. Marvel Entertainment, LLC*, 135 S. Ct. 2401 (2015).

62 *Kimble v. Marvel Entertainment, LLC*, 135 S. Ct. 2407 (2015). In Japan, the JFTC takes a more nuanced approach and opines that when a licensor imposes an obligation to pay royalties even after the rights to the technology have become extinct,

> it generally impedes the free use of technology. It will constitute an unfair trade practice if it tends to impede fair competition. Notwithstanding the above, the royalty payment obligation is thought not to unjustifiably restrain licensees' business activities if it is within the permissible extent of an installment or the deferred payment of royalties.
>
> JFTC, Guidelines for the Use of Intellectual Property under the Antimonopoly Act, 2016, Part 4(5)(iii)

royalties—all kinds of joint ventures—that enable parties to share the risks and rewards of commercializing an invention are also acceptable. Call/make it whatever you like, but just don't call/make it royalty for patents.

2.4.2. Before the Protection Term Expires

IPRs could be terminated prior to their expiration if they don't deserve the protection in the first place, were granted through fraudulent means, failed to achieve the functions that the legislature expects of them, or failed to pay the prescribed fee (registration fees, annuity, etc.). All these have in mind the early returning to the public domain of whatever that should not flow out of it.

Consequently, in many jurisdictions, unworthy granted patents can be invalidated in the post-grant invalidation procedure, and registered trademarks could be invalidated if not used for three consecutive years. Granted patents can also be revoked, forfeited, or invalidated if not implemented domestically within a designated time frame (e.g. India). The US Supreme Court from the twentieth century consistently championed the importance of encouraging patent challenges over contractual arrangements of no challenge.[63] Admittedly, this is also driven by the desire of returning unworthy patents back to the public domain as early as possible.

3. IP Redefined and Reappreciated

A common and succinct definition of IP is that "IP is the product or result of intellectual activity in the industrial, scientific, literary or artistic fields."[64] However, there is more to IP. Initially, IP is an incentive mechanism created by the government to address the issue of market failure. Further, if designed properly, IP could promote dynamic competition with enhanced innovation leading to new creation in terms of products and services of reliable quality that could evoke a sense of happiness among the public.[65] At the end of each IP exercise, a new creation will flow back to the public domain, enriching it even more and non-stop.

3.1. Members

To qualify as members of the IP family new creations must comply with some basic principles (refer to Subsections 4.7 and 4.8 of Chapter 4 for more details).

63 Merges, R. (2022). *American Patent Law—A Business and Economic History* (p. 492). Cambridge University Press. However, he argues that the America Invents Act has changed the incentive picture related to patent challenge, therefore restricts a plausible and sensible contractual agreement, and should therefore be revisited.

64 Ng-Loy, W. (2021). *Law of Intellectual Property of Singapore* (3rd. ed.), [1.1.3]. Sweet & Maxwell.

65 One might wonder what new creation trademark system would bring. Trademarks are known for the function of reducing the search costs of consumers. In addition, trademarks will also stimulate efforts to create new brands and maintain them as symbols of reliable quality and signs of happiness.

Therefore, IP members include patents, utility models, designs, trademarks, copyright (neighboring rights), and plant variety rights. IP members do not include IC layout designs and trade secrets, as there is no systemic guarantee that they will be eventually disclosed and flow back to the public domain. Test data submitted for governmental approval purposes are only disclosed to a narrow circle of people and do not satisfy the sufficient disclosure requirement. They are therefore not member of the IP family. Accordingly, Article 39 of the TRIPS Agreement protects trade secrets and test data submitted for government approval not as exclusive IPRs, but only along the line of curbing unfair competition and unfair commercial use.[66] Publicity right (lack of new creation),[67] and other "collective equitable rights," such as GIs, biodiversity,[68] traditional knowledge, folklore, cultural icons, totems, and the like are not members of the IP family (see Subsection 4.13 of Chapter 4).

3.2. Characteristics

There are some inherent characteristics of IP. They include high fixed costs to acquire (R&D, trials and errors, market acceptance, etc.), the ease of misappropriation in the digitized era where the marginal costs of producing and accessing copies are low or even zero, and there is no wear and tear in the quality of reproduction (infringing goods are just as good as genuine ones).

66 The relevant parts of Article 39 of the TRIPS Agreement provide:

> 1. In the course of ensuring effective protection against unfair competition as provided in Article 10bis of the Paris Convention (1967), Members shall protect undisclosed information in accordance with paragraph 2 and data submitted to governments or governmental agencies in accordance with paragraph 3. 2. Natural and legal persons shall have the possibility of preventing information lawfully within their control from being disclosed to, acquired by, or used by others without their consent in a manner contrary to honest commercial practices. . . 3. Members, when requiring, as a condition of approving the marketing of pharmaceutical or of agricultural chemical products which utilize new chemical entities, the submission of undisclosed test or other data, the origination which involves a considerable effort, shall protect such data against unfair commercial use. In addition, Members shall protect such data against disclosure, except where necessary to protect the public, or unless steps are taken to ensure that the data are protected against unfair commercial use.

67 "Although the right of publicity may have been accepted as an emerging area of intellectual property law in the United States." "The unjust enrichment rationale . . . championed by the US Supreme Court . . . appears to be the most appealing justification for recognizing the right of publicity." See Tan, D. (2017). *The Commercial Appropriation of Fame–A Cultural Analysis of the Right of Publicity and Passing Off* (pp. 41, 62). Cambridge University Press.

68 Korean IP Framework Act recognizes genetic resources as IP:

> The definitions of terms used in this Act shall be as follows: 1. The term "intellectual property" means knowledge, information, technology, the expression of thoughts or feelings, the indication of business or goods, varieties of organism or genetic resources and other intangibles created or discovered by creative activities, experience, etc. of human beings, the value of property of which may be realized.
>
> Article 3(1)

Another key feature of IP is that the actual scope and boundary of IPRs are highly uncertain. In the patent realm, it depends on the actual comparison of claims of patents that are in dispute and their equivalents in patent cases. In the trademark area, the comparison of trademarks and goods and services on which those trademarks are applied, and the determination of the perception of them with regard to the likelihood of confusion and dilution by the relevant public. In the copyright sphere, it depends on the assessment of originality and access possibility of works in question. The defense for IP infringement is also very uncertain, the fair-use defense varies from one area of IP to another.

In the highly connected global economy, if access to essential IP that involves network effects, compatibility with de jure or de facto standards, and popularity-induced indispensableness (e.g. pachinko machines in Japan, premier sports events in the West) is denied, the level of competition and innovation would be more adversely impacted, as opposed to the denial of access to tangible property.[69]

3.3. Economic Significance

In the knowledge economy of our times, IP exceeds conventional property in its economic significance. According to Ocean Tomo, the intangible assets (deducting the tangible assets) of the S&P 500 companies grew exponentially from 17% to 84% of the total assets over the forty-year period of 1975–2015. By July 2020, the intangible assets command 90% of the S&P 500 market value. This trend also holds for the S&P Europe 350 index as well, albeit to a lesser extent, with an increase from 71% in 2015 to 74% in 2020.[70]

The US and EU started to estimate the economic significance of IP in their respective economies around 2012. The US Department of Commerce issued "Intellectual Property and the US Economy: Industries in Focus." The report identified the industries that rely most heavily on IP as IP-intensive and estimated their contribution to the US economy. The latest report shows that IP-intensive industries in the US accounted for 41% of domestic economic activity, or output, in 2019. Altogether the IP-intensive industries accounted for 63 million jobs, or 44% of all US employment in 2019. About 33%, or more than 47 million jobs, were directly supported by IP-intensive industries. They also indirectly supported—through the supply of intermediate goods and services—an additional 15.5 million jobs, accounting for the remaining 11% of the total.[71]

The latest report published by the EPO and the EUIPO shows a similar trend. IP-intensive industries generated 29.7% of all jobs in the EU in 2017–19. This

69 Drexl, J. (Ed.). (2008). *Research Handbook on Intellectual Property and Competition Law* (pp. 49–50). Edward Elgar; Hilty, R. (2012). Patent enforcement. In Liu, K.-C., & Hilty, R. (Eds.), *Patent Enforcement* (p. 11). Springer.

70 See https://oceantomo.com/intangible-asset-market-value-study

71 USPTO. *Intellectual Property and the U.S. Economy* (3rd ed.), at: https://www.uspto.gov/sites/default/files/documents/uspto-ip-us-economy-third-edition.pdf.

means they directly employed more than 61 million people in the EU. In addition, another 20 million jobs were generated in industries that supply goods and services to IPR-intensive businesses, adding up to a total number of 82 million IPR-dependent jobs (39.4%). PR-intensive industries generated EUR 6.4 trillion in 2017–19, or more than 47% of the EU's GDP. These industries also accounted for most of the EU's trade with the rest of the world and generated a trade surplus of EUR 224 billion.[72]

4. IP and Protection Against Unfair Competition

Since the Revision Conference of The Hague in 1925, the Paris Convention has "the repression of unfair competition" as one of the objects of the protection of industrial property, due to the consideration that "in many cases infringement of industrial property rights . . . will at the same time be an act of unfair competition," (Article 1(2))[73] without qualifying "the repression of unfair competition" as IP. The TRIPS Agreement adheres to this non-IP stance towards protection against unfair competition when it defines "intellectual property" as referring "to all categories of intellectual property that are the subject of Sections 1 through 7 of Part II (Article 1(2)), excluding Section 8 (Control of Anti-competitive Practices in Contractual Licences)."

The TRIPS Agreement does not touch upon the relationship between the protection of IP and the protection against unfair competition, whereas the Paris Convention stipulates that the former has the latter as one of its objects. This almost one-hundred-year-old provision of the Paris Convention seems hard to apprehend. Why IP protection's objects could include "the repression of unfair competition," as IP is mostly about entitlement to encourage creation and its exploitation that would benefit human society and enrich the public domain?

Rather, there has been some complementarity between IP protection and the repression of unfair competition, especially in jurisdictions where their law of trademarks is developed from the broader law of unfair competition. IP regimes generally started later than unfair competition law and were unable, due to incomplete or limited provisions, to cover many non-IP-infringing but culpable practices. In many economies, unfair competition law was applied to stop some of these non-IP-infringing but unfair practices. For example, the unauthorized use of other's well-known marks on dissimilar goods before the TRIPS Agreement was not covered by many national trademark laws and could only be prevented by unfair competition law. Then it would have been meaningful had the Paris Convention reminded us that unfair competition law can come to the rescue. However, after

72 EPO & EUIPO. (2022). *Intellectual Property Rights Intensive Industries and Economic Performance in the European Union*, at: https://www.epo.org/en/news-events/press-centre/press-release/2022/452248.

73 See Bodenhausen, G. (1968). *Guide to the Application of the Paris Convention for the Protection of Industrial Property, as Revised at Stockholm in 1967* (p. 23). WIPO, at: https://www.wipo.int/edocs/pubdocs/en/intproperty/611/wipo_pub_611.pdf.

the establishment of the WTO, IP regimes have witnessed expansion in protection globally and more and more national trademark regimes become stand-alone laws separated from the general unfair competition law. This complementarity started to wane in many jurisdictions, as their respective IP regimes have exhaustively dealt with the disputes they targeted, leaving no lacuna for unfair competition law to fill.[74]

Noteworthy is that beginning in 1994, the Japanese Unfair Competition Prevention Act (UCPA) prohibits acts of assigning, leasing, displaying for the purpose of assignment or leasing, exporting or importing goods which imitate the configuration (excluding configuration that is indispensable for ensuring the function of said goods) of another person's goods as "unfair competition." (Article 2 (1)(iii)(a)). However, there are problems with protecting IP-related interests with unfair competition law, as it is not "entitlement" law. Therefore, UCPA puts a three-year time limit on such protection.[75] In other words, a slavish copy of the configuration of others' goods, which are not IP-protected, within three years from the date they were first sold in Japan is an act of unfair competition in Japan.

5. IP as Part of the National Innovation System

National states commonly set up their own national innovation system which includes diverse components, such as market competition, subsidies to basic research, rewards, prizes, grants, higher education, infrastructure (commercialization, logistics), IP, etc. IP is just part of that complicated national innovation system.

On top of those, there are I(ntellectual) P(roducts) without IP, such as creation by chef cooks, magicians,[76] comedians, and fashion,[77] which are protected by the

74 It is why Russia does not include the protection against unfair competition in Part IV of its Civil Code that incorporated all IP laws. "Following the Russian legal tradition, the Federal Law No. 135-Fz provides protection against unfair competition with administrative, rather than civil legal tools." See Lisitsa, V. (2016). IP law in Russia, development, problems, and perspectives. *WIPO-WTO Colloquium Papers*, 62, at: https://www.wto.org/english/tratop_e/trips_e/colloquium_papers_e/2016/chapter_7_2016_e.pdf (2016).

75 Article 19(1) No. 5(a) of Japanese UCPA provides:

> The provisions of Articles 3 through 15, Article 21 (excluding the part under Article 21, paragraph (2), item (vii)), and Article 22 do not apply to the act prescribed in the relevant of the following items for the classification of unfair competition set forth in that item: (v)(a) the act of transferring, leasing, displaying for the purpose of transfer or lease, exporting or importing goods that imitate the form of goods if three years have elapsed since the date they were first sold in Japan.

76 Dougherty, J. (2018). Now you own it, now you don't—or do you? Copyright and related rights in magic productions and performances after *Teller v. Dogge*. Loyola Law School. *Los Angeles Legal Studies Research Paper No. 2018–12*, 2, at: https://papers.ssrn.com/sol3/papers.cfm?abstract_id=3151843.

77 Raustiala and Sprigman explain enlighteningly how the fashion industry curiously survives, and even thrives, in the face of extensive copying, see Raustiala, K., & Sprigman, C.J. (2021). Faster fashion: The piracy paradox and its perils. *Cardozo Arts & Entertainment*, *39*, 537 et seq.

self-regulation of the businesses. Last but not least, many creations are made out of altruism for the common good of society and do not need any protection.

Moreover, IP, as part of the national innovation system, does not and should not be used to protect and prolong existing business models and ways of life. For example, IP should not stand in the way of cloud computing and streaming as they replace physical copies, or block file-sharing as it takes over buying or getting licensed, hampers eBooks as they squeeze out printed ones, or hinder live concerts and live events as they phase out the sale of records or canned music, or slow down hand-held mobile devices' individualization of the use and enjoyment of works.

6. IP's Position Within the General Legal System

IP is an equal component of a comprehensive legal system, not trumping every other law as *lex specialis*, where the arch-principles of proportionality, basic human rights, consumer protection, respect for the private sphere, and international free trade prevail. Unfortunately, as Balganesh points out "The dominant scholarly trend in the field today resists acknowledging the derivative nature of intellectual property and its symbiotic relationship with other areas."[78] With the entrenchment of IP laws and the setting up of specialized IP courts,[79] some unnerving IP exceptionalism can be observed rising.

Echoing this concern are the 37 decisions that the US Supreme Court rendered between 2006 and 2020, which "reflect a project of eliminating 'patent exceptionalism' and assimilating patent doctrine to general legal principles . . . bringing patent law in conformity with general legal standards."[80] The USCAFC, which enjoys the unified national jurisdiction of patent disputes, has "had mangled the contours of general legal doctrines when applying those doctrines to patent cases, forcing the Supreme Court to run down many of its stray rulings."[81]

78 Balganesh, S. (2022). The genius of common-law intellectual property. *The Journal of Legal Studies*, *50*, S102.

79 One of the characteristics of IP laws in major Asian economies, see Liu, K.-C. (2022). *IP Laws and Regimes in Major Asian Economies—Combing Through Thousand Threads of IP to Peace in Asia* (p. 4). Routledge.

80 Lee, P. (2016). The supreme assimilation of patent law. *Michigan Law Review*, *114*, 1413, at: https://repository.law.umich.edu/mlr/vol114/iss8/2.

81 Merges, R. (2022). *American Patent Law—A Business and Economic History* (p. 447). Cambridge University Press.

3 Market Competition and Competition Law

1. Introduction: Competition and Competition Law

For market economies, which are doubtful of an almighty planner, competition is the preferred discovery process for optimal allocation of limited resources to enrich human societies. Competition is again not an end, but a tool to serve a higher end, an end that is bigger than any individual's gains or losses. Just like IP, competition enriches the public domain on which every human being is dependent. We cheer for winners of that process, not because of heroism, but achievements that elevate human status. We also cherish those who did not win immediately, as they might be the next winners. That said, competition is not synonymous with social Darwinism that excludes the weaker losers, but a continuous effort to boost higher human performance. No matter how important it is, competition is just one human leg and needs another leg of cooperation to drive societal progress.

To achieve its purpose, competition must be free and fair. Competition is to unleash the greatest potential of market players, therefore it should be free, free from restraint, collusion, distortion, concentrated power through money games, such as anti-competitive mergers, and bullying by abusing dominant market position. Free competition also encompasses free access to the public domain, the right to free copying, and competition by imitation. Free competition must, of course, respect other people's rights, including IPRs, so that competition by substitution can also take place. But competition should be as free as possible, as free as the blue sea for everything to set sail, needing only to avoid sporadic small islands of (IP) rights. Free competition has to be supplemented by fair competition that is free from untruthful, misleading, unfair, and reproachable/unethical competition. Internationally, free and fair competition means free and fair trade.

For more than a century, market competition has been the scrutiny subject of anti-trust law and unfair competition law (collectively competition law). Competition law has two branches, one general and the other sector-specific. General competition law has no special concerns for the success or failure of any given business sector. It has broadly termed legislative standards, therefore its detailed rulemaking is often left to independent agencies with broad general market-related expertise and courts. General competition law is thus quite far removed from democratic

DOI: 10.4324/9781003597766-4

control.[1] It mostly intervenes ex-post, with some exceptions, such as requiring prior notice under merger control, so that enterprises have the maximum freedom in conducting businesses.

In addition, there are myriad sector-specific competition laws due to many considerations, such as insufficient competition caused by hard-to-break network effects, and asymmetric bargaining power between incumbent dominant players and new market entrants or consumers at large. If the success or failure of the sector is of societal, economic, or strategic importance (such as radio, TV, telecom, digital platforms, etc.) to regulators, they will enact sector-specific competition laws to proactively intervene ex-ante. Sector-specific competition laws are often fraught with regulatory considerations to attain certain goals, whether regulating monopolies, liberalizing/de-monopolizing markets, price control,[2] or fostering competition in networked industries. It is common that special agencies are set up to enforce sector-specific competition laws (e.g., USFCC, German Federal Network Agency) and are policy-oriented and politics-influenced. The regulatory agency has a narrower scope of expertise and runs higher risks of being captured by its regulatees and interest groups.

But unlike IP laws, which are internationally harmonized under a plethora of international treaties, competition law is not harmonized on a global scale.

2. Market and the Relevant Markets

2.1. Market and Types of Market

Market is the place or platform, real or virtual, where competition for goods or services takes place. Basically, there are three types of markets according to their concentration level. The first is the free (competitive) market where near-perfect competition reigns. It means free market entry and existence. Market demand and supply reach their equilibrium through the invisible hand of the market. The second is the oligopolistic market where it is dominated by a small number of players (oligopolists). One of the features of an oligopolistic market for homogeneous products which are perfect substitutes for each other is that there will be little or no price

1 Ackermann, T. (2023). Private rights and public autonomy in a fragmented world: Why an institutional perspective on intellectual property and competition laws matters. *GRUR International*, 209.

2

> There is also a widely accepted view that competition authorities are ill-suited to carry out price controls, a task which should be better left to sector-specific regulators. Because they intervene on an ad hoc basis, i.e. to sanction specific anticompetitive behavior, competition authorities cannot easily transform themselves into price regulators. Price regulation is a long-term effort which requires quasi-permanent supervision."
>
> Geradin, D. (2007)

The necessary limits to the control of "excessive" prices by competition authorities—a view from Europe. *Tilburg University Legal Studies Working Paper*, 1–44, at: https://papers.ssrn.com/sol3/papers.cfm?abstract_id=1022678.

competition if the only two firms in the market produce at constant marginal costs. Then neither firm has any reason to raise prices as it will lose all its customers to the other firm. Nor will they cut prices, as it will only force the other firm to follow suit, which will offset the first firm's advantage brought by the price cut and lower the overall price level of the two firms.[3] The gasoline market is one good example of an oligopolistic market in many economies.

A monopolistic market is the third type of market, where the monopolist enterprise faces no competition or has a dominant position to exclude competition in the relevant market for a significant period. It can be a single firm monopoly that is dominated by one enterprise. For example, the search engine market is dominated by Google, which enjoys a global market share of 81.95% as of January 2024.[4] Even Amazon, despite being the online retail giant itself and appearing as the first organic result when netizens key in "amazon," pays Google to secure that its "Amazon" will pop up as the first result of keyword search. This shows the monopolistic power Google has in the search engine market.

A monopolistic market can also be a joint monopoly held by several undertakings, which are legally and economically independent of each other, provided that—from an economic point of view—they present themselves or act together on a relevant market as a collective entity. "The existence of an agreement or of other links in law is not indispensable to a finding of a collective position of dominance. Such a finding may be based on other connecting factors."[5] A typical case where such connecting factors exist would be the joint monopoly formed by Philips, Sony, and Taiyo Yuden through the CD-R patent pool and joint licensing scheme alluded to in Subsection 5.1 of Chapter 1.

2.2. The Relevant Markets

Market regulation is normally targeted at one specific or relevant market. Therefore, defining the relevant market is the first step, also for the application of competition law. The market will be relevant if it provides products or services that are substitutable by reason of their characteristics, prices, intended use, and geographic and temporal availability. With regard to technical products and services, there could be up to four relevant markets: the relevant R&D market, the relevant technology market (composed of patents and know-how), the relevant product market, and the relevant after-service market. Finding the right relevant market is not always easy.

With the rise of the internet, two-sided or even multi-sided markets become prevalent. Two-sided markets are online platforms that interconnect two or multiple distinct user groups that used to transact directly with one another. Examples

3 This is according to the Bertrand duopoly equilibrium, see https://en.wikipedia.org/wiki/Bertrand_competition.

4 See https://gs.statcounter.com/search-engine-market-share/desktop/united-states-of-america.

5 EC, Guidelines on market analysis and the assessment of significant market power under the EU regulatory framework for electronic communications networks and services (2018/C 159/01), at 3.2.

of two-sided markets include credit cards (composed of cardholders and merchants), healthcare organizations (composed of patients and doctors), and apps on smartphones (composed of end-users and developers), with the last one having the capacity to become the mega two-sided market that would absorb all other sub-two-sided markets.

A key feature of two-sided markets is the novel pricing strategies and business models they employ. In order to attract one group of users, online platforms typically subsidize the other group of users.[6] For example, users of communication apps, such as WhatsApp, Line, and WeChat, get their service for free and quickly aggregate to become big customer bases to attract advertisers who then fund the system. The search engine market also follows the same pattern.

In dealing with any two-sided market, it is necessary to consider the two distinct user groups and the platform that interconnects between the two as the relevant market.[7] In the PRC, Alibaba had forced its users to choose between Alibaba and its competitors through the "one of the two" restriction. State Administration for Market Regulation (SAMR) found in April 2021 that such practice constitutes monopolization and fined Alibaba RMB 18,228 billion, 4% of its 2019 domestic sales volume. The relevant market that SAMR determined is the "online retail service platform market within China"—a two-sided market that connects businesses on the service platform and consumers.[8]

2.3. Measurement of Market Power: The Herfindal-Hirschman (HHI) Index

The now most used measure by antitrust agencies, for example, USDOJ, FTC, and the EC, for market power is the so-called HHI Index. Named after economists Orris Herfindahl and Albert Hirschman, the Herfindal-Hirschman (HHI) Index is the sum of the squares of the market shares of the 50 largest firms (or all the firms if fewer than 50) within the industry. The sum can range from zero to ten thousand points, moving from a huge number of very small firms to a single monopolistic producer. Increases in the HHI indicate an increase in market power. HHI gives more weight to larger firms.

In the US, since 1982 the DOJ and FTC refer to mergers with HHI above one thousand as concentrated markets, with HHI between one thousand and eighteen hundred as "moderately concentrated" and above eighteen hundred as "highly concentrated." Transactions that increase the HHI by more than one hundred points in

6 In the telecom industry there has long been riddled with practices of cross-subsidization, where one telecom service provider charges one group of users, such as urban users, for one specific service above costs or at artificially higher prices to ease the financial burden of another group of users, such as rural users. Long distance telecom service has also been charged exorbitant fees to underwrite low monthly rates for local telecom service. See Nuechterlein, J., and Weiser, P. (2012). *The Digital Crossroads* (2nd ed., 38–528). MIT Press.

7 Rysman, M. (2009). The economics of two-sided markets. *Journal of Economic Perspectives, 125*, at: https://pubs.aeaweb.org/doi/pdfplus/10.1257/jep.23.3.125.

8 See http://www.xinhuanet.com/english/2021-04/10/c_139871057.htm.

highly concentrated markets are presumed by them to substantially lessen competition or tend to create a monopoly.[9]

In the EU, however, the EC sees the HHI Index slightly differently. It is unlikely to identify horizontal competition concerns in a market with a post-merger HHI below one thousand. The EC is also unlikely to identify horizontal competition concerns in a merger with a post-merger HHI between one thousand and two thousand and a delta below two hundred and fifty, or a merger with a post-merger HHI above two thousand and a delta below one hundred and fifty, barring special circumstances.[10]

3. General Competition Law

More and more countries have adopted/enacted general competition laws. There has been an exponential increase of competition laws in national legal systems in recent years, accounting for more than 127 jurisdictions as of 2021.[11] The proliferation of general competition law means that the protection of market competition has become a universal truism.

3.1. Why Regulating Market?

Government regulation takes place for many reasons, mostly to protect public interests, such as health and safety, public security, morality, taxation, positive externality (in getting rid of public nuisances such as pollution, traffic congestion, etc.), access to knowledge and justice, freedom of expression, incentives for innovation and its sharing (IP), and the functioning market competition.

Although the market can work its magic, "markets often don't work well . . . markets don't exist in a vacuum, and have to be structured."[12] "Whenever information is imperfect and markets incomplete, which is to say always, and especially in developing countries, then the invisible hand works most imperfectly."[13] As a matter of fact, market failure happens, and quite often: prudential markets (trust,

9 DOJ & FTC, Merger Guidelines §2.1 (2023). Between 2010 and 2023, DOJ and FTC raised the thresholds: an HHI of less than 1,500 to be a competitive marketplace, an HHI of 1,500 to 2,500 to be a moderately concentrated marketplace, and an HHI of 2,500 or greater to be a highly concentrated marketplace. Mergers that increase the HHI by more than 200 points in highly concentrated markets raise antitrust concerns, as they are assumed to enhance market power. The Guidelines returns to the original standards adopted in 1982 as DOJ and FTC are of the opinion that "the original HHI thresholds better reflect both the law and the risks of competitive harm suggested by market structure."

10 EC, Guidelines on the assessment of horizontal mergers under the Council Regulation on the control of concentrations between undertakings, Official Journal C 031, 05/02/2004, paragraphs 19–20.

11 Godinho I, M., and Marques, N.C. (2021). Competition criminal law: An international and global trend? *SHS Web of Conferences 92, 03011/Globalization and Its Socio-Economic Consequences 2020*, at: https://www.shs-conferences.org/articles/shsconf/pdf/2021/03/shsconf_glob20_03011.pdf.

12 Stiglitz, J. (2018). Globalization and its discontents revisited. *Norton*, xliii.

13 Stiglitz, J. (2018). Globalization and its discontents revisited. *Norton*, 169.

insurance, investment, etc.) due to the inherent moral hazards, public utilities (urban transportation market, water, electricity, etc.) due to natural monopoly issues (more than one supplier of the same service would cause wasteful duplication), network industries (railroad, telecom, etc.) due to exorbitant sunk costs and network effects (people locked in by the network due to prohibitive switching costs), and professional markets (judicial, public heath, accounting, etc.) due to information asymmetry.

Even in the US, which is believed to be the most competitive market, there are quite a few oligopolistic markets: three providers (Verizon, AT&T Mobility, T-Mobile) control over 99% of the cellular telephone service market as of 2023.[14] Five movie studios receive almost 80–85% of American film revenues.[15] ASCAP and BMI together represent approximately 90% of the public performance licensing market.[16] The five largest brewers, including Anheuser-Bush and Miller Coors, account for nearly 80% of the market share.[17] The smartphone market is a duopoly by Apple and Samsung with a combined market share of 86%.[18] Oligopolistic markets are hotbeds for anti-competitive behavior that requires oversight from competition law.

Globally speaking, oligopolistic markets are common. In the music industry, Universal Music Group, Sony Music Entertainment, and Warner Music Group had a collective global market share of some 65–70% in 2014.[19] The accountancy market is dominated by the big four: KPMG, Deloitte Touche Tohmatsu, PricewaterhouseCoopers, and Ernst &Young. Three credit rating agencies (Standard & Poor's, Moody's, and Fitch Group) dominate the entire credit rating industry.[20] Sixty percent of the commercial seed market is currently controlled by the big four seed companies: Bayer, Corteva, Sinochem, and BASF.[21]

3.2. Legal Protection of Free Competition

Free competition is a protectable institution by antitrust law because it facilitates productive and distributive efficiency, and enhances consumer welfare by increasing

14 See https://www.statista.com/statistics/199359/market-share-of-wireless-carriers-in-the-us-by-subscriptions/.
15 See https://en.wikipedia.org/wiki/Major_film_studios.
16 Delrahim, M. (January 2021) *"And the Beat Goes On": The Future of the ASCAP/BMI Consent Decrees*, at: https://www.justice.gov/opa/speech/file/1355241/download.
17 Codog, A. (2019). The antitrust roadblock: Preventing consolidation of the craft beer market. *The University of the Pacific Law Review*, *50*, 407.
18 Zahran, O. (January 2022). *Apple, Samsung, and the Irrelevance of the American Smartphone Market*, at: https://omarzahran.medium.com/apple-samsung-and-the-irrelevance-of-the-american-smartphone-market.
19 See https://en.wikipedia.org/wiki/Record_label.
20 Finny, D. (November 2023). *Credit Rating Agencies: Overview and History*, at: https://www.investopedia.com/articles/bonds/09/history-credit-rating-agencies.asp.
21 Pesticide, Seed, and Digital Agriculture Industry Concentrates Wealth and Power, Threatens Health posted on 13 January 2023, at: https://beyondpesticides.org/dailynewsblog/2023/01/pesticide-seed-and-digital-agriculture-industry-concentrates-wealth-and-power-threatens-health/.

more choices and better quality at lower prices. Commercial competition acts as a check-and-balance to commercial power and establishment, which if unchecked will result in collusion with political power and encroach on democracy.[22]

3.2.1. *The US Approach*

The English common law of restraint of trade is the direct predecessor to modern competition law later developed in the US by the Sherman Act of 1890. At the time of its passage, "trust" was synonymous with monopolistic practice, because it was a popular way for monopolists to overcome prohibitions in Ohio state against oil corporations owning stock in other corporations with their overflowing oil money and a way for cartel participants to create enforceable agreements. That's why the Act is also known as anti-trust law. The Sherman Act is extremely short (eight sections in total) and succinct from its inception, which gives courts exceptional authority to shape the law and reconsider precedents based on better economic analysis.

A. SECTION 1, SHERMAN ACT BANS CARTEL ACTIVITIES

The Sherman Act first bans any and all collusion, whether contract, combination (trust or otherwise) or conspiracy, in restraint of trade or commerce.[23] When the Sherman Act was passed, the penal punishment was only a misdemeanor punishable by up to a year in prison. Congress amended the Sherman Act in 1974 to increase penalties and make cartel activity a felony subject to three-year imprisonment. Maximum penalties were again increased to up to ten years by a 2004 amendment to the Sherman Act.[24]

22 Nazi Germany and Japan before WWII are two classical examples of concentrated economic power entrenching concentrated political power and vice versa. Therefore, the Ally issued decartelization decrees in 1947 in Germany and Japan to break apart concentrated economic power to pave way for democratization to take hold. The Japanese Antimonopoly and Fair Trade Maintenance Act was legislated in 1947. Germany enacted its Act Against Restraints of Competition in 1957, which entered into force on January 1, 1958.

23 Section 1 of the Sherman Act provides:

> Every contract, combination in the form of trust or otherwise, or conspiracy, in restraint of trade or commerce among the several States, or with foreign nations, is declared to be illegal. Every person who shall make any contract or engage in any combination or conspiracy hereby declared to be illegal shall be deemed guilty of a felony, and, on conviction thereof, shall be punished by fine not exceeding $100,000,000 if a corporation, or, if any other person, $1,000,000, or by imprisonment not exceeding 10 years, or by both said punishments, in the discretion of the court.

24 During the first seventy years of the Sherman Act, prison sentences were very rarely imposed in cases involving ordinary cartel activity. A 1967 law review article reflected the general consensus that cartel activities were "not crimes of moral turpitude" and thus were "classified as malum prohibitum (wrong [as or because] prohibited) crimes rather than mala in se crimes." In the early 1970s, individuals were incarcerated after 8% of successful cartel prosecutions, and imprisoned individuals served an average of 44 days. During 1975–80, prison sentences were imposed nearly

Courts adopt the rule of reason approach when applying Section 1 of the Sherman Act and apply "its three-step, burden-shifting framework." Step 1: The plaintiff has the initial burden to show that "the challenged restraint has a substantial anticompetitive effect that harms consumers in the relevant market." Step 2: The burden shifts to the defendant to show a procompetitive rationale for the restraint. Step 3: The burden shifts back to the plaintiff to demonstrate that the procompetitive efficiencies could be reasonably achieved through less anticompetitive means.[25] In this juncture, it is worthwhile to point out that in the case involving Fashion Originators' Guild alluded to in Subsection 6.2 Chapter 1, joint efforts to police and punish those who copied and sold registered dress designs were struck down by the Supreme Court in 1941 as a violation of Section 1 of the Sherman Act.[26]

B. SECTION 2 OF THE SHERMAN ACT PENALIZES MONOPOLIZATION

Section 2 prohibits monopolization and attempts to categorize monopolization as a felony.[27] There are two elements of monopolization. (I) The possession of monopoly power in the relevant market. (II) The willful acquisition or maintenance of that power "through exclusionary conduct 'as distinguished from growth or development as a consequence of a superior product, business acumen, or historic accident."[28] Section 2 is a species of restraint of trade under Section 1.

To prevent and cure monopolization, competition authority could break up the over-sized monopolies. The first divestiture took place in 1911 when Standard Oil was ordered to be broken into 33 different companies.[29] The second large-scale divestiture happened some seventy years later. The USDOJ had long suspected the then monopoly in the US telecommunication market, American Telephone &

---

three times as often under the felony statute as under the misdemeanor statute. In addition, the average term for individuals sentenced to prison under the felony statute was more than three times that for individuals sentenced under the misdemeanor statute. In the early 1980s, individuals were incarcerated after 29% of successful cartel prosecutions, and the imprisoned individuals served an average of 120 days. Sanctions actually imposed have continued to increase. During 200507, the average term of incarceration for all crimes prosecuted by the Antitrust Division was 703 days. During this period, 76% of convicted individuals were sentenced to terms of incarceration. See Stucke, M. (2006). Morality and antitrust. *UTK Law Faculty Publications*, 773, at: https://ir.law.utk.edu/utklaw_facpubs/773 (460 et seq.).

25 *Ohio v. Am. Express*, 138 S. Ct. 2274, 2284 (2018).

26 *Fashion Originators' Guild of Am. v. FTC*, 312 US 457 (1941).

27 Section 2 Sherman Act provides that:

> Every person who shall monopolize, or attempt to monopolize, or combine or conspire with any other person or persons, to monopolize any part of the trade or commerce among the several States, or with foreign nations, shall be deemed guilty of a felony, and, on conviction thereof, shall be punished by fine not exceeding $100,000,000 if a corporation, or, if any other person, $1,000,000, or by imprisonment not exceeding 10 years, or by both said punishments, in the discretion of the court.

28 *US v. Grinnell Corp.*, 384 US 563 (1966).

29 *Standard Oil Co. of New Jersey v. US*, 221 US 1 (1910).

Telegraph Company (AT&T), of monopolizing the telecommunication market and accused it in 1974 of levering the monopoly in its bottleneck local exchange facilities to unfairly create and sustain monopolies in the competitive interexchange service and tried to break up AT&T. On January 6, 1982, a consent decree was reached between AT&T and DOJ, and accepted by Judge Herald Greene with two-times revision, effective on January 1, 1984. According to the decree, AT&T divested itself of seven regional Bell holding companies.[30]

C. SECTION 7 OF THE CLAYTON ACT BANS MERGERS THAT SUBSTANTIALLY LESSEN COMPETITION

The Clayton Act addresses specific practices that the Sherman Act does not clearly prohibit, such as mergers and interlocking directorates (that is, the same person making business decisions for competing companies). Section 7 of the Act prohibits mergers and acquisitions whose effect "may be substantially to lessen competition, or to tend to create a monopoly." As amended by the Robinson-Patman Act of 1936, the Clayton Act also bans certain discriminatory prices, services, and allowances in dealings between merchants. The Clayton Act was amended again in 1976 by the Hart-Scott-Rodino Antitrust Improvements Act to require companies planning large mergers or acquisitions to notify the government of their plans in advance.

As the Supreme Court has explained, "Section 7 itself creates a relatively expansive definition of antitrust liability: To show that a merger is unlawful, a plaintiff needs only prove that its effect 'may be substantially to lessen competition.'"[31] This is because "[t]he grand design of . . . Section 7, as to stock acquisitions [and] the acquisition of assets, was to arrest incipient threats to competition which the [more broadly applicable] Sherman Act did not ordinarily reach."[32]

The antitrust agencies have remained inactive in curbing anti-competitive mergers in the last two decades. Only recently, the DOJ and FTC in the 2023 merger guidelines exhibit a determination to end this "green light" era of not enforcing antitrust laws.[33]

30 Nuechterlein, J., & Weiser, P. (2012). *The Digital Crossroads* (2nd ed., pp. 44–528). MIT Press.

31 *California v. Am. Stores Co.*, 495 U.S. 271, 284 (1990) (quoting 15 USC §8 with emphasis, citing Brown Shoe, 370 US at 323).

32 *US v. Penn-Olin Chemical Co.*, 378 US 158, 170–71 (1964).

33 A comment by Tim Wu, cited from the editorial of the New York Times on August 26, 2023, The Americans Pay a Price for Corporate Consolidation, at: https://www.nytimes.com/2023/08/26/opinion/biden-lina-khan-ftc.html.

3.2.2. The EU Approach

A. ARTICLE 101 TFEU BANS THE PREVENTION, RESTRICTION OR DISTORTION OF COMPETITION

Following Section 1 of the US Sherman Act, Article 101 of the TFEU prohibits cartel activities. In so doing, it has made progress, compared with the former, in better-defining cartel: "all agreements between undertakings, decisions by associations of undertakings and concerted practices which may affect trade between Member States and which have as their object or effect the prevention, restriction or distortion of competition within the internal market." Article 101 then gives detailed and enumerative examples of cartels: price fixing, limiting, or controlling production (markets, technical development, or investment), sharing of markets or sources of supply, discrimination, and tie-ins.

Article 101 however has certain flexibilities to exempt cartel that contributes to improving the production or distribution of goods or to promoting technical or economic progress, while allowing consumers a fair share of the resulting benefit. It is also mindful of the danger that such exemption might be misused and therefore adheres to the proportionality principle widely applied in the EU regulatory context by requiring that the concerned restrictions must be indispensable to the attainment of these objectives and may not afford undertakings in question the possibility of eliminating competition in respect of a substantial part of the products in question.[34]

To provide guidance on the understanding of Article 101, the European Commission (EC) issued the 2011 Guidelines on the applicability of Article 101 of the Treaty on the Functioning of the EU to horizontal cooperation agreements (Horizontal Guidelines), replacing guidelines on the applicability of Article 81 of the EC Treaty to horizontal cooperation agreements (2001/C 3/02) in 2001.

34 Article 101 TFEU prescribes:

> 1. The following shall be prohibited as incompatible with the internal market: all agreements between undertakings, decisions by associations of undertakings and concerted practices which may affect trade between Member States and which have as their object or effect the prevention, restriction or distortion of competition within the internal market, and in particular those which: (a) directly or indirectly fix purchase or selling prices or any other trading conditions; (b) limit or control production, markets, technical development, or investment; (c) share markets or sources of supply; (d) apply dissimilar conditions to equivalent transactions with other trading parties, thereby placing them at a competitive disadvantage; (e) make the conclusion of contracts subject to acceptance by the other parties of supplementary obligations which, by their nature or according to commercial usage, have no connection with the subject of such contracts. 2. Any agreements or decisions prohibited shall be void. 3. The provisions of paragraph 1 may, be declared inapplicable to any agreement which contributes to improving the production or distribution of goods or to promoting technical or economic progress, while allowing consumers a fair share of the resulting benefit, which does not: (a) impose on the undertakings concerned restrictions which are not indispensable to the attainment of these objectives; (b) afford such undertakings the possibility of eliminating competition in respect of a substantial part of the products in question.

B. ARTICLE 102 TFEU BANS ABUSE OF DOMINANT POSITION

Any abuse by one or more undertakings of a dominant position within the internal market or in a substantial part of it shall be prohibited as incompatible with the internal market in so far as it may affect trade between Member States. Such abuse may, in particular, consist in: (I) directly or indirectly imposing unfair purchase or selling prices or other unfair trading conditions; (II) limiting production, markets or technical development to the prejudice of consumers; (III) applying dissimilar conditions to equivalent transactions with other trading parties, thereby placing them at a competitive disadvantage;(IV) making the conclusion of contracts subject to acceptance by the other parties of supplementary obligations which, by their nature or according to commercial usage, have no connection with the subject of such contracts.

The EC has made frequent use of Article 102 to batter the abuse of dominance. Google cases are especially noteworthy. In March 2015 the EC issued a formal Statement of Objections to Google, alleging the company has committed multiple violations of European antitrust law. The EC first reached a conclusion in June 2017 that Google abused its dominance in the general internet search market in 31 members of the EEA by deploying discriminatory algorithms,[35] which led to a sharp increase of traffic to its websites (45 times in the United Kingdom, 35 times in Germany, 19 times in France, and 29 times in the Netherlands). The EC imposed a fine of €2.42 billion (US$5 billion) on Google.[36]

In July 2018 the EC further found Google has abused its Android market dominance in three key areas and imposed on Google a record-breaking €4.3 billion (US$5 billion) fine: (I) Google has been bundling its search engine and Chrome apps into the operating system. Android has long been considered as open-source software, but Google has slowly added key components into its Google Play Services software and associated agreements. (II) Google has also blocked phone makers from creating devices that run forked versions of Android alongside anti-fragmentation agreements to keep manufacturers on Google's version of Android. (III) Google "made payments to certain large manufacturers and mobile network operators" to exclusively bundle the Google search app on handsets.[37]

35 The position and display of Google's comparison-shopping services and its competitors, in general, search results pages of Google are treated unequally by Google. As for the position, Google uses dedicated algorithms, as opposed to normal generic ones, to identify and demote competing comparison-shopping services in Google's general search results, reducing their ranking and visibility drastically. Google uses at least two kinds of dedicated algorithms to conduct anti-competitive practices, and only one has been disclosed, the other anonymized. The disclosed one, Panda, was introduced in the US in February 2011, and subsequently extended to all English language queries worldwide on April 11, 2011, and to all general search queries across the EEA on August 12, 2011. The visibility of the most important comparison-shopping services in Google's general search results pages dropped suddenly after the launch of the Panda algorithm in the respective EEA country.

36 EC decision of June 27, 2017, AT.39740 Google Search (Shopping).

37 EC decision of July 81, 2018, AT.40099—Google Android.

The EC dealt Google yet another blow in March 2019 by imposing a fine of €1.49 billion (US$1.69 billion) for stifling competition in the online advertisement sector. The EC found Google had placed exclusivity contracts on website owners, stopping them from including search results from Google's rivals, Google had asked publishers to seek permission on how rival ads were displayed, and Google had prevented rivals from being able to "compete and innovate fairly" in the online ad market.[38]

C. MERGER CONTROL BANS CONCENTRATION THAT SIGNIFICANTLY IMPEDES EFFECTIVE COMPETITION

According to Council Regulation (EC) No. 139/2004 of January 20, 2004, on the control of concentrations between undertakings (the EC Merger Regulation), concentration that would significantly impede effective competition, in the common market or in a substantial part of it, in particular as a result of the creation or strengthening of a dominant position, shall be declared incompatible with the common market (Article 2(3)). The EC in principle only examines larger mergers with an EU dimension, meaning that the merging firms reach certain turnover thresholds (Article 1(2) and (3)). The EC may either unconditionally clear the merger, approve the merger subject to remedies, or prohibit the merger if no adequate remedies to the competition concerns have been proposed by the merging parties.

3.2.3. *The Divide Between the US and the EU: Abuse of a Dominant Position*

There is a fundamental difference between US and EU antitrust law, namely the US does not have any specific regulation on the abuse of dominant position while EU antitrust law (including Japan, Korea, PRC, Singapore, and Taiwan) does. According to the latter, it is not in itself illegal for an undertaking to be in a dominant position and such a dominant undertaking is entitled to compete on the merits. However, a dominant undertaking has a special responsibility not to allow its conduct to impair genuine and undistorted competition in the common market.

38 In addition to selling advertising on its own search page, Google also has a business of brokering advertising space on other websites that also include a search box like newspapers, blogs, or travel sites. This allows the owners of those websites to make money in much the same way Google does on its own site—by selling space next to search results. These other websites rely on an advertising broker. Google is by far the biggest of those brokers, with its platform "AdSense for Search." This market is important because it could serve as an entry point for competitors, including other search providers and online advertising platforms. By gaining a foothold in online advertising brokerage, they could grow their business and try to challenge Google in the general search advertising market. Google is dominant in online advertising brokerage market, with market shares in Europe of above 70% since 2006. And there are high barriers to entry, which make it hard for new competitors to come in. See https://ec.europa.eu/commission/presscorner/detail/en/statement_19_1774.

In the last twenty years, basically, all the US tech giants, such as Microsoft,[39] Facebook,[40] Google, Qualcomm,[41] and Apple,[42] have been investigated and fined by the EC for the abuse of dominance while unchallenged by the US antitrust agencies. This has caused disaccord between the US and the EU. From around 2017 onwards, the DOJ and the FTC started investigating Qualcomm,[43] Amazon, Apple, Google and Meta, the parent company of Instagram and WhatsApp, for monopolistic behavior. The government has sued all five companies—Google twice, once over the search engine market and the other over online advertising.[44] At long last, the US District Court for the District of Columbia found in August 2024 that Google had abused a monopoly over the search business.[45]

3.3. Legal Protection of Fair Competition

Section 5 of the Federal Trade Commission Act (USFTCA), enacted in 1914, remains just as succinct as its antitrust counterpart and prohibits "unfair or deceptive" methods and acts.[46] The relationship between Section 5 of the USFTCA

39 *MS v. The EC* decided by the EU Court of First Instance (Grand Chamber) Case T-201/04 (September 17, 2007) which upheld a decision by the EC that found MS abusing its market dominance by refusing to supply and authorize the use of interoperability information, among others.

40 In Germany, the Federal Cartel Office (Bundeskartelamt) found Facebook forcing users, via its terms of service, to give consent to the merging of personal data that Facebook collects inside and outside of its social media platform an exploitative abusive use of its dominance. Bundeskartellamt decision No. B6–22/16 of February 6, 2019. See https://www.bundeskartellamt.de/SharedDocs/Entscheidung/EN/Fallberichte/Missbrauchsaufsicht/2019/B6-22–16.

41 EC decision C (2018) 240 (decided on January 24, 2018).

42 On March 4, 2024, the EC fined Apple over €1.8 billion for abusing its dominant position on the market for the distribution of music streaming apps to iPhone and iPad users ("iOS users") through its App Store. In particular, the EC found that Apple applied restrictions on app developers preventing them from informing iOS users about alternative and cheaper music subscription services available outside of the app ("anti-steering provisions"). See https://ec.europa.eu/commission/presscorner/detail/en/ip_24_1161 Amazon narrowly escaped its anti-trust liability by making commitments to the EC in 2022.

43 In 2017 the USFTC charges Qualcomm with violating the Section 5 FTCA ("unfair methods of competition") with District Court for the Northern District of California. The court decided for the FTC which was revoked by the Ninth Circuit in *FTC. v. Qualcomm Inc.*, D.C. No. 19–16122 at 55 (9th Cir. 11 Aug. 2020).

44 Kang, C., & McCabe, D. (2024). The US antitrust case against Google is just the start. *New York Times*, at: https://www.nytimes.com/2024/05/03/technology/google-apple-amazon-meta-antitrust.html.

45 https://www.nytimes.com/2024/08/05/technology/google-antitrust-ruling.html.

46 Section 5 of the USFTCA provides:

> (1) Unfair methods of competition in or affecting commerce, and unfair or deceptive acts or practices in or affecting commerce, are hereby declared unlawful. (2) The Federal Trade Commission is hereby empowered and directed to prevent persons, partnerships, or corporations from using unfair methods of competition in or affecting commerce and unfair or deceptive acts or practices in or affecting commerce.

and Sections 1 and 2 of the Sherman Act can be so understood: (I) "Unfair methods of competition" under the FTCA includes "violations of the Sherman Act."[47]

> All of the committee reports and the statements of those in charge of the Trade Commission Act reveal an abiding purpose to vest both the Commission and the courts with adequate powers to hit at every trade practice, then existing or thereafter contrived, which restrained competition or might lead to such restraint if not stopped in its incipient stages.[48]

In civil law jurisdictions, unfair competition law also provides a broad protection against any and all "unfair commercial practices," typified by Article 3(1) of the German Unfair Competition Prevention Act. Noteworthy is that civil law jurisdictions have codified many of their case law on unfair competition, such as the Annex of German Unfair Competition Prevention Act which lists thirty-two practices that are always illegal vis-à-vis consumers.

At this juncture, it suffices to point out one possible unfair trade practice in the context of IP licensing. For the alleged reason of policing under-reporting and correctly calculating royalty that is to be paid by the licensee, IP holders tend to demand detailed and sensitive information regarding output and prices to be reported by the licensees. However, legal disputes could arise when the IP holders are also competing with the licensees. In the CD-R case, Philips required the licensees of its CD-R patents to provide detailed "list of manufacturing equipment, suppliers, dates of installing and testing" and "sales report in writing" (breaking down into countries, product specifications, buyers, and trademarks used) 30 days after the end of each quarter. Which was found in April 2006 by the TFTC as a violation of the general clause against unfair competition, namely Article 25 of the TFTA and imposed a fine of NT$ 6 million.[49] However, the Taipei Administrative High Court did not see the "list of manufacturing equipment, suppliers, dates of installing and testing" as trade secrets of the licensees because the licensor knew already the manufacturing procedures (the same across all CD-R manufacturers) and equipment, and many other factors (e.g. orders, actual work dispatch and operation, and prices of dyes and PCs) contributed to the price determination of CD-R. At the same time, the Court found a violation of Article 25 of the FTA in Philips' demand of the information about the identification of CD-R buyers and the trademarks used by the buyers to be contained in the "written sales report." For the Court, these were sensitive business information and unrelated to the calculation of royalty, not even after taking into account the common phenomenon of underreporting by

47 *FTC v. Cement Inst.*, 333 US 683, 692 (1948).

48 *FTC v. Cement Inst.*, 333 US 683, 692 (1948), 694.

49 The TFTC Gong-Chu-Zhi 095045 Decision (April 26, 2006), at: http://www.ftc.gov.tw/uploadDecision/2005302–0950426_002_095d045.pdf.

the licensees, which can be dealt with through other lawful means. The Supreme Administrative Court upheld this decision.[50]

3.4. Competition Law's View on IP

3.4.1. The US's Ambivalence Towards Patents (From Pro-Competition to Pro-IP)

The US has a very succinct antitrust law. It does not address IP at all. However, the antitrust law in action, or court practice, has probably the longest history of checking patents. This has to do with the fact that the US is the cradle of modern competition law. "Progressive Era[51] antitrust law developed a deep and lasting interest in how business firms licensed and otherwise used their patents."[52] This "Progressive Era policing of patent licensing gave way to much more aggressive attacks . . ."[53] that took place between 1930 and 1960, where the US "antitrust law looked closely and skeptically at all manners of patent-related contracts."[54] "Patent ownership seemed to many like simply an excuse to perpetrate power abuses on contractual partners."[55]

In the 1980s, innovation and patents returned to favor in the US. The Court of Appeals for the Federal Circuit (CAFC) was set up in 1982 as the only appellate-level court with the jurisdiction to hear patent case appeals.[56]

This shift from pro-competition to pro-IP eventually led to growing secondary market for patents and its side-effects, patent trolls. The 2011 American Invents Act gave birth to cheaper patent challenges and reduced the settlement leverage trolls have counted on.[57] However, this pro-IP stance seems unwavering as of this writing (see supra 3.2.3).

50 The Supreme Administrative Court rejected both the appeals filed by the TFTC and Philips for their failing to raise an issue of law, see Ruling Caizi No. 2027, No. 2028, ruled on September 9, 2010.

51 The Progressive Era (1896–1917) in the US "was a period of widespread social activism and political reform across the United States focused on defeating corruption, monopoly, waste, and inefficiency" see https://en.wikipedia.org/wiki/Progressive_Era.

52 Merges, R. (2022). *American Patent Law—A Business and Economic History* (p. 40). Cambridge University Press.

53 Merges, R. (2022). *American Patent Law—A Business and Economic History* (p. 41). Cambridge University Press.

54 Merges, R. (2022). *American Patent Law—A Business and Economic History* (p. 22). Cambridge University Press.

55 Merges, R. (2022). *American Patent Law—A Business and Economic History* (p. 41). Cambridge University Press.

56 The decisions of the CAFC, particularly in regard to patent cases, are unique in that they are binding precedent throughout the US within the bounds of the court's subject-matter jurisdiction. This is unlike the other courts of appeals as the authority of their decisions is restricted by geographic location and thus there may be differing judicial standards depending on location.

57 Merges, R. (2022). *American Patent Law—A Business and Economic History* (pp. 41–42). Cambridge University Press.

3.4.2. The Singling Out of IP by Some National Competition Laws

The GATT 1947 only deals with the relationship between the enforcement of measures relating to the protection of patents, trademarks, copyrights, and free trade. It allows the former so long as it is necessary and does not constitute arbitrary or unjustifiable discrimination or a disguised restriction on international trade and is not inconsistent with the provisions of the GATT.[58]

When Japan enacted its first Antimonopoly and Fair Trade Maintenance Act in 1947, it must have drawn lessons from Article XX of the GATT. Therefore, it has singled out the exercise of IP, which was followed by Korea, and referenced by Taiwan, India,[59] and China,[60] provided that it does not exclude or restrict market competition.

In Germany, there has been a period of forty years (1965–2005) in which the exercise of copyrights by collecting societies was exempted from its competition law. When enacting the Act on the Management of Copyright and Related Rights[61] in 1965, the German parliament perceived collective management of copyright through collecting societies as indispensable for the exercise of copyrights and therefore provided them with immunity from the cartel prohibition in Article 24 which introduced Article 102a into the Competition Act.[62] Article 102a was later changed to Article 30 in 1998, after adjusting to the decision of the CJEU.[63] Article

58 Article XX (General Exception s) of the GATT stipulates:

> Subject to the requirement that such measures are not applied in a manner which would constitute a means of arbitrary or unjustifiable discrimination between countries where the same conditions prevail, or a disguised restriction on international trade, nothing in this Agreement shall be construed to prevent the adoption or enforcement by any contracting party of measures: (d) necessary to secure compliance with laws or regulations which are not inconsistent with the provisions of this Agreement, including those relating to . . . the protection of patents, trademarks and copyrights, and the prevention of deceptive practices.

59 Article 21 of the Japanese Anti-Monopolization Act, Article 59 (Exercise of Right to Intangible Property) of the Monopoly Regulation and Fair Trade Act of South Korea, Article 45 of Taiwan's Fair Trade Act, Section 3(5) of the Indian Competition Act (2002).

60 Exemplified by Article 68 of Chinese Anti-monopolization Law:

> This Law does not govern the conduct of business operators to exercise their intellectual property rights under laws and relevant administrative regulations on intellectual property rights; however, business operators' conduct to eliminate or restrict market competition by abusing their intellectual property rights shall be governed by this Law.

61 Its German title reads as "Gesetz über die Wahrnehmung von Urheberrechten und verwandten Schutzrechten."

62 BGBl. I S. 1294.

63 Article 30 specifically provided that the formation of collective copyright management organizations which were under the scrutiny of the Act on the Management of Copyright and Related Rights and the necessary agreements and resolutions which these organizations made in order to effectively manage copyright and neighboring rights and had been reported to the Ministry of Law were exempted from the prohibition of cartel and resale price maintenance. Inclusive agreements (Gesamtverträge) that had been set by Munich Higher Regional Court (Oblerlandesgericht) were under the scrutiny of the Federal Cartel Office if they were misused. See https://lexetius.com/GWB/30,4.

30 was deleted in 2005 for the simple sake of EU harmonization in competition law and does not mean any change in the legal assessment of the mentioned activities.[64]

However, the singling out of the exercise of IP serves no meaningful purpose and should be deleted,[65] as the exercise of IP should be handled equally as the exercise of any other tangible or intangible rights by competition law.

3.5. Competition Authorities' View on IP and Its Exercise

3.5.1. General Approach: Treating IP Equally and Its Licensing Favorably

The DOJ and FTC issued the Antitrust Guidelines for the Licensing of Intellectual Property in 1995 and updated it in 2017 (US Antitrust-IP Guidelines) which treat IP equally just as any other property but looks at IP licensing favorably. This approach has three components: First, agreements involving IP can be analyzed using the same antitrust rules applied to agreements involving any other property. The exercise of IP is thus neither particularly free from scrutiny under the antitrust laws nor particularly suspect under them. The two US agencies recognize that the licensing of IP is often global. Second, an IP does not necessarily create market power (the ability to profitably maintain prices above or output below competitive levels for a significant period of time). Third, licensing (including cross-licensing) or transferring IP can facilitate integration of the licensed property with complementary factors of production. This integration can lead to more efficient exploitation of the IP, benefiting consumers through the reduction of costs and the introduction of new products.[66]

The TTBER and Article 101 Guidelines are in essence similar to that of the US, with slightly different wording:

> The fact that IP laws grant exclusive rights of exploitation does not imply that IP rights are immune from competition law intervention. Article 101 of the Treaty is in particular applicable to agreements whereby the holder licenses another undertaking to exploit its intellectual property rights. Nor does it imply that there is an inherent conflict between IP rights and the

64 See Schricker/Loewenheim/Reinbothe, UrhG (6. Aufl. 2020), Einl. VGG Rn 17, 44.

65 Liu, K.-C. (2019). As a matter of standard for Asia and beyond? In Liu, K.-C., & Hilty, R. (Eds.), *SEPs, SSOs and FRAND–Asian and Global Perspectives on Fostering Innovation in Interconnectivity* (pp. 16–17). Routledge.

66 The PRC in the Anti-Monopoly Guideline on Intellectual Property Abuse issued by the State Council Anti-Monopoly Commission in 2019 (Chinese Guidelines on IP Abuse) subscribes almost to all three components (Article 2 and the introduction to Chapter 2). TFTC endorses only the second component in Guidelines on Technology Licensing Agreements (Taiwanese Tech Licensing Guidelines) promulgated on January 20, 2001 (latest amendment in 2016). KFTC mentions only the third component in its Review Guidelines on Unfair Exercise of Intellectual Property Rights issued in 2000 (last amendment on March 23, 2016, Korean IP Guidelines) 2.E. So does JFTC's Guidelines for the Use of Intellectual Property under the Antimonopoly Act (Japanese IP Guidelines) issued on September 28, 2007, revised in 2016 and 2023.

Union competition rules (Point 7). There is no presumption that intellectual property rights and license agreements as such give rise to competition concerns. Most license agreements do not restrict competition and create pro-competitive efficiencies. Indeed, licensing as such is pro-competitive as it leads to dissemination of technology and promotes innovation by the licensor and licensee(s). In addition, even licence agreements that do restrict competition may often give rise to pro-competitive efficiencies, which must be considered under Article 101(3) and balanced against the negative effects on competition. The great majority of license agreements are therefore compatible with Article 101(Point 9).

3.5.2. Applying Rule of Reason to Analyze IP Exercise

Due to its ability to better accommodate the rationale behind IP regime establishment and its shifting dynamics and to demystify IP as having no absolute or natural rights, the rule of reason is replacing the per se rule (per se legal or illegal).

A. THE US

Courts in the 1960s and 1970s adopted the per se rule of patent misuse, routinely refusing to enforce patents where extension of the monopoly-type abuse was demonstrated, without requiring evidence of anticompetitive effect, ultimately leading to the "Nine No-Nos,"[67] conducts presumed to be per se illegal. This is a pro-competition approach. 1986 *Windsurfing International, Inc. v. AMF, Inc.*[68] represents a watershed case, in which the alleged infringer in resorting to patent misuse was required to 'show that the patentee has impermissibly broadened the "physical or temporal scope" of the patent grant with anticompetitive effect. This changed to be very pro-IP. Skepticism against the patent misuse doctrine was ushered in. Congress enacted the 1988 Patent Misuse Reform Act.

The wholesale rule of reason approach to IP originated from the Department of Justice of the US when it appointed UC Berkeley economics professor Richard Gilbert as its Deputy Assistant Attorney General for Economics in 1993, and was the driving force behind the famous US Antitrust-IP Guidelines. Both agencies affirm

67 Homiller, D.P. (2006). Patent misuse in patent pool licensing: From national harrow to "The Nine No-Nos" to not likely. *Duke Law and Technology Review*, 7. at: http://www.law.duke.edu/journals/dltr/articles/2006dltr0007.html#37. The Nine No-Nos were (I) Requiring a licensee to purchase unpatented materials from the licensor (tying). (II) Requiring a licensee to assign to the licensor patents issued to the licensee after the licensing arrangement is executed. (III) Restricting a purchaser of a patented product in the resale of that product. (IV) Restricting a licensee's freedom to deal in products or services outside the scope of the patent. (V) Agreeing with a licensee that the licensor will not, without the licensee's consent, grant further licenses to any other person. (VI) Requiring that the licensee accept a "package" license. (VII) Requiring royalties not reasonably related to the licensee's sales of products covered by the patent. (VIII) Restricting the licensee's sales of (unpatented) goods made with the licensed patented process. (IX) Requiring a licensee to adhere to specified or minimum prices in the sale of the licensed products.

68 828 F.2d 755 (Fed. Cir. 1987).

that "Our modernized IP Licensing Guidelines continue to apply an effects-based analysis that puts the focus on evaluating harm to competition, not on harm to any individual competitor, and support procompetitive intellectual property licensing that can promote innovation," and their continued "commitment to an economically grounded approach to antitrust analysis of IP licensing."[69]

B. THE EU

Beginning from the 1999 Umbrella Regulation on vertical agreements, the EC started to depart from the previous legalistic approach and introduced the new market-share approach.[70] The EC takes up an "economic-based approach" to IP most notably in its Regulation (EC) No. 772/2004 of April 27, 2004, on the application of Article 81(3) of the Treaty to categories of technology transfer agreements (Technology Transfer Block Exemption Regulation, TTBER Regulation),[71] TTBER Regulation was updated by Commission Regulation (EU) No. 316/2014 of March 21, 2014, on the application of Article 101(3) of the Treaty on the Functioning of the European Union to categories of technology transfer agreements (effective on May 1, 2014, and shall expire on April 30, 2026).[72]

In order to provide guidance on the application of the TTBER as well as on the application of Article 101 to technology transfer agreements that fall outside the scope of the TTBER, the EC issued guidelines on the application of Article 101 of the Treaty on the Functioning of the European Union to technology transfer agreements (2014/C 89/03) (TTBER and Article 101 Guidelines). The standards set forth in these two guidelines follow the rule of reason, as they "must be applied in the light of the circumstances specific to each case. This excludes a mechanical application. Each case must be assessed on its own facts and these guidelines must be applied reasonably and flexibly." (Point 3, TTBER and Article 101 Guidelines).

69 See USDOJ press release of January 13, 2017, at https://www.justice.gov/opa/pr/doj-and-ftc-issue-updated-antitrust-guidelines-licensing-intellectual-property.

70 Drexl, J. (2008). Is there a "'more economic approach" to intellectual property and competition law? In Drexl, J. (Ed.), *Research Handbook on Intellectual Property and Competition Law* (p. 29). Edward Elgar Publishing.

71 Commission Regulation 772/2004 on the application of Article 81(3) of the Treaty to Categories of Technology Transfer Agreements, 2004 O.J.(L123)11, at: http://eur-lex.europa.eu/LexUriServ/LexUriServ.do?uri=CELEX:32004R0772:EN:HTML. All references to Articles 81 and 82 EC should be understood as references to the current Articles 101 and 102 of the Treaty on the Functioning of the European Union as renamed by the Treaty of Lisbon, which entered into force on December 1, 2009.

72 The EC is currently conducting an evaluation to help it decide whether to let TTBER Regulation expire, prolong its duration, or revise it. The TTBER Regulation has a rather limited scope of application. First, the Council Regulation 19/66 did not empower the Commission to block exempt technology transfer agreements concluded between more than two undertakings. Consequently, the TTBER Regulation only deals with technology transfer agreements between a licensor and a licensee. Second, the TTBER does not cover all IP and is limited to licensing agreements that involve 'technology rights' which means know-how and the following rights, or a combination thereof, including applications for or applications for registration of (I) patents, (II) utility models, (III) design rights, (IV) topographies of semiconductor products, (V) supplementary protection certificates for medicinal products or other products for which such supplementary protection certificates may be obtained, (VI) plant breeder's certificates, and (VII) software copyrights (Article 1).

C. MAJOR ASIAN ECONOMIES

General competition authorities in major Asian economies in principle stand by the rule of reason approach. However, if IP holders are dominant market players, such as SEP patentees, and have undertaken certain anti-competitive behavior, such as the three numbers discussed in Subsection 4.7 of Chapter 9, these authorities might fall back to the per se illegal approach.

In Japan,[73] the IP Guidelines deals "solely with intellectual property concerned with technology." It is meant to comprehensively specify the principles by which the Antimonopoly Act is applied to restrictions pertaining to the use of technology. The Japanese IP Guidelines adopt the flexible rule of reason approach, with diminishing categorical classification.[74] The Korean IP Guidelines also follow the rule of reason approach to apply the Korean Monopoly Regulation and Fair Trade Act (MRFTA) to a conduct that externally and formally constitutes an exercise of IPRs but goes beyond the purpose of the IPRs system (to encourage invention and creation) in case such conduct restricts competition in the technology market, goods market, etc.[75] It is stated as one of its basic principles that:

> When an exercise of IPRs increases both anti-competitiveness and effectiveness, whether the exercise violates the Act or not in principle is determined after comparing the two effects through the fair comparison of the interests. When the effectiveness of the exercise concerned outweighs the anti-competitiveness, the exercise does not violate the Act.[76]

On one occasion, the KFTC has imposed sanctions for abusing patent rights that violated Article 23(1)4 of the Monopoly Regulation and Fair Trade Act (unfairly taking advantage of its bargaining position): Dolby, a SEP patentee and has made a FRAND commitment, blocked Kaon Media since June 2018, from using their patented technology through the BP3 platform in order to urge Kaon Media to agree to their audit results, which negatively affected Kaon Media's development and production of new set-top boxes.[77]

73 For a comprehensive description of the development of the interface between IP and competition law in Japan before 2005, see Heath, C. (2007). The interface between competition law and intellectual property in Japan. In Anderman, S.D. (Ed.), *The Interface Between Intellectual Property Rights and Competition Policy* (pp. 250, 250–311). Cambridge University Press.

74 Shibata, J. (2008). Patent and know-how licenses under the Japanese Antimonopoly Act. In Drexl, J. (Ed.), *Research Handbook on Intellectual Property and Competition Law* (pp. 201, 211). Edward Elgar Publishing.

75 OECD, Licensing of IP rights and competition law—Note by Korea (2019), Paragraph 6 at https://one.oecd.org/document/DAF/COMP/WD(2019)23/en/pdf.

76 Korean IP Guidelines II 2 D.

77 KFTC, decision on August 13, 2021, at: https://www.ftc.go.kr/solution/skin/doc.html?fn=41df21daf54e51d748da25dbe955857b2cea57b795e548c4bbf447e7fde1389a&rs=/fileupload/data/result/BBSMSTR_000000002402/.

Taiwanese Tech Licensing Guidelines also endorses the rule of reason approach:

> In reviewing technology licensing arrangements, in addition to the reasonableness of the provisions of such arrangements, the Commission shall consider the market power of the licensor with regard to the licensed technology, the market position of the parties to the arrangement at a relevant market and the status of that market, the degree of influence to which the licensing arrangement will increase opportunities for utilization of the technology or exclude competition, the degree of difficulty of access to the relevant market, the length of the term of limitations under the licensing arrangement, and international or industry precedents applicable to the relevant market.[78]

Chinese Guidelines on IPR Abuse takes a similar position:

> When assessing whether business operators have abused IPRs to exclude or restrict competition, the following basic principle shall be adhered to: To evaluate the positive impact of the relevant behavior on efficiency and innovation based on circumstances of individual cases.
>
> Article 2(4)

3.5.3. An Intervention Threshold

IP agreements would only harm competition if there was sufficient market power backing. Thus, it is a popular practice among jurisdictions to set up an intervention threshold (safety zone or harbor) that would exclude IP agreements of minor market significance from scrutiny. The US, the EU, the PRC, and Japan have set up an intervention threshold of market share.

Under the US Antitrust-IP Guidelines, except under extraordinary circumstances, the USDOJ and the USFTC will not challenge a restraint in an IP licensing arrangement if (I) the restraint is not *prima facie* anticompetitive[79] and (II) the licensor and its licensees collectively account for no more than 20% of each relevant market significantly affected by the restraint. The EU block-exempts technology agreements by parties whose combined market share does not exceed 20% of the affected relevant technology and product market when they are competing undertakings. Where the undertakings parties to the agreements are not competing undertakings and the market share of each of the parties does not exceed 30% of the affected relevant technology and product market, the block exemption will also apply (Article 3 TTBER Regulation).

78 See id. Point 4(3).

79 According to footnote 59 of the US IP Licensing Guidelines, "facially anticompetitive" refers to restraints that normally warrant per se treatment, as well as other restraints of a kind that would always or almost always tend to reduce output or increase prices.

Article 13 of Chinese Guidelines on IP Abuse also provides a numeric safe harbor: IP-license-related agreements by business operators, which satisfy any of the following requirements, are generally not monopoly agreements prohibited by Antimonopoly Law (Articles 13(1)6 and 14(3)), provided that there is no opposing evidence proving that the agreement at issue has restrained or excluded market competition:

> 1. The combined market shares of the business operators in question on the relevant market is less than 20% if they are non-competing; 2. The business operator or its transaction partner each has less than 30% market share of any of the relevant markets affected by the IP-related agreement; 3. There are four or more substitutive technologies other than those controlled by parties of the licensing agreement that can be acquired at reasonable costs from other independent business operators on the relevant market in case the market shares of business operators are hard to come by, market shares could not accurately reflect the market position of business operators.

The Japanese IP Guidelines adopt a 20% threshold of sorts.[80] It lists cases where restrictions may have major impacts on competition (acts between competitors and when influential technologies are involved) and cases where restrictions are deemed to have a minor effect in reducing competition. In principle, restrictions pertaining to the use of technology are deemed to have a minor effect in reducing competition when the entrepreneurs using the technology subject to the restrictions in the business activity have a share in the product market of 20% or less in total. This is not applicable, however, to the conduct of restricting sale prices, sales quantity, market share, sales territories or customers for the product incorporating the technology or to the conduct of restricting research and development activities or obliging entrepreneurs to assign rights or grant exclusive licenses for improved technology. The impact of a particular restriction on competition in the technology market is also deemed to have a minor effect in reducing competition if the product share is in principle 20% or less in total.[81]

4. Sector-Specific Competition Laws

In the following, three sector-specific competition laws that have more intersection with IP will be discussed.

80 See Yen, T.-T. (2009). The rules of technology licensing agreements under Japanese antimonopoly law-reflections on Taiwan's Fair Trade Act (in Chinese). *Fair Trade Quarterly*, *17*, 99, 108 et seq.; Wakui, M. (2004). Standardization and patent pools in Japan. In Taplin, R. (Ed.), *Valuing Intellectual Property in Japan, Britian and the US* (pp. 81, 99). Routledge.

81 Japanese IP Guidelines Part 2(4) and (5).

4.1. Communication Laws

Telecommunication is of great importance for the economy since the early twentieth century. Therefore, a sector-specific competition law that values government planning over competition was widely enacted throughout the world, with the US leading with its 1934 Communications Act. After a long period of no policy to promote technological progress, and no incentives for innovation, the tide to favor competition and innovation in the telecommunications industry was ushered in by the 1982 AT&T divestiture case in the US as a result of a consent decree with the USDOJ. The divestiture broke AT&T's local exchange services into seven carriers, leaving AT&T as a long-distance and equipment company.

Finally, the US enacted the Telecommunications Act of 1996 to induce competition. It intends to eliminate the monopolies enjoyed by the inheritors of AT&T's local franchises. The Act both prohibits state and local regulation that impedes the provision of telecommunications service (Section 253(a)) and obligates incumbent carriers to allow competitors to enter their local markets (Section 251).

Section 251 of the Act imposes a large number of duties upon incumbent local exchange carriers—above and beyond those basic responsibilities it imposes upon all carriers, including providing access to rights-of-way[82] and three kinds of access. Perhaps most intrusive is the duty to offer access to unbundled network elements on "just, reasonable, and non-discriminatory" terms,[83] a phrase that the USFCC has interpreted to mean a price reflecting long-run incremental cost.[84] A rival can interconnect its own facilities with those of the incumbent LEC, or it can simply purchase services at wholesale rates from the incumbent and resell them to consumers.[85]

4.2. Broadcasting Laws

Another area of sector-specific competition law that relates to IP law and the theme of this book is broadcasting law. In this regard, the US is the global trendsetter as well. Regular commercial TV network programming began in the US in 1948.[86] The US has a decentralized and market-oriented television system. The USFCC encourages diversity in broadcasting through its Broadcast Ownership Rules (2024

82 See 47 USC §251(b)(2)(4).

83 See 47 USC §251(c)(3).

84 *Verizon Communications Inc. v. FCC*, 535 US (2002), 495–496.

85 See Nuechterlein, J., & Weiser, P. (2012). *The Digital Crossroads* (2nd ed., pp. 44–528). MIT Press.

86 After the invention of radio by Marconi in 1895, radio stations mushroomed in the early 20th century. In the US, hundreds of stations began broadcasting in the 1920s. Regulation was almost non-existent. However, this led to the tragedy of commons, the SOS call from Titanic was drowned and unheard by the authorities. The US enacted the Radio Act of 1927 which required that spectrum had to be owned and licensed by the Federal Radio Commission. A comprehensive federal licensing scheme was put in place.

latest review). The Rules prohibit, among other things, a merger between any two of the big four broadcast television networks: ABC, CBS, Fox, and NBC.[87]

In 1965, the FCC began to regulate Cable TV (CATV), a closed system only accessible to subscribers who pay. When CATV reached high market penetration, traditional terrestrial TV became dependent on CATV to access its audience. Therefore, the US enacted the 1992 Cable Television Consumer Protection and Competition Act to introduce must-carry regulation, requiring that locally licensed television stations must be carried on a cable provider's system. A broadcast station cannot charge a CATV provider license fee for the program content retransmitted on the cable network under the rule.[88] The Act also empowers the FCC to prescribe rules and regulations to enhance effective competition so that no operator can unfairly impede the flow of video programming from video programmers to consumers.

4.3. Law on Data

The EU Data Act is a sector-specific regulation to enhance access to data.[89] It puts forward a set of rules to ensure that users of a product or related service in the Union can access, in a timely manner, the data generated by the use of that product or related service and that those users can use the data, including by sharing them with third parties of their choice. Specifically, where data cannot be directly accessed by the user from the product, the data holder shall make available to the user the data generated by its use of a product or related service without undue delay, free of charge, continuously, and in real-time.

> Trade secrets shall only be disclosed provided that all specific necessary measures are taken to preserve the confidentiality of trade secrets in particular with respect to third parties. The data holder and the user can agree measures to preserve the confidentiality of the shared data, in particular in relation to third parties.
>
> Article 4(3)

The user shall not use the data obtained pursuant to a request referred to in Article 4(1) to develop a product that competes with the product from which the data originate." (Article 4(4) see Subsection 2.3.3 of Chapter 12).

However, these data-access-ensuring measures, especially Article 4(4), might conflict with IP and trade secret protection. How these conflicts will play out and be resolved is still too early to tell.

87 See https://docs.fcc.gov/public/attachments/DA-24-144A1.pdf.

88 See https://en.wikipedia.org/wiki/Must-carry.

89 Regulation (EU) 2023/2854 of the European Parliament and of the Council of December 13, 2023, on harmonized rules on fair access to and use of data and amending Regulation (EU) 2017/2394 and Directive (EU) 2020/1828 (Data Act).

4 An IP Code, Its Principles and a More Balanced International IP Regime

1. Codification as a Means of State-Building

Modern-day states are built decisively through codification, the birth of great civil codes in the 19th and 20th centuries, is a powerful testament. It starts with the French Civil Code (1804) and continues to the Civil Code of the People's Republic of China (2020).[1] France gained its international significance in modern history through the inspiring Napoleonic Code (French Civil Code). The code is not just about private rights, it forbade privileges based on birth, allowed freedom of religion, and specified that government jobs should go to the most qualified. It was drafted by a commission of four eminent jurists under the direct involvement of Napoléon (therefore Napoleonic Code) and entered into force on March 21, 1804.[2] The Code, with its stress on clearly written and accessible law, was a major step in replacing the previous patchwork of feudal laws. It is one of the few documents that has influenced the whole world.[3] This function of helping state-building lives on as more and more states are emerging.

Of course, codification also serves a plethora of other vital functions, such as providing predictability, easy access to and therefore democratization of law, strengthening people's trust in the legal systems, social reform,[4] and summarizing

1 Great civil codes of the world include at least French Civil Code (1804), Austrian Civil Code (1811), Netherlands Civil Code (1838), Italian Civil Code (1865), Portuguese Civil Code (1867), Swiss Law on Obligations (1881), Spanish Civil Code (1889), Japanese Civil Code (1898), German Civil Code (1900), Swiss Civil Code (1911), Brazilian Civil Code (1916), Soviet Union Civil Code (1922), Turkish Civil Code (1926), Civil Code (1930) of Republic of China, Italian Civil Code (1942), Egyptian Civil Code (1949). Soviet Union Civil Code (1964), Netherlands Civil Code (1992), Russian Civil Code (1994), German reform of obligation law (2002), Brazilian Civil code (2003, French reform of obligation law (2016), and Civil Code of the PRC (2020).

2 See Zweigert, K., & Kötz, H. (1998). *An Introduction to Comparative Law* (3rd ed., pp. 86, 87). Oxford University Press.

3 The German Civil Code of 1900, almost a century later than the French Civil Code, is also instrumental to the state-building of modern-day Germany.

4 Jeremy Bentham (1747–1832), although trained in the common law jurisdiction, forcefully advocates comprehensive codification of the common law into a coherent set of statutes, only through which thorough reform of English legal life is possible. See Zweigert, K., & Kötz, H. (1998). *An Introduction to Comparative Law* (3rd ed., p. 197). Oxford University Press.

DOI: 10.4324/9781003597766-5

case law to build new legal doctrines. Codification also facilitates legal transplants across national borders. As our world is getting more complex all the time, so is codification. Without codification, our lives will be ungovernable.

2. The Need of an IP Code

IP laws as they now are stand generally in isolation from each other,[5] and lack overarching guiding principles that could lead to coherent legislation, interpretation, and application of individual IP provisions when dealing with similar or even the same topics, such as exhaustion, fair use, compulsory license, damages, etc. It is also imperative to find ways to democratize IP laws, namely providing easily accessible and understandable principles of IP laws, reducing the complexity of IP laws, and deciphering the legal labyrinth created by interest groups and lobbyists.[6]

Therefore, some national states have made efforts to codify IP laws either into one combined piece of law or into their respective civil code. Admittedly, these countries are minority.

Yet, there are substantial negative effects of not having a unified IP code.

2.1. Divergent Regulation of the Same/Similar Problems

Simply due to a lack of systemic planning by the parliament, uneven regulation of the same or similar problems is commonplace. For example, in Taiwan, the predetermined or statutory damages for IP infringement are hugely divergent. Taiwan's Patent Act does not recognize predetermined damages for patent infringement. In contrast, Taiwan's Copyright Act recognizes statutory damages between NT$ 10,000 and NT$ 1 million which the courts may increase to NT$ 5 million for serious cases (Article 88). Taiwan's Trademark Act foresees a different statutory damages regime: not more than 1,500 times of the unit retail price of the infringing

5 In Japan, however, the Trademark Act applies many articles of the Patent Act by analogy. For example, Article 13 provides:

> The provisions of Paragraphs (1) to (4) of Article 43, 43–2(2) and (3) of the Patent Act shall apply mutatis mutandis to an application for trademark registration. . . . (2) The provisions of Articles 33 and paragraphs (4) to (7) of Article 34 (Right to obtain a patent) of the Patent Act shall apply mutatis mutandis to the rights deriving from an application for trademark registration."

Article 35 further provides:

> Article 73 (co-ownership), 76 (Lapse of patent rights in absence of heir), 97(1) (waiver), and 98(1)(i) and 98(2) (Effect of registration) of the Patent Act shall apply mutatis mutandis to trademark rights. In this case, the term "transfer (excluding those by general succession including inheritance)" in Article 98 (1)(i) of the Patent Act shall be deemed to be replaced with "division and transfer (excluding those by general succession including inheritance).

6 However, Copyright Act of Singapore has 541 sections in total, making it probably the longest copyright act on earth. It is an understatement to say, "should be obvious just from the sheer length of the Copyright Act 2021 . . . copyright law is not an easy subject to either grasp or to explain." Llewelyn, D. et al. (2023). *Modern Law of Copyright in Singapore*, 17.1. Academy Publishing.

goods; if over 1,500 pieces of infringing goods were found, the amount of damages shall be a lump sum of the market value of the infringing goods; or the equivalent amount of royalty that may be collected from using the trademark. The court may, at its discretion, reduce the amount of the mentioned damages if it is apparently disproportionate (Article 71).

With regards to exhaustion of IPRs, Taiwan's IP laws swing from international exhaustion (trademark, patent, and integrated circuits), national exhaustion (plant variety), and extremely narrow national exhaustion (copyright).[7]

If there were a codified IP Code that brings all IP laws under one roof with general principles applicable to all IPRs, the same and similar legal issues would principally be handled in the same or similar manner, unless there are justified reasons for exceptional treatment.

2.2. *Arm-Twisting by Lobbyists Made Easier*

Lobbying is done mostly in invisible ways and through sophisticated chains of networks, for example, competitiveness campaigns, sponsored research, donating chair professorship and awards, subsidized conferences, visits, and financed legal opinions. IP laws are heavily lobbied.[8] Special provisions tailored to special interests. Without the guidance of an IP Code, lobbyists can ravage the IP landscape at will. This concern is magnified in countries where there is no oversight mechanism for lobbyists and lobbying activities in place.

2.3. *Neglecting the Importance of Procedural IP Law and Prescribing Wrong Cure*

IP laws have both substantive parts and procedural parts on which the former rely for its implementation. Failing procedural IP laws is sometimes the root cause for unsuccessful substantive IP laws and rights. However, often the linkage and interdependence of the two is overlooked. For example, provisions on collective management of copyright remain neglected in many jurisdictions, with the French IP Code as one of the exceptional few. As a result, policymakers keep on prescribing wrong cure for the insufficient protection of substantive copyright, by recognizing more substantive rights, longer protection terms, and stronger penal punishment. The cure of the problem lies in securing functional collecting societies that bridge between the infinite users, works, ways of use, and rightsholders, through which copyright can live up to its promise of providing incentives to new creation and its sharing.

7 For more see Liu, K.-C. (2022). *IP Laws and Regimes in Major Asian Economies— Combing Through Thousand Threads of IP to Peace in Asia* (pp. 203–210). Routledge.

8 For example, in the US, Hollywood or the entertainment industry has successfully lobbied multiple extensions of copyright protection terms. Pharmaceutical and information technology industries are behind many of the patent reforms. See Merges, R. (2022). *American Patent Law—A Business and Economic History* (p. 42). Cambridge University Press.

In certain jurisdictions, there are other procedural IP provisions that are decisive for the substantive IP laws, such as the powerful IP Case Adjudication Act in Taiwan.[9]

Only with a comprehensive IP code, where substantive IP laws are integrated with procedural ones into a code, will we appreciate that substantive IPs must be supported by procedural IP laws. The fix of the former is only needed or justified when the latter has been perfectly implemented and improved. A set of functional procedural IP laws can provide the infrastructural foundation for further expanding substantive IP rights.

3. Codification of IP

There are at least four different types of IP codifications. The first type is an all-encompassing and stand-alone IP code, with or without general provisions. The second type is all-encompassing but not stand-alone IP code. The third type is composed of industrial property code and copyright law. The fourth type is mostly for the purpose of summarizing, streamlining, and setting up national IP policies, which will affect IPRs and their materialization.

3.1. All-Encompassing and Stand-Alone IP Code

3.1.1. Without General Provisions

Take the French IP Code (Code de la propriété intellectuelle) for example. It was formalized by Law No. 92-597 of July 1, 1992, which consolidated 23 laws. It is without a section of general provisions, following its Civil Code tradition. Nevertheless, the Code is the most comprehensive one, covering copyright (La propriété littéraire et artistique) and industrial property rights (Deuxième partie: La propriété industrielle). It deals with procedural or organizational aspects of the two groups of rights, namely collective management organizations of copyright, patent office, patent attorneys, and their association.

The French IP Code is not just a random compilation of IP laws, but rather a reorganization and streamlining of them. Although it lacks a section of general provisions, some argue that a more flattened and non-hierarchical structure between

9 For example, Article 19(1) of the Act allows courts to appoint a verifier in patent infringement cases to verify the documents or devices or equipment held or managed by the opposing party or a third party:

> To determine the truthfulness of a factum probandum in a patent infringement case, the court may, upon motion filed by a party, appoint a verifier to verify the documents or devices or equipment held or managed by the opposing party or a third party, unless the time or costs required for the verification or the burden on the verified party is obviously disproportionate.

its constituting chapters was created, which will make the system more open to constant changes.[10]

3.1.2. With General Provisions on IP

It is interesting to see that two Asian countries have enacted all-encompassing and stand-alone IP Code: the Philippines and Vietnam. IP Code of the Philippines was enacted in 1997. Section 2 declares a wide-ranging state policy on IP:

> The State recognizes that an effective intellectual and industrial property system is vital to the development of domestic and creative activity, facilitates transfer of technology, attracts foreign investments, and ensures market access for our products. It shall protect and secure the exclusive rights of scientists, inventors, artists and other gifted citizens to their IP and creations, particularly when beneficial to the people, for such periods as provided in this Act. The use of IP bears a social function. To this end, the State shall promote the diffusion of knowledge and information for the promotion of national development and progress and the common good.

Vietnam enacted its all-encompassing IP Code in 2005, which distinguishes copyright from industrial property rights and includes them both (Article 6). Part I of the Code contains 12 general provisions that deal with the scope, subjects of application, subject matters of IP, interpretation of terms, application of IP laws and other laws, bases for the emergence and establishment of IPRs, contents of state management of IP and its responsibilities, and IP fees and charges, among others.

Noteworthy are its limitations on IPR:

> The exercise of IPRs must neither be prejudicial to the State's interests, public interests, legitimate interests, and interests of other organizations and individuals, nor violate any other provisions of law. In the circumstances where the achievement of defense, security and people's life-related objectives and other interests of the State and society specified in this Law should be guaranteed, the State may prohibit or restrict the exercise of IPRs by the holders or compel the licensing with appropriate terms. Article 7(2)(3)

Vietnamese IP Code articulates that the state's IP policies are

> to recognize and protect IPRs on the basis of harmonizing benefits of IPR holders and public interests; not to protect IP objects which are contrary to the social ethics and public order and prejudicial to defense and security, and to encourage and promote activities of creation and utilization of intellectual

10 Cao, X.M., & Zhang, J.H. (2010). (Eds.). *Research on Codification of IPRs (in Chinese)* (pp. 75–76). Peking University Press.

assets in order to contribute to the socio-economic development and the improvement of the people's material and spiritual life. (Article 8)

One distinct feature of the Vietnamese IP Code is that it does not contain criminal punishment for IP infringement. Rather, the 2015 Criminal Code under Article 225 (Infringement of copyrights and relevant rights) and Article 226 (Infringement of industrial property rights) foresee such provision.

3.2. All-Encompassing but not Stand-Alone IP Code

3.2.1. Russia

In Russia, the codification of laws on IP was done within civil law because the legal regulation of IP is primarily performed in the sphere of civil law. Part IV of the Civil Code of the Russian Federation, effective since January 1, 2008, entitled "Rights to the Results of Intellectual Activities and Means of Individualization," brings together a variety of previous Russian laws on IP[11] which were unrelated and incompatible with each other and other laws, artificially isolated from the rest of its components, including the fundamental and general rules of civil law. The codification was the best way to duly integrate IP law into civil law and harmonize the relevant rules, as well as to greatly simplify their use and enhance their credibility and stability.[12]

Some assess that Part IV is a good example of codification; it is the full version of the systematization of IP law. It lays down the general provisions relating to all forms of IP and excludes the further need for specific laws on certain types of IP. It also ensures uniformity of legal regulation, eliminates unnecessary differences, unifies the terminology, and provides for the correlation and possible application of general rules of civil law.[13]

11 Such as Civil Code of RSFSR of June 11, 1964 (sections IV–VI), Law of Russia "On Copyright and Related Rights" of July 9, 1993, "On Breeding Achievements" of August 6, 1993, "On Legal Protection of Computer Programs and Databases" of September 23, 1992, Patent Law of Russia of September 23, 1992, Law of Russia "On Trademarks, Service Marks and Indications of Origins of Goods" of September 23, 1992, Law "On Legal Protection of Topologies of Integrated Circuits" of September 23, 1992, see Lisitsa, V. (2016). IP law in Russia, development, problems, and perspectives. *WIPO-WTO Colloquium Papers*, 59, at: https://www.wto.org/english/tratop_e/trips_e/colloquium_papers_e/2016/chapter_7_2016_e.pdf.

12 Lisitsa, V. (2016). IP law in Russia, development, problems, and perspectives. *WIPO-WTO Colloquium Papers*, 60, at: https://www.wto.org/english/tratop_e/trips_e/colloquium_papers_e/2016/chapter_7_2016_e.pdf, 60.

13 Lisitsa, V. (2016). IP law in Russia, development, problems and perspectives. *WIPO-WTO Colloquium Papers*, 60, at: https://www.wto.org/english/tratop_e/trips_e/colloquium_papers_e/2016/chapter_7_2016_e.pdf

3.2.2. China?

In China, there is no IP Code, although its Civil Code does have provisions governing some aspects of IP-related issues.[14] That said, there has always been strong unwavering advocacy from academic heavyweights for IP codification, either as part of its Civil Code[15] or as a stand-alone IP Code. One recent example is that Professor Wu Handong advocated since 2010 for a comprehensive IP Code with seven parts and several hundred articles.[16] We are better advised not to underestimate China's drive to codification, both to be true to its civil law tradition and, more importantly, to more scientifically regulate the complicated social, commercial, and technical fabrics of the country. We never know if and when China decides top-down to incorporate all its scattered IP laws into one IP Code.

3.3. All-Encompassing Industrial Property Code Plus Copyright Law

Some jurisdictions have an all-encompassing industrial property law, covering all industrial property matters, and a copyright law, for example, Turkey and Italy. Turkey Industrial Property Law (Law No. 6769 of December 22, 2016, on Industrial Property, effective January 10, 2017) and Copyright Act. The Industrial

14 Such as Article 123 of China's Civil Code which recognizes IP rights as property rights, among others.

15 Liu Chuntian strongly promotes that:

> China, as the mega economy that rises swiftly in the last couple of decades and a late comer society of rule of law, should grasp the moment, ride on the tide of history, surpass forefathers, break away from old mold, and pave the way to modernization of the Civil Code. Furthermore, China should codify IP laws into the Civil Law and lay a well-established legal foundation for the long-term strategy of innovation-driven development in China.

Liu, C. T., and Liu, K-C. (2019). On the necessity of incorporating IP laws into the civil law of China and how. In Liu, K-C. and Racherla, U. (Eds.), *Innovation, Economic Development and IPR in China and India—A Study of Six Economic Sectors* (pp. 25–37). Springer. Zheng Chengsi, although against the incorporation of IP Part into the Civil Code, proposed in 2002 under the mandate of the Legal Working Committee, People's Congress an IP Part with six chapters to be incorporated into the then-discussed Chinese Civil Code, believing that his proposal will enhance and not hinder the constant improvement of the Civil Code. There were 86 articles in total, Chapter 1 General Provisions (22 articles), Chapter 2 Authors' and Disseminators' Rights (13 articles), Chapter 3 Patents (23 articles), Chapter 4 Trademarks (18 articles), Chapter 5 Trade Secrets (3 articles), and Chapter 6 Protection Against Unfair Competition (5 articles). See Zheng, C.S. (2007). *On Intellectual Property* (3rd. ed.) (in Chinese), 55–58. Law Press China.

16 Part 1 general provisions (12 articles), Part 2 literature rights (copyrights, neighboring rights, and collective management organizations), Part 3 patents and other proprietary rights (invention patents, utility models and designs, rights over technology knowledge (trade secrets, IC layout designs, and new plant variety rights), Part 4 rights over commercial signs (trademark rights, trade name rights, geographic indication, and domain name rights), Part 5 other rights (traditional knowledge, biodiversity, and unfair competition), Part 6 administrative agency, judiciary, and remedies (three instances of IP courts, national IP office, infringement, and remedies), and Part 7 (transitional provisions). See Cao, X.M., and Zhang, J.H. (2010) (Eds.). *Research on Codification of IPRs* (in Chinese) (pp. 282–412). Peking University Press.

Property Law foresees three "Preliminary Provisions" that deal with the purpose, scope, definitions, and persons that will benefit from protection. Italy promulgated the Industrial Property Code in 2005 and the Copyright Act. The IP Code has six general provisions that define industrial property rights, their establishment and acquisition, the treatment of foreigners, priority, exhaustion, and joint ownership (Title I).

3.4. Act on National IP Policy

3.4.1. Japan IP Basic Act 2002

In its efforts to revitalize its stagnant economy, the Japanese looked back to their success story in the second half of the 19th century where they catapulted Japan from a third-world country to the first world with a complete set of IP laws. Japan enacted IP Basic Act in 2002 which does not affect private party rights and duties but gives direction to IP policy by setting forth a fundamental mission with respect to Japan's national strategy. It also sets forth the roles of government, industry, and academics in executing the strategy, while listing measures necessary to accomplish the individual groups' missions. The Basic IP Law gave the Japanese government the power to establish an IP Strategy Headquarters within the Cabinet to be chaired by the Prime Minister himself.[17]

3.4.2. Korean Framework Act on IP

Following the Japanese footprint, Korea enacted its Framework Act on IP in 2011 (last amended 2022). The Act has an elevated purpose, namely:

> contribute to the economic, social and cultural development of the Republic of Korea and the improvement of people's quality of life by formulating basic government policies and establishing the system for promotion thereof in order to facilitate creation, protection and utilization of intellectual property and create the foundations thereof, thus enabling the value of intellectual property to be displayed in our society to the fullest extent.
>
> Article 1[18]

The Framework Act generously recognizes IP:

> The term 'intellectual property' means knowledge, information, technology, the expression of thoughts or feelings, the indication of business or goods,

17 Takanaka, T. (2009). Success or failure? Japan's national strategy on intellectual property and evaluation of its impact from the comparative law perspective. *Washington University Global Studies Law Review, 1*.

18 At: https://www.wipo.int/wipolex/en/text/588922

> varieties of organism or genetic resources and other intangibles created or discovered by creative activities, experience, etc. of human beings, the value of property of which may be realized.
>
> Article 3(1)

The Act then suggests the possibility of the so-called "new IP," which reads open-ended: "The term 'new intellectual property' means intellectual property that appears in new fields in line with economic, social or cultural changes or the development of science and technology." (Article 3(2)). However, "intellectual property right" has to be "recognized or protected according to Acts and subordinate statutes, treaties, etc." (Article 3(3)).

Article 5(1) (Relations with Other Acts) establishes the principle that all other Acts related to IP must comply with this Framework Act ("Where other Acts related to intellectual property are enacted or amended, they shall satisfy the objectives and basic principles of this Act.")

The Framework Act on IP urges the Government to promote policies related to IP,[19] to formulate Masterplan for National IP (Article 8) and Action Plan for National IP (Article 9), to vitalize the procedures for settlement of disputes other than trials (Article 22), to promote the utilization of IP (Article 25), and to foster IP service industry (Article 26). This piece of the Act has been instrumental in catapulting Korea to a strong IP player on the global stage.[20]

4. Principles of an IP Code

An ideal IP Code in the sense of de lege ferenda, must have a section of general principles which govern or guide the interpretation and application of individual and specific IP provisions, rather than just window-dressing declaration only.[21]

19 Article 2 of the Korean Framework Act on IP provides:

> The Government shall promote policies related to intellectual property according to the following basic principles: 1. To promote the creation of excellent intellectual property by encouraging creators of intellectual property, such as writers, inventors, technicians, and artists to engage in their activities creatively and stably; 2. To protect intellectual property in an effective and stable manner, promote the utilization and the reasonable and fair use thereof; 3. To build up foundations to promote the creation, protection and utilization of intellectual property by promoting the social environment that values intellectual property and fostering professional human resources and related industries; 4. To contribute to the common development of the international community by bringing harmony between domestic norms and international norms on intellectual property and supporting the strengthening of intellectual property-related aptitude of developing countries.

20 Ahn, K-H. (2022). Korea's intellectual property protection strategy and its implication for ASEAN. In Chen, L., and Kimura, F. (Eds.), *Intellectual Property Rights and ASEAN Development in the Digital Age* (pp. 172–250). Routledge.

21 Some suggest that the General Provisions and Basic Principles of the TRIPS Agreement should be taken as binding rules, see Kur, A., & Levin, M. (Eds.). (2011). *Intellectual Property Rights in a Fair World Trade System Proposals for Reform of TRIPS* (pp. 529–640). Edward Elgar Publishing.

The IP Code can include at least the following fifteen principles which can be applied to different IPRs with varying degree,[22] like a sliding scale of sorts, according to the respective nature of the right at issue. Sometimes, some of the principles might even entirely disapply for certain IP (e.g., no compulsory license of trademark rights and no sharing of economic fruits with trademark owners), which, however, does not affect the core nature of IP.

This could be comparable to the determination of the likelihood of confusion between trademarks. There are a host of factors to be considered, such as the similarity of goods and services (factoring in again prices, sales channels, complementarity, etc.) and the similarity of marks (factoring in the dominant part of marks and then the ultimate holistic observation, etc.) at issue. The missing of one factor or even several factors in one specific case, will not necessarily affect the final conclusion of the likelihood of confusion. The decisive point is to conduct "a global assessment or appreciation," and to see an interdependence between these fifteen principles, which are not to be treated as a "watertight compartment," therefore a lesser degree or even non-existence of one principle can be offset or compensated by a greater degree of other principles.[23]

4.1. *Technical Neutrality*

In the world of fast advancing technologies, it is imperative to treat all technologies equally, or with neutrality, rather than responding to technologies differently. However, often we come across IP regimes that run counter to this principle. To name a few:

4.1.1. *Wrongful Special Treatment of Semiconductor Technology*

The rise of the semiconductor technology and industry in 1960 has catapulted human progress limitlessly. The protection of integrated circuits (IC) layouts or chip topographies (the design of chips) was an uncharted territory. It was feared that IC-layout designs would not be protected by copyright law due to their technical function, patent protection requires lengthy examination, and chip pirates would arise. To find a quick fix, in the US, Intel and the Semiconductor Industry Association lobbied for a sui generis law and treaty, which led to the world's first-ever Semiconductor Chip Protection Act of 1984 (SCPA). The SCPA is a sui generis regime tailor-made for the semiconductor industry. Although it is codified in Title 17 of the US Code (copyrights), it is neither a copyright nor patent law.

22 These fifteen principles are too complex to Richard Epstein who believes in the virtue of simplicity and is of the opinion that some five or six simple rules suffice: "self-ownership, or autonomy; first possession; voluntary exchange; protection against aggression; limited privilege for cases of necessity; and takings of property for public use on payment of just compensation." See Epstein, R. (1995). *Simple Rules for a Complex World* (p. 53). Harvard University Press.

23 Mellor, J. et al. (2023). *Kerly's Law of Trade Marks and Trade Names*(17th ed.), 11–056. Sweet & Maxwell; CJEU, Sabel v. Puma [1997] E.C.R.1–6191.

It resembles utility model law and copyright law as it requires no examination. It differs from copyright law in that it requires registration. The SCPA provides only ten years protection upon registration.

The SCPA is a dubious law, to say the least. For two reasons. First, IC-layout design rightsholder could eventually double charge (or double dip). It can charge infringers for actual or statutory damages[24] and then charge "innocent purchasers," who purchase semiconductor chip products in good faith and without having notice of protection with respect to the semiconductor chip products, "a reasonable royalty on each unit of the infringing semiconductor chip product" for infringement liability with respect to the importation or distribution of units of infringing semiconductor chip products.[25] Second, the SCPA provides only very limited access to deposited materials about the IC-layout designs, which will be discussed in detail in Subsection 4.7.

Notwithstanding the mentioned flaws, the US pushed for the Washington Treaty on Intellectual Property in Respect of Integrated Circuits (IPIC Treaty) in 1989 and applied a "carrot and stick scheme" to induce and pressure foreign nations to follow suit. As a result, both major and smaller economies (such as Hong Kong, Vietnam, Malaysia, etc.) have enacted domestic special law (such as Australia, Canada, the EU, India, Japan, Korea, Taiwan) or regulation (such as the PRC).[26] The TRIPS Agreement also eagerly anticipates that the IPIC Treaty would take effect and incorporates many of its provisions.[27] However, there are only a handful of economies can manufacture chips and the IPIC Treaty has not yet entered into force (ratified or acceded to only by Bosnia and Herzegovina, Egypt and Saint Lucia). Ironically, not even the initiator, the US, has ratified it.

Forty years after the enactment of the SCPA, IC-layout design regimes around the globe have now proven to be of no practical use or significance. Take the US for example, the world champion in IC design, the number of registered IC-layout designs is unbelievably low, between 2010–2022 there were only 646 mask works registered in the US Copyright Office,[28] far fewer than patents filed and granted. There is no case law that applies the SCPA. Taiwan, the world leader in semiconductor manufacturing, has also a small number of registered IC-layout designs,[29] no case law (litigation is not worth the buck!).

24 17 U.S. Code § 911—Civil actions.

25 17 U.S. Code § 907—Limitation on exclusive rights: innocent infringement.

26 Regulations on IC-Layout Designs was promulgated by the State Council and not a statute enacted by the People's Congress.

27 Article 35 (Relation to the IPIC Treaty) of the TRIPS Agreement provides "Members agree to provide protection to the layout-designs (topographies) of integrated circuits (referred to in this Agreement as "layout-designs") in accordance with Articles 2 through 7 (other than Paragraph 3 of Article 6), Article 12 and Paragraph 3 of Article 16 of the Treaty on Intellectual Property in Respect of Integrated Circuits and, in addition, to comply with the following provisions."

28 Cited from Protecting Semiconductor Chip Design under the Semiconductor Chip Protection Act of 1984 (SCPA)—Part I (Registration and Inspection) (11 January 2023) at https://www.lexology.com/search.

29 Between 2013–2022, there were only 1,045 registered IC layout designs in Taiwan.

Now chip production has become capital-intensive[30] and technology-driven, there is no room for petty pirates and piracy. It begs the question "do we still need IC-layout design protection law?"[31] and "do we still need the IPIC Treaty?" In hindsight, isn't the sui generis law the result of not following the technical neutrality principle? The way forward would be to abolish the sui generis protection of IC layout designs and to rely on the good old model of patent law.[32]

In this light, Article 31(c) of the TRIPS Agreement's special treatment of semiconductor technology (limiting the scope and duration of compulsory use of semiconductor patents only to be for public non-commercial use or to remedy a practice determined after judicial or administrative process to be anti-competitive) looks ostensibly unjustified and unnecessary. This is nothing but the result of lobbying by interest groups.

4.1.2. Obsolete Legislation on Optical Disks

In its efforts to curb rampant copyright piracy via optical dicks, the US has imposed on its major trading partners, such as Malaysia, Hong Kong, the Philippines, Taiwan, Singapore, Serbia, etc., stringent sui generis optical disc laws which punish unreported CD manufacturing. The US also demanded them to revise their respective copyright law to raise the criminal punishment for copyright infringement committed via optical discs.[33] This is again a blatant violation of the technical neutrality principle. It is now obsoleted by the progress of wireless streaming

30 Take TSMC, No. 1 in high-end chip OEM production, for example. It is projected to invest US $37 billion in capital expenditure in 2025, marking a 15.6% increase from the projected US $32 billion in 2024. See Yeh, A. *Surging TSMC 2nm Demand to Spark Chip Investment Race in 2025*, at: https://www.digitimes.com/news/a20240703VL210/2025–2nm-capex-demand-investment-tsmc.

31 For brilliant case study of practice of IC-layout protection and the development of chip industry in Taiwan see Chang, T.-P. (2009). Empirical study of the twelve-year practice of Taiwan integrated circuits layout protection law (in Chinese). *Tech Law Review, 6*, 75–111. And in the PRC see Liu, J.C. (2023). From exclusivity to getting paid: The evolution of the entitlement mode for IC layout designs (in Chinese). *Peking University Law Journal, 35(5)*, 1364–1380.

32 Liu Jianchen convincingly argues that a sui generis right for IC layout designs:

> the deviation of the developments of the chip industry from legislative purposes causes right holders less and less reliant on this exclusive right, as evidenced by the small number of cases regarding layout design infringement worldwide. Under these circumstances, modifying those ill-fitted institutions is of limited practical significance.

However, rather than suggesting its abolition he advocated:

> "a fundamental reform of the entitlement mode of chip design is indispensable. A compensatory liability-rule regime . . . can be justified in terms of features of cumulative innovation in the chip industry, the freedom of imitation, and most importantly, preserving chip designers minimum incentive to continue conducting creative activities." Well-intentioned this suggestion might be, it is not practicable.
>
> id.

33 Liu, K.-C. (2022). *IP Laws and Regimes in Major Asian Economies— Combing Through Thousand Threads of IP to Peace in Asia* (p. 6). Routledge.

enabled by ubiquitous IoT. Now these outdated sui generis laws and copyright laws in those economies are nothing but the relics of the long phased-out optical discs.

4.2. Limited Criminal Punishment

IP infringement is a tricky thing to determine in advance, given the lack of public notice in copyright, astronomical number of patents and even more claims, and the whimsically changing perception of the relevant public about the likelihood of confusion and dilution. The actual boundary of IP and its encroachment are highly amorphous and unpredictable. This makes IP infringement an unsuitable candidate for criminal punishment which is meant to influence in advance people's future behaviors. In addition, to punish IP infringement with criminal penalty is an intrusion of state power into private disputes, which can only be justified in exceptional cases. Therefore, the use of criminal punishment for IP infringement should be very limited.

Article 61 of the TRIPS Agreement requires members to provide criminal punishment at least for willful trademark counterfeiting and copyright piracy on a commercial scale.[34] However, sweeping criminalization of IP infringement can be observed in the Western jurisdictions typified by Germany and many major Asian jurisdictions. In practice, there has been relatively rare criminal prosecution of IP infringement in Western countries. On the contrary, criminal prosecution of IP infringement, excluding patent infringement, is not uncommon or even rampant in some major Asian jurisdictions, to quick fix new emerging societal issues due to pressure of their major trading partner, the US.

It is suggested that members of the WTO re-examine and take a hard look at their criminal provisions and practice for IP infringement and to incrementally decriminalize IP crimes that are not "malum in se (evil in and of itself)." This minimalist approach towards criminal punishment of IP infringement corresponds with the basic principle of modesty for criminal law and the defining features of IP.[35] Article 61 of the TRIPS Agreement should be revised to add cautionary notes that the actual use and even overuse of criminal punishment can lead to distortion of IPRs as private rights and market competition.

34 Article 61 of the TRIPS Agreement stipulates "Members shall provide for criminal procedures and penalties to be applied at least in cases of willful trademark counterfeiting or copyright piracy on a commercial scale."

35 Liu, K.-C. et al. (2024). Civil follows criminal or criminal follows civil procedure as models to deal with IP infringement: Asian vis-à-vis Western approaches. In Hilty, R. M. et al., (Eds.), *Kreation Innovation Märkte—Creation Innovation Markets* (pp. 663–739). Springer.

4.3. Numerus Clausus and Specificity in the Recognition of IP

IP laws should follow the numerus clausus (closed number) in the recognition of IPRs. This principle requires that only Congress may create new forms of IP,[36] after cool calculation of the regulatory impacts that follow heated debate. This principle can also preserve the maximum freedom for the general public.[37]

In addition, the congressional recognition of IPRs must be specific, not so broadly termed as to be open-ended, defeating the numerus clausus requirement. In this context, Article 10(1) of Chinese Copyright Law serves as a bad example. After enumerating four moral rights (the right to publish, authorship, alteration and integrity) and twelve economic rights, it loosey recognizes for the first time since 2021 open-ended copyrights: "Other rights that should be enjoyed by authors." It will open the Pandora box! Furthermore, the recognition of any new IPRs has to be based on express parliamentary decisions, which cannot be delegated to administrative agencies or courts, however professional or wise they might be.

4.4. Open-Ended Exceptions and Limitations

As will be discussed in Subsection 5.2, the three-step test is a poor standard for marking limitations and exceptions and should be interpreted as the proportionality principle. The proportionality principle would allow the legislative and especially the judiciary to introduce open-ended limitations to all IPRs,[38] until it is otherwise expressly stipulated by IP laws enacted by Congress. For example, under the US Semiconductor Chip Protection Act of 1984, there is not an express statutory fair use defense for an alleged infringement of mask work, it is still allowable for the courts to find a similar defense that applies to mask work.

This grand doctrinal postulate would secure the maximum freedom for the public. In the trademark area, some European scholars are already advocating the

36 Merrill, T. W., & Smith, H. (2000). Optimal standardization in the law of property: The numerus clausus principle. *The Yale Law Journal, 110,* 19.

37 Although Merrill and H. Smith observed that in the US common law, the numerus clausus is probably at its weakest in the area of IP, as there are some notable exceptions in which judicial creativity in fashioning new IP interests, such as the doctrine of misappropriation of information and a "right of publicity," has been Sanctioned (Merrill, T.W., & Smith, H. (2000). Optimal standardization in the law of property: The numerus clausus principle. *The Yale Law Journal, 110,* 19–20.), the doctrine of misappropriation of information and publicity right are not members of the IP family according to my general theory of IP (see Subsection 3.1 of Chapter 2).

38 Henning Grosse Ruse-Khan similarly argues that although national legislators are better placed to integrate the overlaps, tensions, and conflicts between competing norms, they require "the introduction of something akin to a general exception rule into TRIPS, for example by simply deleting the TRIPS consistency test from Article 8(1)." See Ruse-Khan, H.G. (2016). *The Protection of Intellectual Property in International Law* (pp. 14, 21). Oxford University Press.

adaptation of an open-ended clause to the provision on trademark rights limitations.[39] The same rationale should also apply to copyrights and patents.

However, we have to be prepared that this principle will not be implemented overnight. Every so often, national legislature and courts don't seem to be able to understand/apply open-ended limitations properly.[40] In addition, the relationship between the general fair use clause and individual fair use clauses varies from jurisdiction to jurisdiction.[41] In this regard, the guidance of a general theory of IP will help jurisdictions to overcome this difficulty:[42] specific permitted fair uses are to be supplemented by the overarching general fair use provision so that there will be more liberal application of individual fair use clauses.

4.5. Only Prospective Extension of Protection Term

There is an ever-lasting temptation for IP holders to prolong the protection term of IP and apply the extension to existent and future creation, as it will bring a windfall to those protected rightsholders at no costs. Which triggers endless rent-seeking

39 They advocate that:

> in order to keep pace with technological developments and to allow the adaptation of the law to changing circumstances, an open-ended clause should be added to the provision on limitations which allows courts to develop appropriate new defences on a case-by-case basis in circumstances where the purposes, objectives and fundamental principles underlying the existing legislation warrant permitting third party use notwithstanding the lack of an express limitation. The application of this open-ended clause should not be pre-empted by the existence of more specific limitations. Its scope must not be confined to non-commercial use.
>
> Senftleben, M. et al. (2014)

Recommendation on measures to safeguard freedom of expression and undistorted competition in EU trade mark law 2015. *European Intellectual Property Review, 2015*, 337–344.

40 For example, Taiwan and Korea have transplanted the US open-ended fair use model in their copyright law in 1993 and 2012 respectively. However, in Taiwan, there have been few court decisions that applied the general fair use clause of Article 65(2). Korea confusingly combines it with the three-step test, which only limits the open-ended fair use. Generally speaking, the general fair use clause is used only tentatively in Korea and Taiwan. See Liu, K.-C. (2022). *IP Laws and Regimes in Major Asian Economies – Combing Through Thousand Threads of IP to Peace in Asia* (pp. 97–98). Routledge. Singapore, as an Asian common law jurisdiction, also introduced the US-styled fair use into its Copyright Act in 2005. However, "this should not be taken as indicative that American jurisprudence will now be more persuasive than hitherto . . . the development and theoretic underpinnings of US copyright law differ in material ways from those of Singapore's." Llewelyn, D. et al. (2023). *Modern Law of Copyright in Singapore*, 9.26. Academy Publishing.

41 Under the Korean Copyright Act, "If any act is covered by the listed exceptions, then there is no room for the fair use test in Article 35–3 to apply." However, in Singapore, the specific permitted uses are supplemented by the overarching general fair use provision.

42 In Taiwan there is the double limitation (or marginalization) issue, as some specific fair use articles already contain the condition "within a reasonable scope." Similarly, double limitation (or marginalization) did happen in Malaysia, when High Court of Malaya wrongly read into the individual fair use limitations additional restrictions not intended by the legislature. See Liu, K.-C. (2022). *IP Laws and Regimes in Major Asian Economies—Combing Through Thousand Threads of IP to Peace in Asia* (pp. 101–102). Routledge.

campaigns. This has repeatedly happened in the entertainment industry, which leads to term extensions time and again.[43]

The 1998 Sonny Bono Copyright Term Extension Act (CTEA) in the US extends the protection terms and applies them to existent works. Eric Eldred, joined by a group of commercial and non-commercial interests, which relied on the public domain for their works, challenged unconstitutionality for violating Article I, Section 8, Clause 8 of the US Constitution which empowers Congress to enact federal laws to recognize patent and copyright rights "for limited times." The Supreme Court held in a seven to two decision the CTEA was constitutional.[44] However, if we look at the issue from the viewpoint of incentivizing new creation, then applying the term extension to existent creations retroactively would be counter to the step one principle of the three-step exchange theorem here proposed, namely, granting IP to provide incentive for the creation, dissemination and use of new creations. Existent creations were already made, and do not need any ex-post incentive.

4.6. *To Enable Fair Sharing of Economic Fruits Derived from One's Creation*

4.6.1. *Theoretic Discussion*

The economic fruits of the protected objects should be more fairly distributed to the actual creators (however, this principle does not apply to trademarks). Only then, the promise of incentivizing new creation and its sharing can materialize. Admittedly, traditional IP laws and treaties do not care whether the IP incentive loop closes and leaves creators to take care of their rights through contracts. However, this is less than satisfactory. This suggested principle should have its bearing on the design of IP regimes.

There is now a proposal for a clause for the international copyright community and treaty to consider, which demands that:

> The contracting parties must guarantee that, in the case of severe affectation of the creator's dignity, or in case of severe disproportion between the financial gains obtained by the secondary rightsholders of the copyright and the creator's remuneration, the given contracts related to such situation could

43 For example, Micky Mouse and Mini Mouse in Steamboat Willi (cartoon movie) was created in 1928 and could have entered the public domain in 1955. However, its copyright was extended multiple times due to the lobby by Walt Disney and went into public domain only in 2024. See https://en.wikipedia.org/wiki/Steamboat_Willie.

44 The majority opinion written by Justice Ginsburg relied heavily on the Copyright Acts of 1790, 1831, 1909, and 1976 as precedent for retroactive extensions. One of the arguments supporting the act was the life expectancy has significantly increased among the human population since the 18th century, and therefore copyright law needed extending as well, 537 U.S. 186 (2003).

be reversed by the judiciary. Such guarantee may not be waivable and is of public order.[45]

4.6.2. In Patent Area

The employees' right to equitable sharing of extraordinary revenues derived from their invention during the course of employment, in addition to paid salary, benefits, and promotion in company's echelon, widely recognized in major European economies,[46] France, Italy,[47] Germany,[48] the UK, etc.[49] reflects the same consideration. Unfortunately, in Asia, employees still have a long way to go before they can leave the struggle of employee-turned Nobel laureate Shuji Nakamura from Japan behind in history.[50]

45 Alvarez-Amezquita, D., & Vallejo-Trujillo, F. (2023). Limiting freedom of contract: Next step for copyright treaties in the exploitation of intellectual property rights. In Schovsbo, J. (Ed.), *Search of the Right Balance* (p. 239). Edward Elgar Publishing.

46 By contrast, the most innovative country according to WIPO's Innovation Index, Switzerland, does not have a similar law. However, Hans Ullrich reminds us that a comparison between small, highly industrialized Switzerland, and Germany and the UK are misleading, as patenting activity varies considerably by regional industrial structure. See Ullrich, H. (2023). Harmonization of employee invention laws: The black hole of the EU's innovation policy. In Ghidin, G., & Falce, V. (Eds.), *Reforming Intellectual Property* (p. 245). Edward Elgar Publishing, footnote 70.

47 Ullrich, H. (2023). Harmonization of employee invention laws: The black hole of the EU's innovation policy. In Ghidin, G., & Falce, V. (Eds.), *Reforming Intellectual Property* (pp. 228–352). Edward Elgar Publishing.

48 Germany's participatory democracy under the strong influence of labor unions is keen in securing employees their fair share in the economic fruits of their invention granted during the course of employment. Therefore, Germany enacted the Act on Employee's Inventions.

49 In the UK, the birthplace of the Industrial Revolution, the Patents Act of 1977 also provides employee inventors with a statutory right to compensation when their inventions are exploited by their employer (Section 40). It is however assessed that this statutory right has "been construed in such a way as to provide little direct benefit to employees." See Bently, L. et al. (2018). *Intellectual Property Law* (5th ed., p. 691). Oxford University Press.

50 While working for Nichia, Nakamura invented the first high brightness gallium nitride (GaN) LED whose brilliant blue light is the key to white LED lighting which went into production in 1993. In 1999, he left Nichia to become a professor at the University of California at Santa Barbara in the United States In 2001, Nakamura sued his former employer Nichia over his bonus for the discovery. Nakamura claimed that he received only ¥20,000 (about US $180) for his discovery of "404 patent." Nakamura originally won an award of ¥20 billion (about US $200 million); Nichia appealed the award and the parties settled in 2005 for ¥840 million (about US $8.1 million), the then-largest bonus ever paid by a Japanese company, an amount only enough to cover legal expenses incurred by Nakamura. Nakamura was awarded the Nobel Prize in 2014 for the invention of efficient blue LED. See https://en.wikipedia.org/wiki/Shuji_Nakamura.

4.6.3. In Copyright Area

In the copyright area,

> The digital revolution . . . offers substantial opportunities to reduce, virtually to the costs of electricity, the transaction costs . . . thus making it possible for revenues to be returned to creators with a degree of perfection unavailable even to the CMOs.[51]

Therefore, we should enable fair sharing of economic fruits derived from one's works: "The success of any structural reform of copyright should be judged in part on whether sustainable financial flows to authors are restored."[52] In this regard, the German Copyright Act sets world-leading examples for others to learn from.

A. TO EMPOWER COLLECTING SOCIETIES TO COLLECT AND REDISTRIBUTE LEVIES

German Copyright Act utilizes the well-developed collecting societies to introduce a series of so-called "rights only exercisable by collecting societies,"[53] which empower them to collect and redistribute the collected levies to individual copyright holders, guaranteeing them equitable remuneration, rather than unpaid for free "fair use." These rights include authors' right to equitable remuneration from the resale of artist works (Article 26(1) and (3)),[54] for rental of records or video tapes (Article 27(1)), for lending trough public institutions (Article 27(2)),[55] for reproducing and distributing radio comments and newspaper articles (Article

51 Goldstein, P. (2015). Future platforms for copyright licensing. *IIC, 46,* 153–154.

52 Gervais, D. (2017). *(Re)Structuring Copyright—A Comprehensive Path to International Copyright Reform* (p. 191). Edward Elgar Publishing. In this juncture, it is worth pointing out that the International Instrument on Permitted Uses in Copyright Law proposed by a group of IP scholars emphasizes the importance of economic participation of the creator even in fair use of his works "Contracting Parties shall ensure that the creator of a work is entitled to a reasonable share of any remuneration or compensation paid for the permitted use of that work." See Hilty, R. et al. (2021). International instrument on permitted uses in copyright law. *IIC, 52,* 62–67, at: https://link.springer.com/article/10.1007/s40319-020-00999-8.

53 In German these rights are called "Verwertungsgesellschaften-pflichtige Rechte."

54 Article 26(1) and (2) German Copyright Act provide:

> (1) If the original of an artistic work or of a photographic work is resold and if an art dealer or an auctioneer is involved as purchaser, vendor or intermediary, the vendor is to pay the author a share of the selling price. . . . The obligation under sentence 1 does not apply where the selling price amounts to less than 400 euros.

55 Article 27(1) and (2) German Copyright Act provide:

> (1) Where the author has granted rental rights (article 17) in respect of a video or audio recording to the producer of the audio recording or of a film, the lessor is, nevertheless, required to pay the author equitable remuneration for the rental. The claim for remuneration may not be waived. It may be assigned in advance only to a collecting society. (2) The author is to be paid equitable remuneration for the lending of those originals or copies of a work whose dissemination is permitted under article 17 (2) if the originals or copies are lent through a publicly accessible institution (library, collection of video or audio recordings or other originals or copies thereof).

49(1)),[56] for reproduction apparatus (Article 54h(1) and (2)),[57] and for permitted uses for teaching, science and institutions (Article 60h(1) and (4)).[58]

B. TO RECOGNIZE STANDALONE AUTHORS' EX-POST RIGHTS

Authors, if standing alone, often stand to be exploited by commercial users of their works. Many authors nowadays are therefore united via collecting societies or even unionized. Whether the copyright regime should poke its nose into the plight of standalone authors, who are not represented by collective management organizations, is a highly controversial policy issue. On this, Germany again took the first bold move in 2002 by first declaring that "Copyright protects the author in his or her intellectual and personal relationships to the work and in respect of the use of the work. It also serves to ensure equitable remuneration for the use of the work." (Article 11). German Copyright Act then further recognizes a host of ex-post rights for standalone authors, including those who are in an employment relationship, to strengthen their contractual position,[59] for example, the right to require the other party to consent to a modification of the agreement, if the agreed remuneration is not equitable (Article 32(1)),[60] if the agreed remuneration is conspicuously disproportionate to the proceeds and benefits derived from the use of

56 Article 49(1) German Copyright Act provides:

> (1) It is permitted to reproduce and distribute individual broadcast commentaries and individual articles, as well as illustrations published in connection therewith, from newspapers and other information sheets devoted solely to current affairs in other newspapers or information sheets of this kind, and it is permitted to communicate such commentaries, articles and illustrations to the public if they concern current political, economic or religious issues and do not contain a statement reserving rights. The author is to be paid equitable remuneration for the reproduction, distribution and communication to the public, unless the reproduction, distribution and communication to the public is of short extracts of several commentaries or articles in the form of an overview. Claims may be asserted only through a collecting society.

57 Article 54h(1) and (2) German Copyright Act provide:

> (1) Claims under sections 54 to 54c, section 54e (2) and sections 54f and 54g may be asserted only through a collecting society. (2) Each rightholder is entitled to an equitable share of the remuneration paid pursuant to sections 54 to 54c. Insofar as works are protected by technical measures pursuant to section 95a, they are not taken into account when income is distributed.

58 Article 60h(1) and (4) German Copyright Act provide "(1) Authors are entitled to equitable remuneration for uses in accordance with this Subdivision. Reproductions are to be remunerated in accordance with sections 54 to 54c. (4) Claims to equitable remuneration may only be asserted through a collecting society."

59 Schricker/Loewenheim/Peifer, §111 UrhG Rn. 1 and 2 (C.H. Beck 6. Aufl. 2020).

60 Article 32(1) German Copyright Act provides:

> The author shall have a right to the contractually agreed remuneration for the granting of rights of use and permission to use the work. If the amount of the remuneration has not been determined, equitable remuneration shall be deemed to have been agreed. If the agreed remuneration is not equitable, the author may require the other party to consent to a modification of the agreement so that the author is granted equitable remuneration.

the work,[61] and the right to separate equitable remuneration from exploitation that was not anticipated by the parties while concluding the contract.[62]

German law has influenced the 2019 EU Digital Single Market Directive (DSM Directive),[63] which establishes the principle of appropriate and proportionate remuneration for authors and performers and demands that "Member States shall ensure that where authors and performers license or transfer their exclusive rights for the exploitation of their works or other subject matter, they are entitled to receive appropriate and proportionate remuneration." (Article 18(1)). The DSM Directive further entitles the author to an adjustment of the contractual remuneration:

> Member States shall ensure that, in the absence of an applicable collective bargaining agreement providing for a mechanism comparable to that set out in this Article, authors and performers or their representatives are entitled to claim additional, appropriate and fair remuneration from the party with whom they entered into a contract for the exploitation of their rights, or from the successors in title of such party, when the remuneration originally agreed turns out to be disproportionately low compared to all the subsequent relevant revenues derived from the exploitation of the works or performances.
>
> Article 20(1)[64]

C. TO RECOGNIZE PRESS PUBLISHERS' NEIGHBORING RIGHT

German Copyright Act was the first to introduce a levy on search engines in 2013. Articles 87f and 87g introduce a neighboring right for the press publisher, namely exclusive right of making available his press products online for commercial

61 Article 32a(1) German Copyright Act provides:

> (1) Where the author has granted a right of use to another party on conditions which, taking into account the author's entire relationship with the other party, result in the agreed remuneration being conspicuously disproportionate to the proceeds and benefits derived from the use of the work, the other party shall be obliged, at the author's request, to consent to a modification of the agreement which grants the author further equitable participation appropriate to the circumstances. It shall be irrelevant whether the parties to the agreement had foreseen or could have foreseen the amount of the proceeds or benefits obtained.

62 Article 32c German Copyright Act provides:

> The author shall be entitled to separate equitable remuneration where the other contracting party commences a new type of use of the author's work, pursuant to section 31a, which was agreed upon, but still unknown, at the time the contract was concluded. Section 32 (2) and (4) shall apply accordingly. The other contracting party shall, without delay, inform the author about the commencement of the new type of use of his work.

63 Directive (EU) 2019/790 of the European Parliament and of the Council of 17 April 2019 on copyright and related rights in the Digital Single Market and amending Directives 96/9/EC and 2001/29/EC (Text with EEA relevance).

64 These EU initiatives have found support from some US scholars, for example, Ginsburg, J. (2023). Authors' remuneration: reforms to wish for. In Ghidini, G., & Falce, V. (Eds.), *Reforming Intellectual Property* (pp. 125–128). Edward Elgar Publishing.

purposes for one year. The publisher should provide the authors of those products a fair share of the collected revenues (Article 87h). Acting alone the German model did not work.[65]

Collective efforts ensued and bore fruits. The EU's DSM Directive follows the German "solo run"[66] and provides publishers of press publications with a two-year neighboring right for the online use of their press publications by service providers.[67] This is pushed through not without criticism.[68] However, to be fair, to charge a levy on search engines is not anti-online innovation but makes the online ecology sustainable. In response, Google has already voluntarily reached agreements with over 1,500 publications across 15 countries in Europe as of June 15, 2023, to comply with the Directive.[69]

D. TO INTRODUCE AI LEVY SYSTEM?

In the era of generative AI, every author's works are being used, either through licensing, text-data-mining, or actual scraping, to train machine that leads to the generative AI, which brings economic fruits and revenues for providers of generative AI services. It is only just and equitable that authors are to share the revenues "to compensate . . . for the reduction in their market share and income."

But how to share is the crucial issue. Some scholars are advocating that:

> Copyright law could serve as a tool to introduce an output-oriented AI levy system and ensure the payment of equitable remuneration . . . the new revenue stream could be used to finance social and cultural funds that improve the working and living conditions of flesh-and-blood authors.[70]

65 In August 2014, the German press sued Google, Yahoo, and 1&1 for violating this neighboring right and asked for fees. Google brought suit to the German Constitutional Court challenging the constitutionality on the grounds of freedom of the press/speech and threatened to delink the German press. The German press was forced to grant Google, etc. an interim revocable one-time license.

66 Schricker/Loewenheim/Stieper, Vor §§87f ff. UrhG Rn. 1, 14 (C.H. Beck 6. Aufl. 2020).

67 Article 15 of Directive on Copyright in the Digital Single Market (Protection of press publications concerning online uses) stipulates that:

> 1. Member States shall provide publishers of press publications with the right provided for in Article 2 and Article 3(2) of Directive 2001/29/EC for the online use of their press publications by information society service. . . . 4. The rights provided for in paragraph 1 shall expire two years after the press publication is published. . . . 5. Member States shall provide that authors of works incorporated in a press publication receive an appropriate share of the revenues that press publishers receive for the use of their press publications by information society service providers.

68 Some impugns the new right as the emperor's new clothes: "The negotiation basis that the right provides is neither clear, nor capable of correcting bargaining imbalances, as it is unable to force relevant platforms to the negotiation table." See Furgal, U. (2023). The emperor has no clothes: How the press publishers' right implementation exposes its shortcomings. *GRUR International*, 650.

69 See https://blog.google/products/news/google-news-regulation/.

70 See Senftleben, M. (2023). Generative AI and author remuneration. *International Review of Intellectual Property and Competition Law*, *54*, 535–1560, at SSRN: https://ssrn.com/abstract=4478370.

In principle, this could be an acceptable suggestion, depending on how it is worked out in detail. One could also ask whether we need to introduce broader corporate social responsibility (see Subsection 5.1 of Chapter 11) with a global framework to deal with the fairness aspect of AI.

4.7. Sufficient Disclosure of the Protected Subject Matter

The protected object of IP must be sufficiently disclosed, at least made available upon request for a fee,[71] mostly for the purpose of notifying (typically in the case of trademarks), inspiring the public (copyright, patents, and the likes), and public oversight (whether there are unworthy patents, trademarks, etc.). Patents are a classical example of sufficient disclosure. The word patent originates from the Latin "patere," which means "to lay open," to make available for public inspection. It is a shortened version of the term "letters patent," which was an open document or instrument issued by a monarch or government granting exclusive rights to a person, predating the modern patent system.[72] Therefore, patent applicants are required to sufficiently disclose their invention so that anyone skilled in the art can implement the invention without the help of the inventors (enablement).

The idea and practice of registering and publishing registered trademarks are dominant world over. Admittedly, copyrighted works are too many to register ad disclose, nevertheless the underlying justification of why expression of idea deserves the protection of copyright points to the need to disclose its content, to notify and inspire others. Some jurisdictions provide favorable treatment to copyright owners to encourage registration and publication of works.[73] At any rate, IPR holders need to prove the actual existence of claimed subject matters before they can proceed to exercise IPRs.

However, under pressure from the US, some jurisdictions introduced the so-called "data exclusivity" for test data submitted for drug approval purposes. For example, Singapore and Taiwan recognize a data exclusivity period of five years. Throughout the entire period of data exclusivity, generic companies are not allowed to file for market approval of pharmaceuticals, regardless of whether the original drug is protected by patent rights or not. However, these data should be made available for public oversight of drugs and can be relied upon by generic manufacturers after paying costs-corresponding fees for drug approval purposes. More correctly, the Law Commission of India on Trade Secrets rejects data exclusivity:

> The TRIPS Agreement does not explicitly endorse data exclusivity or patent linkage in the manner desired by developed nations. Prior to the negotiation

71 In the case discussed in Subsection 4.1 of Chapter 1 Microsoft made the interoperability information available for a one-time fee of €10,000.

72 See https://en.wikipedia.org/wiki/Patent.

73 For example, in the US, under 17 USC §412, statutory damages, attorney fees, and court costs are only available for works that were registered with the Copyright Office prior to infringement, or within three months of publication.

of the TRIPS Agreement, many countries permitted the reliance on originator test data to approve generic products. In tum, simply proving bio-equivalence, meaning that their product was chemically identical to the original product, was enough for generic manufacturers. This approach was consumer friendly as it facilitated the introduction of generics into the market immediately after the patent expiration. The significance of maintaining this traditional approach is emphasized by recent reports such as the UN High-Level Panel Report on Access to Medicines, the WIPO Development Agenda, and WHO Studies, all of which stress the importance of ensuring access to medicines.[74]

Another example of insufficient disclosure is IC layout design, as exemplified by the US which leads the world in protecting such designs. Different from copyright, registration and deposition of material is a must for acquiring IC layout design. Therefore, more disclosure is expected, so that the public can benefit from those designs. However, the deposited material of a mask work is subject to inspection only under limited conditions: (I) An individual/entity is allowed to make an appointment with the Copyright Office to inspect the deposited material by a written request to the Office's Records Research and Certification Section. However, the individual/entity must physically appear at the Copyright Office in Washington D.C. to inspect but is not allowed to make any copy; (II) when the mask work is involved in litigation; (III) When a court order is issued to inspect the deposited materials.[75]

4.8. Working or Licensing the Protected Subject Matter

To fulfill its inspiration promise, IP holders need to work the IP-protected subject matters, if they are not self-evident such as works in the copyright field, or at least license others to. Although this is not expressly mandated by any international IP treaties, we can glimpse it in provisions addressing the issue of non-use, such as

74 The Law Commission of India. (2024). *Trade Secrets and Economic Espionage*. Report, 194–195.

75 Cited from Protecting Semiconductor Chip Design under the Semiconductor Chip Protection Act of 1984 (SCPA)—Part I (Registration and Inspection) (January 11, 2023), at: https://www.lexology.com/search.

compulsory license to use patents and copyrighted works[76] and cancellation of registered trademark for unjustified non-use.[77]

Patents need to be implemented so that the technical progress can take root and its benefits materialized, leading to more investment in R&D and innovation, and eventually more and better products and services. In this regard, Section 83 of the Indian Patent Act is the most enlightening and classical legislature and should be followed by others:

> 83 in exercising the powers conferred by this Chapter, regard shall be had to the following general considerations, namely; (a) that patents are granted to encourage inventions and to secure that the inventions are worked in India on a commercial scale and to the fullest extent that is reasonably practicable without undue delay; (b) that they are not granted merely to enable patentees to enjoy a monopoly for the importation of the patented article;. . .(g) that patents are granted to make the benefit of the patented invention available at reasonably affordable prices to the public.

4.9. Allowing Free Fair Use of the Protected Subject Matter

If users of IP-protected products and services are difficult to locate, the usage is hard to detect, the enforcement costs are high, and exclusive rights have been therefore adopted as the form of protection for IP, then IP holders are expected to allow the so-called "fair use" of their products and services. "Fair use" is by definition free of any charge, which is mainly out of the reality that the users and their usage are hard to identify, and the costs of asking them to pay are prohibitive, such as private and personal use (including reproduction). It is not particularly "fair," ("fair use" is a misnomer) but a pragmatic tolerance to find interim peace with the using public.

76 Article 5A(2) and(4) of the Paris Convention stipulate that:

> Each country of the Union shall have the right to take legislative measures providing for the grant of compulsory licenses to prevent the abuses which might result from the exercise of the exclusive rights conferred by the patent, for example, failure to work. (4) A compulsory license may not be applied for on the ground of failure to work or insufficient working before the expiration of a period of four years from the date of filing of the patent application or three years from the date of the grant of the patent, whichever period expires last; it shall be refused if the patentee justifies his inaction by legitimate reasons. Such a compulsory license shall be non-exclusive and shall not be transferable, even in the form of the grant of a sub-license, except with that part of the enterprise or goodwill which exploits such license.
>
> Articles 11bis(2), 13(1), and 12 of the Berne Convention

For more see Subsections 3.1 and 4.1 of Chapter 5.

77 Article 5C(1) of the Paris Convention provides: "If, in any country, use of the registered mark is compulsory, the registration may be cancelled only after a reasonable period, and then only if the person concerned does not justify his inaction."

Free fair use can further be based on other public interests, such as education, access to knowledge, and promoting market competition. Free fair use is called for to facilitate open science, free exchange of creative ideas and follow-on research and its application when voluntary licensing, cross-licensing and patent pools cannot solve the problem of worldwide proliferation of patents and copyrighted works (software in particular), and forfeiture of unused or underused patents would be too strong a cure to prescribe.

However, we should caution against the over-zealous pursuit of public interests at the expense of IP holders. If technology and business models are available, fair use is better to be replaced by "fared" use, such as use under compulsory license. For example, public lending by libraries is serving important public interests, but should not happen at the expense of copyright holders. Therefore, a fee should be collected for authors of works when feasible.

4.10. Allowing Fared Compulsory/Statutory Use of the Protected Subject Matter

Free fair use, as indispensable as it is, has its problems and limitations. Free fair use as expansively applied by the US courts in the copyright field (so long the use of the existent works is transformative it is fair use),[78] is quite difficult for other jurisdictions to follow, for at least two reasons. First, they often do not have unconditional protection of free speech and free press as the First Amendment in the US. Second, such wholesale free fair use of others, especially competitors, works by deep-pocketed conglomerates, amounts to gross unfairness to copyright holders in many jurisdictions. In addition, fair use needs to be worked out on a case-by-case basis and is therefore rather uncertain and unpredictable.

Use under compulsory/statutory licensing then comes into play, as it is by far the least intrusive and the most pro-competition method. Such compulsory use enhances the utilization of existent creation after paying reasonable remuneration to their creators, which in turn will lead to more and better creation.[79] Compulsory licensing over the medium to longer term can only benefit rightsholders, as it expands the base for licensing exponentially and encourages innovative usage. As a result, compulsory licensing can generate much more than enough revenue to offset the initial losses from not being able to charge as much as rightsholders would have. "Substantial financial rewards can come from giving up some control,

78 Yet another recent example is the *Google LLC v. Oracle America* case, where the US Supreme Court unsurprisingly held Google's act of copying 15,000 lines of Java software transformative, non-infringing, and free fair use, see *Google LLC v. Oracle America, Inc.*, 593 US ___ (2021).

79 In the Oracle refusing to license Google case discussed in Subsection 4.4 of Chapter 1, Oracle should be required to issue a license to Google in return for reasonable remuneration. This way, Oracle could get rewarded by well-resourced Google, and Google could develop its platform without being conscience-stricken.

in the form of liability rules. This is a lesson the music industry might want to contemplate as it struggles to adjust to new technologies."[80]

What is more, public life as we are now living is unthinkable without compulsory licenses. Never before has the issue of patent/software blockage and of (forward and backward) compatibility become so important in the interconnected world. The daily routine of interconnection and roaming among telecom and internet users is only possible with the help of compulsory license of incumbent dominant players' assets, including IP, and facilities. SSOs' FRAND Licensing of SEPs Policy is in essence yet another compulsory license of SEPs (see Chapter 9).[81] Therefore, it is incumbent on all IP holders, except trademark holders, to allow fared compulsory/statutory use of the protected subject matter of their IPRs.

4.11. No Abuse of IP

4.11.1. National Practices

Very early on patent abuse has been a grave concern in the US. The US courts have been the vanguard in sanctioning patent misuse. In 1917, the Supreme Court held that, because a patent grant is limited to the invention described in the claims, the patent law does not empower the patent owner to extend the scope of the patent monopoly by restricting the use of the patented article to materials necessary for their operation but forming no part of the patented invention, or to place downstream restrictions on the articles making them subject to conditions as to use.[82] *Carbice Corp. v. American Patents Development Corp.* clarified that requiring patent licensees to buy other products as a condition of a patent license ("product tying") was patent misuse.[83] *Brulotte v. Thys Co.* established that attempting to collect royalties after a patent expired was misuse,[84] which was again confirmed by the Supreme Court in 2015.[85]

The CAFC has characterized patent misuse as the patentee's act of "impermissibly broadening the 'physical or temporal scope' of the patent grant with anticompetitive effect."[86] However, given that a patent grant entitles the patentee to impose a broad range of conditions in licensing the right to practice the patent, the doctrine of patent misuse "has largely been confined to a handful of specific practices by

80 McLeod, K., & DiCola, P. (2011). *Creative License: The Law and Culture of Digital Sampling* (p. 262). Duke University Press.

81 Not to mention that compulsory license can bring down high-priced patented drugs also in advanced countries. However, this is not the competition-related aspect of compulsory license that this volume aims at.

82 *Motion Picture Patents Co. v. Universal Film Co.*, 243 US 516 (1917).

83 *Carbice Corp. v. Patents Development Corp.*, 283 US 27 (1931).

84 *Brulotte v. Thys Co.*, 379 US 29 (1964).

85 *Kimble v. Marvel Entertainment, LLC*, 576 US 446 (2015). The US Congress acted in the opposite direction by limiting the patent misuse affirmative defense in both 1952 and 1998, resulting in 35 USC §271(d) of the Patent Act.

86 *Princo Corp. v. International Trade Commission*, 616 F.3d 1318, 1328 (Fed. Cir. 2010, "Princo II").

which the patentee seemed to be trying to 'extend' his patent grant beyond its statutory limits."[87] Patent misuse is not available to a presumptive infringer simply because a patentee engages in some kind of wrongful commercial conduct, even conduct that may have anticompetitive effects.[88]

In Asia, the patent misuse doctrine is expressly adopted in Japanese patent law.[89] In India, "that the patent right is not abused by the patentee or person deriving title or interest on patent from the patentee" is listed as one of the "general principles applicable to working of patented inventions in India."[90] China's Patent Law unequivocally points to the check that competition law plays on the misuse of patent rights:

> The application and exercise of patent rights should follow the principle of good faith. Patent shall not be misused to hurt public interests or the legitimate interests of others. The misuse of patent to eliminate or restrict market competition shall be governed by the Antimonopoly Law. (Article 20)

In the copyright filed, the International Instrument on Permitted Uses in Copyright Law proposed by a group of IP scholars expresses their desire to "control anticompetitive practices" by copyright holders.[91] In the US the patent misuse doctrine was extended to copyright law in 1948 for the first time.[92] It was adopted by various circuit courts. One illustrative example of copyright misuse is when the timepiece maker Omega tried to stop parallel import by Costco Wholesale which undercut the price for its popular "Seamaster" watches (cutting from US $1,995 down to US $1,299.99), by registering its mark as copyrighted works, and leveraging copyright's limited monopoly to block the import of its genuine Seamaster watches. The case was rejected by the District Court for the Eastern District of California as abuse of copyright and hence unenforceable.[93] However, the contours and scope of the copyright misuse doctrine remain to be explicitly recognized by the US Supreme Court.

87 *Princo Corp. v. International Trade Commission*, 616 F.3d 1318, 1328 (Fed. Cir. 2010, "Princo II"), 1329.

88 *Princo Corp. v. International Trade Commission*, 616 F.3d 1318, 1328 (Fed. Cir. 2010, "Princo II"), 1329.

89 Nakayama, I. (2017). Recognizing the abuse of rights defense and the invalidation defense. In Liu, K.-C. (Ed.), *Annotated Leading Patent Cases in Major Asian Jurisdictions* (pp. 20–32). City University of HK Press.

90 Section 83(f) of Indian Patents Act.

91 See Hilty, R. et al. (2021). International instrument on permitted uses in copyright law. *IIC, 52*, 62–67, at: https://link.springer.com/article/10.1007/s40319-020-00999-8.

92 *M. Witmark Sons v. Jensen*, 80 F.Supp. 843, 850 (D. Minn. 1948).

93 *Omega S.A. v. Costco Wholesale Corp.*, No. 04–05443, (E.D. Cal. Nov. 9, 2011), which was upheld (776 F.3d 692 (9th Cir. 2015)) but based on the first sale doctrine recognized by *Kirtsaeng v. John Wiley & Sons, Inc.*, according to which distribution and importation rights exhaust after the first sale, regardless of where the item was manufactured or first sold.

In the field of trademark, no abuse of trademark rights shall be allowed. Courts in Japan, Korea and China have already extended the basic legal principle of no abuse of rights enshrined in their civil law to the realm of trademark law.[94]

4.11.2. A Theory of No Abuse of IP

From the perspective of establishing a principle of IP law, we can justifiably set up an axiom that IP shall not be abused/misused. IPRs have a much stronger propensity of overshooting their boundaries and, therefore of being abused, as they are driven by powerful interest groups (such as IFPI, big pharma companies, Hollywood/Bollywood, Silicon Valley, etc.) and sometimes even coupled with actual criminal punishment, at least in Asian economies, or the threat thereof. Therefore, IP abuse/misuse should be dealt with seriously and systemically. Article 8(2) of the TRIPS Agreement therefore expressly allows members to take appropriate measures to prevent IP abuse: "Appropriate measures . . . may be needed to prevent the abuse of intellectual property rights by right holders or the resort to practices which unreasonably restrain trade or adversely affect the international transfer of technology."

IP abuse can lie simply in its non-use which violates Principle 8, namely, to work or license the protected subject matter. Based on a similar foundation, the Paris Convention added in 1925 Article 5A(2) and (4) which recognizes that failure to work or non-use, including insufficient working or use, could be an abuse of patent right for members to permit compulsory license as a remedy.

IP can further be misused if it violates Principles 7, 9, and 10, and will be subject to invalidation, compulsory license, and statutory license. There can be IP abuse without finding an antitrust violation. IP abuse/misuse sometimes, but not always, can cause anticompetitive concerns and even antitrust violations when committed by dominant market players.

4.12. IP Holders are Expected to Help Reduce Compliance Costs

The uncountable number of IPRs and the legal complications of their exercise make the compliance costs unmanageable, which has shaken people's acceptance of IPRs. More should be expected of IP holders than just allowing free fair use and fared compulsory use by others. They are expected to take proactive measures to help reduce such costs. It is only in their best self-interests if IP holders could devise, set up, maintain, and improve mechanisms that are conducive to easy compliance with IPRs and could thereby reduce related costs.[95]

94 Liu, K.-C. (2022). *IP Laws and Regimes in Major Asian Economies—Combing Through Thousand Threads of IP to Peace in Asia* (pp. 75–77). Routledge.

95 Patry, W. (2011). *How to Fix Copyright* (p. 262). Oxford University Press. Patry argues similarly: "Copyright owners should also support the good guys by providing reasonably priced, convenient authorized goods. If they don't, no copyright law can help them."

IP holders should be encouraged and even required to organize their right enforcement/exercise in such a way that makes IP holders and their IP-protected subject matters easily accessible, the terms and conditions for their use transparent (e.g. to publicize patent portfolios or provide search service for a fee). Whenever possible, IP holders should utilize collective management mechanisms, such as collective copyright management organizations (collecting societies) and patent pools. The UK CDPA 1988 has similar considerations when it provides exceptions to copyright infringements that are designed to encourage collective licensing schemes which are conducted for groups of rights-owners.[96]

IP holders should be constantly reminded of the importance of investing more to devise smarter business models that make payment, collection, and distribution of IP-generated revenues easy.

4.13. IP as Rights of Individuals

IP is for the encouragement of human creation by individuals. Therefore, IPRs are rights of individuals. They are different from collective rights, such as GIs, rights for communities, and ethnicity groups (e.g., Maori people in New Zealand, Seediq people in Taiwan, etc.). These collective rights intersect with other aspects of human activities and are not to be protected absolutely.

GIs are mostly about upholding consumers' trust in the use of well-known GIs and preserving traditional ways of producing agrarian products. We human beings migrate/emigrate throughout history and carry with us all kinds of symbols and memories wherever we go and whatever we do. An absolute ban on people's using GIs, from which they themselves originated, in any plainly descriptive way would amount to deprivation of their cultural and ethnic identity. Therefore, the absolute protection of GI for wine and spirits without the likelihood of confusion is simply not justified.

In addition, TK, biodiversity, folklore, cultural icons, or totems are without a doubt worthy of legal protection. However, they are less about boosting new human creations as IP requires than they are about collective rights and interests of people and preserving traditional wisdom, cultural identity, and ways of life, and therefore do not belong to the IP family. The legal mechanism for their protection can be more aptly dubbed as "collective equitable rights."

96 See Llewelyn, D., & Aplin, T. (2023). *Intellectual Property: Patents, Copyright, Trade Marks and Allied Rights* (10th ed.), 12–045. Sweet & Maxwell.

4.14. IPRs as Negative Exclusive Rights/Equitable Liability Rights

Frank Easterbrook, judge of the United States Court of Appeals for the Seventh Circuit and one of the most cited appellate judges in the US, noted already in 1990:

> Patents are not monopolies. . . . Patent gives a right to exclude; just as the law of trespass does with real property. . . . A patent *may* create a monopoly—just as an auto manufacturer *may* own all of the auto production facilities—but property and monopoly usually differ.[97] Old rhetoric about intellectual property equating to monopoly seemed to have vanished, replaced by a recognition that a right to exclude in intellectual property is no different in principle from the right to exclude in physical property. . . . Old cases holding that copyrights and patents are monopolies . . . were condemned to benign neglect.[98]

IPRs can take the form of negative exclusive rights and the weaker form of right to remuneration.

4.14.1. Negative Exclusive IP

IPR mostly take the form of negative exclusive rights, which are first and foremost the right to exclude others from using IP-protected creations without the consent or authorization of their owners. As to whether the IP owner can actually commercialize their creation and put them on the market is dependent on other governmental regulations.[99] For example, a patented drug still needs to be approved by the health authority before the patentee can manufacture and sell the drug. Similarly, the patentee of an effective explosive still needs to undergo a government review process before the manufacture and sale of the explosives.

Exclusive IP right is different from property right on tangible goods, where the owner of a thing has the positive right, within the statutory limits, to freely use it, profit from it, dispose of it, and exclude the interference from others.[100] Section 108 (Nature of copyright) of Singapore Copyright Act 2021 drives this point home:

> 108. (1) Where a copyright owner has the exclusive right to do an act —(a) the right is a right to exclude others from doing that act (or authorising the doing of that act) without the authorisation of the copyright owner; and (b) it

97 Easterbrook, F.H. (1990). Intellectual property is still property. *Harvard Journal of Law and Public Policy, 13(1),* 108–118. In Mossoff, A. (Ed.). (2013). *Intellectual Property and Property Rights* (pp. 27–36). Edward Elgar Publishing.

98 Easterbrook, F.H. (1990). Intellectual property is still property. *Harvard Journal of Law and Public Policy, 13(1),* 108–118. In Mossoff, A. (Ed.). (2013). *Intellectual Property and Property Rights* (p. 30). Edward Elgar Publishing.

99 Although historically patent rights and copyrights were often granted with monopolistic privileges (in the UK, etc.), IPR as an exclusive right is not a monopoly right.

100 Article 903, German Civil Code is a classic example: "The owner of a thing may, to the extent that a statute or third-party rights do not conflict with this, deal with the thing at his discretion and

> is declared that the right is not a positive right of the copyright owner to do that act. (2) To avoid doubt, where a copyright owner has the right to be paid equitable remuneration for the doing of an act, the right is not a positive right of the copyright owner to do that act.[101]

However, it is crucial to point out that the right to exclude has also become conditional, and not absolute. In other words, there will be no automatic issuance of injunctive relief if it would be disproportionally harsh on the infringing party. The trendsetter is undoubtedly the *eBay Inc. v. MercExchange, L.L.C.* in the US.[102] The US Supreme Court unanimously held that an injunction should not be automatically issued based on a finding of patent infringement. Instead, a federal court must weigh in on what the Court described as the four-factor test traditionally used to determine if an injunction should be issued. That test requires a plaintiff to demonstrate:

> (1) that it has suffered an irreparable injury; (2) that remedies available at law are inadequate to compensate for that injury; (3) that considering the balance of hardships between the plaintiff and defendant, a remedy in equity is warranted; and (4) that the public interest would not be disserved by a permanent injunction.

German courts are renowned for their friendliness towards patentees, against the background that German industries are often patentees themselves, and regularly issue preliminary injunctive relief before reaching substantive decisions on infringement. However, the tide has changed for German industries (especially the car industry) as they become more often the defendants accused of infringing (foreign) patentees' rights embodied in components and risk being prevented from manufacturing or selling the complex products that incorporate these components. In the 2016 Wärmetauscher (heat exchanger) judgment, in which a German car manufacturer argued that a patent infringement on a minor component (heat exchanger) should not impede the sale of the entire car. The Federal Court of Justice confirmed the injunction in the case, it stated that as a matter of principle, proportionality and the interests of both parties must be considered to some degree when granting an injunction.[103]

After years of debate, Germany finally revised its Patent Act in June 2021 which codifies the Federal Court of Justice's concerns over the automatic issuance of injunction. Now Article 139(1) expressly allows an exception to the injunction in cases where the issuance of an injunction would lead to disproportionate

---

exclude others from every influence." Article 765 of the Civil Code of Taiwan and Article 240 (the exclusive right of direct control) of the PRC's Civil Code follow the German model.

101 Therefore, some call this "a right to exclude but not to do," see Llewelyn, D. et al. (2023). *Modern Law of Copyright in Singapore* (p. 16). Academy Publishing.

102 547 US 388 (2006).

103 Germen Federal Court of Justice X ZR 114/13 (decided on May 10, 2016).

hardship not justified by the exclusive right nature of a patent for the infringer or third parties, after taking into consideration the special circumstances of the individual cases and the requirement of good faith. In other words, an unrestricted and automatic issuance of an injunction will no longer be the case in Germany.[104] This change could signal the beginning of a paradigm shift for all IPRs, including copyright, trademark, etc.

4.14.2. Equitable Liability Rights

IPR can also take the form of equitable liability rights that do not empower rightsholders to exclude but to demand payment for equity purposes. These include droit de suite (resale rights for artists), remuneration for public lending (compensating authors for possible decreased sale of their works), levies for reproduction machines (compensating authors for increased possibility of right infringement), and right to equitable sharing (if ever recognized).

Equitable liability rights can boost the use of new creations, especially when usage can be recorded and traced with the help of technology, such as IoT.

4.15. Unenforceability of IPRs

IPRs like any other rights can ask courts to enforce their rights in principle. However, as a principle of IP, courts in some situations can refuse to lend a helping hand, so that IPRs although remain tradeable and licensable, cannot seek the help of courts in case of a dispute. Unenforceability can be a general one that cannot be enforced against any person, exhaustion being an example, and also be a specific one that cannot be enforced against specific persons.

4.15.1. General Unenforceability: When Exhausted

The intangible nature of IPRs can be misused to haunt the after fate of IP-protected goods and affect their later transactions. Therefore, the IP exhaustion theory was established to draw an end to the exercise of IPRs: After the legitimate first sale by the IP holder or a third party they authorized, the right to exercise IP exhausts, not the IPRs per se. Exclusive rights exhaust, but not equitable liability rights.

As will be argued in Subsection 5.3, the TRIPS Agreement should be revised to adopt the international exhaustion principle for all IPRs in principle. Consequently, Members of the WTO should adopt the international exhaustion principle as well. However, if adopting national exhaustion suits national developmental needs better, Members can be allowed to change course. But they are advised to conduct

104 However, case law after the amendment thus far shows that "Regional courts unmoved by new disproportionality amendment to the German Patent Act," see D. Skiebe at https://www.iam-media.com/article/regional-courts-unmoved-new-disproportionality-amendment-the-german-patent-act (8 March 2023).

periodic reviews to assess whether national exhaustion has indeed achieved its goal and change back to the international exhaustion principle when the assessment result is a no.

4.15.2. Individual Unenforceability: When Abused

When an IP is being exercised to the extent of abuse/misuse, courts cannot be its accomplice by enforcing it, among other legal consequences and remedies. Therefore, the US Supreme Court has long held that patent misuse made the patent unenforceable.[105] Likewise, Courts in Japan, Korea and China will not enforce abused trademark rights (see Subsection 4.11.1). Especially when the determination of IP validity and IP infringement is bifurcated in different courts in some civil law jurisdictions, such as Germany, Japan, Korea, Taiwan, and the PRC, the finding of invalid IP has only effects in the specific case. The actual and general invalidation of IP must be separately declared by the other competent authority or court.

In cases where the exercise of IP, mostly through licensing agreements, has been found by the authorities to be violating antitrust law, what impact would the finding have on such IP licensing agreements? The question was answered with a categorical no in Taiwan: the licensing agreement is still valid notwithstanding the determination that abusively high royalty demanded by a dominant patent pool has violated the Fair Trade Act. In the ensuing civil lawsuit, after the antitrust cases were finalized, brought by patentee Philips against Princo, a Taiwanese licensee, for royalty payment, the Shinju District Court awarded Philips the full royalty as agreed in the licensing agreement: (calculated by the minimum of ¥10 times the amount of CD-Rs produced by Princo, with a monthly interest of 2% for delayed payment (an annual interest of 24%), despite Philips has been found to have abused its dominance by refusing to negotiate the reduction of royalty. The decision was upheld by TIPCC and the Supreme Court.[106]

Clearly, there is legal schizophrenia at work which treats competition law and IP law as two unrelated fields of law. This is clearly ignorant of the internal linkage between the two, as IP is part of the mechanism of market regulation. What has been decided by competition law must ripple through to the exercise of IP. For example, an anti-competitive and abusive royalty is not void but should be reduced.

More correctly, the German Federal Court of Justice acknowledges a co-relationship between antitrust law and patent law in the "Orange-Book-Standard" decision and came to a different conclusion in a similar case involving Philips and Princo: damages that the patentee can demand from an unauthorized infringer who

105 For example, *Morton Salt Co. v. G.S. Suppiger Co.*, 314 US 488 (1942).

106 For criticism see Liu, K.-C. (2017). IP court contradicted the TFTC's decision on abuse of monopolistic market power. In Liu, K.-C. (Ed.), *Annotated Leading Patent Cases in Major Asian Jurisdictions* (pp. 269–271). City University of HK Press.

has a right to compulsory license according to the competition law are limited to an amount that is uncontroversial according to the German Antitrust Law.[107]

5. A More Balanced International IP Regime

Joseph Stiglitz critically points out that the TRIPS Agreement reflects the triumph of corporate interests in the US and Europe over the broader interests of billions of people in the developing world. To Stiglitz, the TRIPS Agreement suffers from governance deficit, the voices of special interests are heard too loudly. Lobbyists work hard to bury their self-serving provisions in long and complex trade agreements.[108]

The world community should be repeatedly reminded that one size does not fit all, as the circumstances of developed, developing and least developed countries differ. We can have more innovation with more social justice at lower costs to developing and the least developed countries. International IP regime must show deference to Article 27 of the Universal Declaration of Human Rights which solemnly proclaims that:

> Everyone has the right freely to participate in the cultural life of the community, to enjoy the arts and to share in scientific advancement and its benefits. Everyone has the right to the protection of the moral and material interests resulting from any scientific, literary or artistic production of which he is the author.

The international IP community must therefore treat the TRIPS Agreement with the understanding that we do not live in a uniform world where everything is immediately (short-termism) and rigidly the same. Non-conformity of the TRIPS Agreement by those who are in need is not necessarily bad in the longer term for those abiders. For example, non-conformity that makes medicines and knowledge readily available to developing and the least developed countries would not impose extra costs on the developed countries but would bring huge benefits to the former, namely increased health, literacy (a value of its own), and productivity, which in turn would induce increased purchase power, appreciation for, and purchase of products and services from developed countries.

To make our international IP regime more ideally balanced, the following measures are worth taking by the TRIPS Agreement:

5.1. To Adopt Moderate Moral Rights

To protect or not to protect the personal or moral relationship between the creator and his creation is the lasting divergent point between the civil law (recognizing

107 The German Federal Court of Justice KZR 39/06 (decided on May 6, 2009).

108 Stiglitz, J. (2018). *Globalization and Its Discontents Revisited—Anti-Globalization in the Era of Trump* (pp. 4, 40–528). Norton.

moral rights) and common law approach (imposing duty not to attribute false authorship of work or identity of performer of performance to copyright).[109] The civil-law-oriented Berne Convention protects the right to authorship (attribution) and the integrity right (against distortion) (Article 6bis) but does not protect the right to disclosure or divulgation.[110]

Article 4ter of the Paris Convention provides the inventor the right to be mentioned as inventor: "The inventor shall have the right to be mentioned as such in the patent." The TRIPS Agreement follows suit and recognizes inventors' right to inventorship.[111]

However, moral rights are so heavily protected in some countries, especially France, that they become "immoral" as they have been used to inhibit the use and interpretation of works time and again, thus stifling the freedom of artistic expression.[112] These outrageous experiences must have horrified the common-law-dominated TRIPS Agreement that decided not to protect at all the moral rights of authors.[113]

However, the TRIPS Agreement should recognize and protect the two moral rights of authors, the right to be identified and the integrity right, recognized by the Berne Convention, as even the arch-doubter of them, the UK, has flipped its stance. The proviso of Article 9(1) should be deleted. However, it should limit the protection of moral rights to "cases of real injury,"[114] so that entrepreneurs will not

109 For example, Singapore Copyright Act before its 2021 amendment had prohibited false attribution of authorship. Section 188 stipulated:

> (1) Where a person commits a breach of a duty owed by him to another person by virtue of this Part, the breach shall not be enforceable by criminal proceedings but the other person may bring an action in respect of the breach. (2) The relief that a court may grant in an action under subsection (1) shall include an injunction (subject to such terms, if any, as the court thinks fit) and damages.
>
> Ng-Loy, W. (2021). *Law of Intellectual Property of Singapore* (3rd ed.), 5.2.8. Sweet & Maxwell

110 However, quite a few jurisdictions expressly recognize such a right, for example, Japan, PRC, and Taiwan.

111 Article 2(1) of the TRIPS Agreement mandates that "In respect of Parts II, III and IV of this Agreement, Members shall comply with Articles 1 through 12, and Article 19, of the Paris Convention (1967)."

112 In 1987 the fabled movie director John Huston sued to prevent the "Asphalt Jungle" he directed in 1950 from being colorized and shown. Five different French courts first prevented screening, then allowed it only if the director's objections were publicized, and finally levied hefty fines. A French Court set aside Anne Bragance's contractual obligations of renouncing her moral rights in a book she had ghostwritten for Prince Michael of Greece. See Baldwin, P. (2014). *The Copyright War—Three Centuries of Trans-Atlantic Battle* (pp. 1, 2). Princeton University Press.

113 Article 9(1) of the TRIPS Agreement stipulates:

> Members shall comply with Articles 1 through 21 of the Berne Convention (1971) and the Appendix thereto. However, Members shall not have rights or obligations under this Agreement in respect of the rights conferred under Article 6bis of that Convention or of the rights derived therefrom.

114 Llewelyn, D., & Aplin, T. (2023). *Intellectual Property: Patents, Copyright, Trade Marks and Allied Rights* (10th ed.), 12–073. Sweet & Maxwell.

be "held to ransom as infringers of moral rights,"[115] thus affecting market competition. Moral rights should not be allowed to "restrict artistic possibilities . . . give authors an aesthetic veto."[116] For example, new forms of presenting (silent v. sound, black-and-white v. colored, two-dimensional v. 3D, analogue v. digital, standard v. high definition, etc.) existent works, their new interpretation or follow-up creation shall never be stymied by moral rights, as they diversify and enrich our cultural experiences, expressions, and choices, without damaging the original works.

5.2. To Interpret the Three-Step Test as Proportionality Principle

The three-step test principle is the overarching principle of limiting all IPRs according to the TRIPS Agreement. This principle is followed by most members of the WTO, with the US Copyright Act and its followers as exceptions.[117] The US has notably a unique open-ended free fair-use doctrine that was developed by courts over the years and has been codified in Section 107 of the Copyright Act in 1976. This arguably can be the trendsetter for not just copyright but also other IPRs as well for the brave new world ahead.

Section 107 of the US Copyright Act stipulates that in determining whether the use made of a work in any particular case is a fair use the following four factors need to be considered: (I) the purpose and character of the use, including whether such use is of a commercial nature or is for nonprofit educational purposes; (II) the nature of the copyrighted work; (III) the amount and substantiality of the portion used in relation to the copyrighted work as a whole; and (IV) the effect of the use upon the potential market for or value of the copyrighted work.

The US did not change its liberal fair use doctrine when it joined the Berne Convention in 1988. Nor did the US change its stance when leading the adoption of the three-step test by the TRIPS Agreement. Which can only mean that in the context of the TRIPS Agreement, the three-step test does not require limitations and exceptions to be interpreted narrowly as the legal saying "Exceptio est strictissimae interpretationnis" goes. The three-step test is to be interpreted according to the objectives and purposes of IP laws. It constitutes an indivisible entirety, which is to be considered holistically in a comprehensive overall assessment.[118] The test is merely a poor attempt to express what is the widely accepted principle of proportionality under modern parlance. The limitation of IPRs is allowable by all means, but we should not overdo it so that the purpose of having IP would be defeated.

115 Llewelyn, D., & Aplin, T. (2023). *Intellectual Property: Patents, Copyright, Trade Marks and Allied Rights* (10th ed.), 12–094. Sweet & Maxwell.

116 Baldwin, P. (2014). *The Copyright War–Three Centuries of Trans-Atlantic Battle* (p. 30). Princeton University Press.

117 As a result of the US Singapore Free Trade Agreement, Singapore deviated from the UK tradition and adopted the US fair use doctrine (Section 191 of the Singapore Copyright Act 2021).

118 The Max Planck Institute for Innovation and Competition (2008). *The Declaration of a Balanced Interpretation of the "Three-Step Test" in Copyright Law*, at: https://www.ip.mpg.de/en/research/research-news/declaration-three-step-test.html.

5.3. To Uphold Free Trade

Free trade is the hallmark of the international community after World War II, and should also be upheld, rather than hampered, by IP. National IP border measures in the name of IP protection can harass free trade, as they could suspend transit or disallow imported goods. To safeguard traffic in transit, the GATT demands, but only generally, that traffic in transit shall not be subject to any unnecessary delays or restriction and customs duties, except charges for transportation or administrative expenses entailed by transit.[119] The first sentence of Article 51 of the TRIPS Agreement provides pointedly that Members shall adopt procedures to enable a rightsholder to lodge an application in writing with competent authorities, administrative or judicial, for the suspension by the customs authorities of the release into free circulation of counterfeit trademark or pirated copyright goods. However, "It is understood that there shall be no obligation to apply such procedures to imports of goods put on the market in another country by or with the consent of the rightsholder, or to goods in transit." (Note 13)

Against this backdrop, it is unfortunate to see the TRIPS Agreement take the hands-off approach to the exhaustion issue (Article 6), and some jurisdictions stop the parallel import of genuine goods by insisting that the consent given by the rightsholder in a foreign jurisdiction is irrelevant and extra consent must be sought from the local rightsholder or that the two rightsholders must be one and the same or have some legal relationship.

In a truly global trading system, any first legitimate sale of IP-protected goods and services in any part of the global market should ripple through the rest and thereby exhaust the right to exercise the IP involved. It is imperative that the TRIPS Agreement be revised to expressly and principally subscribe to the international exhaustion principle unless some other international IP agreements provide otherwise.[120] So that WTO Members do not fragment the global market into numerous national markets and practice price discrimination to maximize their profits at the costs of consumers. This would uphold free trade, including free parallel import of genuine goods and boost market competition.[121]

119 Article V(3) of the GATT demands:

> Any contracting party may require traffic in transit through its territory be entered at the proper custom house, but, except in cases of failure to comply with applicable customs laws and regulations, such traffic coming from or going to other territory of other contracting parties shall not be subject to any unnecessary delays or restriction and shall be exempt from customs duties and from all transit duties or other charges imposed in respect of transit, except charges for transportation or those commensurate with administrative expenses entailed by transit or with the cost of services rendered traffic in transit exempted from border control.

120 The 1991 version of the International Convention for the Protection of New Varieties of Plants adopts the domestic exhaustion principle (Articles 14(1) and 16(1)), not the international exhaustion principle.

121 In this juncture, it is worthy of pointing out that the International Instrument on Permitted Uses in Copyright Law proposed by a group of IP scholars emphasizes the importance of free circulation:

> Contracting Parties shall ensure that further circulation of goods is not unduly impeded by copyright. 2. In particular, if copies of a protected work are made available in tangible form or on data

Domestic IP holders can still prevail over imported products by superior marketing strategies, such as effective branding, product differentiation, nationwide after-service network, etc., rather than stopping legitimate parallel import of genuine goods, which hurts consumer welfare.

5.4. To Define Abuse of IP and to Usher in Competition Law

Article 8(2) of the TRIPS Agreement although expansively allows members to take measures to prevent the abuse of IPRs, it fails to define IP abuse or give clues to its understanding. It also failed to expressly mention that competition law could play an important role if abuse of IP restrains and even excludes market competition. Article 8(2) of the TRIPS Agreement should be revised to define abuse of IP as acts violating at least Principles 7 to 10, namely insufficient disclosure, not working or licensing, hindering free fair use or fared compulsory use of the protected subject matters. Further, Article 8(2) of the TRIPS Agreement should be revised to usher in competition law: if the abuse of IPRs leads to the restrain or exclusion of competition, it must be inhibited by competition law.[122]

> carriers by the right holder or with the right holder's consent, it shall be permitted to a) re-sell such copies within the territory where they were subject to an authorized sale; b) offer such copies for public lending by public service institutions.
>
> Hilty, R. et al. (2021). International instrument on permitted uses in copyright law. *IIC, 52,* 62–67, at: https://link.springer.com/article/10.1007/s40319-020-00999-8

122 A group of European IP scholars advocates a new Article 8b(1) for the TRIPS Agreement that specifically addresses the interface issue between IP and competition law:

> 1. For the purposes of maintaining a fair balance between intellectual property rights and free competition:(a) Members shall provide for legislative or administrative measures, in particular, in the form of limitations of the rights or in the form of compulsory licenses, if the use of the product protected by an intellectual property right is indispensable for competition in the relevant market, unless the application of such measures would have a significantly negative effect on the incentives to invest in research and development; (b) Members should further provide for remedies if the use of an intellectual property right results in the abuse of a dominant position on the relevant market or in behavior violating anti-trust principles.
>
> Kur, A., & Levin, M. (Eds.). (2011). Intellectual Property Rights in a Fair World Trade System Proposals for Reform of TRIPS (pp. 465–467). Edward Elgar Publishing

However, it is already commonplace for WTO Members to foresee limitations of IPRs or compulsory license of IPRs (see Chapter 5), therefore the proposed Article 8b(1)(a) appears unnecessary. In addition, more than 127 jurisdictions now have competition laws in place (see Chapter 3) that can remedy the abuse of dominant position or anti-competitive behavior, the proposed Article 8b(1)(b) is not forthcoming enough.

Part II

Compulsory License of IPRs to Further Competition

Thus far, the significance of compulsory licensing of IP for daily public life has been sparely appreciated. Based on one of the principles of an ideal IP Code discussed in Subsection 4.10 of Chapter 4, "Allowing Fared Compulsory and Statutory Use of the Protected Subject Matter," this part of the book dedicates two chapters to advocate a competition-oriented compulsory license that could be applicable to all IPRs,[1] excluding however trademarks[2] and GIs,[3] as an overarching principle of IP for the purpose of preserving and enhancing competition.

Chapter 5 examines most international IP treaties and national IP regimes and practices on compulsory licensing. Chapter 6 continues to examine international and national regimes on the compulsory licensing of plant variety rights, the compulsory licensing of IP through competition law, justify competition-oriented compulsory licensing of all IPRs, excluding trademarks, and provide suggestions for making compulsory license work and improving the TRIPS Agreement.

1 Although in my understanding of IP, trade secret protection, GIs, and IC-layout designs do not belong to the IP family (see Subsection 3.1 of Chapter 2). However, IC-layout designs are subject to compulsory licensing under international and national regimes, and so could trade secrets. Therefore, they are discussed in Chapters 5 and 6.

2 I have advocated for compulsory license of trademark for vaccines in the context of the pandemic and pointed out a de facto compulsory license of trademark case in the PRC (Liu, K.-C. (2022) *IP Laws and Regimes in Major Asian Economies—Combing Through Thousand Threads of IP to Peace in Asia* (p. 81) Routledge). However, admittedly, these situations are not related to the preservation of competition, and I cannot think of any situation where the compulsory license of a trademark is justified and needed for the preservation of competition. Therefore, trademarks are excluded from compulsory license in my proposal.

3 I have argued in Subsection 4.13 of Chapter 4 that GIs do not belong to the IP family.

DOI: 10.4324/9781003597766-6

5 International IP Treaties and National IP Regimes on Compulsory Licensing

1. Introduction

Traditionally, the issue of compulsory licensing dwells mainly in the field of patents, and IP professionals feel reluctant to address compulsory licensing of IPRs. However, this is an incomplete and even incorrect view about IP laws, especially compulsory licensing regimes. The time has come for us to embrace compulsory IP licensing as an important tool for preserving and enhancing market competition.

Two international documents are heralding the message. On April 27, 2023, the EC proposed a regulation on compulsory licensing for crisis management which aims at creating, at EU level, an efficient compulsory licensing framework to address EU crises.[1] This initiative is ostensibly too narrow in its scope. Some scholars have already made the suggestion that: "The objective should not merely be to patch up the system so that it works in times of crisis, but to design a well-orchestrated legal framework that promotes European market integration."[2]

More noteworthy for the global community is the Proposals for Amendment of TRIPS by a group of European IP scholars that advocate for a new Article 8b to be added to the TRIPS Agreement, which generally proposes compulsory license as a limitation to all IPRs so that they can maintain balance with free competition (see Subsection 10.3 of Chapter 6).

Compulsory licensing refers to the use of protected IP without the consent of rightsholders upon payment of a reasonable remuneration.[3] If the remuneration is left to be negotiated, it is compulsory license proper or compulsory license in the narrower sense. If no negotiation is needed and the remuneration is fixed in advance, it is then a statutory license or part of the broader compulsory license. In any case, the exclusivity conferred by IP is downgraded from exclusive right to remuneration right.

1 At https://single-market-economy.ec.europa.eu/system/files/2023-04/COM_2023_224_1_EN_ACT_part1_v11.pdf.

2 Lamping, M. et al., (2023). Revisiting the framework for compulsory licensing of patents in the European Union—reflections on the European Commission's initiative. *GRUR International*, 472.

3 No international convention ever defines the meaning of compulsory licenses.

DOI: 10.4324/9781003597766-7

2. Why is Compulsory Trademark Licensing Not Allowed?

The TRIPS Agreement is the first international treaty to mention and ban compulsory licensing of trademarks. Article 21 stipulates that: "it being understood that the compulsory licensing of trademarks shall not be permitted." Two common justifications for such exclusion: First, the purpose of a trademark is to distinguish the goods or services of one undertaking from those of another,

> it would be nonsensical to let a third party to use that link as identifying the product or service without the consent of (and control by) the trademark owner. In other words, compulsory trademark licensing would lead to the danger of confusion of consumers as to source of the goods.[4]

Second, compulsory trademark licensing would deprive the trademark owner of the chance to control the quality of the goods that would bear his/her trademark and constitute a disincentive to provide consumers with high-quality goods.[5]

It is evident that in principle compulsory trademark license should not be allowed and the TRIPS Agreement should not have had the need to spend one article to unnecessarily legislate such a ban. Then where does Article 21 derive from? In this context, it is worth pointing out that in 1976 the USFTC staff had twice proposed to impose compulsory trademark license to remedy monopoly concerns. One of its administrative judges, Daniel Hanscom, made such a proposal to remedy monopolization which would order lemonade monopoly brand ReaLemon to license its trademark to its competitors at the royalty rate of one-half of one percent of dollar sales, for ten years. Similarly, another USFTC staff had also sought a compulsory trademark license in an action against the major cereal manufacturers which had dominated the relevant market of cereal through intensive brand and product differentiation and proposed that Kellogg, General Mills, and General Foods license for twenty years their existing trademarks royalty-free and to provide formulas and methods of production to any firm willing to comply with quality control standards.[6] Perhaps these incidents at the USFTC were so terrifying for many well-known trademark owners and their lobbyists that they drove the TRIPS Agreement to enact Article 21.

4 Kur, A. (1996). TRIPS and trademark law. In Beier, F.-K., and Schricker, G. (Eds.), *From GATTS to TRIPS: The Agreement on Trade-Related Aspects of Intellectual Property Rights* (p. 114). Wiley-VCH.

5 Regibeau, P., and Rockett, K. (2007). The relationship between intellectual property law and competition law: An economic approach. In Anderman, S. (Ed.), *The Interface between Intellectual Property Rights and Competition Policy* (p. 544). Cambridge University Press.

6 Cited from Dobb, S. (1977). Compulsory trademark license as a remedy for monopolization. *Catholic University Law Review*, *26*, 603. See also Leaffer, M. (2006). Sixty years of the Lanham Act: The decline and demise of monopoly phobia. In Hansen, H. (Ed.), *US Intellectual Property Law and Policy* (pp. 85–86). Edward Elgar Publishing.

The categorical exclusion of compulsory trademark licensing by the TRIPS Agreement has found support:

> The purpose of a trademark being its ability to distinguish the goods or services of one undertaking from those of another, it would be nonsensical to let a third party use that link as identifying the product or service without the consent (and control by) the trademark owner.[7]

However, there might be scenarios in which compulsory trademark licensing is not only justified but also imperative, either for respecting the status quo or public health.[8]

3. Compulsory Patent/Utility Model Licensing

By the early 1990s, about 100 countries had some form of compulsory patent licensing regime.[9] The actual granting of compulsory licenses is rather rare. In Asia, the actual grant of compulsory patent licenses is very limited.[10] To many people's surprise, Canada as a member of G7 has issued the greatest number of compulsory patent licenses, 613 in total between 1969 and 1992,[11] probably more than the aggregate number of issued compulsory licenses of the rest of the world.

3.1. International Treaties

3.1.1. Paris Convention: General Compulsory Patent Licensing to Prevent Patent Abuse

The Paris Convention foresees a general recognition of compulsory patent licensing that is also keen on the preservation of market competition. It started from the

7 Gervais, D. (2021). *TRIPS Agreement: Drafting History and Analysis* (5th ed.), 3.111. Sweet & Maxwell.

8 Liu, K.-C. (2022). *IP Laws and Regimes in Major Asian Economies—Combing Through Thousand Threads of IP to Peace in Asia* (p. 81). Routledge.

9 Reichman, J., & Hasenzahl, C. (2003). *Non-voluntary Licensing of Patented Inventions—Historical Perspective. Legal Framework under TRIPS and an Overview of the Practice in Canada and the USA* (p. 12), at: https://unctad.org/system/files/official-document/ictsd2003ipd5_en.pdf.

10 There is no issued compulsory patent license in China, Hong Kong, Indonesia, Japan, Korea, and Singapore. There are one in India, two in Malaysia, three in the Philippines, three in Taiwan, and seven in Thailand. See Liu, K.-C. (2022). *IP Laws and Regimes in Major Asian Economies—Combing Through Thousand Threads of IP to Peace in Asia* (pp. 38–46). Routledge. Worth pointing out is that Japan has a de facto compulsory in 1997 where the JFTC held that the refusal to license pooled patents by patentees holding a market share of 90% amounted to an unlawful attempt at monopolization and ordered the patent pool to cease the refusal of licenses to non-members, without ordering the grant of a license. The decision was upheld by the Tokyo High Court in 2003. See Heath, C. (2017). Patent pools, refusal to license and abuse of a dominant position. In Liu, K.-C. (Ed.), *Annotated Leading Patent Cases in Major Asian Jurisdictions* (pp. 129–143). City University of HK Press.

11 Reichman, J., & Hasenzahl, C. (2003). *Non-voluntary Licensing of Patented Inventions—Historical Perspective, Legal Framework under TRIPS and an Overview of the Practice in Canada and the USA* (p. 4), at: https://unctad.org/system/files/official-document/ictsd2003ipd5_en.pdf.

1925 Hague revision where a new provision on compulsory license, namely Article 5A(2), was inserted on the request and pressure of the industry. Prior thereto, many patent laws had forfeiture clauses for lack of working. Compulsory licenses were regarded by industrial representatives, such as the International Chamber of Commerce, at the negotiation table as the only appropriate sanction for the non-working of patents.[12] Article 5A stipulates a general purpose for compulsory patent licensing, namely to "prevent the abuses" which might result from the exercise of the exclusive rights conferred by the patent,[13] for example, failure to work, including insufficient work.

> Other examples of such abuses may exist in cases where the owner of the patent . . . refuses to grant licenses on reasonable terms and thereby hampers industrial development, or does not supply the national markets with sufficient quantities of the patented product, or demands excessive prices for such products.[14]

Article 5A of the Paris Convention has led to the worldwide acceptance of compulsory patent licensing regime.[15] Article 5A(2) is to be applied mutatis mutandis, to utility models, according to Article 5A(5) added in 1934. Therefore, compulsory licenses can also be used to prevent abuse of utility models.

3.1.2. The TRIPS Agreement[16]

A. OVERT DOUBLE-STANDARD BY LEADING DEVELOPED COUNTRIES AND UNDERLYING US HOSTILITY

After categorically denying compulsory trademark license in Article 21, the TRIPS Agreement foresees a general clause on compulsory patent license in Article 31. Unfortunately, although appreciating the importance of protecting market

12 Menescal, A. (2005). Those behind the TRIPS Agreement: The influence of the ICC and the AIPPI on international intellectual property decisions. *Intellectual Property Quarterly, 2,* 161.

13 In cases where the grant of compulsory licenses would not have been sufficient to prevent the said abuses, forfeiture of the patent can be provided for. No proceedings for the forfeiture or revocation of a patent may be instituted before the expiration of two years from the grant of the first compulsory license. A compulsory license may not be applied for before the expiration of a period of four years from the date of filing of the patent application or three years from the date of the grant of the patent, whichever period expires last; it shall be refused if the patentee justifies his inaction by legitimate reasons. Such a compulsory license shall be non-exclusive and non-transferable, even in the form of the grant of a sub-license, except with that part of the enterprise or goodwill which exploits such license.

14 Bodenhausen, G. (1968). *Guide to the Application of the Paris Convention for the Protection of Industrial Property* (p. 71). WIPO.

15 Harnisch, S. (2010). *Die Zwangslizenz im südafrikanischen und deutschen Patentrecht* (p. 59). BWV Berliner-Wissenschaft.

16 TRIPS Agreement obliges all Members to comply with Articles 1 to 12 and 19 of the Paris Convention (Article 2(1)).

competition by compulsory license in their respective domestic territories, leading developed countries take a double-standard[17] approach in the making of Article 31 of the TRIPS Agreement by making strenuous efforts to limit the Members' power to grant compulsory licenses "on the broad and generic ground of promoting the public interest."[18] Article 31 does not even use the right terminology, "compulsory licenses."[19] TRIPs Agreement does not define or limit the substantial grounds where "use without authorization of the right holder" may be granted. Article 31(a) only allows compulsory patent license based on "individual merits" of the case and does not mention the regime of "compulsory license as of right" stipulated in the UK Patents Act (see infra Subsection 3.2.3).

B. STRICT PROCEDURAL RULES AND SEMI-CONDUCTOR INDUSTRY UNFAIRLY FAVORED

Article 31 establishes only strict procedural safeguards. "The hostility of the US to the very idea of compulsory patent licensing lies beneath these provisions."[20] The safeguards were so strict that it led to an explosion of objections from developing countries over the effective denial of access to medicines to combat epidemics.[21]

In addition, Article 31(c) first confines the scope and duration of compulsory licenses to the purpose for which it was authorized, and further limits them in the case of semi-conductor technology to only for public non-commercial use or remedying a practice determined after judicial or administrative process to be anti-competitive. This is the result of interest group lobbying, a naked compromise that dents the ideal of international IP norms.

17 The EU can also be faulted with a double-standard practice in contrast to its case law concerning the application of Article 102 of the TFEU to refuse to license (Volvo, Magill, IMS Health, and Microsoft), the EU has reacted strongly against the decision of the TIPO to grant compulsory license against Phillips. It demanded that Taiwan revise provisions on compulsory license and "ensure that precedential effects of the measures are eliminated, including ensuring that the compulsory licenses are revoked in their entirety" within two months from the transmission of the report to the TIPO. Under such a threat, the TIPO did undertake to revise the provisions, the result of which is critically unsatisfactory. See Liu, K.-C. (2010). The Taiwanese Philips CD-R cases: abuses of a monopolistic position, cartel, and compulsory patent licensing. In Heath, C., & Sanders, A. (Eds.), *Landmark Intellectual Property Cases and Their Legacy*, 92 et seq. Aspen Publishing.

18 Reichman, J., and Hasenzahl, C. (2003). *Non-voluntary Licensing of Patented Inventions—Historical Perspective, Legal Framework under TRIPS and an Overview of the Practice in Canada and the USA* (p. 2), at: https://unctad.org/system/files/official-document/ictsd2003ipd5_en.pdf.

19 Instead, Article 31 of the TRIPS Agreement uses the opaque wording of "other use without authorization of the right holder."

20 Llewelyn, D., & Aplin, T. (2023). *Intellectual Property: Patents, Copyright, Trade Marks and Allied Rights* (10th ed.), 7–042. Sweet & Maxwell.

21 Llewelyn, D., & Aplin, T. (2023). *Intellectual Property: Patents, Copyright, Trade Marks and Allied Rights* (10th ed.), 7–042. Sweet & Maxwell.

C. COMPULSORY DEPENDENCY LICENSES HAVE TO PASS HIGH BAR

Following the underlying hostility towards compulsory licenses, the regime on compulsory dependency licenses has been made practically impossible by the extra high bar set up by Article 31(l).[22] It requires that the dependent patent "shall involve an important technical advance of considerable economic significance in relation to the invention claimed in the first patent." The institutions in charge of the grating of compulsory dependence licenses, whether (generalist or specialist) courts or the PTOs, will have a hard time defining "an important technical advance of considerable economic significance," as these are foreign to the three basic criteria of patentability, namely novelty, non-obviousness, and industrial applicability, and involve economic assessment. Therefore, compulsory dependency licenses have always been of an extremely limited practical significance, and there is limited case law and only little literature on Article 31(l) TRIPS.

From the specific perspective of a comparison to the treatment of free derivative use in copyright law, it is suggested that Article 31(l) TRIPS be interpreted in a "relative" and flexible manner, which can help to lead to a broader field of application of this provision.[23] However, from the perspective of the principle that IP holders are to "allow fared compulsory and statutory use of the protected subject matter," then we'd think the better of this high bar.

D. MEMBERS' RIGHT TO GRANT COMPULSORY LICENSE REASSURED

The public outrage accumulated over time culminated in the 2001 Doha Declaration on the TRIPS Agreement and Public Health, which firmly reassures that "Each member has the right to grant compulsory licenses and the freedom to determine the grounds upon which such licenses are granted." (Paragraph 5(b)). The Declaration ushered in the amendment of the TRIPS Agreement by the Protocol of December 6, 2005, that entered into force on January 23, 2017. The amendment inserted a new Article 31bis into the TRIPS Agreement as well as an Annex and Appendix. These provide the legal basis for WTO members to grant compulsory licenses for the production and export[24] of affordable generic medicines to other

22 Article 31(l) of the TRIPS Agreement stipulates:

> where such use is authorized to permit the exploitation of a patent ("the second patent") which cannot be exploited without infringing another patent ("the first patent"), the following additional conditions shall apply: (i) the invention claimed in the second patent shall involve an important technical advance of considerable economic significance in relation to the invention claimed in the first patent; (ii) the owner of the first patent shall be entitled to a cross-license on reasonable terms to use the invention claimed in the second patent; and (iii) the use authorized in respect of the first patent shall be non-assignable except with the assignment of the second patent.

23 Leistner, M. (2015). The requirements for compulsory dependency licenses: Learning from the transformative use doctrine in copyright law. In Liu, K.-C., Hilty, R. (Eds.), *Compulsory Licensing—Practical Experiences and Ways Forward* (pp. 227–458). Springer.

24 It was feared that the trade of drugs made under compulsory licenses would eventually come into the US and spoil the market there. However, the problem of generic drugs being exported to the US,

members "with insufficient or no manufacturing capacities in the pharmaceutical sector" for their patients.[25]

3.2. *Major National Regimes*

In the following, only the compulsory patent/utility model license regime from the US, UK, and Germany will be discussed.

3.2.1. The US

Generally speaking, the US has never adopted a statutory regime of compulsory license to curb patent misuse. Nor has Congress ever enacted a law that generally authorizes compulsory licensing of patents in the public interest.[26] However, the antitrust authorities, the FTC and the DOJ,[27] and courts, from district courts[28] to the Supreme Court,[29] made aggressive use of compulsory patent licensing in order to regulate misuse of patent rights and antitrust concerns.[30] US District Court for the Southern District of New York forcefully puts it: "We decree compulsory licensing because the patent rights which were granted the defendants were misused."[31]

Such an approach culminated in the 2006 eBay decision by the US Supreme Court,[32] which established a high threshold for issuing permanent injunctive relief in cases where patents have been infringed. According to eBay, no permanent

---

while present, is limited. The pharmaceutical industry is one of the most regulated in the world, with most of the costs being paid by insurance companies and governments. So, incentives for buying drugs made under compulsory licenses are weak, and it is not easy to do so.

25 It is suggested that members circumvent the cumbersome Article 31bis system by utilizing the flexibility of Article 31(k) (where such use is permitted to remedy a practice determined after judicial or administrative process to be anti-competitive) to make compulsory licenses available. See Ong, B. (2015). Compulsory licenses of pharmaceutical patents to remedy anti-competitive practices under Article 31(k) of the TRIPS agreement: Can competition law facilitate access to essential medicines? In Liu, K.-C., & Hilty, R. (Eds.), *Compulsory Licensing—Practical Experiences and Ways Forward* (pp. 246–458). Springer.

26 Reichman, J., & Hasenzahl, C. (2003). *Non-voluntary Licensing of Patented Inventions—Historical Perspective, Legal Framework under TRIPS and an Overview of the Practice in Canada and the USA* (p. 21), at: https://unctad.org/system/files/official-document/ictsd2003ipd5_en.pdf.

27 For example, the USDOJ settled with Comcast/NBCU in 2011 which allows the merger at issue according to the Clayton Act under the condition that Comcast/NBCU to make the estimated 30 satellite-delivered national networks and 14 satellite-delivered RSNs it controls available to competitors until January 2018, at: https://www.justice.gov/opa/pr/justice-department-allows-comcast-nbcu-joint-venture-proceed-conditions.

28 For example, *US v. Imperial Chemical Industries*, 105 F.Supp. 215 (1952). The case was brought to my attention by Merges, R. (2022). *American Patent Law—A Business and Economic History* (p. 298). Cambridge University Press.

29 For example, *United States v. National Lead Co.*, 332 US 319 (1947).

30 Reichman, J., & Hasenzahl, C. (2003). *Non-voluntary Licensing of Patented Inventions—Historical Perspective, Legal Framework under TRIPS and an Overview of the Practice in Canada and the USA* (pp. 2, 4, 5), at: https://unctad.org/system/files/official-document/ictsd2003ipd5_en.pdf.

31 *US v. Imperial Chemical Industries*, 105 F.Supp. 222 (1952).

32 *eBay v. MercExchange*, 547 US 388 (2006).

injunction will be issued immediately after the adjudication of infringement and validity of patents and copyrights. Rather, the plaintiff must first demonstrate the following four factors are fulfilled before he/she can stop the alleged infringer from carrying on its use of the IP he/she owned: (I) that it has suffered an irreparable injury; (II) that remedies available at law, such as monetary damages, are inadequate to compensate for that injury; (III) that, considering the balance of hardships between the plaintiff and defendant, a remedy in equity is warranted; and (IV) that the public interest would not be disserved by a permanent injunction. Clearly, if the plaintiff fails to satisfy the four-factor test, the alleged infringer can continue the use of the IP until the courts come to a final determination. Before that, it was as if a de facto compulsory license had been granted.[33]

3.2.2. The UK

A. STATUTORY PROVISIONS AND PRACTICE

In the UK, the Patents Act of 1883 already recognized compulsory licenses.[34] The Patents Act of 1977 gives the comptroller the power to grant a compulsory license in the following five situations, provided that three years have lapsed after the patent grant: (I) where, either, domestic demand for a patented product is not being met on reasonable terms; where the exploitation of another patented invention, which is technically and economically important, is being prevented or hindered; or in the case of unreasonable conditions imposed upon licensing of the patent, prejudicing the development or establishment of commercial or industrial activities in the UK (Section 48A(1));[35] (II) following a report of the Competition and Markets Authority (CMA) that an undesirable monopolistic situation exists or an anti-competitive practice is operating against the public interest (Section 51); (III) for Crown use (Sections 55–59); (IV) in relation to biotechnological inventions; and (V) public health grounds.[36] The UK's compulsory license system requires careful investigation of the circumstances before granting and therefore is not much used.[37] The order granting

33 The eBay decision has changed the practice of federal district courts in refusing injunction applications. In several cases, the refusal was on the grounds that the plaintiff was a non-practising entity, or the patent covered only one small component of a complex device. As an alternative to injunctions, these courts fixed a reasonable royalty that the infringer would have to pay the plaintiff to continue using the patent. See Seaman, C. (2016). Permanent injunctions in patent litigation after eBay: An empirical study. *Iowa Law Review, 101*, 1949.

34 From 1919 to 1977 a special provision existed in the UK which made compulsory licenses for food and drug patents available as of right save exceptionally. See Llewelyn, D., and Aplin, T. (2023). *Intellectual Property: Patents, Copyright, Trade Marks and Allied Rights* (10th ed.), 7–040. Sweet & Maxwell.

35 Section 48 differentiates between patents with WTO owners and patents with non-WTO owners, and foresees more cumbersome grounds on which compulsory licenses will be granted in the case of WTO owners. Given the large number of WTO Members, it suffices to point only to Section 48A(1).

36 Bently, L. et al. (2018). *Intellectual Property Law* (5th ed., p. 685). Oxford University Press.

37 Between 1959–1968, only two compulsory licenses were granted under the general provisions of the Patents Act. Four special compulsory licenses were granted for food and medicine. See Llewelyn, D., & Aplin, T. (2023). *Intellectual Property: Patents, Copyright, Trade Marks and Allied Rights*

the license is subject to review by the Patents Court. The supposed effect of compulsory licensing provisions in the UK today is "mainly in terrorem."[38]

B. NOTEWORTHY PROVISIONS

The UK compulsory patent license regime is noteworthy for its provisions on the eligibility of the applicant, the two forms of compulsory license, and the sweeping discretionary power of the Comptroller. This unparalleled legislation should have been introduced to the world during the drafting of the TRIPS Agreement.

a. The Eligibility of the Applicant From a contract law perspective, the licensee who has signed a voluntary license agreement might later be barred or estopped from filing an application for compulsory license over the same patent. To rule out such an uncertainty Section 48(3) expressly stipulates that:

> An application may be made . . . even though the applicant is already the holder of a licence under the patent; and no person shall be estopped or barred from alleging any of the matters specified in the relevant grounds by reason of any admission made by him, whether in such a licence or otherwise, or by reason of his having accepted a licence.

b. Two Forms of Compulsory License There are two forms of compulsory license, the more usual individual license and the rarer form of license of right. The individual compulsory patent license could be granted not only to the applicant but also to "customers of the applicant" that the comptroller sees fit (Section 49(1)). Another form of compulsory patent license is one of right when the Minister applies to the Comptroller to have the patent endorsed as a license of right in response to a CMA report that an undesirable monopolistic situation exists or an anti-competitive practice is operating against the public interest (Section 50A(2)). Under the license of right, the patentee "must license all comers on terms which, if they cannot be agreed, will be fixed by the Comptroller."[39]

(10th ed.), 7–048. Sweet & Maxwell. The last reported case of a granted compulsory license dates back to 1971. See T. Amin, Practical Experiences with Compulsory Licensing in the UK, ASEAN Workshop on Compulsory Licensing to Increase Access to Antiretrovirals (ARVs) and Diagnostic Reagents, Kuala Lumpur, Malaysia 2006. Since 2000, there have been four applications for compulsory patent license, two were withdrawn and two were dismissed by a joint decision of the comptroller, see Bently, L. et al. (2018). *Intellectual Property Law* (5th ed., p. 684). Oxford University Press, footnote 81.

38 Llewelyn, D., & Aplin, T. (2023). *Intellectual Property: Patents, Copyright, Trade Marks and Allied Rights* (10th ed.), 7–040. Sweet & Maxwell; Bently, L. et al. (2018). *Intellectual Property Law* (5th ed., p. 684). Oxford University Press, footnote 81.

39 Llewelyn, D., & Aplin, T. (2023). *Intellectual Property: Patents, Copyright, Trade Marks and Allied Rights* (10th ed.), 4–025. Sweet & Maxwell.

c. Sweeping Discretionary Power of the Comptroller The comptroller is given sweeping discretionary power in the granting of compulsory patent licenses. In case of an application filed according to Section 48, the comptroller may order the existing license to be cancelled (if they order the grant of a license to the applicant), or simply order the existing license to be amended, without granting a compulsory license (Section 49(1)). The comptroller may, in case of an application under Section 50A(2), cancel or modify any condition restricting the use of the invention by the licensee or the right of the proprietor to grant other licenses. The comptroller may, instead or in addition, make an entry in the register to the effect that licenses under the patent are to be available as of right.

The comptroller can thus decidedly intervene into the license agreements between the parties, ranging from amending, modifying, to cancelling them, and to making an entry in the patent register of a compulsory license as of right.

3.2.3. Germany

A. INVENTION PATENTS

a. Ordinary Compulsory License Joseph Kohler commented more than 120 years ago that the then German Patent Law was "exceedingly incomplete" because it lacked direct compulsory license and foresaw only forfeiture of a patent in case the patentee did not exercise his/her right.[40] The Patent Act of 1911 for the first time recognized the granting of compulsory license by courts. There has been a drastic change in view about compulsory patent licensing in Germany. According to the current Article 24 of the Patent Act, there are two kinds of compulsory licenses, one for public interests and the other for dependent patents. A non-exclusive authorization to commercially exploit an invention shall be granted by the Federal Patent Court in individual cases (I) if the applicant for a license has unsuccessfully endeavored for a reasonable period of time to obtain from the patentee consent to exploit the invention under reasonable conditions common in trade, and (II) public interest commands a granting of compulsory licensing (Subsection 1). If the applicant cannot exploit his patent without infringing on another patent of an earlier date, and if his invention in comparison with that of the earlier invention comprises an important technical advance of considerable commercial significance, and the conditions listed in Subsection 1(1) are met, he/she shall have the right to ask the patentee of the earlier invention to grant compulsory license (Subsection 2). In addition, where the proprietor of the patent does not apply the patented invention in Germany or does not do so predominantly, compulsory licenses under Subsection 1 may be granted to ensure an adequate supply of the patented product on the German market. Import is thus equivalent to the use of the patent in Germany (Subsection 5).

40 Kohler, J. (1900). *Handbuch des deutschen patentrechts in rechtsvergleichender darstellung* (p. 618). J. Bensheimer.

In the "Polyferon" case, the Federal Court of Justice, in annulling the granted compulsory license, elaborates that from the exclusive position of a rightsholder alone, no public interest can be established, even if the rightsholder enjoys a de facto monopolistic position. Therefore, special circumstances must exist in order to satisfy the public interest requirement. What may come within the purview of special circumstances besides abuse of patent rights includes technical, economic, social-political, and medical perspectives, which can certainly include the maintenance of market competition.[41]

Commendably, the German Federal Court of Justice took a liberal stance in interpreting the TRIPS Agreement in the "Orange-Book-Standard" decision (May 6, 2009).[42] It started from the assumption that Article 31 of the TRIPS Agreement in principle grants the right to use the patent without authorization from the patentee, so long as the permission is based on the circumstances of individual cases. In addition, the condition of Article 31(b) (on reasonable commercial terms and conditions) is satisfied if the license-seeker prior to the commencement of the use has tried fruitlessly to acquire a license on non-discriminating terms (Paragraph 28), which should be applicable to the interpretation of Article 24(1) of the Patent Act.

b. Interim Compulsory License Pursuant to Article 85(1) the German Patent Act, in pending proceedings for the grant of a compulsory license, the plaintiff may be allowed by way of a preliminary injunction to exploit a patented invention if it demonstrates to the satisfaction of the court that the requirements of Article 24 of the Patent Act for the grant of a compulsory license are being met and that an immediate grant is urgently required in the public interest.

In the Raltegravir case,[43] the Federal Court of Justice affirms that a relatively small group of patients and the hesitant behavior of the license seeker do not affect the recognition of "public interest." The public interest requirement for the issuance of compulsory license can exist even when only a relatively small group of patients is affected. This is especially the case when this group is exposed to especially high risk if the medicine at dispute is no longer at their disposal. In the interest-weighing process according to Article 85, the hesitant behavior (zögerliches Verhalten) of the license seeker will be taken into consideration. However, such a behavior will not automatically speak against the existence of public interest.

41 German Federal Court of Justice XZR 26/09 (decided on December 5, 1995).

42 German Federal Court of Justice KZR 39/06 (decided on May 6, 2009).

43 The antiretroviral drug, based on Raltegravir, has been the object of a prolonged court fight between Japanese drug company Shionogi and its US competitor Merck. Merck, since 2008, has sold Isentress on the German market. It is used for treatments of HIV patients to reduce the amount of virus cells in the body while increasing the number of CD4 T cells. See German Federal Court of Justice X ZB 2/17 (decided on July 11, 2017).

c. De Facto Compulsory License to Avoid Disproportionate Hardship Article 139(1) of the German Patent Act since June 2021 expressly allows an exception to the automatic injunction in cases where the issuance of an injunction would lead to disproportionate hardship not justified by the exclusive right nature of a patent for the infringer or third parties, after taking into considerations the special circumstances of the individual cases and the requirement of good faith.

Article 139(1) continues to provide that, in case that injunction is exceptionally not granted, the claimant is to be awarded reasonable monetary remuneration (ein angemessener Ausgleich in Geld), without prejudice to the claim for infringement damages recognized in Article 139(2). The application of Article 139(1) will impose a de facto compulsory patent license on the infringed patent holder, as the defendant can continue its use after paying a reasonable monetary remuneration.

d. Practice Between 1923 and 1943, there were 295 applications for compulsory licensing and 25 grants.[44] Since then, according to the statistics of the Federal Patent Court, from 1961 (the year in which the court was founded) onwards, there were only 22 applications and one grant in 1994 ("Polyferon") which was later evoked by the Federal Court of Justice in 1996, and another interim compulsory license granted according to Article 85 (Raltegravir) for the HIV drug Isentress, which was upheld by the Federal Court of Justice in 2017.[45]

B. Utility Models Article 20 of the German Utility Model Act (Gebruachmustergesetz) stipulates that Article 24 of the Patent Act is to be applied to utility models by analogy. The current Article 20 was based on the 1998 Second Patent Revision Act.[46] There is rarely a compulsory license for utility models in Germany.

4. Compulsory Copyright Licensing

4.1. International Treaties

Economically speaking, performers, phonogram producers, collecting societies, music publishers, and broadcasting organizations are in a vertical relationship of supply and demand of content and service. It is not uncommon that the negotiations between these groups stall and lead to stalemate, sending the transaction costs for the use of copyrighted works skyrocketing; an intervention from the law is therefore desirable. The Berne Convention, the Rome Convention for the Protection of Performers, Producers of Phonograms and Broadcasting Organizations (1961), and the TRIPS Agreement[47] recognize compulsory copyright licensing only in

44 Kübel, C. (2004). *Zwangslizenzen im Immaterialgüter-und Wettbewerbsrecht* (p. 93). Carl Heymanns.

45 Benkard/Kober-Dehm, Patentgesetz, §24 Rdnr. 4 (C.H. Beck 12. Aufl. 2023).

46 Mes, P. PatG und Gebrauchmustergesetz, §20 Rdnr. 2 (C.H. Beck 5. Aufl. 2020).

47 Article 9(1) of the TRIPS Agreement takes over Articles 1 through 21 and the Appendix of the Berne Convention (1971).

enumerated cases which aim at preserving market competition for broadcasting and recording industries.[48]

4.1.1. The Berne Convention

The Berne Convention recognizes two compulsory copyright licenses to counterbalance dominant collecting societies and music publishers. The Berne Convention allows its members to impose two specific types of compulsory licensing. However, there is no Conventional obligation for Union members to impose compulsory license.[49] One compulsory license is on the right of broadcasting, communication to the public by wire, rebroadcasting, and public communication by loudspeakers and the like (Article 11bis(2)),[50] the other is on the right of recording musical works (Article 13(1) and (2)),[51] although the term "compulsory license" was mentioned only in the title, not the text, of Articles 11bis(2) and 13(1) and (2).

48 In respect of the communication to the public of television broadcasts if such communication is made in places accessible to the public against payment of an entrance fee, the Rome Convention foresees a possibility of compulsory licensing and even statutory licensing that would limit broadcasting organizations' right of public communication (13(d)). See Lewinski, S.V. (2008). *International Copyright Law and Policy*, 6.69. Oxford University Press.

49 See Ricketson, S., & Ginsburg, J. (2005). *International Copyright and Neighbouring Rights—The Berne Convention and Beyond* (Vol. I, 13.71, 2nd ed.). Oxford University Press.

50 Article 11bis(2)

> It shall be a matter for legislation in the countries of the Union to determine the conditions under which the rights mentioned in the preceding paragraph may be exercised, but these conditions shall apply only in the countries where they have been prescribed. They shall not in any circumstances be prejudicial to the moral rights of the author, nor to his right to obtain equitable remuneration which, in the absence of agreement, shall be fixed by competent authority. [W]as inserted at the Rome Revision Conference (1928) when the right of broadcasting was first introduced. It was based on "a French amendment which avoided any reference to the recognition of a Conventional compulsory license, but proposed reserving to national legislation the power to regulate the conditions under which the broadcasting right could be exercised." See Ricketson, S., & Ginsburg, J. (2005). *International Copyright and Neighbouring Rights—The Berne Convention and Beyond* (Vol. I, 13.68, 2nd ed.). Oxford University Press.

51 Article 13(1) and (2) of the Berne Convention provides: (1) Each country of the Union may impose for itself reservations and conditions on the exclusive right granted to the author of a musical work and to the author of any words, the recording of which together with the musical work has already been authorized by the latter, to authorize the sound recording of that musical work, together with such words, if any; but all such reservations and conditions shall apply only in the countries which have imposed them and shall not, in any circumstances, be prejudicial to the rights of these authors to obtain equitable remuneration which, in the absence of agreement, shall be fixed by competent authority. (2) Recordings of musical works made in a country of the Union in accordance with Article 13(3) of the Conventions signed at Rome on June 2, 1928, and at Brussels on June 26, 1948, may be reproduced in that country without the permission of the author of the musical work until a date two years after that country becomes bound by this Act.

Both compulsory licensing was done "in the interests of the public."[52] More specifically, they are "for the benefit of particular groups of the society," namely broadcasting organizations and phonogram producers to counterbalance the dominant position of collecting societies and music publishers which "usually exercised monopolistic practices."[53] That means exactly the preservation of competition. As of 2011, only 15 of the 164 parties of the Berne Convention have availed themselves of enjoying the benefit of these compulsory licenses.[54]

4.1.2. The Rome Convention

The Rome Convention recognizes two compulsory licenses for broadcasting organizations.

A. REBROADCASTING, FIXATION, AND THE REPRODUCTION OF SUCH FIXATION OF PERFORMANCE FOR BROADCASTING PURPOSES

To protect the performing artists Article 7(1) of the Rome Convention grants them the possibility of preventing the exploitation of their performance if they have not consented thereto.[55] This is considerably a lower level of protection as compared to the rights of phonogram producers and the broadcasting organizations which include the right to authorize and prohibit.[56]

52 WIPO. (1978). *Guide to the Berne Convention for the Protection of Literary and Artistic Works* (pp. 11–16). WIPO.

53 Lewinski, S. V. (2008). *International Copyright Law and Policy*, 5.193. Oxford University Press.

54 Silva, A. (2012). Beyond the unrealistic solution for development provided by the Appendix of the Berne Convention on copyright. *PIJIP Research Paper No. 2012–08 American University Washington College of Law*, Washington, at: https://digitalcommons.wcl.american.edu/cgi/viewcontent.cgi?article=1032&context=research.

55 Article 7(1) of the Rome Convention provides:

> 1. The protection provided for performers by this Convention shall include the possibility of preventing: (a) the broadcasting and the communication to the public, without their consent, of their performance, except where the performance used in the broadcasting or the public communication is itself already a broadcast performance or is made from a fixation; (b) the fixation, without their consent, of their unfixed performance; (c) the reproduction, without their consent, of a fixation of their performance: (i) if the original fixation itself was made without their consent; (ii) if the reproduction is made for purposes different from those for which the performers gave their consent; (iii) if the original fixation was made in accordance with the provisions of Article 15, and the reproduction is made for purposes different from those referred to in those provisions.

56 Article 10 of the Rome Convention provides "Producers of phonograms shall enjoy the right to authorize or prohibit the direct or indirect reproduction of their phonograms." Article 13 stipulates: Broadcasting organizations shall enjoy the right to authorize or prohibit: (a) the rebroadcasting of their broadcasts; (b) the fixation of their broadcasts; (c) the reproduction: (i) of fixations, made without their consent, of their broadcasts; (ii) of fixations, made in accordance with the provisions of Article 15, of their broadcasts, if the reproduction is made for purposes different from those referred to in those provisions; (d) the communication to the public of their television broadcasts if such communication is made in places accessible to the public against payment of an entrance fee; it shall

Once performing artists consented to the use of their performance, such possibility is no longer available to them. Rather, it is up to the contracting states to provide protection against rebroadcasting, fixation for broadcasting purposes and the reproduction of such fixation for broadcasting purposes (Article 7, Paragraph 2(2)). In so providing, the contracting states can provide for compulsory licenses to use the performance.

B. SECONDARY USES OF PHONOGRAMS

The use of phonograms which have been published for commercial purposes by broadcasting organizations is economically the most important situation that the Rome Convention was called upon to regulate. According to Article 12,[57] such phonograms are made available to broadcasting organizations, provided that a single remuneration shall be paid by the user to the performers, or the producers of the phonograms, or to both. The allocation of that payment between the parties is left to domestic legislation.

4.2. Major National Regimes

Preserving market competition is a major concern for the US, UK, and German copyright law.

4.2.1. The US

The US Copyright Act contains numerous compulsory and statutory licensing mechanisms in Sections 108 through 122 and 1004[58] to prevent the delay and expenses of negotiation with copyright owners that would make a voluntary licensing impracticable.[59] As a consequence, the fees that copyright owners may collect from innumerable types of consumers of their products are controlled to varying degrees by administrative agencies and courts.[60] Pursuant to Section 801, the Library of Congress shall appoint three full-time Copyright Royalty Judges to the Copyright Royalty Board (CRB). The CRB's duties include determining and adjusting the terms and rates of royalty payments that are subject to statutory

be a matter for the domestic law of the State where protection of this right is claimed to determine the conditions under which it may be exercised.

57 Article 12 [Secondary Uses of Phonograms] of the Rome Convention stipulates:

> If a phonogram published for commercial purposes, or a reproduction of such phonogram, is used directly for broadcasting or for any communication to the public, a single equitable remuneration shall be paid by the user to the performers, or to the producers of the phonograms, or to both. Domestic law may, in the absence of agreement between these parties, lay down the conditions as to the sharing of this remuneration.

58 Section 107 differs from Sections 108 through 122 in that it requires ongoing reassessment while the latter rests on the assumption that the relevant cost-and-benefit calculus remains constant, id., 12.15.

59 Goldstein, P. (2005). *Goldstein on Copyright* (3rd ed.). Aspen Publishers.

60 Fisher, W. (2004). Promises to keep, technology, law, and the future of entertainment. *Stanford Law and Politics*, 184.

or compulsory licenses, as provided in Sections 112(e) (ephemeral recordings by transmitting organizations), 114 (non-interactive webcasting), 115 (for making and distributing phonorecords to the public for private use), 116 (for public performances by means of coin-operated phonorecord players), 118 (for non-commercial broadcasting by public broadcasting entities), 119 (for secondary transmission of superstations and network stations for private home viewing) and 1004 (royalty payment for digital audio recording devices).

In response to the rise of piano rolls, the Copyright Act of 1909 extended the rights of musical works owners, in part, by granting rights to the mechanical reproductions of a composition. Congress also created the compulsory "mechanical license," allowing anyone to make a mechanical reproduction of a musical work without the knowledge or consent of the copyright owner, provided that the licensee meets certain qualifications for the license and that the copyright owner is compensated through a statutorily established royalty rate.[61] The term "mechanical license" has stuck although the reproduction and distribution of a work no longer involve actual mechanical reproduction. Currently, mechanical rates for physical phonorecords and permanent downloads are 9.1 cents per song or 1.75 cents per minute of playing time, whichever is greater.[62]

The Small Webcaster Settlement Act of 2002 (SWSA) was enacted to provide relief to small and non-commercial webcasters after the first statutory royalties for webcasting were set by the Copyright Arbitration Royalty Panel. Pursuant to the SWSA, small commercial and non-commercial webcasters reached agreements with SoundExchange, since 2003 the non-profit and sole organization designated by the US Library of Congress to collect and distribute digital performance royalties for sound recordings. It pays featured and non-featured artists and master rights (recording) owners for the non-interactive use of sound recordings under the statutory licenses. Copyright Royalty and Distribution Reform Act of 2004 makes extensive changes to the procedural framework for adjudicating royalty rates for compulsory licenses under the Copyright Act. Compulsory licenses facilitate innumerable copyright-related activities, including digital transmissions of sound recordings in webcasting. While the 2002 SWSA was limited to small and noncommercial webcasters, the Webcaster Settlement Act of 2008 makes the negotiation procedure available to all webcasters regardless of size or commercial nature. Under the 2008 Act, agreements with SoundExchange will apply to all copyright owners of sound recordings, including the approximately 5% of copyright owners that are not directly represented by SoundExchange. Thus, webcasters would need to reach only one agreement, and they would be covered for all sound recordings they might perform.

In 2018 the Music Modernization Act (MMA) was signed into law.[63] The MMA replaced the previous policy-oriented Section 801(b)(1) rate-setting standard,

61 Linn, N. (2023). Mechanical licenses and the willing buyer/willing seller standard: establishing royalty rates in a vacuum of knowledge. *Cardozo Journal of Arts and Entertainment Law, 40(1)*, 319.

62 Linn, N. (2023). Mechanical licenses and the willing buyer/willing seller standard: establishing royalty rates in a vacuum of knowledge. *Cardozo Journal of Arts and Entertainment Law, 40(1)*, 321.

63 This omnibus legislation is comprised of three key titles: Title I—Musical Works Modernization; Title II—Classics Protection and Access; and Title III—Allocation for Music Producers.

adopting a willing buyer/willing seller standard for mechanical royalty determinations, eliminating the fourth consideration of Section 801(b)(1) analysis and allowing the CRB to consider all relevant market data to determine a fair rate between a hypothetical willing buyer and willing seller.[64] SoundExchange has paid more than $11 billion in distributions to date (May 2024).[65]

4.2.2. The UK

In the UK, there is no longer any rule allowing for general compulsory copyright licenses equivalent to those for patents, nor the "statutory right . . . to make their own recordings to record a work bearing musical copyright."[66] However, according to the Copyright, Designs and Patents Act of 1988 (CDPA) there are several distinctive categories of compulsory copyright licenses. One is that the Minister has the power to reduce the exclusive rental right into a right to reasonable royalty.[67] The second category deals with the compulsory license for the inclusion of any sound recording into a broadcast.[68] The third category of compulsory license aims at the control of monopoly: the Minister and the CMA are given the power to cancel or modify the licensing agreement, and the power to provide that licenses shall be available as of right to control anti-competitive or monopolistic practices.[69] The

64 The policy-oriented §801(b)(1) standard that was previously used for mechanical licenses, including in Phonorecords III required the CRB to determine a royalty rate that would achieve the following objectives: (I) To maximize the availability of creative works to the public. (II) To afford the copyright owner a fair return for his or her creative work and the copyright user a fair income under existing economic conditions. (III) To reflect the relative roles of the copyright owner and the copyright user in the product made available to the public with respect to relative creative contribution, technological contribution, capital investment, cost, risk, and contribution to the opening of new markets for creative expression and media for their communication. (IV) To minimize any disruptive impact on the structure of the industries involved and on generally prevailing industry practices.

65 See https://www.soundexchange.com/who-we-are/#about-us.

66 Llewelyn, D., & Aplin, T. (2023). *Intellectual Property: Patents, Copyright, Trade Marks and Allied Rights* (10th ed.), 13–047. Sweet & Maxwell.

67 Section 66(1) of CDPA provides:

> The Secretary of State may by order provide that in such cases as may be specified in the order the lending to the public of copies of literary, dramatic, musical or artistic works, sound recordings or films shall be treated as licensed by the copyright owner subject only to the payment of such reasonable royalty or other payment as may be agreed or determined in default of agreement by the Copyright Tribunal. Llewelyn, D., & Aplin, T. (2023). *Intellectual Property: Patents, Copyright, Trade Marks and Allied Rights* (10th ed.), 12–045. Sweet & Maxwell

68 Section 135C of CDPA.

69 Section 144 of the CDPA 1988 is about powers that the Minister can exercise in consequence of the report of CMA: (1) Subsection (1A) applies where whatever needs to be remedied, mitigated, or prevented by the Secretary of State or (as the case may be) the CMA . . . consists of or includes—(a) conditions in licences granted by the owner of copyright in a work restricting the use of the work by the licensee or the right of the copyright owner to grant other licences; or (b) a refusal of a copyright owner to grant licenses on reasonable terms. (1A) The powers conferred by Schedule 8 to the Enterprise Act 2002 include "power to cancel or modify those conditions and, instead or in addition, to provide that licences in respect of the copyright shall be available as of right."

terms of all three categories of compulsory license shall, in default of agreement, be settled by the Copyright Tribunal on an application by the person requiring the license.

4.2.3. Germany

The German Act on the Management of Copyright and Related Rights by Collecting Societies foresees a whole range of obligations of CMOs that amount to compulsory license of copyrighted works: obligation to conclude contract (Article 34), to conclude inclusive agreements with associations of users at reasonable conditions (Article 35), to allow use after conditional payment (Article 37), to set tariffs (Article 38), and to set them on the basis of the pecuniary benefits, etc. (Article 39) (see Subsection 3.1.5 of Chapter 8).

5. Compulsory Design Licensing

5.1. The Paris Convention

The Paris Convention is silent on whether design patents are subject to compulsory license as well. However, there is a historical episode that happened in the 1934 London conference. The host country, the UK, and the International Bureau had jointly made a proposal to expressly prohibit compulsory license for design patents. However, the proposal was rejected, due to objections from Czechoslovakia and Yugoslavia.[70] This shows that members' sovereignty in deciding whether to recognize compulsory design license remains unrestricted.

5.2. Major National Regimes

Compulsory license of designs is recognized at least in the UK, Germany, and Japan.

In the UK, the CDPA 1988 subjects both unregistered designs[71] and registered designs[72] to compulsory license. Germany has evolved from one general

70 Ricketson, S. (2015). *The Paris Convention for the Protection of Industrial Property*, 11.26, 11.27. Oxford University Press.

71 Section 238 CDPA 1988 is about powers exercisable for protection of the public interest and provides "(1) Subsection (1A) applies where whatever needs to be remedied, mitigated or prevented by the Secretary of State or (as the case may be) the Competition and Markets Authority . . . consists of or includes—(a) conditions in licences granted by an unregistered design right owner restricting the use of the design by the licensee or the right of the design right owner to grant other licences, or (b) a refusal of a design right owner to grant licences on reasonable terms. (1A) The powers (by the Secretary of State, the CMA) conferred by Schedule 8 to the Enterprise Act 2002 include power to cancel or modify those conditions and, instead or in addition, to provide that licences in respect of the design right shall be available as of right. (3) The terms of a licence available by virtue of this section shall, in default of agreement, be settled by the comptroller."

72 Section 270 CDPA 1988 provides the same powers exercisable for protection of the public interest when it comes to registered designs "(3) it appears to the registrar that the matters operate or

compulsory design license to a specific one. Article 20 of the Design Act had previously provided that the provisions of the Patent Act on the grant and revoke or adjustment of remuneration by court decision of a compulsory license (Article 24) and on the procedure (Articles 81–99, 110–122a) be applied mutatis mutandis to registered designs. However, it was deleted after the 2014 amendment. The current Design Act has a special "repairs clause" which exempts spare parts used for repair purposes from design protection. However, consumers are to be duly informed about the origin of the product used for repair (Article 40a of the German Design Act).[73] Japan also foresees compulsory licensing of design rights to be issued by the Commissioner of the JPO.[74]

---

operated or may be expected to operate against the public interest include—(a) conditions in licences granted in respect of a registered design by its proprietor restricting the use of the design by the licensee or the right of the proprietor to grant other licences, or (b) a refusal by the proprietor of a registered design to grant licences on reasonable terms, he may by order cancel or modify any such condition or may, instead or in addition, make an entry in the register to the effect that licences in respect of the design are to be available as of right. (4) The terms of a licence available by virtue of this section shall, in default of agreement, be settled by the registrar on an application by the person requiring the licence; and terms so settled shall authorise the licensee to do everything which would be an infringement of the right in the registered design in the absence of a licence."

73 Article 40a of German Design Act provides:

> (1) Protection as a design does not exist for a design incorporated in or applied to a product which constitutes a component part of a complex product used for the sole purpose of enabling the repair of that complex product so as to restore its original appearance. This does not apply if the main purpose for which the aforementioned component is put on the market is other than the repair of the complex product. (2) Subsection (1) only applies if consumers are duly informed, by means of an identification mark or in other appropriate form, about the origin of the product used for repair purposes so that they are able, with full knowledge of the facts, to make an informed choice between competing products.

74 Article 72 of the Japanese Patent Act provides:

> Where a patented invention uses another person's patented invention, registered utility model, registered design or design similar thereto for which an application was filed prior to the date of filing of the said patent application, or where the patent right is in conflict with another person's design right or trademark right obtained based on an application filed prior to the date of filing of the said patent application, the patentee, exclusive licensee or non-exclusive licensees may not work the patented invention as a business.

Article 92 of the Japanese Patent Act provides:

> (1) Where a patented invention falls under any of the cases as provided in Article 72, the patentee or exclusive licensee may request the other person under the said Article to hold consultations to discuss granting a non-exclusive license to work the patented invention, the utility model right or the design right. (3) Where no agreement is reached by consultations or no consultations are able to be held as provided in paragraph (1), the patentee or the exclusive licensee may request the Commissioner of the Patent Office for an award.

6. Compulsory IC-Layout Design Licensing

The US Semiconductor Chip Protection Act of 1984 does not recognize compulsory IC-layout design licensing. However, it is recognized at least in the PRC[75] and Taiwan.[76] No actual issuance of any such compulsory license was known.

The Washington Treaty on Intellectual Property in Respect of Integrated Circuits in 1989 (IPIC), not expected to enter into force, generously recognizes compulsory license of IC-layout designs to secure free competition and to prevent abuses by rightsholders:

> (3) (a) . . . any Contracting Party may, in its legislation, provide for the possibility of its executive or judicial authority granting a non-exclusive license, in circumstances that are not ordinary, for the performance of any of the acts referred to in paragraph (1) by a third party without the authorization of the holder of the right ("non-voluntary license"), after unsuccessful efforts, made by the said third party in line with normal commercial practices, to obtain such authorization, where the granting of the non-voluntary license is found, by the granting authority, to be necessary to safeguard a national purpose deemed to be vital by that authority; the non-voluntary license shall be available for exploitation only in the territory of that country and shall be subject to the payment of an equitable remuneration by the third party to the holder of the right. (b) The provisions of this Treaty shall not affect the freedom of any Contracting Party to apply measures, including the granting, after a formal proceeding by its executive or judicial authority, of a nonvoluntary license, in application of its laws in order to secure free competition and to prevent abuses by the holder of the right. (c) The granting of any non-voluntary license . . . shall be subject to judicial review. Any non-voluntary . . . shall be revoked when the conditions . . . cease to exist.

This broad recognition of compulsory IC-layout design license is one of the major reasons why the IPIC Treaty failed to attract sufficient members to take effect (Article 6(3)). However, compulsory license, whether broadly or narrowly defined,

75 In the PRC, Regulations on IC-Layout Designs allow non-voluntary licensing of IC-layout designs by China National IP Administration in cases of national emergency and extreme situations, public interests, and remedying unfair competition decided by courts or agencies in charge of overseeing and inspecting unfair competition (Article 25).

76 Article 24(1) and (2) of Taiwan's Integrated Circuit Layout Protection Act similarly provides: (1) For a use to promote nonprofit public interests in a circuit layout, the agency in charge of circuit layout affairs may, upon application, grant to an applicant a compulsory license to the circuit layout rights. The compulsory license shall be granted primarily to supply the demand of the domestic market. (2) If an owner of the circuit layout rights is found to have engaged in unfair competition, which has been irrevocably confirmed by the court or the Fair Trade Commission, the competent authority of circuit layout affairs may, upon application, grant an applicant a compulsory license to the circuit layout rights, notwithstanding the absence of the condition set forth in the preceding Paragraph.

is a tool destined not to be used given the nature of the IC-layout design and manufacturing (see Subsection 4.1 of Chapter 4).[77]

7. Compulsory Plant Variety Rights Licensing

Both the international treaty for the protection of new plant varieties and domestic regimes of major economies recognize the compulsory license of plant variety rights for public interests which can include the preservation and fostering of market competition, among others.

7.1. The International Convention for the Protection of New Varieties of Plants

The International Convention for the Protection of New Varieties of Plants was adopted on December 2, 1961, came into force on August 10, 1968, is administered by the International Union for the Protection of New Varieties of Plants (UPOV),[78] therefore known as the UPOV Convention. The UPOV Convention allows compulsory licensing of plant variety rights for public interest purposes with equitable remuneration since its inception in 1961 (Article 9). Its 1991 version remains unchanged in that stance (Restrictions on the Exercise of the Breeder's Right):

> [Public interest] Except where expressly provided in this Convention, no Contracting Party may restrict the free exercise of a breeder's right for reasons other than of public interest. (2) [Equitable remuneration] When any such restriction has the effect of authorizing a third party to perform any act for which the breeder's authorization is required, the Contracting Party concerned shall take all measures necessary to ensure that the breeder receives equitable remuneration.
>
> (Article 17)

7.2. Major National Regimes

7.2.1. The US

In the US, the Plant Variety Protection Act of 1970 (PVPA) grants protection similar to that available through patents, but plant patents are limited to asexually reproduced plants. To safeguard the "public interest in wide usage" the PVPA allows the Department of Agriculture to make an "open to use" declaration: to declare a protected variety open to use on the basis of equitable remuneration to

77 Feuerstein, K. (1992). Chips off the trade bloc: International harmonization of the laws on semiconductor chips. *Fordham Intellectual Property, Media and Entertainment Law Journal, 2*, 137, at: https://ir.lawnet.fordham.edu/iplj/vol2/iss2/4.

78 It has 79 members as of February 2024, according to https://www.upov.int/members/en/.

the owner, upon finding that such a declaration is necessary in order to ensure an adequate supply of fiber, food, or feed and that the owner is unwilling or unable to meet public demand at a reasonably fair price. Such declaration may be, with or without limitation, with or without designation of what the remuneration is to be; and shall be subject to review (any finding that the price is not reasonable being reviewable) and shall remain in effect not more than two years. In the event litigation is required to collect such remuneration, a higher rate may be allowed by the court (Section 44). The "open to use" declaration is a compulsory license and the users of such declaration need not be limited to individual applicants or cases.

7.2.2. The EU

The EU Council Regulation No. 2100/94 of 27 July 1994 on community plant variety rights recognizes the community plant variety rights and "compulsory exploitation right" which shall be granted to one or more persons by the Community Plant Variety Office, on application by that person or those persons, but only on grounds of public interest and after consulting the Administrative Council. On application by a Member State, by the Commission or by an organization set up at the community level and registered by the Commission, a compulsory exploitation right may be granted, either to a category of persons satisfying specific requirements or to anyone in one or more Member States or throughout the Community. It may be granted only on grounds of public interest and with the approval of the Administrative Council (Article 29(1) and (2)).[79]

The EU 1998 Directive on the legal protection of biotechnological inventions further recognizes "compulsory cross-licensing" to solve the dependence issue between a patent concerning a biotechnological invention and a plant variety, provided prior good-faith negotiation for a voluntary license has failed and the plant variety or the invention constitutes significant technical progress of considerable economic interest compared with the invention claimed in the patent or the protected plant variety (Article 12).

7.2.3. In Asia

Compulsory license of plant variety rights is commonly recognized. For example, in Japan, if a registered variety has not been adequately exploited continuously for two years, or if the exploitation of a registered variety is particularly necessary for the public interest, then any person who intends to exploit that registered variety may initiate consultation, and further apply to the Minister of Agriculture, Forestry and Fisheries for arbitration when consultation failed. Unless the Minister finds the exploitation of a registered variety particularly necessary for the public interest, he/she must not issue an award through arbitration to the effect that a non-exclusive

79 Article 24(3) of the German Patent Act recognizes compulsory license mutatis mutandis where a plant breeder cannot obtain or exploit a plant variety right without infringing an earlier patent.

exploitation license should be established on that registered variety, etc. if there are any justifiable grounds for the registered variety, etc. not to have been appropriately exploited (Article 28(5) of Plant Variety Protection and Seed Act).

Taiwan's Plant Variety and Plant Seed Act provides broad compulsory licensing of plant variety rights: when coping with grave national situations, making non-profit use for the enhancement of the public interest, failing good-faith voluntary licensing negotiation to produce agreement, remedying rightsholders' anti-competitive or unfair competition. Compulsory licensing of plant variety rights is limited to mainly satisfying domestic market needs, except for remedying anti-competitive or unfair competition (Article 30).[80]

8. Compulsory Licensing of Trade Secrets

In addition to the Indian Law Commission's suggestion in The Protection of Trade Secrets Bill 2024 that the government could issue compulsory license of trade secrets in circumstances of national emergency or extreme urgency,[81] trade secrets can also be compulsorily licensed to certain neutral, independent, and professional third-party mechanisms to help market competition in very exceptional and limited situations.

These mechanisms include, for example, the competence center under the designated SSOs discussed in Chapter 10 and the authentication agency discussed in Chapter 11. If managed well, the secrecy of the trade secrets in question can still be largely preserved.

80 In the PRC, there is no enacted law, but Regulations on New Plant Varieties promulgated by the State Council. It empowers the approving authority to grant compulsory license for national or public interests and register and publish it. The licensee must pay the rightsholder reasonable fees to be negotiated by both parties. If no agreement can be reached, the approving authority shall decide. The rightsholder can appeal the decisions of the approving authority with people's courts within three months since receiving the notice (Article 11).

81 Article 6 of The Protection of Trade Secrets Bill 2024 suggested by the Indian Law Commission stipulates:

> (l) The Central Government, if it is satisfied, that there exist circumstances of national emergency or extreme urgency involving substantial public interest, including situations of public health emergency, national security etc., may require the holder of trade secret to issue compulsory license for use of his trade secret to third parties or to the Government. (2) Any license issued under sub-section (l) shall be subject to such license fee having regard to the nature and value of trade secret, the expenditure incurred by the holder of trade secret in developing and maintaining the trade secret, and may be subject to such other conditions and in such form as may be prescribed. (3) Any person, legal or natural, acquiring a trade secret as a consequence of operation of sub-section (1), shall have a duty to maintain confidentiality of the information so received and shall not disclose it further whether during or after termination of such license or use. (4) The license granted under this section may be terminated by the Government at any time after the circumstances specified in sub-section (l) cease to exist.

6 Competition-Oriented Compulsory Licensing of IPRs—Except Trademarks and GIs

1. Compulsory IP Licensing Through Competition Law

1.1. General Competition Law

Competition law can also be applied and lead to compulsory license of IPRs. In this regard, the essential facility (EF) doctrine developed in the US and accepted globally[1] could serve as the key test for compulsory licensing of IPRs, except trademarks. In the following, the discussion of national general competition laws will be limited to the US, the EU, and Germany, as they have more articulate case law.

1 For example, the Chinese antitrust authority, the State Administration of Market Regulation (SAMR) follows the essential facilities doctrine, however, without using the terminology. In its Regulations Against Abuse of IPR to Exclude and Restrain Competition revised in 2023, Article 10 stipulates "(1) A dominant business operator shall not refuse without due course to license other business operators to use its IPRs on reasonable terms and conditions while exercising those rights to exclude or restrain competition. (2) In determining the act prohibited by the preceding paragraph the following factors shall be taken into consideration: (i) the IPR at issue is reasonably not to be replaced and is indispensable for other business operators to participate in market competition; (2) the adversary effects on market competition or innovation, and harm to consumer interests or public interests as a result refusal to license the IPR; (3) the issuance of a license to use the IPR would not cause unreasonable damages to the business operator." So far there is no reported case to which the SMAR applied this article. However, the Ningbo Intermediate Court in 2021 ruled in *Ningbo Ketian Magnet Co., Ltd. v. Hitachi Metals, Ltd.* that a patent holder's refusal to license patents for producing rare-earth magnets to competitors constituted an abuse of dominance in violation of China's Antimonopoly Law, see (2014) ZheYonZhiChuZi No. 582 (decided on April 23, 2021). In 2023, the IP Court of the SPC overruled the decision for lack of market dominance of the defendant but did not touch upon the issue of abuse of dominance as a result of refusal to license, see (2021) ZuiGaoFaZhiMinZhong No.1413 (decided on December 14, 2023). Noteworthy though, the IP Court discussed and denied both the technical and economic indispensability of the patents at issue. In Japan, JFTC Recommendation Decision No. 5 of 1997 on August 6, 1997, found the association managing patents and other rights relating to the manufacture of pachinko machines restrained any third party from entering the market by refusing to grant licenses, and violated Article 3 of the Antimonopoly Act.

DOI: 10.4324/9781003597766-8

1.1.1. The US

The leading case for the EF doctrine is *MCI Communications v. AT&T*, adjudicated by the 7th Circuit in 1983,[2] which sets out a four-part test for an EF claim: (I) control of the EF by a monopolist; (II) competitor's inability practically or reasonably to duplicate the EF; (III) the denial of the use of the facilities to a competitor; and (IV) the feasibility of providing the facilities. A monopolist by denying access to the EF can extend its monopoly from one stage of production to another, and from one market into another. In such cases, firms controlling the EF bear the obligation to make the facilities available to their competitors on non-discriminatory terms. Although the EF doctrine has been criticized by influential writers and not yet recognized by the Supreme Court,[3] several Federal Circuit Courts do endorse and apply the EF doctrine.[4]

The Supreme Court reiterated its reservations about the EF doctrine in *Verizon Communications Inc. v Law Offices of Curtis V. Trinko, LLP* (Trinko), and took a very narrow view of the indispensable requirement, namely unavailability of access to the EF should be denied where a state or federal agency has effective power to compel its sharing and to regulate its scope and terms. For this reason, the 1996 Telecommunications Act's extensive provision for access made the application of the EF doctrine unnecessary:[5]

> We conclude that Verizon's alleged insufficient assistance in the provision of service to rivals is not a recognized antitrust claim under this Court's existing refusal-to-deal precedents. This conclusion would be unchanged even if we considered to be established law the 'essential facilities' doctrine crafted by some lower courts. *We have never recognized such a doctrine, and we find no need to either recognize it or repudiate it here.* It suffices for present purposes to note that the indispensable requirement for invoking the doctrine is the unavailability of access to the "essential facilities"; where access exists, the doctrine serves no purpose. . . . The 1996 Act's extensive provision for access makes it unnecessary to impose a judicial doctrine of forced access.[6]

2 *MCI Communications Corp. v. AT&T Co.*, 708 F. 2d 1080, 1132–33 (7th Cir. 1983).

3 In *Aspen Skiing v. Aspen Highlands Skiing*, 472 US 585 (1985), footnote 44, the US Supreme Court held: "Given our conclusion that the evidence amply supports the verdict under the instructions as given by the trial court, we find it unnecessary to consider the possible relevance of the "essential facilities" doctrine, or the somewhat hypothetical question whether non-exclusionary conduct could ever constitute an abuse of monopoly power if motivated by an anticompetitive purpose. If, as we have assumed, no monopolist monopolizes unconscious of what he is doing, that case is unlikely to arise."

4 *Alaska Airlines Inc. v. United Airlines Inc.*, 948 F.2d 536 (9th Cir. 1991); *Laurel Sand & Gravel, Inc v. CSX Transportation, Inc.*, 924 F.2d 539 (4th Cir. 1991); *Covad Communications Co v. BellSouth Corp.*, 299 F.3d 1272 (11th Cir. 2002); *Paladin Associates, In. v. Montana Power Co.*, 328 F.3d 1145 (9th Cir. 2003).

5 540 US 398 (2004).

6 540 US 408.

The Trinko case explicitly mentions the Aspen Skiing case, in which the refusal to continue an existing contractual relationship compensated at retail price violated Section 2 of the Sherman Act, as the only exception to the right to refuse to deal with other firms ("Aspen Skiing is at or near the outer boundary of Section 2 liability"[7]). In contrast thereto, refusal to commence dealing in products that had never been offered would presumably not violate Section 2 of the Sherman Act. The Trinko case has been rightly criticized as a myth assuming all markets are contestable[8] and therefore "backward-looking and a late success of the traditional Chicago School."[9] However, the Trinko case does not rule out the space, very limited as it might be, for lower courts to continue applying the EF doctrine to the refusal to continue an existing contractual relationship.

1.1.2. The EC and the CJEU

The EC adopted the EF doctrine in the 1990s.[10] In its Access Notice from 1998, the Commission set out a full-fledged essential facilities doctrine that markedly resembled that expressed by some US circuit courts.[11] The CJEU also takes converging views with US circuit courts in demanding that the facility in question must be virtually indispensable to competition in another relevant market, although without using the term EF.[12] However, the CJEU constantly requires that the refusal to license prevents the emergence of a new product.[13] This approach is followed by the European Court of First Instance (Grand Chamber) in the 2007 Microsoft case:

> The refusal by an undertaking holding a dominant position to license a third party to use a product covered by an intellectual property right cannot in

7 540 US 406.

8 Jablon, R., Hegedus, M., & Flynn, S. (2005). Dispelling myths: A real world perspective on Trinko. *Antitrust Bulletin, 50*, 590.

9 Drexl, J. (2004). IMS Health and Trinko—Antitrust placebo for consumers instead of sound economics in refusal-to-deal cases. *IIC, 35*, 797.

10 Sealink/B&I—Holyhead 1992 (9) Common Market Law Reports, 255.

11 1998 Access Notice, Para. 91: —In order to determine whether access should be ordered under the competition rules, account will be taken of a breach by the dominant company of the following elements, taken cumulatively: (a) access to the facility in question is generally essential in order for companies to compete on that related market; (b) there is sufficient capacity available to provide access; (c) the facility owner fails to satisfy demand in an existing service or product market, blocks the emergence of a potential new service or product, or impedes competition on an existing or potential service or product market;(d) the company seeking access is prepared to pay the reasonable and non-discriminatory price and will otherwise in all respects accept non-discriminatory terms and conditions; there is no objective justification for refusing to provide access.

12 Joined cases C-241/91 P and C-242/91 P, 1995 ECR I-743 (decided on April 6, 1995).

13 The additional requirement of a new product being prevented seems unjustified since competition by substitution of a new product (dynamic efficiency) is excluded by the refusal, then at least competition by imitation shall be allowed to achieve allocative efficiency, see Drexl, J. (2004). IMS Health and Trinko–antitrust placebo for consumers instead of sound economics in refusal-to-deal cases. *IIC, 35*, 806.

itself constitute an abuse of a dominant position. . . . It is only in exceptional circumstances that the exercise of the exclusive right by the owner of the intellectual property right may give rise to such an abuse and that, accordingly, it is permissible, in the public interest in maintaining effective competition on the market, to encroach upon the exclusive right of the holder of the intellectual property right by requiring him to grant licences to third parties seeking to enter or remain on that market.

The following circumstances, in particular, must be considered to be exceptional: in the first place, the refusal relates to a product or service indispensable to the exercise of a particular activity on a neighboring market; in the second place, the refusal is of such a kind as to exclude any effective competition on that neighboring market; in the third place, the refusal prevents the appearance of a new product for which there is potential consumer demand.[14]

1.1.3. Germany

Germany first introduced the EF doctrine into individual laws on network industries (railroads, telecommunications, electricity, airport, and post) to facilitate access,[15] then in 1999 into the Law against Constraints of Competition, namely Article 19(4) No. 4. It serves as one of the examples of abuse of dominant position, however, is not applicable to IP according to the legislative reasoning:

In particular, it is an abuse of dominance when the dominant undertaking for goods or services refuses another undertaking access to its own network or infrastructure facilities at reasonable prices, without the shared use of which it is de facto or de jure impossible for the latter to compete against the dominant undertaking in the upstream or downstream market.

In the 2004 "Spundfass" (tight drum) decision of the German Federal Court of Justice had a chance to interpret Article 19(4) No. 4 and its relationship with the compulsory license regime of the Patent Act.[16] The case involved an indus-

14 Case T-201/04 *Microsoft Corp. v. EC* (decided on September 17, 2007), paras. 6 and 643.

15 Fuchs in Immenga/Mestmäcker, §19 Rdnr. 257 (C.H. Beck, GWB 6. Aufl., 2020).

16 For an English translation of the case and comment by Matthias Leistner at 36 IIC 741–752 (2005). The case involved an industry standard developed jointly by four leading companies in the chemical industry in Germany, which are all members of the "Association of Chemical Industry (VCI)," namely the plaintiff, K, S, and vL. The technical method based on the patent held by plaintiff was adopted in the "VCI framework conditions for the new L-ring-bottle, 31.7.1990" endorsed by major players such as BASF, Bayer, Hoechst, and Hüls. The plaintiff granted licenses to K, S, and vL free of charge, and to other bottle manufacturers in return for a royalty. However, on July 17, 1996, the plaintiff declined to license its patent to the defendant, which was a subsidiary of an Italian bottle maker and sued the defendant for patent infringement. On February 9, 1999, the plaintiff obtained an injunction from Düsseldorf district court which prohibited the sale of the bottles in question. The defendant justified its use of the patent by claiming that the plaintiff was obliged to grant a free

try standard developed jointly by four leading companies in the chemical industry in Germany, which are all members of the "Association of Chemical Industry (VCI)," namely the plaintiff, K, S, and vL. The technical method based on the patent held by plaintiff was adopted in the "VCI framework conditions for the new L-ring-bottle, 31.7.1990" endorsed by major players such as BASF, Bayer, Hoechst, and Hüls. The plaintiff granted licenses to K, S, and vL free of charge, and to other bottle manufacturers in return for a royalty. However, on July 17, 1996, the plaintiff declined to license its patent to the defendant, which was a subsidiary of an Italian bottle maker and sued the defendant for patent infringement. On February 9, 1999, the plaintiff obtained an injunction from Düsseldorf district court which prohibited the sale of the bottles in question. The defendant justified its use of the patent by claiming that the plaintiff was obliged to grant a free license. The District Court ruled in the plaintiff's favor. The defendant appealed the decision and filed a counterclaim for the free use of the patent. Both the appeal and the counterclaim were rejected by the Appellate Court. But the Federal Court of Justice overruled the decision and remanded the case back to the Appellate Court.

The Federal Court of Justice first established that the licensing of the patent at issue is for itself a relevant market and separated from the downstream relevant product (L-ring-bottles) market. It then determined that the use of the patented method cannot be replaced by another technical arrangement for the chemical industry, because the "VCI framework conditions for the new L-ring-bottle" could only be met by following the patented teaching, and most companies in the German chemical industry would buy only bottles complying with the VCI framework conditions. The Court further reasoned that a patent also protects the potential to expand the formal exclusive position in the market to a commercial monopoly. So, in principle, there is a significant leeway for the justification of unequal treatment of undertakings seeking to license the patent. However, when on top of the market dominance by the patent additional circumstances would make unequal treatment a threat to the freedom of competition protected by the Act against Constraints of Competition, stricter requirements must apply. In the present case, the market dominance was not just based on the patent, but also on the fact that the access to the downstream product market required compliance with the patented method. As the market-dominating enterprise arbitrarily denied access to the downstream market, it fell afoul of competition rules. By holding that IP rights incorporated in standards can be "infrastructure facilities," the Federal Court of Justice went in fact beyond the original intent of Article 19(4) No. 4 which excludes IP rights from being made subject to forced access.

The Court also clarified that because Article 20(1) of the Act against Constraints of Competition and Article 24 of the Patent Act serve different purposes and have

license. The district court ruled in the plaintiff's favor. The defendant appealed the decision and filed a counterclaim for the free use of the patent. Both the appeal and the counterclaim were rejected by the Appellate Court. But the Federal Court of Justice overruled the decision and remanded the case back to the Appellate Court.

different pre-conditions, compulsory access due to the abuse of dominant position or unjustifiable discrimination may be ordered based on the former notwithstanding the exclusive jurisdiction of the Federal Patent Court to grant compulsory licenses under Article 24 of the Patent Act.[17]

In the 2009 "Orange-Book-Standard" case the Federal Court of Justice followed its pro-patentee approach to avoiding holdout by the license-seeker by applying Article 20(3) of the Act against Constraints of Competition[18] to the injunctive relief filed by the dominant patentee. It ruled that such application could have violated Article 20(3), provided however that (I) the defendant has made an unconditional offer to sign the licensing agreement and (II) started paying royalties into an escrow account for patentee or provided guarantee for royalty payment.[19] As a remedy for such a violation, a compulsory license of the patent could be ordered.

1.2. Secor-Specific Competition Law: Communications Law

1.2.1. The WTO Reference Paper

The daily routine of interconnection and roaming is only possible with the help of compulsory license of incumbent dominant players' assets, including IP, and facilities. Therefore, the General Agreement on Trade in Services (GATS) of the WTO puts trade in telecommunications within its ambit. An Annex on Telecommunications (AT) was adopted which provides foreign suppliers with access to and use of public telecommunications networks and services on reasonable and non-discriminatory terms:[20]

> Each Member shall ensure that any service supplier of any other Member is accorded access to and use of public telecommunications transport networks and services on reasonable and non-discriminatory terms and conditions, for the supply of a service included in its Schedule. (Paragraph 5(a))

However, the term "access and use" does not cover interconnection, that is, the physical and logical linking of two competing telecommunications networks.[21] During the post-Uruguay Round negotiations in basic telecommunications, the negotiation group agreed on a set of definitions and principles on the regulatory framework for the basic telecommunications services that were summarized on April 24, 1996, as the Reference Paper (RP). The RP is a unique document in the

17 German Federal Court of Justice KZR 40/02 (decided on July 13, 2004).

18 Article 20(3) Act against Constraints of Competition prohibits conduct of undertakings with relative or superior market power against small or medium-sized enterprises: "Undertakings with superior market power in relation to small and medium-sized competitors may not abuse their market position to impede such competitors directly or indirectly in an unfair manner."

19 German Federal Court of Justice KZR 39/06 (decided on May 6, 2009), Para. 33.

20 Mathew, B. (2003). *The WTO Agreements on Telecommunications* (p. 52). Lang.

21 Mathew, B. (2003). *The WTO Agreements on Telecommunications* (p. 52). Lang, 103.

history of the WTO in the sense that it is a binding document derived from Article XVIII GATS,[22] rather than an amendment to GATS or AT which would require ratification by two-thirds of WTO members.

At least 82 WTO members have subscribed to this additional regulatory commitment as of August 2021. The RP defines essential facilities as facilities of a public telecommunications transport network or service that, (I) are exclusively or predominantly provided by a single or limited number of suppliers; and (II) cannot feasibly be economically or technically substituted to provide a service. A supplier which has the ability to materially affect the terms of participation in the relevant market for basic telecommunications services as a result of control over essential facilities is characterized as a major supplier. Major suppliers are subject to the obligation of interconnecting with other suppliers according to Paragraph 2 of the RP.[23]

1.2.2. The US

As mentioned in Subsection 4.1 of Chapter 3, the 1996 US Telecommunications Act imposes many duties on incumbent monopolistic LECs to share their essential facilities with their competitors, such as providing access to rights-of-way and three kinds of access, including the duty to offer access to unbundled network elements on "just, reasonable, and non-discriminatory" terms. A rival can interconnect its own facilities with those of the incumbent LEC, or it can simply purchase services at wholesale rates from the incumbent and resell them to consumers. The Act also imposes upon incumbents the duty to allow physical collocation.

The FCC began in 2008 to intervene in contractual arrangements between satellite cable programming vendors, cable operators, and satellite broadcast programming vendors, as these would control the distribution of programming. In accordance with the Program Access Rule added by the 1992 Cable Television Consumer Protection and Competition Act, the FCC requires that exclusive contracts between cable operators, satellite cable programming vendors in which a cable operator has an attributable interest or satellite broadcast programming

22 Article XVIII GATS reads: "Members may negotiate measures affecting trade in services, <u>including</u> those regarding qualifications, standards or licensing matters."

23 Paragraph 2.1 first delineates the general coverage of interconnection. Paragraph 2.2 then articulates the ways in which interconnection with major suppliers at any technically feasible point is to be ensured: "(I) under non-discriminatory terms, conditions (including technical standards and specifications) and rates and of a quality no less favorable than that provided for its own services or for similar services of non-affiliated service suppliers or for its subsidiaries or other affiliates; (II) in a timely fashion, on terms, conditions (including technical standards and specifications) and cost-oriented rates that are transparent, reasonable, having regard to economic feasibility, and sufficiently unbundled so that the supplier need not pay for network components or facilities that it does not require for the service to be provided; and (III) upon request, at points in addition to the network termination points offered to the majority of users, subject to charges that reflect the cost of construction of necessary additional facilities."

vendors in which a cable operator has an attributable interest in an area served by a cable operator must be approved by the FCC in advance. The purpose of the Program Access Rule is to prevent exclusive contracts from constraining or even blocking the use of copyrighted works. Under the Rule, cable companies are required in many contexts to make their own programming available on reasonable terms to providers of rival platforms, a de facto compulsory licensing mechanism.[24] In addition, the must-carry regulation under the 1992 Cable Television Consumer Protection and Competition Act is, in essence, a compulsory license-like arrangement between a CATV provider's system and local TV stations. Just that it is for free.

1.2.3. The UK

The issue of ensuring fair and effective competition has been an acute problem in the live broadcasting of premium sports events, due to the following reasons: (I) They retain an enduring appeal for many UK consumers; (II) access to this content has driven the development of pay TV in the UK; and (III) for many years Sky had held the exclusive rights to broadcast many of the most sought-after premium sports and therefore had market power in the wholesale of these channels. After reckoning the fact that Sky's market position was unlikely to change in the following few years, the Office of Communications (Ofcom) on March 31, 2010, exercised its powers under Section 316 of the Communications Act to ensure fair and effective competition and issued the "Pay TV Statement."

The Pay TV Statement foresaw a coming market failure and therefore imposed compulsory license on Sky by requiring Sky to offer the most important sports channels, Sky Sports 1 and Sky Sports 2, to retailers on platforms other than Sky's at wholesale prices set by Ofcom and approved Arqiva's request for Sky to offer its own pay TV services on digital terrestrial TV (Picnic), but conditional on a wholesale must-offer obligation on Sky Sports 1 and 2 being put in place. This conclusion was also conditional on any movie channels included in Picnic being offered to other digital terrestrial TV retailers.[25] After a period of about five years, Ofcom removed the wholesale must-offer obligation from Sky in 2015, given that existing pay TV providers have grown (BT and TalkTalk), new providers have entered (e.g., EE), or planned to enter (e.g., Vodafone), and there was also wider availability of sports content.[26]

24 Nuechterlein, J., & Weiser, P. (2005). *Digital Crossroads* (p. 370). MIT Press.

25 Ofcom, Pay TV Statement 2010, at: https://www.ofcom.org.uk/__data/assets/pdf_file/0021/55470/paytv_statement.pdf, 1–2.

26 Ofcom, Review of the pay TV wholesale must-offer obligation 2015, at: https://www.ofcom.org.uk/__data/assets/pdf_file/0022/76081/Review-of-the-pay-TV-wholesale-must-offer-obligation-pdf, 3

2. Theoretical Analysis of a Competition-Oriented Compulsory Licensing

2.1. Justification

The German IP polymath Joseph Kohler argued in 1900 for compulsory patent licensing from the perspective of social obligation of the patentee "to work one's patents" pursuant to the then German Patent Act. He reasoned that:

> the underlying idea of such a statutory principle is the following: when one is free to exercise his/her right or not to, it is then just when his/her slowness does not bring significant disadvantages to the general public. However, when it does, the individual may not deprive the people of the cultural achievements by not exercising (his/her right). The exercise of rights then becomes a social obligation. This applies whenever the right-owner possesses a monopolistic position, so as not to deprive the country or his/her fellow men of the whole legal regime. (Rechtsgut)[27]

Therefore, we can identify inherent competition policy considerations in the compulsory licensing regimes of international IP treaties,[28] ad hoc and haphazard yet undoubtedly for preserving market competition, especially when IP rightsholders and commercial exploiters find themselves in gridlock and cannot agree on the terms and conditions of licensing (such as the constellation in the recorded music industry and broadcasting industry). IP laws of IP-advanced countries also endorse a broad scope of compulsory licensing of IPRs.

This chapter advocates and argues for a general compulsory licensing doctrine that should be considered as an inherent and integral element of all IPRs, except trademarks, for preserving and fostering market competition.[29] An IP-internal compulsory license regime should be generally established around the theme of preserving and fostering of market competition.[30] In other words, future IPs should internalize competition policy considerations.

2.1.1. Patents/Utility Models

Along with worldwide rampant proliferation of patents comes the threat to the ideals of open science and free exchange of creative ideas and to follow on research

27 Kohler, J. (1900). *Handbuch des deutschen patentrechts in rechtsvergleichender darstellung* (p. 613). J. Bensheimer.

28 Hilty, R. (2009). Renaissance der Zwangzlizezen im Urheberrecht? *GRUR*, 633, 641–642.

29 Other public interest considerations, such as the prevention of and dealing with epidemics, and access to information for education purposes (arguably education is undeniably the basis for competition, however, it is a bit moot), that could also trigger compulsory license will not be discussed. Therefore, this chapter will not discuss the Appendix of the Berne Convention which foresees compulsory license for developing members in an overly strict, complex, and ambiguous manner.

30 Hilty, R. (2009). Renaissance der Zwangzlizenzen im Urheberrecht. *GRUR*, 643.

and its application.[31] Never before, has the issue of patent blockage and compatibility (forward and backward) become so important. Cross-licensing and patent pools have limited alleviating effects.[32]

Various types of exemptions as solutions for the anti-commons and blockage problem, ranging from a fair use exception to the exclusive rights of patents, to an opt-in exemption, and to forfeiture, have been proposed.[33] However, compulsory patent licensing is by far the least intrusive and the most easy-to-operate method. Therefore, it would be desirable to recognize that the maintenance of competition is a public policy objective worthy of protection via compulsory patent licensing.[34] The same can be said of utility models.

2.1.2. Copyright and Other IPRs

Traditionally, copyright has little to do with competition law due to its less exclusive character. But the time has changed. Copyright can impede competition much the same way as patents, exemplified by the Microsoft case discussed in Subsection 4.1 of Chapter 1.[35] The European Copyright Code proposed by the Wittem Group in 2010 rightly points out this danger and advocates that copyright law should reflect the core (European) principles and values of law, including freedom of competition (freedom of expression and information as well, Preamble).[36] It therefore suggests that compulsory license be granted for the use of news articles, scientific works, industrial designs, computer programs, and databases against payment of a negotiated remuneration,[37] provided that

> (i) the use is indispensable to compete on a derivative market; (ii) the owner of the copyright in the work has refused to license the use on reasonable

31 Wang, L.-D. (2008). Biomedical upstream patenting and scientific research: The case for compulsory licenses bearing reach-through royalties. *Yale Journal of Law and Technology*, *10*, 253.

32 Wang, L.-D. (2008). Biomedical upstream patenting and scientific research: The case for compulsory licenses bearing reach-through royalties. *Yale Journal of Law and Technology*, *10*, 307–312.

33 For a summary of all the suggestions, see Wang, L.-D. (2008). Biomedical upstream patenting and scientific research: The case for compulsory licenses bearing reach-through royalties. *Yale Journal of Law and Technology*, *10*, 315–318.

34 Liu, K.-C. (2008). Rationalizing the regime of compulsory patent licensing by the essential facilities doctrine. *IIC*, *39(7)*, 757, 773; Podszun, R. (2010). Lizenzverweigerung-Ernstfall im Verhältnis von Kartell-und Immaterialgüterrecht. In Matousek, P., Mueller, E., & Thanner, T. (Eds.), *Jahrbuch Kartell und Wettbewerbsrecht* (pp. 57, 74). NWV.

35 For a discussion of this topic see Ramello, G.B. (2003). Copyrights and antitrust issues. In Gordon, W.J., & Watt, R. (Eds.), *The Economics of Copyright* (pp. 118–147). Edward Elgar Publishing.

36 The European Copyright Code is the result of the Wittem Project established in 2002 as collaboration between copyright scholars across the EU concerned with the future development of European copyright law. Its Drafting Committee is composed of Lionel Bently, Thomas Dreier, Reto Hilty, Bernt Hugenholtz, Antoon Quaedvlieg, Alain Strowel, and Dirk Visser. Available at: http://www.copyrightcode.eu.

37 According to footnote 54 of the European Copyright Code, the term negotiated remuneration means that the compulsory license fee is to be negotiated in individual cases and therefore does not imply a role for collective rights management.

> terms, leading to the elimination of competition in the relevant market, and (iii) the use does not unreasonably prejudice the legitimate interests of the owner of the copyright in the work. (Article 5.4)

Other IPRs, such as designs, registered and unregistered alike, IC-layout designs, and plant variety rights, all have similar competition concerns, and should be subject to compulsory licensing as well.

2.2. Functions

2.2.1. To Restore an Integral Part of IP

Currently, advanced countries have in general better integrated compulsory license with their respective economic and social life. However, IP less-developed countries, which are at the besiege of a hostile international environment, are easily tempted to constantly, consciously, or not, narrow down the scope of compulsory licensing (Taiwan as an example),[38] and deterred from applying compulsory licensing to preserve and foster competition. "Developing countries that wish to retain their autonomous powers to exploit the flexibility inherent in the TRIPS standards will sooner or later have to devise appropriate national and regional strategies for sustaining and enhancing this autonomy."[39] Only with the help of a generalized theory and doctrine can compulsory licensing be reinstated to IP family, so that especially developing countries can embrace compulsory licensing to preserve competition in their domestic markets.

2.2.2. To Alleviate the Over-Burdened Fair Use

Fair use as an overarching limitation to IP rights can be highly uncertain country by country, sometimes its application can be even less certain than throwing at a dartboard. Once recognized as fair use, no compensation or remuneration is required at all. However, this in many cases may not be really "fair" to rightsholders. This is the zero-sum dilemma of fair use, which may reduce the application of fair use exceptions or push its use to the extreme.

During pandemics, such as SARS (Severe Acute Respiratory Syndrome) and COVID-19, which tend to happen more frequently, the noble call for "waiver of patent"[40] is something equivalent to free fair use and simply not feasible and pale.

38 Liu, K.-C. (2015). Compulsory license and government use in Taiwan-A regress. In Liu, K.-C., & Hilty, R. (Eds.), *Compulsory Licensing—Practical Experiences and Ways Forward, Max Planck Asian Intellectual Property Law Series* (pp. 79–93). Springer.

39 Reichman, J., & Hasenzahl, C. (2003). *Non-voluntary Licensing of Patented Inventions—Historical Perspective. Legal Framework under TRIPS and an Overview of the Practice in Canada and the USA* (p. 12), at: https://unctad.org/system/files/official-document/ictsd2003ipd5_en.pdf.

40 In 2020 India and South Africa started the initiative for a broad waiver of all IPRs protecting COVID-19 vaccines, as well as the rights over therapeutics and diagnostics. See Gabriele, S. (2022).

By contrast, compulsory license is not that extreme, it enhances availability of IP-protected subject matters with reasonable remuneration for rightsholders and can alleviate the over-burdened fair use, making patented vaccines available at affordable prices. The WTO adopted the Ministerial Decision on the TRIPS Agreement on June 17, 2022, to expressly recognize or reiterate that all developing country members as eligible members may authorize compulsory license of the subject matter of a patent, including ingredients and processes, required for the production and supply of COVID-19 vaccines.[41]

2.2.3. To Accelerate Voluntary Licensing

One can assume that the general possibility of granting a compulsory license alone poses a deterrent effect and enhances rightsholders' readiness to sign a licensing agreement.[42] Therefore, the ultimate goal of compulsory licensing is not to deprive IP holders of their rights, but only to function as the last resort to stimulate the patentee into working or voluntarily licensing the patent. From the perspective of royalty negotiation, compulsory license functions as a shift from entirely ex-ante (before use) negotiation to partially ex-ante and partially ex-post (after use) negotiation.

As such, compulsory license does not sabotage but rather accelerates voluntary licensing, because it avoids excessive costs incurred by prolonged negotiation.

> Patent negotiations can be complex and time-consuming. Resources devoted to negotiating in the ex-ante period must be taken from other projects and activities. Complete and detailed ex-ante negotiations come with opportunity costs. When these are high enough—when devoting resources to negotiating ex-ante would starve or drain a crucial activity such as product development—it makes sense to wait.[43]

Moreover, the partially ex-post approach in compulsory license to determining royalties can provide parties better basis upon which to estimate the real value of the

What Happened to the COVID-19 Vaccine Patent Waiver? at: https://blog.petrieflom.law.harvard.edu/2022/11/08/what-happened-to-the-covid-19-vaccine-patent-waiver/.

41 See https://docs.wto.org/dol2fe/Pages/SS/directdoc.aspx?filename=q:/WT/MIN22/30.pdf&Open=True.

42 Bently, L., & Sherman, B. (2014). *Intellectual Property Law* (4th ed., p. 651). Oxford University Press. However, some argue that "How far the threat of applying to the Comptroller enhances the bargaining position of would-be voluntary licensees cannot be measured. Neither can it be discounted." See Llewelyn, D., & Aplin, T. (2023). *Intellectual Property: Patents, Copyright, Trade Marks and Allied Rights* (10th ed., p. 294), 7–049. Sweet & Maxwell.

43 Merges, R. (2021). After the trolls: Patent litigation as ex-post market-making. *Akron Law Review, 54*, 559.

patents used because concrete outcomes derived from the actual use of patents will be at the parties' disposal.

> The more information the parties have, the more likely there will be some potential agreements that they both will think acceptable given the facts. In technical terms, revealed information increases the chances that the "bargaining ranges" of the parties will overlap.[44]

2.2.4. To Create Multiple Wins

It is human nature to make improvement to existent creation. In the 19th century, German composers could freely set the poems of others to music, leading to the special genre of Lieder. Franz Schubert composed the music of the Schoene Muellerin and the Winterreise without the permission of Wilhelm Mueller, and the Elkoenig without the permission of Johann von Goethe. However, the 1965 Copyright Act shut down the leeway with its rigid copyright, which regrettably led to the decline of Lieder.[45] This is a triple loss for authors of literate works, composers, and the art world.

In addition, modern public-listed corporations often run on short-term, quarterly, or even monthly,[46] basis and tend to grasp for immediate returns and get impatient about long-term rewards. The shorter their appointment is termed, the more impatient CEOs will become. Short-termism is bound to fail to apprehend the long-term benefits of helping competitors and fostering a competitive environment.

Suppose I was the author of the song "Happy Birthday," allegedly the most popular song on earth, and I intuitively would tend to refuse to license it to my competitors. If that happens, the world will be bored by my singing as no others are allowed to sing, the sale of my songs will plummet, and others are prevented from enriching this song. However, if I am required by law to issue licenses to my competitors, then there will be more competition, cultural diversity, and even more revenue for me, as my competitors will have to pay me royalty every time they compete with me. This will create a win-win-win situation. Essentially, compulsory license help us overcome our human nature of short-termism.

44 Merges, R. (2021). After the trolls: Patent litigation as ex-post market-making. *Akron Law Review, 54*, 562.

45 Baldwin, P. (2014). *The Copyright War—Three Centuries of Trans-Atlantic Battle* (p. 5). Princeton University Press.

46 In the popular exchange-traded funds (ETF), which is a type of investment fund that is also an exchange-traded product, sector there are a plethora of major firms, including State Street Global Advisors, Vanguard Group, and BlackRock that pay out monthly dividends. See https://www.investopedia.com/investing/monthly-dividend-etfs/.

3. To Solve Two Thorny Issues

3.1. To Determine the Reasonable Remuneration

Perhaps the most commonly raised objection against compulsory license is that it is impossible to determine the reasonable remuneration to be paid to IP rightsholders. The German Federal Court of Justice states in the "Orange-Book-Standard" decision that if the license-seeker alleges that the royalty demanded by the patentee was excessively high reaching the extent of abuse, or the patentee refused to specify the royalty, then the license-seeker should be allowed to determine a reasonable royalty in accordance with equitable standards. Otherwise, the license-seeker would risk overpaying the patentee in order to satisfy the requirement of making an unconditional offer to sign a licensing agreement.[47]

There are at least three separate methods to determine reasonable compensation, which can be used individually, alternatively, and/or cumulatively.

3.1.1. Looking into the Original Licensing Agreement

Oftentimes some proxies for a fair remuneration can be found readily available by looking into the original licensing agreement between the parties at dispute. In the Phillips CD-R cases in Taiwan, for example, the agreed method of calculating royalty was initially 3% of the net sales price. It was only supplemented by a price-floor clause, namely not lower than ¥10 per disc. When ¥10 per disc becomes anti-competitively high, the 3% of net sales price could be the fallback presumption for being the reasonable remuneration. Of course, the patentee can argue otherwise and deny such an assumption of *prima facie* reasonableness. However, the burden of proof shall rest with him/her to substantiate the denial.

3.1.2. License Analogy

Another common method of determining royalty rate for compulsory license is by comparison with relevant or comparable rates charged by the patentee or other players in the industry for similar licenses.

In the context of employees' invention derived from the course of employment in Germany, the minister of Labour and Social Affairs (Der Bundesminister für Arbeit und Soziales) issued Guidelines on Compensation for Employees' Invention[48] (in 1959 and revised in 1983) to mediate the differences between employers and employees over the to be paid remuneration. The Guidelines adopt the "license analogy" (Liznenanalogie) method. The Arbitration Panel under the German Patent and Trademark Office will be called upon when employees and employers cannot

47 BGH KZR 39/06 (decided May 6, 2009), paragraphs 38, 39.

48 The German title is "Richtlinien für die Vergütung von Arbeitnehmererfindungen im privaten Dienst."

reach agreement on the amount of compensation.[49] In order to discharge its duty, the Arbitration Panel has been actively collecting license rates from different branches, classifying them according to the international patent classification. The Panel also publishes Licensing Rates for Technical Inventions (Lizenzsätze für technische Erfindungen). In more than sixty years this practice has proved to a success.[50]

3.1.3. Twenty-Five Percent Classic Rule

In addition, a fairly simple and straightforward "25 Percent Classic Rule'" ("Classic Rule") has been established and adopted by US courts over the last 40 years, according to which the licensee pays a royalty rate equivalent to 25% of his/her expected profits for the product that incorporates the IP at issue until the CAFC decided otherwise in 2011 in *Unilock v. Microsoft*.

> This court now holds as a matter of Federal Circuit law that the 25 percent rule of thumb is a fundamentally flawed tool for determining a baseline royalty rate in a hypothetical negotiation. Evidence relying on the 25 percent rule of thumb is thus inadmissible under Daubert and the Federal Rules of Evidence, because it fails to tie a reasonable royalty base to the facts of the case at issue.[51]

However, the leading proponent of the Classic 25 Percent Rule for the last fifty years, Robert Goldscheider rebutted: this rule is not a "wooden and inflexible methodology" and as a sensitive methodology, whose widespread acceptance has been merited and guaranteed its longevity in the licensing profession, "it will, regardless of how courts view the admissibility of the Classic 25% Rule, continue to guide the outcome of thousands of IP licensing transaction (not involving litigation) throughout the world."[52]

The Classic Rule has been useful not only in valuating patents but also in valuating copyright, trade secrets and know-how contexts.[53] The focus of the Rule is placed on long-term and fully-loaded profits.[54] More specifically, one empirical study suggests that:

> the reported royalty rates across industries do not converge with the rates generated by the 25 percent rule at industry level, although they generally fall

49 Article 28 of the German Act on Employees' Inventions.

50 Hellebrand, O., & Rabe, Di-H. (2021). *Lizenzsätze für technische Erfindungen* (6 Aufl.). Carl Heymanns.

51 632 F.3d 1315 (Fed. Cir. 2011).

52 Goldscheider, R. (2011). The classic 25% rule and the art of intellectual property licensing. *Duke Law and Technology Review*, *10*, 1–23.

53 Goldscheider, R., Jarosz, J., & Mulhern, C. (2007). Use of the twenty-five percent rule in valuating intellectual property. In Parr, R. (Ed.), *Royalty Rates for Licensing Intellectual Property* (p. 31). Wiley.

54 Goldscheider, R., Jarosz, J., & Mulhern, C. (2007). Use of the twenty-five percent rule in valuating intellectual property. In Parr, R. (Ed.), *Royalty Rates for Licensing Intellectual Property* (p. 34). Wiley.

> between 25 percent of gross profit margins and 25 percent of operating profit margins. Also, the EBITDA (earnings before interest, taxes, depreciation, and amortization) margin seems to be a more reasonable base upon which to apply the 25 percent rule compared to gross margin and EBIT (earnings before interest and taxes) margin.[55]

It is fair to say that the Classic 25% Rule serves as a good starting point for royalty negotiations and calculation of reasonable remuneration.

In the situation where a number of complementary patents held by different patentees, the Rule might not be applicable. It is because the question of how to calculate the expected profits of these patents which are in many different hands is simply insolvable. In this case, it is similar to the licensing of a group of essential patents, not necessarily SEPs. Then the discussion about a lump-sum or aggregate royalty at 3.2 of Chapter 10 is likely more applicable.[56]

3.2. To Issue the Absolutely Necessary Ancillary Orders

Compulsory licenses are always granted with conditions and limitations, such as the period, place and price, and arrangements for averting the likelihood of confusion and assuring quality. For example, if a vaccine was made with a compulsory license of a patent, then it is likely that such a license came with the condition that the manufacturer be subject to the surveillance of the patentee, and products so made should not be represented in a confusingly similar way as those of the patentee.[57]

Once issued, a compulsory license should be implemented effectively and fairly by the licensee. The licensee should be allowed to apply with the issuing agency for ancillary orders that are required to make such a license work. Many licensees lack the capacity to implement the issued compulsory license and are therefore dependent on licensors for assistance. Then know-how assistance/transfer orders conditioned on the payment of a reasonable fee could be in order.

However, this is a strong interference into the patentee's sphere and could be done only in exceptional cases, especially when and only to the extent that providing such assistance is easily within the patentee's capacity. Then, such know-how assistance/transfer orders could be issued. The enforcement of these orders could be by imposing fines and/or exempting third parties who have access to the necessary

55 Kemmerer, J., & Lu, J. (November 2012). *Profitability and Royalty Rates Across Industries: Some Preliminary Evidence*. KPMG Global Valuation Institute, at: https://papers.ssrn.com/sol3/papers.cfm?abstract_id=1141865.

56 Some argue for a compulsory license system that charges reach-through royalties, which are measured by the contribution that patented research inputs make to the individual research, see Wang, L.-D. (2008). Biomedical upstream patenting and scientific research: The case for compulsory licenses bearing reach-through royalties. *Yale Journal of Law and Technology, 10*, 251.

57 Wang, L.-D. (2015). Ancillary orders of compulsory licensing and their compatibility with the TRIPS agreement. In Liu, K.-C., & Hilty, R. (Eds.), *Compulsory Licensing—Practical Experiences and Ways Forward* (pp. 197–198). Springer.

information from trade secret infringement liability if they release the information to the licensee.[58]

For example, the US Supreme Court allowed the sharing of certain information at a reasonable charge by one defendant with another defendant which is its leading competitor:

> The District Court (for the Southern District of New York) did not exceed its discretion in requiring that, during a period of three years, defendants make available to licensees under their patents at a reasonable charge, certain information in writing as to the methods and processes used by the licensor at the date of licensing. . . . Since the public interest requires that the court be permitted to produce the most effective and generally fair decree that it can devise to give effect simultaneously to the antitrust laws and the patent laws, the decree represents a permissible exercise of judicial discretion—even though it includes, within narrow limits, disclosure of technical information by one defendant to another defendant which is its leading competitor.[59]

4. To Revise the TRIPS Agreement

Preamble(e) of the TRIPS Agreement already recognizes, "the underlying public policy objectives of national systems for the protection of intellectual property, including developmental and technological objectives." Article 7 further recognizes economic welfare as a public policy objective, so that the protection and enforcement of IPRs should contribute to the promotion of technological innovation and to the transfer and dissemination of technology, to the mutual advantage of producers and users of technological knowledge and in a manner conducive to social and economic welfare, and to a balance of rights and obligations.

However, this declaratory statement alone is not enough to make compulsory license a workable institution that furthers the balance between IPR protection and public interest. A new Article 8bis, to generally allow compulsory licensing of IP, which would obviate Article 31,[60] is needed. It could stipulate:

1. Each member has the right to grant compulsory licenses of IP and the freedom to determine the grounds upon which such licensees are granted.[61]

58 Wang, L.-D. (2015). Ancillary orders of compulsory licensing and their compatibility with the TRIPS agreement. In Liu, K.-C., & Hilty, R. (Eds.), *Compulsory Licensing—Practical Experiences and Ways Forward* (pp. 196–197). Springer.

59 *United States v. National Lead Co.*, 332 US 353, 358 (1947).

60 Alternatively, Article 31 of the TRIPs Agreement can be revised by deleting the carveout of semi-conductor technology, the requirements that cripple the compulsory license of dependent patents and allow it to be applied to other IP by analogy.

61 Borrowed from 5(b) Declaration on the TRIPS agreement and public health adopted on November 14, 2001 by the WTO.

2. Members may issue individual compulsory license, especially in the following situations:

   (1) Where domestic demand for IP (except trademarks and GIs)-protected products or service is not being met on reasonable terms, or the development or establishment of commercial or industrial activities in the Member is prejudiced by unreasonable licensing conditions imposed upon of IP,
   (2) Where an essential patent held by a dominant undertaking, which is indispensable for others to compete against the dominant undertaking in the upstream or downstream market due to legal (e.g. de jure standards) or factual reasons (competitor's inability practically or reasonably to duplicate the essential patent), but was refused without justifiable reasons to license those good-faith license-seekers who failed to reach voluntary licensing agreement after a reasonable period of negotiation on reasonable conditions.
   (3) Where a later IP (the second IP) cannot be exploited without infringing another prior IP (the first IP).

3. The licensee of a compulsory license must deposit or pay the reasonable remuneration before using the IP at issue for the benefit of the rightsholders.
4. In the case of compulsory licensing of the dependent second IP, the owner of the first IP shall be entitled to a cross-license on similar terms to use the second IP.
5. Members may also make compulsory license available as of right by for example making a registration on the IP registry.

The need of a compulsory license can be equally existent for many other license seekers who are in the same or similar situation as the applicant or grantee of a compulsory license. It is pointless and wasteful to ask them to go through individual application procedures again and again. Therefore, the UK adopted the license of right mechanism in its patent, design, and copyright regimes, and the US adopted the "open to use" declaration in its Plant Variety Protection Act of 1970.

The TRIPS Agreement should be amended to expressly allow compulsory license as a right so that non-applicants and non-complainants could resort automatically to the compulsory licenses granted to the applicants or complainants. Consequently, a non-applicant, who has previously concluded a voluntary licensing agreement with the patentee, may replace it with the later compulsory one.

Part III

Aggregating IP

The large number of IPRs and their intricate inner relationship hampers compliance even by professional people. IP thicket arises when too many IPs covering individual elements of a product are separately owned by different entities,[1] resembling the issue of anti-common in real property when there is excessive fragmentation of ownership in a single parcel of land. Therefore, efforts must be made to aggregate IPRs to ease the licensing of IPRs.[2] However, this inevitably involves concentration of rights in an organized fashion, which can restrain or even exclude market competition. Again, the theme of the book is touched upon.

Therefore, the third Part of the book dedicates two chapters to discussing how the right balance between licensing efficiency and free and fair competition can be found. Chapter 7 dives into patent pools, the oldest and most effective arrangement for aggregating patents, leaving a related mechanism, the FRAND licensing of SEPs through SSOs, to the fourth part of the book after Chapter 8 that takes on work pools and trademark pool of sorts, the database of well-known trademarks.

1 Shapiro, C. (2001). Navigating the patent thicket: Cross licenses, patent pools, and standard-setting. In Jaffe, A., Lerner, J., and Stern, S. (Eds.), *Innovation Policy and the Economy* (Vol. 1, pp. 119–121). MIT Press.

2 With similar concern in mind, Richard Gilbert discusses the benefits, costs and antitrust safeguards of the so-called collective rights organizations which include at least patent pools, copyright collectives and cross-licensing arrangements, See Gilbert, R. (2017). *Collective Rights Organizations: A Guide to Benefits, Costs and Antitrust Safeguards*, at SSRN: https://ssrn.com/abstract=2904739.

DOI: 10.4324/9781003597766-9

7 Patent Pools

1. The Development and Function of Patent Pools[1]

Patent pools are "licensing arrangements in which multiple patent owners agree to license their patents to each other, third parties, or both" and "have existed in some form for nearly two centuries,[2] dating back to the sewing machine war of the 1850s in the US that was solved by the privately formed Sewing Machine Combination of 1856 until its last patent expired in 1877."[3]

In the early 20th century, America witnessed two major patent pools which have lasted very long and cemented the global leadership of the US industry. One was the Automobile Manufacturers Association (AMA) formed by the auto industry in 1914.

The auto industry is a complex one with thousands of components that can be covered by hundreds of patents in the hands of dispersed patent holders. However, auto patent litigation never seems to have grown beyond a manageable level, mostly due to AMA. AMA is an industry-wide, royalty-free patent-sharing arrangement that encourages peace and waiver by including only "commodity" patents, and preserves incentives to perform pioneering R&D by excluding revolutionary patents from the pool.[4] The other major patent pool was The Manufacturers' Aircraft Association (MAA) mandated by the government in 1917 when the American aircraft industry was stymied by the difficulties of sorting out the patents of the Wright Brothers and Glenn Curtiss and could not keep up with the need of World War I. The MAA also runs on a royalty-free basis yet allows members to ask for a

1 Patent pools for drugs, such as Medicines Patent Pool, are for life-saving purpose that is not related to the theme of the volume and will therefore not be discussed.

2 Jurata, J., & Luken, E. (2021). Glory days: Do the anti-competitive risks of standards-essential patent pools outweigh their procompetitive benefits? *San Diego Law Review, 58*, 418, at SSRN: https://ssrn.com/abstract=3622615.

3 Mossoff, A. (2011). The rise and fall of the first American patent thicket: The sewing machine war of the 1850s. *Arizona Law Review, 53*, 166, at: https://papers.ssrn.com/sol3/papers.cfm?abstract_id=1354849.

4 Mossoff, A. (2011). The rise and fall of the first American patent thicket: The sewing machine war of the 1850s. *Arizona Law Review, 53*, 166, at: https://papers.ssrn.com/sol3/papers.cfm?abstract_id=1354849, 325–327.

DOI: 10.4324/9781003597766-10

special royalty for making an extra contribution to the pool which will be decided by a board of arbitration.[5]

Both the AMA and MAA have played a significant role in the growth and development of the American industry. Both were challenged by overzealous antitrust enforcement in the 1960s. The AMA was eventually abandoned[6] and the MAA was dissolved in 1977.[7] Patent pools later proliferated internationally and have become a critically effective mechanism for both the deployment of new technology and patent enforcement.

More recently, many patent pools from two areas, namely audio and video pools[8] and mobile telecom pools,[9] were assessed by the USDOJ pursuant to its Business Review Procedure.[10]

Patent pools provide "one-stop-shopping" services to multiple parties on both sides of patent licensing games that ease up the take-up of new technologies, standards, and products. Patent pools set and charge a single price for use of the pooled patents and are therefore "more formal than FRAND commitments"[11] and therefore "comparatively rare compared to FRAND commitments."[12] Patent pools solve the patent thicket issue by offering transparency, clarity, cost-saving, and assurance of no holdup by patentees.[13] "Patent pools function according to liability rules," as "they provide a regularized transactional mechanism in place of the statutory property rule baseline which requires an individual bargain for each transaction."[14]

5 Mossoff, A. (2011). The rise and fall of the first American patent thicket: The sewing machine war of the 1850s. *Arizona Law Review*, *53*, 166, at: https://papers.ssrn.com/sol3/papers.cfm?abstract_id=1354849, 326.

6 Mossoff, A. (2011). The rise and fall of the first American patent thicket: The sewing machine war of the 1850s. *Arizona Law Review*, *53*, 166, at: https://papers.ssrn.com/sol3/papers.cfm?abstract_id=1354849, 328.

7 See https://en.wikipedia.org/wiki/Manufacturers_Aircraft_Association.

8 For example, the MPEG (Moving Picture Experts Group) patent pool is to digital video and audio compression technologies. These technologies are used in a wide range of applications, such as digital television, DVD, and the internet. The MPEG patent pool was created in 1988, as the MPEG group was developing the first set of international standards for digital video and audio compression. These patents cover key technologies such as video and audio compression, digital rights management, and other related technologies. See https://en.wikipedia.org/wiki/Moving_Picture_Experts_Group.

9 For example, in 1998, five vertically integrated companies—Ericsson, Nokia, IBM, Toshiba, and Intel—formed the Bluetooth Special Interest Group to promote the Bluetooth short-range wireless communications technology. See https://en.wikipedia.org/wiki/Bluetooth_Special_Interest_Group. 3GPP (3G Patent Platform) for third-generation cellular technologies was formed in 1999. See https://www.justice.gov/sites/default/files/atr/legacy/2014/01/08/302201.pdf.

10 28 C.F.R. §50.6.

11 Merges, R. (2022). *American Patent Law—A Business and Economic History* (p. 430). Cambridge University Press.

12 Merges, R. (2022). *American Patent Law—A Business and Economic History* (p. 430). Cambridge University Press, 431.

13 Merges, R. (2022). *American Patent Law—A Business and Economic History* (p. 430). Cambridge University Press, 431.

14 Merges, R. (1998). *Institutions for Intellectual Property Transactions: The Case of Patent Pools* (p. 17), at: https://lawcat.berkeley.edu/record/1116665.

Technology sharing of complementary patents through patent pools can also improve product quality and variety.[15]

That said, patent pools also have inherent anti-trust concerns when they "facilitate price fixing, market division, or some other restraint in the product market."[16] In actual licensing practice, patent pools have conducted anti-competitive behavior. For example, the patent pool One-Blue sent notice to three major customers of its licensee Imation in Japan who were engaged in the sales of recordable BDs that were manufactured and sold by Imation. This notice informed them that One-Blue licensors had the right to seek an injunction against their conduct of infringement on the relevant patent right. Upon receipt of such notice, one of the three customer retailers suspended the sale of the recordable BDs manufactured and sold by Imation. The JFTC found that One-Blue's conduct falls under Paragraph 14 (Interference with a Competitor's Transactions) of the "Designation of Unfair Trade Practices," consequently being in violation of Article 19 of the AMA.[17]

The following sections survey how the US, the EU, and four major Asian economies (Japan, Korea, Taiwan, and the PRC) weigh on patent pools and some of their licensing agreements from competition law perspectives, which is based on their general approach of treating IP licensing favorably and applying the rule of reason in their analysis of IP exercise (see Subsection 3.5 of Chapter 3).

2. The US

2.1. Rule of Reason

The first patent pool case to reach the US Supreme Court was *E. Bement & Sons v. National Harrow Company* in 1902. However, what followed was a convoluted history, as court decisions

> did little to clarify when collective rights organizations had benefits or costs for upstream technology markets when the agreements did not restrict competition in downstream product markets. Courts often failed to investigate whether CROs licensed rights that were substitutes or complements.

Greater clarity was finally achieved in the mid-1990s through a series of policy statements from antitrust enforcement agencies.[18]

15 Hovenkamp, E., & Hovenkamp, H. (2017). *Patent Pools and Related Technology Sharing* (p. 2), at: https://scholarship.law.upenn.edu/faculty_scholarship/1766/.

16 Hovenkamp, E. (2015). Antitrust and the patent system: A reexamination. *OSLJ Ohio State Law Journal, 76*, 531, at: https://scholarship.law.upenn.edu/faculty_scholarship/1820.

17 JFTC. (November 2016). *Closing the Investigation on the Suspected Violation by One-Blue*. LLC of the Antimonopoly Act, at: https://www.jftc.go.jp/en/pressreleases/yearly-2016/November/161118_files/161118.pdf. However, because the relevant violation already ceased to exist, there was no necessity to issue a cease-and-desist order. Therefore, the JFTC has decided to close the investigation on the case.

18 Gilbert, R. (2017). *Collective Rights Organizations: A Guide to Benefits, Costs and Antitrust Safeguards* (pp. 4–7), at SSRN: https://ssrn.com/abstract=2904739.

The US Antitrust-IP Guidelines look at patent pools favorably: "These arrangements may provide procompetitive benefits by integrating complementary technologies, reducing transaction costs, clearing blocking positions, and avoiding costly infringement litigation. By promoting the dissemination of technology, cross-licensing and pooling arrangements are often procompetitive."[19] It also cautions that:

> pooling arrangements can have anticompetitive effects in certain circumstances. For example, collective price or output restraints in pooling arrangements, such as the joint marketing of pooled intellectual property rights with collective price setting or coordinated output restrictions, may be deemed unlawful if they do not contribute to an efficiency-enhancing integration of economic activity among the participants.[20]

2.2. Lenient Practice

The DOJ has approved almost all proposed patent pools through a series of business review letters issued since the late 1990s,[21] with one exception.[22] It opines that those pools have more justifications than risks as they were structured as follows:

> the portfolio was limited to technically essential patents, which, by definition, are not in competition with each other; an independent expert assessed

19 US Antitrust-IP Guidelines, 30. The US courts also recognize that patent pools formed by companies to provide access to standardized technology can have pro-competitive efficiencies in the reduced transaction costs, litigation expenses, and uncertainty in the context of bringing new products to the market. *U.S. Philips v. International Trade Commission*, 424 F.3d 1179, 1192 (Fed. Cir. 2005).

20 US Antitrust-IP Guidelines, 30. The US courts also recognize that patent pools formed by companies to provide access to standardized technology can have pro-competitive efficiencies in the reduced transaction costs, litigation expenses, and uncertainty in the context of bringing new products to the market. *U.S. Philips v. International Trade Commission*, 424 F.3d 1179, 1192 (Fed. Cir. 2005).

21 Merges, R. (2022). *American Patent Law—A Business and Economic History* (p. 432). Cambridge University Press.

22 The DOJ declined to issue favorable guidance in a Business Review Letter for Intellectual Property Exchange International (IPXI). IPXI proposed a financial exchange for patents that would offer standardized licenses for defined sets of patents contributed to the exchange under terms and conditions set jointly with patent holders. IPXI anticipated licensing patent portfolios as well as individual patents. The proposal communicated IPXI's intent to identify and exclude competing patents from its licenses, but because IPXI was not designed to license patents for a particular technology, its proposal offered no specific criteria for "essential." Although the DOJ recognized that IPXI could potentially produce certain efficiencies, it identified potential antitrust concerns related to portfolios of substitute patent rights, the absence of provisions for independent licensing, and the sharing of competitively sensitive information. The DOJ decided that it did not know enough to conclude that IPXI's activities would not raise antitrust concerns, and consequently declined to state its enforcement intentions. Cited from Gilbert, R. (2017). *Collective Rights Organizations: A Guide to Benefits, Costs and Antitrust Safeguards* (p. 11), at: SSRN: https://ssrn.com/abstract=2904739.

whether the patents were technically essential; the patents included in the pooled portfolio licenses also remained available for licensing outside of the pool; the patents included in the pool were not expired; licensing was available on a nonexclusive, worldwide basis; and grant-backs were limited to essential patents for the same standard.

The latest patent pool reviewed and approved by the DOJ is probably Avanci founded in 2016. It offers a joint patent-licensing pool platform that aggregates patents declared essential to 2G, 3G, and 4G standards, which are licensed for manufacturing connected vehicles and smart meters. Avanci also licenses SEPs to implement 5G cellular wireless standards for use in automobile vehicles and distribute royalty income among the licensors.[23] To date, the DOJ has not taken any law enforcement action against patent pools.

However, in the US, there is now a resounding call for the DOJ to reconsider Avanci's business review letter, as "the letter undermines bipartisan consensus on standard setting, relies on questionable positions, expresses concerns that real-world events have corroborated,[24] compounds supply-chain problems, and threatens even more foreboding future harms as 5G is more fully deployed."[25]

3. The EU

3.1. Rule of Reason

Generally, the EC is of the opinion that most licensing agreements are pro-competitive[26] and that technology transfer agreements "will usually improve economic efficiency and be pro-competitive as they can reduce duplication of research and development, strengthen the incentive for the initial research and development, spur incremental innovation, facilitate diffusion and generate product

23 https://www.justice.gov/atr/page/file/1298626/dl (July 28, 2020).

24 Real-world events demonstrate that holdup by SEP-licensers exists. These include nineteen lawsuits by three Avanci members against Daimler AG in Germany; lawsuits by five Avanci members against Tesla Inc. in the US, Japan, and Germany; and at least seven lawsuits by seven Avanci members in the US and Germany, see https://media.orrick.com/Media%20Library/public/files/insights/2022/law-360-doj-needs-to-reconsider-prior-administration-avanci-letter.pdf.

25 Letter from former government officials. (October 17, 2022). *Professors, and Academics to DOJ Regarding Avanci Business Review Letter*, at: https://papers.ssrn.com/sol3/papers.cfm?abstract_id=4250512.

26 According to EC, guidelines on the applicability of Article 101 of the Treaty on the Functioning of the European Union to horizontal cooperation agreements (2023/C 259/01) (EC Horizontal Cooperation Guidelines), "Horizontal cooperation agreements can lead to substantial economic benefits, including sustainability benefits, in particular where they combine complementary activities, skills, or assets. Horizontal cooperation can be a means to share risk, save costs, increase investments, pool know-how, enhance product quality and variety, and launch innovation faster. Similarly, horizontal cooperation can be a means to address shortages and disruptions in supply chains or reduce dependencies on particular products, services, and technologies" (Para. 20).

market competition."[27] The EC therefore exempts wholesale from the prohibition of Article 101(1) of the TFEU those technology transfer agreements that do not exceed the market thresholds (20% in the case of agreements between competitors and 30% in the case of agreements between non-competitors) and do not contain hardcore restrictions pursuant to the Technology Transfer Block Exemption Regulation (TTBER Regulation).[28] The EC also issued guidelines on the application of Article 101 of the Treaty on the functioning of the EU to technology transfer agreements (TTBER and Article 101 guidelines)[29] to provide guidance on the application of the TTBER as well as on the application of Article 101 of the TFEU.

According to TTBER and Article 101 guidelines, TTBER Regulation does not cover "Agreements establishing technology pools and setting out the terms and conditions for their operation are not—irrespective of the number of parties," as the agreement to establish the pool does not permit a particular licensee to produce contract products. Such agreements are addressed only by TTBER and Article 101 guidelines (Point 247).

TTBER and Article 101 guidelines take a rule-of-reason approach to patent pools, as they can produce pro-competitive effects and also be restrictive of competition (Points 245 and 246). In assessing the possible competitive risks and efficiencies, the Commission will, inter alia, take account of the transparency of the pool creation process; the selection and nature of the pooled technologies, including the extent to which independent experts are involved in the creation and operation of the pool and whether safeguards against exchange of sensitive information and independent dispute resolution mechanisms have been put in place (Point 248).

3.2. *Pools with Significant Substitute Technologies Are Anti-Competitive*

According to TTBER and Article 101 Guidelines, two basic distinctions are made between (a) technological complements and substitutes; and (b) essential and non-essential technologies (Point 250).[30]

27 Commission Regulation (EU) No. 316/2014 of March 21, 2014, on the application of Article 101(3) of the Treaty on the Functioning of the European Union to categories of technology transfer agreements (TTBER Regulation) (Recital 4).

28 The TTBER Regulation replaces Commission Regulation (EC) No. 772/2004, which defines categories of technology transfer agreements which the Commission regarded as normally satisfying the conditions laid down in Article 101(3) of the Treaty and expired on April 30, 2014. In view of the overall positive experience with the application of that Regulation, and taking into account further experience acquired since its adoption, the TTBER Regulation was adopted and will expire on April 30, 2026.

29 EC, 2014/C 89/3 (Point 2).

30 Two technologies are complements when they are both required to produce the product or carry out the process to which the technologies relate. Conversely, two technologies are substitutes when either technology allows the holder to produce the product or carry out the process to which the technologies relate (Point 251). A technology is essential if there are no viable substitutes (both commercially and technically) for that technology inside or outside the pool and the technology in question constitutes a necessary part of the package of technologies for the purposes of producing the product(s) or carrying out the process(es) to which the pool relates. In addition, a technology is essential if it constitutes a necessary part (that is to say, there are no viable substitutes) of the pooled technologies needed to comply with the standard supported by the pool (standard essential technologies) (Point 252 TTBER and Article 101 Guidelines).

When a pool is composed only of technologies that are essential and therefore by necessity also complements, the creation of the pool as such generally falls outside Article 101(1), irrespective of the market position of the parties. However, the EC is intolerant of patent pools which include significant substitute technologies and reverts almost to the illegal per se rule: "in the case of pools composed solely or predominantly of substitute technologies amounts to a price fixing cartel" (Point 246), and "The inclusion of substitute technologies in the pool generally restricts inter-technology competition since it can amount to collective bundling and lead to price fixing between competitors. As a general rule the Commission considers that the inclusion of significant substitute technologies in the pool constitutes a violation of Article 101(1) of the Treaty. The Commission also considers that it is unlikely that the conditions of Article 101(3) will be fulfilled in the case of pools comprising to a significant extent substitute technologies . . . To alleviate the competition concerns it is not sufficient that the parties remain free to license independently. This is because the parties are likely to have little incentive to license independently in order not to undermine the pool's licensing activity, which allows them to jointly exercise market power." (Point 255 of TTBER and Article 101 Guidelines)

3.3. Pools with Significant Complementary but Non-Essential Patents Are Likely Anti-Competitive

Where significant complementary but non-essential patents are included in the pool there is a risk of foreclosure of third-party technologies. Once a technology is included in the pool and is licensed as part of the package, licensees are likely to have little incentive to license a competing technology when the royalty paid for the package already covers a substitute technology. Moreover, the inclusion of technologies which are not necessary for the purposes of producing the product(s) or carrying out the process(es) to which the technology pool relates or to comply with the standard which includes the pooled technology also forces licensees to pay for technology that they may not need.[31] The inclusion of such complementary technology thus amounts to collective bundling. Where a pool encompasses non-essential technologies, the agreement is likely to be caught by Article 101(1) where the pool has a significant position on any relevant market (Point 262 of TTBER and Article 101 Guidelines).

3.4. Pools With Stronger Market Position Under Stricter Scrutiny

For the EC, "the stronger the market position of the pool the greater the risk of anti-competitive effects; the stronger the market position of the pool, the more

31 EC. (2017). *Setting Out the EU Approach to Standard Essential Patents,* 11 (COM 712 final), at: https://ec.europa.eu/docsroom/documents/26583. European Commission opines that: In this context, SEP holders may offer more patents, including non-SEPs, but cannot require a licensee to accept a licence for these other patents as well. The general non-willingness or nonacceptance to offer or accept all SEPs that a licensee needs may be an indication of bad faith.

likely that agreeing not to license to all potential licensees or to license on discriminatory terms will infringe Article 101" (Point 267 of TTBER and Article 101 Guidelines).

Where the pool has a dominant position on the market, the EC would require that "royalties and other licensing terms should be non-excessive and non-discriminatory and licenses should be non-exclusive. These requirements are necessary to ensure that the pool is open and does not lead to foreclosure and other anti-competitive effects on down-stream markets" (Point 269 of TTBER and Article 101 Guidelines).

3.5. *Safe Harbor for Certain Open and Free Patent Pools*

TTBER and Article 101 Guidelines provide safe harbor for certain open and free patent pools, exempting them from Article 101(1) of TFEU, irrespective of the market position of the parties:

if all the following conditions are fulfilled:

(a) participation in the pool creation process is <u>open to all</u> interested technology rights owners;
(b) <u>sufficient safeguards</u> are adopted to ensure that <u>only essential technologies</u> (which therefore necessarily are also complements) are pooled;
(c) sufficient safeguards are adopted to ensure that exchange of sensitive information (such as pricing and output data) is restricted to what is necessary for the creation and operation of the pool;
(d) the pooled technologies are licensed into the pool <u>on a non-exclusive basis</u>;
(e) the pooled technologies are <u>licensed out to all potential licensees</u> on FRAND terms;
(f) the parties contributing technology to the pool and the licensees are free to challenge the validity and the essentiality of the pooled technologies, and;
(g) the parties contributing technology to the pool and the licensee remain free to develop competing products and technology. (Point 261 of TTBER and Article 101 Guidelines)

4. Japan

JFTC issued the Guidelines on Standardization and Patent Pool Arrangements for patent pools formed for standardization on June 29, 2005.[32] In addition, JFTC issued Guidelines for the Use of Intellectual Property under the Antimonopoly Act (AMA) in 2016 (last amended in 2023) (Japanese IP Guidelines).[33]

32 At https://www.jftc.go.jp/en/legislation_gls/imonopoly_guidelines_files/Patent_Pool.pdf.
33 At https://www.jftc.go.jp/en/legislation_gls/imonopoly_guidelines_files/IPGL_Frand.pdf.

4.1. Highly Intolerant of Patent Pools with Substitute Technologies

According to the Japanese IP Guidelines, "it is an unreasonable restraint of trade if the parties holding the rights to the substitute technologies in a particular technology market establish a patent pool and jointly set forth licensing conditions (including the scope of use of technologies) for their rights to substitute technologies and substantially restrain competition in the field of trade associated with these technologies (Part 3(2) (i)(b)).[34]

4.2. Unjustified Refusal to License Might Lead to Private Monopolization

The Japanese Guidelines deal with the issue of refusal to license the pooled IPRs from the perspective of private monopolization pursuant to the AMA. In a case where entrepreneurs participating in a patent pool refuse to grant a license to any new entrant or any particular existing entrepreneurs without any reasonable grounds, to hinder it from using the technology, the restriction may fall under the exclusion of business activities of other entrepreneurs (Japan IP Guidelines, Part III(1)(i)(a)).

In a case in which entrepreneurs competing with one another in a particular product market establish a patent pool for technologies required to supply their product as a sole body that can grant licenses to other entrepreneurs, its refusal to grant licenses to new entrants or certain existing entrepreneurs without reasonable grounds constitutes conduct of jointly impeding new entries or hampering the business activities of the existing entrepreneurs. It is an unreasonable restraint of trade if this conduct substantially restrains competition in the field of trade of the product in question (Japan IP Guidelines, Part III(2)(i)(d)).

In practice, in the 1997 pachinko machines case the JFTC found the refusal to license patents owned by ten pachinko-manufacturing companies and administered by an association (Japan Amusement Machine Patent Managing Federation) to other pachinko-manufacturing companies a violation of Article 3 of the AMA.[35]

34 In addition, consequent to the enactment of Law No. 51 of 2009 for amending the Antimonopoly Act in 2009, the JFTC formulated the "Guidelines for the Exclusionary Private Monopolization under the Antimonopoly Act" (revised in 2020, Japanese Exclusion Guidelines, at: https://www.jftc.go.jp/en/legislation_gls/imonopoly_guidelines_files/20122501.pdf), which includes refusal to supply as one of the four typical exclusionary conducts. The Japanese Exclusion Guidelines in principle respect an entrepreneur's discretion to select to whom and on what conditions it supplies products. However, if an entrepreneur carries out, beyond a reasonable degree, refusal to supply, imposing restriction on the quantity or contents, or applies discriminatory treatment to the condition or implementation of supply in the upstream market concerning a product necessary for the trading customers to carry out business activities in the downstream market, such conduct may cause difficulty in the business activities in the downstream market of the trading customers who are unable to easily find an alternative supplier in the upstream market, and may undermine competition in the downstream market. Thus, carrying out refusal beyond a reasonable degree concerning a product necessary for the trading customers to carry out business activities in the downstream market may fall under exclusionary conduct (p. 25 et seq).

35 JFTC Recommendation Decision No. 5 of 1997 on 6 August 1997. Cited from Japan IP Guidelines, Part III(1)(i)(a).

5. Korea: Pools with Substitutes or Non-Essential or Invalid Patents Likely Unjust

The Koran IP Guidelines deal with patent pool-related issues in great detail. If the technologies included in the patent pool are a substitute for one another, the exercise of rights related to such a patent pool is likely to be determined as unjust as it can increase costs to a licensee as well as the possibility of unfair collaborative practices among competing enterprises. In addition, if non-essential or invalid patents are included in the joint working of patents, there is a high possibility that the exercise of rights related to the relevant patent pool will be determined as unjust as it can increase a licensee's costs and unfairly allow invalid patents to exist.[36] However, Korean IP Guidelines do not define substitute.

6. Taiwan: No Inclusion of Substitutes into Pools

The TFTC's Guidelines on Technology Licensing Arrangements (Taiwanese Tech Licensing Guidelines)[37] does not address the issue of a patent pool at all. However, it has cleared two patent pools through patentees' forming jointly a new entity in charge of the management of the pooled patents. In 2011 the TFTC cleared the first patent pool. It decided not to oppose the merger between Hitachi, Panasonic, Philips, Samsung, Sony, and CyberLink which takes the form of a new company, One-Blue, with each company controlling one-sixth of its share. One-Blue acts as a licensing agent for the patent pool to license essential blue-ray disc (BD) patents for the manufacturing of backwards-compatible BD products (such as CDs, DVDs, etc.).

The TFTC examined and confirmed that the patent pool will be composed exclusively of patents that will be periodically reviewed by independent patent experts Through periodic review by independent patent experts, this patent pool will exclude substitutive patents and be exclusively composed of essential and complementary patents.[38]

It is evident that the TFTC puts much emphasis on the fact that substitute patents are not included in the patent pool and strives to avoid restraint of licensees' freedom to decide prices, use or challenge the pooled patents, and to research and develop competitive products or technologies. The TFTC cleared the second patent pool of One-Red by LG, Philips, Pioneer, and Sony in 2013, as it is structured and arranged just like One-Blue.[39]

36 Korean IP Guidelines, 21.

37 TFTC Kong-Fa-Zhi No. 10515606031 Order (decided on 24 August 2016), at: https://www.ftc.gov.tw/internet/main/doc/docDetail.aspx?uid=163&docid=227.

38 TFTC Gong-Jie-Zhi No. 100002 Decision (decided on 31 March 2011), 4–5, at: http://www.ftc.gov.tw/uploadDecision/fc229308-2070-4498-9f4e-a845bcea7c55.pdf.

39 TFTC Gong-Jie-Zhi No. 102002 Decision (decided on 24 January 2013), at: https://www.ftc.gov.tw/uploadDecision/328e3fdd-64bd-4e57-a871-a458e35c576f.pdf.

7. The PRC

7.1. Dominant Pools may not Coerce License of Competing/Non-Essential/ Expired Patents

In China, the Anti-monopoly Commission (AMC) of the State Council also takes a rule of reason approach to the patent pool, calling it "joint patent operation," in its Chinese Guidelines on IP Abuse.[40] In addition, the Chinese antitrust authority, State Administration of Market Regulation (SAMR) issued the Regulations Against Abuse of IPR to Exclude, Restrain Competition in 2015 (last revised 2023, Regulations Against IPR Abuse). Article 17 stipulates that:

> (1) Business operators shall not exclude or restrain market competition through patent joint operation when exercising their IPRs. (2) Members of a joint patent operation shall not exchange information sensitive to market competition such as prices, volume, market segregation that would lead to monopolistic agreements prohibited by Articles 17 and 18(1) of AML, unless business operators can prove that the reached agreement meet the exception provisions of Articles 18(2) and (3) and 20 of the AML. (3) Joint patent operation or its members which enjoy market dominance shall not use joint patent operation to conduct the enumerated market-dominance abusing behaviors, including to coercively license competing patents in portfolio (bundled licensing), or to coercively license non-essential patents or expired patents with other patents without due course.[41]

40 Article 26 of Chinese IP Guidelines on IP Abuse provides: "(2) Joint patent operation in general can reduce transaction costs, enhance efficiency in licensing, and have pro-competition effects. However, joint patent operation can also exclude, restrain competition, and its assessment could take into consideration the following factors: (1) the market share of the business operator in the relevant market and its control over the market; (2) Whether there is alternative technology to the patents in the joint operation; (3) Whether members of the patent joint operation are restrained from licensing patents separately or developing technology; (4) Whether business operators exchange information through joint patent operation about prices and volume of products; (5) Whether business operators reach cross-licensing, exclusive grant-back, no-challenge clause or other restraint through joint patent operation;(6) Whether business operators license patents at unreasonably high prices, tie-in, attach unreasonable transaction terms and conditions or practice differentiated treatment through joint patent operation."

41 Other enumerated market-dominance abusing behaviors include (a) To license jointly operated patents at unreasonable high prices; (b) To restrict members of the joint patent operation or its licensees the scope of using the patent without due course; (c) To restrict members of the joint patent operation to license patents as independent licensor without due course; (d) To restrict members of the joint patent operation or its licensees to independently or jointly develop technology that competes with the jointly operated patents without due course; (e) To force the licensee to exclusively grant back its improvement or R&D result to the joint patent operation entity or its members without due course; (f) To prohibit the licensee to challenge the validity of the jointly operated patents without due course; . . . (h) To practice differentiated treatment in transaction terms to members of the joint patent operation who are of the same qualifications or licensees from the same relevant market without due course; (9) To practice other behaviors of abuse of market dominance determined by the SAMR.

7.2. Practice: SAMR Issued "Letter of Reminding and Urging" to Avanci

Noteworthy is that on June 27, 2024, the SAMR initiated the first ever "reminding and urging" procedure in accordance with the newly announced (December 6, 2023) "Notice of Three Notices and One Letter during the antimonopoly procedures"[42] and handed over a letter of reminding and urging to the representatives of the Avanci patent pool. It reminds and urges Avanci to scrutinize, prevent, and inhibit the danger of monopolization during the licensing of SEPs of wireless communication for cars.[43] According to the report, Avanci issues only whole-car level licenses to car manufacturers, which might limit the technical choices and development of spare parts manufacturers, and affect fair competition within the entire industrial chain of car manufacture; in addition, the patent list provided by Avanci lacks transparency and the levels of licensing and their licensing rates remain unclear, which might lead to tie-in or monopolistic conduct of charging unfair high-prices.[44]

It remains to be seen how Avanci responds to this warning letter, as it has seldom been challenged by national antitrust authorities, and whether the SMAR is not satisfied with its response and proceeds to the next stages of ordering correction to be taken by Avanci, interviewing, investigating, and even sanctioning Avanci.

8. The Governance of Patent Pools

Despite the widely acknowledged integrative efficiency-enhancing benefits, patent pools consisting of substitutes held by competitors can facilitate horizontal collusion that would reduce price and inter-technology competition and lead to margin squeeze.[45] To offset these perils and maximize the pro-competitive effects of patent pools, first and foremost, patent pools must be subject to good governance. Good governance of patent pools requires at least no inclusion of substitutes, an independent oversight mechanism, internal and external openness, and firewalls. These principles corroborate with the EU's safe harbour requirement for patent pools.

8.1. No Inclusion of Substitutive Technologies

It has been shown "that patent pools increase welfare when included patents are perfect complements (i.e., they have no value unless they are used together), and

42 Joint Notice by the AMC of the State Council and the SAMR, ShuangFanBanFa (2023) No.1 at: https://www.samr.gov.cn/zw/zfxxgk/fdzdgknr/jzzcxds/art/2023/art_515052484fd94fb1a2d8a648615b4c1c.html. Accordingly, both agencies can issue a letter of reminding and urging. The addressee of the letter has to file a written report with the agencies within the designated timeframe on its corrective measures. If the corrective measures were insufficient or not taken, the agencies can order correction to be made within the designated timeframe by the addressee, interviewing, investigating, and administratively punishing the addressee.

43 See http://www.pw-partners.com/newsinfo/7375596.html?templateId=590244.

44 See https://www.zhichanli.com/p/1021010776.

45 Peritz, R. (2007). Competition policy and its implications for intellectual property rights in the United States. In Anderman, S. D. (Ed.), *The Interface Between Intellectual Property Rights And Competition Policy* (pp. 125–249). Cambridge University Press.

decrease welfare when they are perfect substitutes (i.e., one is as good as the other but no one needs both).[46] While the antitrust agencies surveyed from Sections 3 to 7 all show serious doubt about including substitute patents within a patent pool, the US also exhibits reservation.[47] The inclusion of substitutive technologies would facilitate collusion and foreclose the development of an alternative, substitutive, and therefore competing technology. In practice, however, it can be difficult to distinguish supplementary, complementary, and therefore essential technologies or patents from substitutes, as "many times the patent landscape in an industry falls far short of strict complementarity"[48] or "it is often unclear whether rights are substitutes or complements,"[49] particularly in information technologies where patents have large numbers of claims, and to divide them up into substitutes and complements is often impossible. "Many patents function as both simultaneously."[50] Some even argue that "In sum, the complements/substitutes distinction becomes useless in markets with any significant degree of complexity."[51]

This difficulty is exemplified by the convoluted decisions of the USCAFC in *Princo Corp. v. International Trade Commission* that sprawled over eight years. US Philips licensed on behalf of the CD-R/RW patent pool to CD-R/RW makers,[52] such as Princo, and asked the ITC to ban the import of CD-R/RW manufactured by Princo over alleged infringement of the pooled patents by ceasing to pay the agreed royalty. In defense, Princo raised the issue that while Philips collaborating with Sony on the CD-R/RW standard, Philips proposed an analog solution covered by its Raaymakers patents, and Sony proposed a digital solution covered by its Lagadec patent. Both the Raaymakers and Lagadec patents were included in the pool administered by Philips. The inclusion of the Lagadec patent in the package led to patent misuse through unlawful tying. The ITC ruled that "Philips's package

46 Hovenkamp, E., & Hovenkamp, H. (2017). *Patent Pools and Related Technology Sharing* (p. 2), at: https://scholarship.law.upenn.edu/faculty_scholarship/1766/.

47 Example 9 of the US Antitrust-IP Guidelines discusses where two of the leading manufacturers of a product hold patents that cover alternative circuit designs for the product and assign several of their patents to a separate corporation wholly owned by the two firms. That corporation licenses the patents rights to other consumer product manufacturers and establishes the license royalties. However, the manufacturers assign to the separate corporation only patents that are blocking. None of the patents assigned to the corporation can be used without infringing a patent owned by the other firm: this patent pooling: does not adversely affect competition in the licensed technology among entities that would have been actual or potential competitors in the absence of the licensing arrangement. Moreover, the licensing arrangement is likely to have procompetitive benefits in the use of the technology. Because the manufacturers' patents are blocking, the manufacturers are not in a horizontal relationship with respect to those patents . . . so the patents are not substitutable. (US Antitrust-IP Guidelines, 32)

48 Merges, R. (1998). *Institutions for Intellectual Property Transactions: The Case of Patent Pools* (p. 48), at: https://lawcat.berkeley.edu/record/1116665.

49 Gilbert, R. (26 January 2017). *Collective Rights Organizations: A Guide to Benefits, Costs and Antitrust Safeguards* (p. 13), at: SSRN: https://ssrn.com/abstract=2904739

50 Hovenkamp, E. (2015). Antitrust and the Patent System: A Reexamination. *OSLJ Ohio State Law Journal, 76*, 531, at: https://scholarship.law.upenn.edu/faculty_scholarship/1820.

51 Hovenkamp, E. (2015). Antitrust and the Patent System: A Reexamination. *OSLJ Ohio State Law Journal, 76*, 532, at: https://scholarship.law.upenn.edu/faculty_scholarship/1820.

52 For more details of the patent pool see Subsection 5.1 of Chapter 1.

licensing practice constituted patent misuse for unlawfully tying patents that were essential for the Orange Book standard to licenses for other patents that were not essential."[53]

On appeal, the CAFC reversed and rejected the ITC's finding of Philips's patent misuse by improperly tying nonessential patents to essential ones and under the rule of reason. It concluded that "Philips was simply charging a fixed licensing fee for licensees to manufacture discs under the Orange Book standard." It noted that "including additional patents in the package was the functional equivalent of promising not to sue licensees on any of the patents in the group, which had the advantages of minimizing transaction costs and ensuring against the risk of post-agreement disputes as to whether those additional patents were required to practice the patented technology."[54] It remanded the case to the ITC for further proceedings.

On remand, the ITC rejected Princo's argument and found there was no evidence that the patents in the joint package licenses covered technologies that were close substitutes, or that the pool licensors would have competed in the technology licensing market absent the pooling arrangements. In particular, the ITC rejected Princo's argument that Sony's Lagadec patent should not have been included in the patent packages. The ITC noted Philips's contention that claim 6 of the Lagadec patent covered a portion of the Orange Book standard and therefore was technically a "blocking patent," and explained if Philips was correct that Lagadec was a necessary part of the Orange Book patent package, then "no misuse flows from including the [Lagadec] patent in the joint licenses." Even if a license to the Lagadec patent was not necessary to manufacture Orange Book-compliant discs, there was no merit to Princo's theories of patent misuse based on the Lagadec patent, because:

> there has been no showing that the Lagadec . . . patent competes with another patent in the pool, no showing that the pool licensors would have competed in the technology licensing market absent the pooling arrangement, and no showing of the anti-competitive effect required under a rule of reason analysis.

There was no evidence that Sony would have entered the CD-R/RW market with a system based on the Lagadec technology and no evidence that such a system would have become a significant competitive force in that market.[55]

53 Cited from *Princo Corp. v. International Trade Commission*, 616 F.3d 1323 (Fed. Cir. 2010, "Princo II").

54 Cited from *Princo Corp. v. International Trade Commission*, 616 F.3d 1323 (Fed. Cir. 2010, "Princo II"), 1324.

55 Cited from *Princo Corp. v. International Trade Commission*, 616 F.3d 1323 (Fed. Cir. 2010, "Princo II"), 1325. USITC, In the Matter of Certain Recordable Compact Discs and Rewritable Compact Discs Investigation No. 337-TA-474, April 2004, at: https://www.usitc.gov/publications/337/pub3686.pdf.

On Princo's appeal, a divided panel of the CAFC ruled against the ITC and Philips. Although the panel rejected several of Princo's arguments, it vacated the ITC's remedial orders and remanded the case for further proceedings on (I) whether Lagadec was a potentially workable alternative to the Orange Book technology and (II) whether Princo has established that Sony and Phillips agreed that Lagadec would not be licensed in a manner allowing its development as competitive technology.[56]

Philips, Princo, and the ITC all filed petitions for rehearing en banc. The court granted Philips's and the ITC's, denied Princo's, vacated the court's opinion expressed in "Princo I," and reinstated the appeal.[57]

The CAFC concluded in a seven to two split decision that "the conduct alleged in this case is not the type of conduct that could give rise to the defense of patent misuse" and it, therefore, affirmed the ITC's orders granting relief against Princo.[58] On the issue of substitute technology, the CAFC required that "What Princo had to demonstrate was that there was a 'reasonable probability' that the Lagadec technology, if available for licensing, would have matured into a competitive force in the storage technology market. It was not enough that there was some speculative possibility that Lagadec could have overcome the barriers to its technical feasibility and commercial success and become the basis for competing disc technology.[59] Princo has failed to show that the putative agreement between Sony and Philips not to license the Lagadec technology for non-Orange Book purposes had any market effect at all—actual or prospective. The record and the findings of the ITC made it clear that the Lagadec technology lacked both the <u>technical and the commercial prospects</u> that would have made it a possible basis for a product that could compete with Orange Book-compliant discs.[60]

Following the USCAFC's standard, substitute technology needs to have "reasonable probability" of maturing into a competitive technology, judging from technical and commercial prospects. This is a high bar to pass, virtually crippling the challenge to patent pools that include "substitutive technologies." More appropriate is perhaps to focus on the technical aspects of substitutability of patents at issue, not to weigh on commercial aspects or "the nature of the licensee's products,"[61] as these are too remote from the forming of patent pools and can be highly unpredictable. Even if patent pools include some "substitutes," they can still pass the antitrust scrutiny if they are supplemented with other necessary safeguard mechanisms to

56 See *Princo Corp. v. International Trade Commission*, 563 F.3d 1321 (Fed. Cir. 2009, "Princo I").

57 583 F.3d 1380, 1381 (Fed. Cir. 2009) at https://casetext.com/case/princo-corp-v-intl-trade-comn.

58 Cited from Princo II.

59 See Princo II.

60 See Princo II, 1340. However, the decision abridged patent misuse and created gap with antitrust law. See Wang, L.-D. (2012). Deviated, unsound, and self-retreating: A critical assessment of the *Princo v. ITC* en banc decision. *Marquette Intellectual Property Law Review, 16*, 51.

61 This is wrongly considered by Hovenkamps see Hovenkamp, E., & Hovenkamp, H. (2017). *Patent Pools and Related Technology Sharing* (p. 6), at: https://scholarship.law.upenn.edu/faculty_scholarship/1766/.

make them less prone to foreclosure of other competing technologies as discussed in the following subsections.

8.2. Independent Patent Controller

Many of the surveyed antitrust agencies value the involvement of independent patent controllers to make sure that no substitutive technologies are included in the pool.[62] For the EC, "Another relevant factor in assessing the competitive risks and the efficiencies of technology pools is the extent to which independent experts are involved in the creation and operation of the pool." (Point 256 of TTBER and Article 101 Guidelines) In the US, without exception, all the patent pools to whom the DOJ issued business review letters have engaged an independent expert to exclude substitutive technologies and to admit to the pool only those complementary patents essential to manufacturing products. For KFTC, "In the event that a patent pool is managed by a group of experts independent of patentees, the exercise of rights with respect to such patent pool is unlikely to be determined as unjust."[63] The One-Blue and One-Red patent pools cleared by TFTC employed independent and professional patent practitioners from different countries selected by the Executive Committee composed of all the patentees of the pooled patents. The patent experts will provide their patent evaluation service on an hourly charge basis and the outcome of their evaluations on the patents' essentiality has no bearing on their compensations for the service. Their determination about the essentiality is binding and cannot be overruled by the patentees, the Executive Committee, or One-Blue.[64]

It is therefore imperative to have a neutral third-party expert not bound by the patent pools, to conduct technical evaluation, either upon his own initiative or request, with regard to the essentiality and substitutability of the pooled patents and confidential know-how.

8.3. Charging Reasonable and Non-Discriminatory Royalty

Collective royalty setting is an integral part of pooling agreements for the avoidance of royalty stacking with individual IPR holders charging royalties on top of royalties already charged by other holders, which would make royalties prohibitively high. Sometimes, royalty set by patent pools can be excessive, as pools concentrate market power and luck for their participants and licensees. In the US, the DOJ and FTC generally will not assess the reasonableness of royalties set by a pool and their analysis will focus on the pool's formation and whether its structure

62 Robert Merges cautions "But I would argue that strict complementarity, based on industry standards, should not be deemed essential to future pools." See Merges, R. (1998). *Institutions for Intellectual Property Transactions: The Case of Patent Pools* (p. 49), at: https://lawcat.berkeley.edu/record/1116665.

63 Korean IP Guidelines, 21.

64 TFTC Gong-Jie-Zhi No. 100002 decision (decided on 31 March 2011), 4–5, at: http://www.ftc.gov.tw/uploadDecision/fc229308-2070-4498-9f4e-a845bcea7c55.pdf.

would likely enable pool participants to impair competition.[65] Nor does the CAFC accept the "assumption that a license to fewer than all the patents in a package would presumably carry a lower fee than the package" because it "ignores the reality that the value of any patent package is largely, if not entirely, based on the patents that are essential to the technology in question."[66]

> It is entirely rational for a patentee who has a patent that is essential to particular technology, as well as other patents that are not essential, to charge what the market will bear for the essential patent and to offer the others for free.[67]

However, excessive royalty set by power patent pools is generally a concern for jurisdictions which prohibit the abuse of market dominance and dependence, such as the EU and the four Asian economies surveyed here. Some opine that "The royalty rate might be flat, annualized, or most commonly, an amount based on the number of units that a licensee produces or its revenue."[68]

For good governance of patent pools, royalties set by them should be reasonable and non-discriminatory. Such royalties can send out a clear price signal to on-lookers who are contemplating entering the market but are hesitant due to the uncertainty of royalties. In this regard, the independent patent controller advocated can play a pivotal role by screening non-essential patents and assessing objectively the technical contribution of major invention by different patentees.

8.4. Openness

Since the US antitrust-IP guidelines take a rule of reason approach to patent pools, it opines that:

> Pooling arrangements generally need not be open to all who would like to join. However, exclusion from . . . pooling arrangements among parties that collectively possess market power may, under some circumstances, harm competition. In general, exclusion from a pooling or cross-licensing arrangement among competing technologies is unlikely to have anticompetitive effects unless (1) excluded firms cannot effectively compete in the relevant market for the good incorporating the licensed technologies and (2) the pool participants collectively possess market power in the relevant market. If these circumstances exist, the Agencies will evaluate whether the arrangement's

65 USDOJ and USFTC. (2007). *Antitrust Enforcement and Intellectual Property Rights: Promoting Innovation and Competition by USDOJ and USFTC* (p. 9), at: http://www.justice.gov/atr/public/hearings/ip/222655.htm.

66 *U.S. Philips v. International Trade Commission*, 424 F.3d 1179, 1191 (Fed. Cir. 2005).

67 *U.S. Philips v. International Trade Commission*, 424 F.3d 1179, 1191 (Fed. Cir. 2005).

68 Hovenkamp, E., & Hovenkamp, H. (2017). *Patent Pools and Related Technology Sharing* (p. 10), at: https://scholarship.law.upenn.edu/faculty_scholarship/1766.

> limitations on participation are reasonably related to the efficient development and exploitation of the pooled technologies and will assess the net effect of those limitations in the relevant market.[69]

The openness of patent pools towards stakeholders can be beneficial and generate pro-competitive effects. There are two aspects of openness, internal and external. Internal openness means pools do not limit the freedom and right of their patentee members to license their patents individually. A "clear and public non-exclusivity requirement, particularly when the pool has a large number of members, significantly reduces the collusion risk."[70] Following that line of thought, the 2007 Antitrust Enforcement and Intellectual Property Rights: Promoting Innovation and Competition by USDOJ and USFTC concludes that:

> In general, a refusal to license less than all of a pool's intellectual property will not raise competitive concerns, provided that the licensors retain the ability to license their patents individually and the pool's design is otherwise procompetitive. In this way, licensees are not required to purchase access to more technology than they need.[71]

External openness means transparency of pools to the outside world. Openness towards competition authorities can ease the burden of discerning procompetitive ones from anti-competitive and help prevent patent pools from denaturing into cartels and means to monopolizing the market. Openness to all interested license-seekers, including disclosing clearly the scope and number of pooled patents owned by each licensor, and the terms and conditions of the licensing agreements, would make pooled patents widely available and maximize the utilities of patent pools.

8.5. Firewalls

An antithesis to internal openness needs to be mentioned, namely, the necessity to establish firewalls within patent pools. Often, in the name of overcoming underreporting by the licensee and correct calculation of royalty, competitively sensitive information such as pricing and output data and sales reports are asked to be provided to the pool administrator or licensors.[72] The exchange or provision of such information will lead to collusion among patent pool members who are (potential) competitors. To preempt such attempts, there should be a safeguard mechanism installed in patent pools to prevent departments other than the one overseeing the

69 US Antitrust-IP Guidelines, 31.

70 Hovenkamp, E., & Hovenkamp, H. (2017). *Patent Pools and Related Technology Sharing* (p. 13), at: https://scholarship.law.upenn.edu/faculty_scholarship/1766/.

71 USDOJ and USFTC. (2007). *Antitrust Enforcement and Intellectual Property Rights: Promoting Innovation and Competition* (p. 84), at: http://www.justice.gov/atr/public/hearings/ip/222655.htm.

72 For related discussion see Subsection 3.3 of Chapter 3.

execution of licensing agreements from gaining access to the business secrets of others and using them to gain competitive advantages.

In the US, the MPEG-2 patent pool hired an independent licensing administrator so that the licensors would not be privy to information gathered from other pool participants; in both DVD patent pools, the parties designed "walls" to sufficiently limit access to each other's sensitive information.

Out of similar concerns for the institutional framework governing pool management, the EU Guidelines state:

> In oligopolistic markets exchanges of sensitive information such as pricing and output data may facilitate collusion. In such cases the Commission will take into account to what extent safeguards have been put in place, which ensures that sensitive information is not exchanged. An independent expert or licensing body may play an important role in this respect by ensuring that output and sales data, which may be necessary for the purposes of calculating and verifying royalties is not disclosed to undertakings that compete on affected markets.[73]

In Japan,

> it is important to limit access to confidential information on licensees' business activities gathered by the management organization. It is also advisable to outsource the management of the pooling activities to a third party that has no human or capital connection with participants of the pool.[74]

73 Point 259 of EU TTBER and Article 101 Guidelines.

74 Japanese Guidelines on Standardization and Patent Pool Arrangements, 8–9.

8 Work Pools and Well-Known Trademarks Database

1. Evolution of Modes of Exercising Copyright

The licensing of copyright started from individually negotiated agreements. With the proliferation of copyrights and protected contents and widespread, cross-border exploitation of copyrighted works, the licensing of copyright became collective, feasible only through CMOs if they function properly. Another way of exercising copyright is through entrusting it with a rights-clearance agency, without involving in its operation. The rise of the internet and the ubiquitous penetration of mobile communication devices, especially smartphones, make direct and individual licensing to end users once again practicable. The internet has evolved to be dominated by platforms that intermediate between content creators, aggregators, and (individual and commercial) users and internet platform providers (IPPs) function as de facto CMOs.

2. Individual Licensing of Copyright

Copyright as an exclusive right, by definition, is to be exercised by the individual copyright owners. Whenever possible, copyright owners would prefer to enforce their rights of their own volition. However, technological advancements have greatly enhanced the possibilities of exploiting copyrighted works, especially musical works, video and audio works, and literature works. It became neither feasible nor economical for most rightsholders and the users in this area (with the exception of dramatic works (playwrights, operas) or so-called "grand rights" musical works whose use is confined to a small number of localities)[1] to exploit works on the basis of individual contracts.

However, nowadays almost everyone is subscribing, fee-paying or not, to one or several IPPs and pays a fee to access the internet under their real names, as the popularity of online livelihood demands. Websites of individual or aggregate creators which are accessible to fans and patrons make direct sale, fair trade, license, or subscription of content possible. Creators are regaining access to their fandom. However, this is more of a niche market, rather than the mass and mainstream mode of exercising one's copyrights.

1 Ficsor, M. (2002). *Collective Management of Copyright and Related Rights*, Paragraph 73. WIPO.

DOI: 10.4324/9781003597766-11

3. Work Pools

3.1. CMOs

3.1.1. From National to International

Copyright as an exclusive right is to be exercised by the individual copyright owners. However, technological advancements have greatly enhanced the possibilities of exploiting copyrighted works. It then became neither feasible nor economical for most copyright holders and users to come to terms with the exploitation of works on the basis of individual contracts, with the exception of motion pictures, TV productions, theatrical performances, and other "grand" performances where both parties will make every effort to reach an agreement directly. As early as 1851, an intermediary mechanism between copyright holders and users of musical works was established in France, "Societe des Auteurs, Copositeirs et Editurs des Musique (SACEM)."[2] As the first collecting society, SACEM is still functioning with success. Many countries followed suit and witnessed the emergence and proliferation of CMOs in all kinds of works.

The need and practice of cooperation between CMOs in different countries led to the formation of international non-governmental organizations, the International Confederation of Societies of Authors and Composers (CISAC) established in 1926.[3] As of 2023, CISAC is the world's largest network in the creative sector, with 228 member societies in 119 countries. It indirectly represents more than five million creators within all the artistic repertoires: music, drama, literature, audio-visual works, graphic and visual arts. The total amount of royalties collected by CISAC's member societies in 2021, on their own national collection territories, amounted to more than €9.126 billion; broadcast remains the largest source of global royalty collections, accounting for 38%; digital collections rose +27.9% to €3.12 billion, and account for 32.6% of all global collections (up +49.1% from 2019).[4]

3.1.2. Competition Between National CMOs

From its inception, the French collecting society SACEM has tried to extend its activities to neighboring countries, such as Belgium, Germany, Switzerland, and the UK.[5] That aroused suspicion of cultural imperialism and soon led to the establishment of national CMOs. CMOs have confined their activities in their own countries and concluded reciprocal representation contracts with foreign CMOs to empower the latter to exercise the rights entrusted to them in the relevant foreign

2 Liu, K.-C. (1991). *Das Recht der Urheberrechtsverwertungsgesellschaften* (p. 5). VVF.

3 Ficsor, M. (2002). *Collective Management of Copyright and Related Rights*, Paragraph 29. WIPO.

4 **4** CISAC. *Global Collections Report 2022*, at: https://www.cisac.org/services/reports-and-research/global-collections-report-2022.

5 Liu, K.-C. (1991). *Das Recht der Urheberrechtsverwertungsgesellschaften* (p. 18). VVF.

countries and vice versa. Thus, national CMOs avoided wastefully duplicating collecting mechanisms in foreign countries and secured for each of them an exclusive turf without competition.

Entrenched within respective borders, national CMOs have a de facto monopoly on issuing licenses for exploitations taking place in their territories. However, collective rights management is in essence a service that would best achieve its efficiency through competition among market players, domestic ones as well as foreign. As evidenced by the European experiences, copyright management on a national basis has precluded economies of scale.[6] The loss of the economies of scale would be quite substantial in a world market. The emergence of the internet made cross-border management of copyright all the more urgent.

3.1.3. Functions

A. EFFECTIVE TOOLS TO EXERCISE AUTHORS' RIGHTS

By pooling their individual copyrights in a CMO and mandating it to administer them via a centralized mechanism, authors are in the position to monitor and police the ubiquitous use of their works around the clock and the world over. Thereby, authors gain significant bargaining power to counterbalance the market power of large-scale exploiters and secure better deals with them.

In addition, CMOs also function as unity and solidarity organizations of authors,[7] which aim "to ensure the safeguarding, respect and protection of the moral rights and professional interests attaching to every kind of literary or artistic production."[8] CMOs have proven to be effective and indispensable tools for the exercise of copyrights.

B. REDUCING TRANSACTION COSTS

On a collective basis (such as standardized tariffs, licensing conditions and distribution rules), CMOs reduce the "transaction costs" that would otherwise exist in searching, ascertaining and negotiating individual licenses, monitoring the uses, policing infringements and collecting royalties. CMOs can further reduce transaction costs by concluding licensing agreements with organizations of users.[9] Pursuing this line of rationale, the German Act on the Management of Copyright and Related Rights by Collecting Societies even prescribes that CMOs are obliged to

6 Lueder, T. (2005). Legislative and Policy Developments in the European Union. At *the 13th Annual Fordham Conference on International Intellectual Property Law & Policy*.

7 Lueder, T. (2005). Legislative and Policy Developments in the European Union. At *the 13th Annual Fordham Conference on International Intellectual Property Law & Policy*, 1342.

8 Article 4 of the 2004 Statutes of CISAC. However, the Statutes are no longer available online.

9 Merges, R. (1996). Contracting into liability rules: Intellectual property rights and collective rights organizations. *California Law Review, 84,* 1293(discussing collective rights organizations' impact on reducing transaction costs).

conclude "inclusive contracts" with users' organizations, provided that the number of their members is not too small (Article 35).[10]

C. FACILITATING THE EXPANSION OF COPYRIGHTS

The continual recognition of new copyrights is inherent to the development of copyright law. Increasingly, the speed of copyright expansion depends on the functions that CMOs can offer to copyright holders and users. The more functions and trustworthiness that CMOs exhibit, the more willing is the legislature to recognize new copyrights, such as droit de suite and the right to levies on reproduction devices, which are manageable and enforceable only by a collective mechanism. In Germany, well-developed CMOs did lay the groundwork for a series of so-called "rights only exercisable by CMOs."[11]

D. CULTURAL/SOCIAL FUNCTION

It is a common global practice of the world that CMOs reach beyond collective management to pursue cultural and social functionality. They do this either voluntarily –under the Guidelines of CISAC, up to 10% of the collected license fees may be channelled into the socio-cultural fund (the so-called socio-cultural deduction)[12]—or out of legal obligation. In Germany for example, CMOs are to lay down in their statute that the general assembly of members decides at least on the general policy on deductions in respect of management fees and, where applicable, deductions to promote culturally important works and contributions (Articles 17(1) No. 9 and 32(1)) and set up welfare and assistance schemes (Article 32(2)).

The cultural and social functions of CMOs are particularly important in developing countries, for they can keep a portion of fees collected for foreign CMOs through socio-cultural deductions to achieve cultural and social objectives, not just extracting fees from local users and paying them to foreign CMOs. It is understandable that rightsholders in developed countries may be resistant to this practice. However, such practice is more than just a matter of generosity or solidarity for rightsholders in the developed world, but "may be a matter of foresight or even that of a mere cool-headed calculation in recognizing that, through this, they may better and more efficiently achieve their overall objectives in a globalized world."[13]

10 Martin Kretschmer's critique that "The transaction cost argument does indeed support some form of collective administration but not remotely in the shape of a traditional, membership-based collecting society" is rather questioning the economic rationale of including both authors (composers and lyricists) and publishers in CMOs for music works, since the publishing companies offer enough commercial values to authors to command a full transfer of their copyrights to freely administer these rights as they see fit, without the intervention of authors. See Kretschmer, M. (2002). The failure of property rules in collective administration: Rethinking copyright societies as regulatory instruments. *European Intellectual Property Review, 24(3)*, 127–128.

11 See Subsection 4.6.3 of Chapter 4.

12 Kretschmer, M. (2002). The failure of property rules in collective administration: Rethinking copyright societies as regulatory instruments. *European Intellectual Property Review, 24(3)*, 134.

13 Ficsor, M. (2002). *Collective Management of Copyright and Related Rights*, Paragraph 36. WIPO.

3.1.4. Legal Ramifications

A. CONSTITUTING PROCEDURAL COPYRIGHT LAW

Copyright law as we know it today comprises at least two parts, one of substantive and one of procedural nature. The former deals with the substantive rights of authors, performers, and producers of works; the latter concerns the ways and means of enforcing and managing copyrights and related rights via CMOs. The development of procedural copyright law would surely have an immediate and significant impact on the future of substantive copyright law. The procedural and substantive copyright laws have become inseparable parts of copyright regimes. Ill-functioning CMOs would render the continuous expansion of substantive copyright, especially through Free Trade Agreements in the post-TRIPS era, a senseless legal pursuit and copyright law "omnipresent, distracting, irrelevant."[14]

B. TRANSFORMING COPYRIGHT FROM PROPERTY RIGHT TO LIABILITY RIGHT

If the regime choice between property rules and liability rules is to be made with economic considerations, then the former would be preferred where transaction costs are low, parties involved are few and the value of the asset is difficult to assess, while the latter would be chosen where there are many parties and high transaction costs.[15] Although copyright is commonly perceived as a property right, once under the management of CMOs, which are often subject to a host of regulatory controls, such as compulsory representation, compulsory licensing, the collectivised and tariffed remuneration scheme, copyright to a certain extent is transformed to liability right, a right to receive remuneration.[16]

It has long been suggested that CMOs may have to evolve into a regulatory instrument rewarding creative activity wherever commerce is generated through the use of creative content. In essence, such a suggestion advocates re-thinking the substance of the law of copyright itself as a non-exclusive reward right, deprived of property altogether and akin to a tax system on the users of cultural works.[17]

More and more people come to realize that copyright in its exclusive form is not up to the challenges we are now facing and has to be reformed in a way that is working with and not against the technical and business advancement of the internet.

14 Borrowing from the subtitle of Cornish, W. (2004). *Intellectual Property–Omnipresent, Distracting, Irrelevant*. Oxford University Press.

15 See Subsection 4.14 of Chapter 4.

16 Streeter, T. (1992). Broadcast copyright and the bureaucratization of property. *Cardozo Art & Entertainment Law Journal, 10*, 576.

17 Kretschmer, M. (2002). The failure of property rules in collective administration: Rethinking copyright societies as regulatory instruments. *European Intellectual Property Review, 24(3)*, 135.

3.1.5. Control

A. EX-ANTE CONTROL BY SUI GENERIS LAWS ON CMOS

CMOs resemble patent pool arrangements, in which all the rights needed are gathered together and managed in a uniform manner, to rival the bargaining power of big corporate users and could command market power and restrict market competition, in addition to cultural importance. In many countries, CMOs enjoy legal or factual monopoly for a particular kind of work. Their monopoly power can reach beyond borders through reciprocal representation contracts with other national CMOs. In particular for well-established CMOs "there has been a tendency towards empire-building and inefficient bureaucracy," as notoriously exemplified by excessively high administration costs (up to 25% of the collected fees) of certain CMOs, the one-man rule of GEMA under Erich Schulze from 1947–1995, and the Tournier dynasty over SACEM in France for most of the twentieth century.[18] CMOs are oftentimes plagued with downsides; setting the abuse of market dominance issue aside, opaqueness in operation and underpayment of the actual creators are the two eminent ones.

As the US Copyright Office reports,

> a paramount concern of songwriters and recording artists is transparency in reporting and payment. As digital licensing deals multiply and increase in complexity, it can become quite difficult to follow the money. Songwriters and artists want to ensure that they understand the royalty scheme, are able to track the use of their works, and are paid what they are owed.[19]

Operational opaqueness leads to corruption.[20] In addition, high administrative costs are commonly associated with CMOs, alienating copyright to benefit commercial intermediaries rather than the actual creators.

Therefore, in addition to relying on general competition law (the US), quite a number of jurisdictions either introduce CMO provisions into the copyright law (Korea, Singapore, Thailand, etc.) or enact sui generis regulations (China) or laws (Germany, Taiwan, Japan, etc.) on CMOs.

a. Germany Germany, along with other European countries, has a long history of regulating collecting societies. Germany was also driving the EU Directive on collective management of copyright. Following its traditional approach, the current

18 Kretschmer, M. (2002). The failure of property rules in collective administration: Rethinking copyright societies as regulatory instruments. *European Intellectual Property Review, 24(3)*, 134.

19 US Copyright Office (2015), Copyright and the Music Market Place, 187.

20 One notorious extreme is the Italian CMO, Societá Italiana degli Autoro ed Editorie (SIAE) which reported loss of US $53 million in 1999 even though collections were up. SIAE later again made a US $52.3 million loss by investing in Lehman Brothers which went broke in 2008. See Patry, W. (2011). *How to Fix Copyright* (pp. 181–182). Oxford University Press.

Act on the Management of Copyright and Related Rights by Collecting Societies (Verwertungsgesellschaftengesetz (VGG), effective June 1, 2016) foresees a whole range of obligations to be imposed on CMOs (141 articles in total): Generally, some registration and approval mechanism are put in place to secure a fair operation of such business, to protect those who consign the management of copyright and neighboring rights, to facilitate the exploitation and diffusion of works, performances, phonograms, broadcasts and wire diffusions, and thereby to contribute to the development of culture. It often happens that CMOs cannot agree with commercial users on the royalty and require intervention from the authorities. Some national legislature makes the collective management of certain rights obligatory, and grants protection to creators' societies "in order that they may maintain and strengthen their position and may continue fulfilling all of their complex economic, social and cultural functions."

With the help of information technology, CMOs should be better equipped to monitor the actual use of every work. The distribution of revenues should reflect the actual use of copyrighted works and the costs of administration be more directly allocated to the costs incurred in collecting revenues for particular works, and members should be free to administer particular categories of rights themselves.

CMOs may either be exclusively composed of authors (authors' societies) or commercial rightsholders or be a combination of both groups. In a collecting society that accords membership to authors and commercial rightsholders, it is critically important that these two groups of members can reconcile with each other. In SACEM, for example, changes to membership and distribution rules could only be implemented by mutual consent of both groups. duty to manage rights of rightsholders according to their choice in types of works and other subject matter (Article 9), duty to contract (Article 34), duty to conclude inclusive agreements ("Gesameverträge") with associations of users at reasonable conditions, unless the membership of the association of users is too small (Article 35), duty to allow compulsory use ("the rights of use are deemed to have been granted") by users after paying what is acceptable to them and making conditional payment in the amount exceeding the CMO's claim or has been deposited for its benefit (Article 37), the obligation to set tariffs (Article 38), and to set them on the basis of the pecuniary benefits derived on account of the exploitation or on another basis if there are sufficient indications which can be secured at economically justifiable expense (Article 39), and the obligation (of a collecting society which already grants or offers to grant multi-territorial licenses for online rights in musical works for at least one other collecting society, at the request of a collecting society which itself does not grant or offer to grant any multi-territorial licenses for online rights in musical works) to conclude a representation agreement and to represent the latter (Article 69). CMOs are subject to the supervisory authority of the German Patent and Trademark Office (Article 75) and need to be authorized by it (Article 77).

The German model is based on the background of CMOs being de facto monopolies in their respective area of management. This has worked very well in Germany and German CMOs are leading in the EU.

b. The EU With the single digital market progressing, cross-border operations within the EU become inevitable. This led the European Parliament and the Council to promulgate Directive 2014/26/EU of February 26, 2014, on collective management of copyright and related rights and multi-territorial licensing of rights in musical works for online use in the internal market (45 articles in total), to coordinate the protection of interests of members of CMOs, rightsholders and third parties.

Most importantly, the Directive demands that rightsholders shall have the right to authorize a CMO of their choice to manage the rights, categories of rights or types of works and other subject matter of their choice, for the territories of their choice, irrespective of the Member State of nationality, residence or establishment of either the CMO or the rightsholders. Unless the CMO has objectively justified reasons to refuse management, it shall be obliged to manage such rights, categories of rights or types of works and other subject matter, provided that their management falls within the scope of its activity (Article 5(2)). The Directive further demands that

> Member States shall ensure that any representation agreement between CMOs whereby a CMO mandates another CMO to grant multi-territorial licenses for the online rights in musical works in its own music repertoire is of a non-exclusive nature. The mandated CMO shall manage those online rights on a non-discriminatory basis. (Article 29(1))

c. Taiwan Contrasting the German model is the Taiwanese model. It enacted a sui generis law on CMOs in 1997 which took a heavy-handed approach towards CMOs, wrongly anticipating CMOs becoming as strong as German ones. However, heavy-handedness thwarted collecting societies in Taiwan which are weak in terms of members, collected fees and managed repertoire.[21] In other words, copyrights are not being effectively managed by functional CMOs, and do not generate the kind of revenues that would incentivize new works.

B. EX-POST CONTROL BY COMPETITION LAW

Ex-post control of CMOs via competition law can be observed at least in the US and EU.

a. In the US The music public performance market has long been dominated by the largest and second-largest CMOs, ASCAP and BMI. ASCAP and BMI provide collective licensing services that make significant contributions to many businesses that benefit from immediate access to music, as well as to songwriters, composers, and publishers who would otherwise have to individually license or enforce against

21 Liu, K.-C. (2019). Royalty setting disputes between CMOs, TIPO, and CATV operators. In Liu, K.-C. (Ed.), *Annotated Leading Copyright Cases in Major Asian Jurisdictions* (pp. 124–125). City University of HK Press.

multiple music users. However, they also caused competitive concerns arising from the exclusive, collective, and blanket licensing of individual copyrights. Therefore since 1941, the DOJ entered into the consent decrees with ASCAP and BMI to address these concerns. The crux of the decrees is to encourage competition between ASCAP, BMI, and other performance rights organizations for members and music users, and between ASCAP, BMI, and their respective members to license copyrighted works to music users. The decrees prohibit exclusive licensing and protect the ability of ASCAP and BMI members to license works directly if they wish. The latest review of the consent decree in 2021 decides to keep it going, making governmental oversight last longer than eighty years.[22]

b. In the EU The EC is very mindful of the competition-restrictive effects of practices adopted by CMOs. As early as 1971 the EC ruled that individual rightsholders should be able to join foreign CMOs to manage their rights in countries where individual rightsholders' national CMO merely acts through a reciprocal representation contract with those foreign CMOs.[23] In 1987, the CJEU ruled that an excessive royalty could be an abuse of dominant position:

> It is not impossible, however, that the amount of the royalty, or of the combined royalties, charged by the copyright-management society may be such that Article 86 (currently Article 102 added by the author) applies. The national court . . . held that SACEM must be regarded as an undertaking occupying a dominant position within the common market. It follows that if that undertaking were to engage in abusive practices, in particular by imposing unfair conditions, its conduct would be contrary to Article 86.[24]

The EC further found in 1989 that the practice of CMOs of refusing to grant a license or to entrust their repertoire abroad to CMO other than the one established in the territory in question, first via exclusive-rights clauses in the reciprocal representation contracts, and when such clauses were removed at the request of the EC, then by means of a concerted practice, to be:

> concerted action by national copyright-management societies with the effect of systematically refusing to grant direct access to their repertoires to foreign users must be regarded as mounting to a concerted practice restrictive of competition and capable of affecting trade between the Member States.[25]

22 Statement of the DOJ on the Closing of the Antitrust Division's Review of the ASCAP and BMI Consent Decrees (Remarks by the then Assistant Attorney General Makan Delrahim on 15 January 2021) at https://www.justice.gov/atr/page/file/1355391/dl?inline.

23 O.J. L134, June 20, 1971 (GEMA).

24 Case 402/85, *Basset v. SACEM* (decided on April 9, 1987), Paragraph 19.

25 Case 395/87, *Ministére Public v. Tournier* (decided on 13 July 1989), Paragraph 23.

It continued to determine that:

> for a copyright-management society occupying a dominant position . . . to fix a scale and rate of royalty which is several times greater than that applied by all copyright-management societies in the member countries of the EEC without any objectively justifiable ground and is unrelated to the sums redistributed to the authors, so that the royalty is disproportionate to the economic value of the service provided,

it must be regarded as indicative of abuse of a dominant position.[26]

3.1.6. Empowerment: Extended Collective Licensing

The EU foresees in its Digital Single Market Directive 2019/790 collective licensing with an extended effect that allows Member States to provide that where a CMO enters into a licensing agreement for the exploitation of works or other subject matter: such an agreement can be extended to apply to the rights of rightsholders who have not authorised that collective management organisation to represent them by way of assignment, license or any other contractual arrangement; or with respect to such an agreement, the organisation has a legal mandate or is presumed to represent rightsholders who have not authorised the organisation accordingly (Article 12).

3.2. Rights-Clearance Agency

There are two kinds of agency, one voluntary and the other statutory.

3.2.1. Voluntary

Much later than CMOs, which are operated by members, rights-clearance agencies emerged, as corporate copyright holders (producers and publishers, etc.) chose—in parallel to or independent of the collective exercise of their rights—to commission an agency to clear their rights for them with no or some collectivised elements. The agency has the sole task of collecting and transferring royalties in accordance with individual rates and conditions as quickly and precisely as possible, and as much in proportion with the value and actual use of the works involved as possible.

The rights-clearance agency functions as a platform of licensing and of acquiring licenses.[27] Rights-clearance agency can be more appealing to individual creators, because they do not have to become a member of any CMO and get involved in its daily operation, and need only to sign an authorization agreement, with no extra costs incurred for the operation of CMOs and no subsidies paid to their peers, whether domestic or foreign.

26 Case 395/87, *Ministére Public v. Tournier* (decided on 13 July 1989), Paragraph 38.
27 Ficsor, M. (2002). *Collective Management of Copyright and Related Rights*, Paragraph 37. WIPO.

An example in point would be the Copyright Clearance Centre (CCC) based in the US.[28] CCC is a broker of licenses. The company earns a 15% commission and 15% administrative fee on revenue it collects and passes the remaining 70% to publishers.[29]

3.2.2. Statutory

In the US, surprisingly, there are a couple of statutory rights-clearing agencies, SoundExchange and MLC. The US Small Webcaster Settlement Act of 2002 (SWSA) was enacted to provide relief to small and noncommercial webcasters after the first statutory royalties for webcasting were set by a "Copyright Arbitration Royalty Panel." Pursuant to the SWSA, small commercial and noncommercial webcasters reached agreements with SoundExchange (since 2003 non-profit, the sole organization designated by the US Library of Congress to collect and distribute digital performance royalties for sound recordings, to administer Section 114 sound recording license (scope of exclusive rights in sound recordings). It pays featured and non-featured artists and master rights (recording) owners for the non-interactive use of sound recordings under the statutory licenses. SoundExchange collects and distributes digital performance royalties on behalf of 650,000 creators and growing. Through proprietary music tech solutions that turn data into accurate revenue, SoundExchange has paid more than $11 billion in distributions to date (May 2024).[30]

Whereas the 2002 SWSA was limited to small and noncommercial webcasters, the Webcaster Settlement Act of 2008 makes the negotiation procedure available to all webcasters regardless of size or commercial nature. Under the Act, agreements with SoundExchange will apply to all copyright owners of sound recordings, including the approximately 5% of copyright owners that are not directly represented by SoundExchange. Thus, webcasters would need to reach only one agreement, and they would be covered for all sound recordings they might perform.

After years of deliberation, the US passed the Music Modernization Act (MMA) of 2018. MMA is organized into three key titles: Title I—Music Licensing Modernization Act (Sec. 115); Title II—Classics Protection and Access Act (Sec. 1401); and Title III—Allocation for Music Producers Act (§114(g)).

On July 8, 2019, the US Copyright Office named the Mechanical Licensing Collective (MLC) non-profit to issue blanket mechanical licenses for qualified

28 The House and Senate Reports accompanying the enactment of the 1976 Act recommended the formation of a neutral clearinghouse to facilitate "workable clearance and licensing procedures," a voluntary organization dedicated to "work[ing] out means by which permissions for uses beyond fair use can be obtained easily, quickly, and at reasonable fees." Therefore, CCC was born in 1978 in the US. See Rich, R. B. (2021). History of CCC and relevance to the Texaco case. In Copyright Clearance Center, *Creating Solutions Together: Lessons to Inform the Future of Collective Licensing* (pp. 31–37), at: https://www.copyright.com/wp-content/uploads/2021/01/CCC_CreatingSolutionsTogether_Ebook_2020.pdf.

29 See https://en.wikipedia.org/wiki/Copyright_Clearance_Center.

30 See https://www.soundexchange.com/who-we-are/#about-us.

streaming and download services (digital service providers, DSPs) in the US, such as Spotify, Apple Music, Amazon Music, and Tidal, and collecting royalties due under those licenses and paying music publishers and administrators; ex-US CMOs; and self-administered songwriters, composers, and lyricists. In cases where the MLC is not able to match musical works to copyright owners, the MLC is authorized to distribute the unclaimed royalties to copyright owners identified in the MLC records, based on the relative market shares of such copyright owners as reflected in reports of usage provided by digital music providers for the periods in question. MLC started functioning in January 2021. It has successfully distributed over US $2 billion in royalties by May 2024.[31]

3.3. IPPs Licensing

3.3.1. A Business Model Replacing P2P

The internet and smartphones have become game changers in the realm of copyright licensing. Peer-to-peer (P2P) file sharing of copyrighted content went viral in the 1990s, as it follows the social fact that people like to borrow and share words, ideas, sounds, and images.[32] RIAA in response sued P2P websites for indirect, contributory and/or joint infringement of copyright the world over, one after the other beginning with the 1999 suit against Napster: Scour, Aimster, AudioGalaxy, Morpheus, Grokster, Kazaa, iMesh, and LimeWire, winning many battles but losing the war![33]

Then iTunes by Apple in the late 2000s ushered in streaming services by IPPs. IPPs include music platforms (e.g. Spotify, Amazon Music and Google Play, Apple

31 See https://www.themlc.com/.

32 McLeod, K., & DiCola, P. (2011). *Creative License: The Law and Culture of Digital Sampling* (p. 266). Duke University Press.

33 To deal with the once popular P2P file sharing, the Electronic Frontier Foundation has advocated a voluntary collective licensing regime as a mechanism that would fairly compensate artists and rights holders for P2P file sharing: the music industry forms one or more CMOs, which then offers file-sharing music fans the opportunity to "get legit" in exchange for a reasonable regular payment. So long as they pay, the fans are free to keep doing what they are going to do anyway (Electronic Frontier Foundation. (2008). *A Better Way Forward: Voluntary Collective Licensing of Music File Sharing* (p. 13), at: http://www.eff.org/wp/better-way-forward-voluntary-collective-licensing-music-file-sharing). In the literature, compulsory license model complemented by levy arrangement has also been suggested (Hilman, L. (2013). Fair trade copyright. *Columbia Journal of Law & the Arts, 36(2)*, 191, 194–201, at: ssrn.com/abstract¼2698069). Other proposed solutions include the establishment of a global internet licensing agency (Sterling, J.A.L. (2010)). Online exploitation and licensing. In Bently, L., Suthersanen, U., & Torremanns, P. (Eds.), *Global Copyright* (p. 295). Edward Elgar Publishing), a fair copyright system that encourages users to donate to recording artists on digital platforms and distribute the donations to artists, and the so-called "reverse liability rule," allowing copyright owners a choice between a compulsory license and a reverse liability rule. Under the reverse liability rule, copyright owners can block the use of their works by paying a fee to the government fund that would in return finance some other works. See McLeod, K., & DiCola, P. (2011). *Creative License: The Law and Culture of Digital Sampling* (p. 265). Duke University Press.

Music social), social media (e.g., Facebook, TikTok, Instagram), and multi-media (e.g., YouTube (owned by Google), Netflix). High smartphone penetration makes IPPs appear on smartphones (e.g., Apple, Samsung) as apps.

IPPs are reaching every online user of copyrighted works from anywhere and, therefore, generating unprecedented revenues for rightsholders. IPPS are probably the most important way of exercising copyright in our online world. IPPs' financial model can be based on per-use fee, flat subscription fee, or ads sponsorship as there are users who are willing to pay extra to get access to copyrighted content, users who are undiscerning and used to pay a flat rate to IPPs, and users who are reluctant to make extra payment for any online content.

Compared to other work pools via CMOs and rights-clearance agencies, IPPs have the most powerful technical capability to keep track of users' use of content and are also actually collecting data about that usage, and can provide the ultimate transparency, accountability, and efficiency that were previously unthinkable. With transparent bookkeeping and auditing comes much faster royalty calculation, payment, and distribution.[34]

3.3.2. Oversight of IPPs

A. EQUITY STRUCTURE

One pressing issue would be the transparency in the equity structure of IPPs which are partially held by rights owners. For instance, major labels together reportedly negotiated an 18% stake in the super music IPP Spotify.[35] Such equity deals and whether and how the value received by the labels will negatively impact the royalties that are to be paid to artists and songwriters and therefore must be reported to artists and songwriters.

B. ABUSE OF DOMINANCE

Successful IPPs could enjoy overwhelming market power, and if unchecked would cause more shortcomings than traditional CMOs do. IPPs should establish industry-wide, certified accounting and auditing requirements standards for usage registration, and develop compatible systems that ensure the exchangeability of data among and between IPPs and CMOs.

IPPs on smartphones easily fall prey to the dominant market power of smartphone operators, such as Apple and Samsung, which can be abused. On March 4, 2024, the EC fined Apple over €1.8 billion for abusing its dominant position on the market for the distribution of music streaming apps to iPhone and iPad users ("iOS

34 Pitt, I. (2015). *Direct Licensing and the Music Industry –How Technology, Innovation and Competition Reshaped Copyright Licensing* (p. 162). Springer.

35 Before the Swedish Spotify was launched a number of record companies bought 18% of the company's stocks: Sony BMG (5.8%), Universal Music (4.8%), Warner Music (3.8%) and EMI (1.9%), at: www.swedishwire.com/jobs/680-record-labels-part-owner-of-spotify.

users") through its app store. In particular, Apple applied restrictions on app developers preventing them from informing iOS users about alternative and cheaper music subscription services available outside of the app ("anti-steering provisions").[36]

4. Database of Well-Known Trademarks

4.1. Introduction

The function of a trademark is elastic, as opposed to other IP rights, such as copyright and patent. The more famous and well-known the mark has become, the more protection it deserves as it acquires more functions. The functions of a trademark grow from the core distinction function to include the advertisement function, quality guarantee function and even investment function.

In order to extend protection to marks already known but not registered in the country where protection is sought, the Paris Convention introduced in 1925 the "well-known" marks regime in Article 6bis. Article 6bis limits the protection of well-known marks to prohibit others' registration or use of confusingly similar marks on identical or similar goods (excluding services). Article 16(2) and (3) of the TRIPS Agreement further applies Article 6bis of the Paris Convention to services and dissimilar goods or services. The term well-known mark is widely used by countries the world over. However, since neither the Paris Convention nor the TRIPS Agreement defines the term, the practices of recognizing and protecting well-known marks vary significantly from country to country.[37]

The continual strengthening of the protection for well-known marks has been one of the features of international trademark development in the post-TRIPS era. In many countries, well-known marks can now be granted full trademark rights and protection merely from the fact that they are well-known; well-known marks can also be protected against the likelihood of dilution,[38] and against comparative advertising that is discrediting or denigrating.[39] However, for market latecomers seeking to register or use a new trademark, there is no clear way to determine if a pre-existing mark is well-known. Without this certainty, late-comers cannot calculate the risk of their trademark application being rejected or their use of such a mark constituting trademark infringement.

Therefore, various jurisdictions establish different ways of recognizing and/or listing well-known marks, with divergent effects. This chapter first examines the

36 See https://ec.europa.eu/commission/presscorner/detail/en/ip_24_1161.

37 Mostert, F. (2004). *Famous and Well-Known Marks* (2nd ed., pp. 1–5). INTA NY.

38 According to the US Trademark Dilution Revision Act of 2006, the owner of a famous mark shall be entitled to an injunction against another person who commences to use a mark or trade name in commerce that is likely to cause dilution by blurring or dilution by tarnishment of the famous mark.

39 According to Article 4(d), Directive 2006/114/EC of the European Parliament and of the Council of December 12, 2006, concerning misleading and comparative advertising (codified version), comparative advertising that discredits or denigrates the trademarks, trade names, other distinguishing marks, goods, services, activities, or circumstances of a competitor, shall not be allowed.

various practices of recognizing and/or listing well-known marks. It then evaluates the pros and cons of different models of recognizing and/or listing well-known marks. With the aim of maximizing the usefulness and minimizing the misuse of recognizing and listings, this chapter concludes by advocating the creation of a centralized online database by individual members of the WTO to collect well-known marks cases recognized by authorities in the past five years in their respective jurisdictions.

4.2. Different Ways of Recognizing and Listing Well-Known Marks

In Asia, at least Japan, China, Korea, Taiwan, and India have developed some type of recognizing and/or listing regime for well-known marks. So do the Russian Federation (RF), Ukraine, and Finland in Europe. These practices of recognizing and listing well-known marks can be classified into two main groups: case-independent and case-dependent. "Case-independent" means the authority can determine whether a mark is well-known simply based on applications, even if there is not an actual trademark case involving examination, opposition, infringement, etc. "Case-dependent" means the authority can only determine whether the mark at issue is indeed well-known when there is an actual case pending. Case-independent recognition and listing of well-known marks have certain legal effects in Japan, RF, and India, but function only as an extra service with no legal effect in Finland. Case-dependent listing of well-known marks is without legal effects and can be found in Ukraine, China, and Taiwan.[40]

4.2.1. Case-Independent Recognition and Listing

A prototype of case-independent recognition and listings of well-known marks with legal effect was proposed in 2003 by Lars Smith of the Louisville University Law School. According to Smith, a "Fame Register" should be established and maintained by the USPTO, a Register that is independent from the Principal Register and the Supplemental Register. Applicants who believe that they are in a position of a famous mark may file an application with USPTO requesting that the mark be included in the Fame Register. In contrast to Principal Register applications where USPTO has the burden of proof that a mark is not entitled to registration, applicants for inclusion in the Fame Register bear the burden of proving that their mark is famous and thus entitled to a registration.[41] During the application process, any party with standing may initiate an opposition to challenge the fame determination

40 According to the website of National Office of IP (NOIP), at: https://ipvietnam.gov.vn/web/english/well-known-trademarks if a well-known mark is recognized according to civil procedures or under a recognition.Decision of the NOIP that well-known marks shall be recorded in the list of well-known marks kept at the NOIP. However, as of July 23, 2024, no such list can be found on NOIP's website.

41 Smith, L. (2003). Implementing a registration system for famous trademarks. *Trademark Reporter*, *93*, 1118, 1131.

before registration is issued.[42] If the application is published and not successfully opposed, the application will be subject to automatic review by the Trademark Trial and Appeal Board (TTAB). Automatic review by the TTAB is warranted because of the import and potential significance of fame registration.[43] Registration on the Fame Register affords the owner nationwide protection for ten years from the date of registration and can be renewed.[44] Fame registration should be subject to cancellation on all the grounds listed in Section 14 of the Lanham Act. In addition, Section 14 should be amended to include a new subsection that would permit petitions to cancel fame registration at any time on the grounds that the mark is not, or is no longer, famous.[45]

A. WITH LEGAL EFFECTS

a. Japan: Well-known Marks Registered as Defensive Marks Japan is a member of the Paris Convention (1899) and the WTO (1995). Its Trademark Act and Unfair Competition Prevention Act provide protection for well-known marks.[46] Article 4(1)(x) of the Trademark Act makes a trademark unregistrable which "is identical with, or similar to, another person's trademark which is well-known among consumers as that indicating goods or services in connection with the person's business if the trademark is used in connection with the goods or services or goods or services similar to them." When a well-known mark is registered, it acquires an exclusive right to use the mark for the designated goods or services, just like any other trademarks that are not well-known or have not been used at the time of filing trademark registration application.

Beginning in 1959 the owner of a registered well-known mark has been further allowed by Article 64 of the Trademark Act to register that mark as a defensive mark, without having the intention of using it for goods or services dissimilar to the designated goods or services of the registered well-known mark, in order to pre-empt and prevent other parties from using the defensive mark and thereby causing confusion.[47] Compared with 513 well-known marks registrations in 1982,[48] Japan Patent Office (JPO) recognizes some 1,228 well-known trademarks as of

42 Smith, L. (2003). Implementing a registration system for famous trademarks. *Trademark Reporter, 93*, 1134.

43 Smith, L. (2003). Implementing a registration system for famous trademarks. *Trademark Reporter, 93*, 1137.

44 Smith, L. (2003). Implementing a registration system for famous trademarks. *Trademark Reporter, 93*, 1150.

45 Smith, L. (2003). Implementing a registration system for famous trademarks. *Trademark Reporter, 93*, 1140.

46 Hinkelmann, K. (2019). *Gewerblicher Rechtsschutz in Japan* (3rd ed.). Carl Heymanns Verlag.

47 Doi, T. (2007). Japan. In Mostert, F. (Ed.), *Famous and Well-Known Marks* (2nd ed.), 4–250. INTA NY.

48 Heath, C. (2000). The protection of well-known marks in Japan. In Heath, C., & Liu, K.-C. (Eds.), *The Protection of Well-known Marks in Asia* (p. 83). Springer.

2022 in the application process for defensive marks and publishes them in both Japanese and English on the website of National Centre for Industrial Property Information and Training.[49] The registration could provide easy proof of the fame of the registered mark in a trademark invalidation procedure or an infringement lawsuit. However, the absolute majority of such registered well-known trademarks were applied for before 2004 (1,215), and the remaining 13 were applied for between 2004 and 2016: 2016 (1), 2015 (1), 2012 (2), 2011 (2), 2010 (1), 2007 (1), 2006 (2), 2005 (2), and 2004 (1). It seems to suggest the declining significance and, therefore, interest of defensive trademark registration in Japan.

b. Russian Federation: Granting Indefinite Period of Legal Protection to Generally-Recognized Marks The Russian Federation (RF) became a member of the Paris Convention on July 1, 1965, through its predecessor the Soviet Union. The RF has been a member of the WTO since 2012.[50] The first Russian Trademark Law of 1992 included certain protection for marks considered well-known without spelling out the terms as such. It was not until March 1998 with the promulgation of the Decree of the Government of the RF No. 367, "On the Formation of Supreme Patent Chamber of Russian Agency for Patents and Trademarks," that the Supreme Patent Chamber of Federal Service for Intellectual Property (Rospatent) was empowered to recognize well-known marks upon application.[51] This empowerment of the Rospatent continues with the enactment of Statute of the Federal Service for Intellectual Property in 2017.

In 2002, the Russian Trademark Law was amended and incorporated into Part IV of the Civil Code.[52] According to Article 1508(1), at the request of a person a trademark can be recognized as "a trademark generally-recognized" in the RF by a decision of the Rospatent if such trademark as the result of intensive use of this trademark or this designation had become broadly known in the RF among relevant consumers in respect of the person's goods as of the date indicated in the application.

Article 1508(2) continues to provide that the legal protection for a trademark shall be granted to a generally-recognized trademark and the grant of legal protection to a generally-recognized trademark means the recognition of an exclusive right to the generally-recognized trademark which has infinite duration.[53] Nevertheless, this does not secure a well-known trademark against cancellation

49 See https://www.j-platpat.inpit.go.jp/t0400.

50 Arievich, E., & Hoffman, J. (2007). Russian federation. In Mostert, F. (Ed.), *Famous and Well-Known Marks* (2nd ed.), 4–295. INTA NY.

51 Liu, K.-C., Wang, E., & Tao, X. L. (2009). The use and misuse of well-known marks listings. *International Review of Industrial Property and Competition Law*, *40(6)*, 685–697.

52 An English version of Part IV of the Civil Code with amendments dated 14.07.2022 is available at: https://rospatent.gov.ru/en/documents/grazhdanskiy-kodeks-rossiyskoy-federacii-chast-chetvertaya.

53 Arievich, E., & Hoffman, J. (2007). Russian Federation. In Mostert, F. (Ed.), *Famous and Well-Known Marks* (2nd ed.), 4–305, 4–306. INTA NY.

of recognition due to non-use or the fact that the trademark was recognized as well-known in violations of the requirement of the law.

A trademark deemed generally-recognized shall be entered into the list of generally-recognized trademarks. A certificate for a well-known trademark shall be issued by Rospatent within one month after the trademark is entered into the list of generally-recognized trademarks (Article 1509(2) and (3)). As of this writing,[54] there are some 191 well-known marks on the List, with ten recognized in 2022, three in 2023, and 2024 respectively, and the oldest one recognized in 2005.[55]

c. India In India, a well-known trademark is accorded extra protection and safeguards against passing off and infringement. Traditionally, trademarks could be declared as "well known" by either the civil courts or the Trade Marks Registry during adversarial proceedings wherein the trademark was under challenge through revocation proceedings. The Trade Marks Act does not give the Registry the power to declare marks as well-known in the absence of such proceedings and on mere application by the trademark owner.

However, pursuant to Rule 124 of Trade Mark Rules of 2017, any person may file a request for determination of a trademark as well-known, which is criticized as unconstitutional for lack of legislative delegation and resuming legislative function that cannot be delegated by Parliament to the Executive.[56] The applicant must pay a fee of INR $100,000 (approx. US $1,250), which is prescribed for one mark only. The request shall be accompanied by a statement of case along with all the evidence and documents relied on by the applicant. The Registrar may call further

54 See Federal Institute of Industrial Property, Trademarks, Service Marks, Geographical Indications and Appellations of Origin (Russian). At: https://www1.fips.ru/publication-web/publications/UsrTM?tab=UsrTM&inputDocNumber=&inputDocNumber_from=&inputDocNumber_to=&inputSelectOIS=CKTM&selectOISDocType=AllDocs&_extendedFilter=on&registration_S=&registration_Po=&searchTextBox_applicationNumber=&searchTextBox_applicationNumber_from=&searchTextBox_applicationNumber_to=&publish_S=&publish_Po=&applicationFilling_S=&applicationFilling_Po=&searchTextBox_classifierMktu=&selectFieldGroup_NoticeType=0&selectFieldGroupValue_NoticeType=&searchSortSelect=dtPublish&searchSortDirection=true.

55 After the West imposed sanctions on RF due to its war with Ukraine, some anti-sanction measures were taken by RF, some of which concerned trademarks. The Decree of President No. 322 on the Temporary Procedure for Fulfillment Obligations to Certain Right Holders (effective on May 27, 2022) establishes the temporary procedure for payment of royalties to the foreign IP owners under license agreements, to special ruble accounts with some restrictions to use money from such accounts. This order was adopted to prevent one-side termination of license agreements due to non-payment, because many licensees in Russia cannot fulfill their obligations to pay royalties due to sanctions in the banking system. Foreign IP owners, who are not leaving the Russian market, continue communication with their licensees and provide necessary goods (if any), information (if agreed), brand management (if agreed), and accept license fees, are not affected by this order. See IP and anti-sanctions measures in Russia: myths and reality posted on July 29, 2022, at: https://azalesov.com/analytics/blog/ip-and-anti-sanctions-measures-in-russia-myths-and-reality-3.

56 Reddy, P. (2017). *The 'Well Known' Trademark under the New Trade Mark Rule: Is the New Procedure Constitutional?* at: https://spicyip.com/2017/04/the-well-known-trademark-under-the-new-trade-mark-rules-2017-is-the-new-procedure-constitutional.html.

such documents as they think fit for the determination of a well-known mark. Moreover, before determining a trademark as well-known, the Registrar may invite objections from the general public to be filed within thirty days from the date of invitation of such objection. In case the trademark is determined as well-known, the same shall be published in the trademark journal and included in the list of well-known trademarks maintained by the Registrar.

The Registrar may, at any time, remove the trademark from the list of well-known marks after giving an opportunity of hearing to the concerned party if it is found that a trademark has been erroneously or inadvertently included or is no longer justified to be in the said list.[57] There are 137 recognized well-known marks collected in the list of well-known trademarks as of October 10, 2022.[58] However, that number jumped to 281 in March 2024.[59] It is noteworthy that at a closer look, the list contains a substantial number of well-known marks recognized by courts and even the WIPO Arbitration and Mediation Center (involving the marks "Honda" and "Red Bull"), without giving the reason why they are included. The oldest one was recognized in 1985.

B. WITHOUT LEGAL EFFECTS

In Finland, there is a purely additional information service with regard to trademarks with a reputation. In June 2007 the National Board of Patents and Registration of Finland (NBPR), now the Finnish Patent and Registration Office (PRH), started to establish a list of trademarks with a reputation in Finland. The acceptance of applications began in August 2007. The list is a database separate from the Trademark Register,[60] and one of the PRH's services that are subject to application fee. The proof of reputation must be submitted by the applicant. Market and reputation surveys carried out by an independent and impartial organization, advertising and marketing material, monetary value of the trademark, and court or authority decisions can all be accepted as proof of reputation.

An entry in the list will remain in force for five years. It may be renewed for another five years, provided that the application fee and entry fee are paid and proofs of reputation are submitted. Anyone may request that an entry be removed from the list on the grounds that the entry was a priori or a posteriori contrary to the Finnish Trademark Act.[61]

The List is without legal effect and cannot be taken to a court of law or any other independent judicial organ. If the PRH does not admit a trademark to the list, or

57 Rule 124 of The Trade Mark Regulation, 2017, at: https://ipindia.gov.in/TM-Rules-2017.htm or https://www.wipo.int/wipolex/en/text/468047.

58 See https://www.ipindia.gov.in/IPIndiaAdmin/writereaddata/Portal/Images/pdf/List_of_Well-Known_Trade_Marks_as_of_10.10.2022.pdf.

59 See https://www.ipindia.gov.in/IPIndiaAdmin/writereaddata/Portal/Images/pdf/List_of_Well-Known_Trade_Marks_as_of_18.03.2024.pdf.

60 Myllymäki, T. (2008). List of trademarks with a reputation in Finland. *IPR Info, 1*, 41, at: https://iprinfo.fi/artikkeli/list_of_trademarks_with_a_reputation_in_finland/.

61 PRH. *Trademarks with a Reputation* (latest update 16 August 2022), at: https://www.prh.fi/en/trademarks/trademarks_with_a_reputation.html.

removes a trademark already entered in the list, the rightsholder may only request a re-examination. Marks entered in the list are published in the Trademark Gazette; however, not on the English website of PRH.

The purpose of the list is to serve commerce and industry, agents and all other stakeholders that need information on reputable marks. The list is helpful when conducting preliminary examinations or tests of confusing similarities of trademarks and should thereby have a preventive effect on trademark disputes.

If the PRH while processing an ordinary trademark application finds a confusingly similar mark in the list, it will notify both the person who filed the trademark application and the owner of the earlier trademark with a reputation. The notification is made regardless of the class(es) in which the mark is sought to be registered. However, the PRH will not take the trademark in the list of trademarks with a reputation into consideration as an obstacle to the registration of the application. It is up to the owner of the trademark with a reputation to decide whether to file an opposition later when the applied trademark has been registered. Therefore, for the owner of the trademark with a reputation, the question is of a supervision service.[62] Nevertheless, the list may have relevance in the trademark trials as part of evidence; it may also broaden the actual scope of protection granted for well-known marks by discouraging small and medium companies from pursuing their trademark applications.[63]

4.2.2. Case-Dependent Recognition and Listing

A. UKRAINE

There has been a regime change in Ukraine with regard to the recognition and listing of well-known marks, switching from case-independent recognition and listing of well-known marks with legal effects to case-dependent recognition and listing. Article 25(1) of Ukraine's 1993 law on Protection of Rights to Marks for Goods and Services for the first time provides for the recognition of well-known marks: the protection afforded to a well-known mark is based on the recognition of the mark as a well-known mark by the Appeals Chamber or by courts. The recognition of a well-known mark used to have not just a case-by-case effect, but a general effect throughout the validity period of the trademark certificate, that is, ten years.[64]

However, with the 2020 amendment (Law of Ukraine on Amending Certain Legislative Acts of Ukraine Concerning Strengthening the Security and Protection

62 PRH. *Trademarks with a Reputation* (latest update June 5, 2024), at: https://www.prh.fi/en/trademarks/trademarks_with_a_reputation.html.

63 Pakarinen, M. (2008). The great reputation of your brand can be registered in Finland. *IPR Info, 1*, 43–44.

64 Liu, K.-C., Wang, E., & Tao, X. L. (2009). The use and misuse of well-known marks listings. *International Review of Industrial Property and Competition Law, 40(6)*, 692.

of Rights to Trademarks and Industrial Designs and Combating Patent Abuse),[65] Article 25(4) now provides:

> If the trademark is recognized as well-known under the legal procedure, a person, which trademark is recognized as well-known, shall inform the Institution of such decision. Information on well-known trademarks . . . shall be entered into the list of trademarks well-known in Ukraine and published in the Bulletin. The list of trademarks well-known in Ukraine shall be for reference purposes, available for the public and published on the official website of the Institution.

There is indeed a database "Information about Well-Known Marks in Ukraine" published on the website of the Ukrainian National Office for Intellectual Property and Innovations (UANIPIO).[66] However, the database does not seem to be functioning in reality.

B. CHINA: FROM EX-ANTE RECOGNIZING AND LISTING TO EX-POST LISTING

a. Paradigm Shift The Trademark Law enacted in 1982 was silent on the subject of well-known marks. However, scholars and the administration derived the obligation to protect well-known marks from China's accession to the Paris Convention on March 19, 1985. There has been occasional registration of internationally well-known marks that were deemed descriptive in nature.[67] In the period between August 1996 and December 2001, there was "active and wholesale approval of well-known marks" made exclusively by the Trademark Office (TMO) and its review authority—the Trademark Appeal Board (TAB)—under the National General Administration for Industry and Commerce (NGAIC). The decisions of both the TMO and the TAB were final and judicially non-reviewable.[68]

From December 2001 onward commenced passive and dual recognition by the TMO and TAB on the one hand and courts on the other. The determination of the TMO and TAB could be appealed to the Beijing People's Intermediate Court. The TMO had published on its website well-known marks that it and the TAB had recognized. The publication made no reference to the cases in which the marks were recognized as well-known.

A fever for well-known marks had swept across the nation and resulted in widespread fraud and a hypertrophy of "well-known marks" that were in fact not

65 See https://www.wipo.int/wipolex/en/text/579054.

66 See https://ukrpatent.org/en/articles/bases.

67 Feng, P. (2000). Protection of well-known marks in China. In Heath, C., & Liu, K.-C. (Eds.), *The Protection of Well-Known Marks in Asia* (pp. 31–32). Kluwer Law International.

68 Feng, P. (2000). Protection of well-known marks in China. In Heath, C., & Liu, K.-C. (Eds.), *The Protection of Well-Known Marks in Asia* (pp. 31–32). Kluwer Law International, 34–35.

well-known at all.[69] This misuse of recognizing and/or listing of well-known marks was finally remedied by the 2013 amendment to the Trademark Law. Although the TMO and TAB as well as courts remain empowered as before to recognize well-known marks during trademark examination, the administrative handling of trademark infringement cases, and trademark disputes upon application, and so are courts in trying civil and administrative cases (Article 14(2) to (4)). Article 14(5) now prohibits manufacturers and business operators from using a description of "well-known trademarks" on products, packages, or containers of products, on advertisements, or in exhibitions or commercial activities. Article 53 punishes violation of Article 14(5) with a fine of RMB 100,000.

This swing to the opposite extreme of not allowing the marketing of well-known trademarks typical of China's paradigm shift, is on the one hand not justified as it abridges the freedom of commercial speech. To alleviate public concerns about overly restrictive application of Article 45(5), China National IP Administration (CNIPA) in its Notice on Strengthening the Work of Protecting Well-Known Marks in the Investigation on Cases Violating the Trademark Law, issued in November 2019, distinguishes between proper and illegal use of the wording of "well-known marks":

> Businesses can make descriptive statements during their business activities about the fact that their marks have obtained the protection of well-known marks (proper use added by the author).
>
> If, however, businesses use the wording of "well-known marks" as honorary title and stand it out, with an intention to dilute the legal nature of recognition and protection of well-known marks, to advertise their business or promote their goods or services (illegal use added by the author), then it should be dealt with by Article 45(5).[70]

It is, therefore, correct as some suggest, "a proprietor can advertise the recognition of its well-known mark status as an event on its company websites, WeChat accounts."[71]

b. Providing Low Presumptive Effect to Recognized Well-Known Marks The NGAIC (currently State Administration of Market Regulation (SAMR)) issued the Rules for the Determination and Protection of Well-Known Trademarks in 2003 which was last amended in 2014. Article 16(2) of the Rules grants low presumptive effect to the recognized well-known mark by allowing the TMO, TAB, or the department in charge of trademark infringement cases to rely on the protection

69 For more details see Liu, K.-C., Wang, E., & Tao, X. L. (2009). The use and misuse of well-known marks listings. *International Review of Industrial Property and Competition Law, 40(6)*, 688–690.

70 關於加強查處商標違法案件中馳名商標保護相關工作的通知, at: http://www.gov.cn/zhengce/zhengceku/2019-11/25/content_5455199.html.

71 Ganea, P. et al. (2021). *Intellectual Property Law in China* (2nd ed., p. 251). Kluwer.

record in disputed cases to provide the mark with the protection awarded to the recognized well-known mark after taking relevant evidence into consideration, provided that the scope of protection that the applicant is seeking for a well-known mark is basically the same as that of the recognized well-known mark and that the opposing party does not dispute that the other mark at issue is well-known or disputes without reasons and evidence to rebut the renown of the mark.[72]

c. The Coming Database on Well-Known Marks Aware of the need for local trademark enforcement, the CNIPA resumes an internal listing of well-known marks as early as around 2019. In its Notice on Strengthening the Work of Protecting Well-Known Marks in the Investigation on Cases Violating the Trademark Law, issued in November 2019, the CNIPA demands local authorities to collect well-known marks which have been recognized in their respective jurisdictions and are still in use to compile a list of contact persons for well-known mark cases and to report it to the CNIPA and update the list periodically. The CNIPA shall establish a database on well-known marks, which will be made available to "personnel in charge of trademark administration to support their local law enforcement activities."

The CIPNA further issued on May 11, 2021, the Understanding and Application of the Notice on Strengthening the Work of Protecting Well-Known Marks in the Investigation on Cases Violating the Trademark Law, which shows that as of the first quarter of 2021, the CIPNA has received accumulatively 344 applications from local trademark authorities for recognizing well-known marks and recognized 69 well-known marks.[73]

In its reply issued on July 22, 2021, to No. 4411 suggested that by the fourth meeting of the 13th National People's Congress,[74] the CNIPA is the process of:

> combing through well-known marks that have been recognized by the administrative and are still in use, and establishing a sound database on well-known marks with updates and maintenance, which will also be made available to the general public when conditions are ripe in addition to personnel in charge of trademark administration. CNIPA will also actively work with the People's Supreme Court to establish mechanism for information sharing that enables periodic exchange of information on well-known marks recognized by the administrative and the judiciary.

C. Taiwan Upon suggestion of this author, the Taiwan IP Office (TIPO) has maintained since 2010 a well-structured online database summarizing cases in which well-known marks have been recognized in the last five years. Currently,

72 See http://www.gov.cn/gongbao/content/2014/content_2758497.html.

73 關於加強查處商標違法案件中馳名商標保護相關工作的通知的理解與適用, at: https://www.cnipa.gov.cn/art/2021/5/11/art_66_159291.html.

74 At: https://www.cnipa.gov.cn/art/2021/7/27/art_516_166276.html?xxgkhide=1.

the database contains 3,384 cases. The database is all-inclusive, incorporating all decisions about well-known marks made by the TIPO during rejection, opposition, and invalidation procedures, and by courts of all instances, the competition authority, the Fair Trade Commission, and the administrator of domain names. Most importantly, the database provides relatively detailed reasons for recognizing a well-known trademark.[75]

4.3. *Evaluation of Different Modes of Recognition and Listing of Well-Known Marks*

4.3.1. *The Case-Independent Recognizing and Listing*

A. WITH LEGAL EFFECTS

The foremost merit of the case-independent recognition and listing of well-known marks with legal effect could lie in the certainty that it promises, and the avoidance of case-by-case determination of a well-known mark that would accrue great costs and burden to rightsholders. However, certainty comes only when sufficient time, quality manpower and resources are in place, which is almost impossible. Even if these three elements were in place, no certainty can be maintained forever and could be easily washed away by commercial reality.

As far as the Russian model is concerned, what the RF permits—indefinite protection—simply contravenes the basic trademark principle. In addition, this model is bound to lose touch with changing market conditions. It will artificially prolong the life of marks that are no longer well-known, inhibit the emergence of new marks, and itself becomes an object of contention among interested parties, leading to extra disputes and litigations.

As far as the Japanese model is concerned, the regime of defensive marks seems to be losing its appeal and relevance, as the number of applications is dwindling down. With regards to the Indian model, it seems to be appealing to trademark owners to file for recognition, as the number of recognized well-known marks doubled, from 137 in October 2022 to 281 in March 2024. It reminds us of the fever for well-known marks that had swept across China and resulted in widespread fraud before 2013.

75 TIPO. *Directory and Case Compilation of Well-Known Trademark of the Past 5 Years*, at: https://topic.tipo.gov.tw/trademarks-tw/lp-566-201.html. In Korea, according to Woo, J.-K. (2015). *Trade Marks and Related Rights in Intellectual Property Law in Korea* (2nd ed., p. 126), B. Kim & C. Heath (Eds.). Kluwer, the KIPO began maintaining and updating its Foreign Trademark Directory in 1995. The directory comprehensively listed trademarks of international or domestic fame. For trademarks included in the directory, often the KIPO did not require evidence of well-known status to save time and effort when opposing or rejecting trademark applications. Recently, the directory has become the Booklet of Trademarks Which Are Frequently Infringed, and it now also includes domestic marks. The KIPO continuously updates this booklet "based on the number of raids against counterfeits for the past two to three years." However, no English materials on this topic can be found on the websites of KIPO and its affiliates.

B. WITHOUT LEGAL EFFECTS

A purely informative case-independent recognition and listing of well-known marks by Finnish PRH is itself a schizophrenic contradiction. On the one hand, PRH establishes the list with great effort and yet uses it only for the purpose of notifying the owners of well-known marks, and will not take the list into consideration in any of its decisions.

4.3.2. The Case-Dependent Recognition and Listing

The case-dependent recognition of well-known marks is adversarial and therefore less biased. The listing of well-known marks is of low cost and hence feasible, as IPOs will not be required to invest extra manpower and no additional matching burdens (such as the high fee to finance extra manpower) will be demanded of the rightsholders. The listing of well-known marks can provide a useful guide to market latecomers on how to avoid existent well-known marks when applying for their own trademarks.

The flipside of this model in the eyes of its supporters is that it does not provide absolute certainty. However, a well-structured and maintained database of cases in which well-known marks were recognized can help reduce uncertainty by providing the public with important information that they need. After all, not every mark is as well-known as Apple, Coca Cola or Google. Such a database is all the more desirable in light of ever-expanding protection and an ever-growing number of well-known marks. This is particularly true for those countries where the renown required of well-known marks is low. It is therefore worthwhile to design a mechanism that would provide useful information on how and when well-known marks have been recognized within a certain time frame.[76]

4.4. Recommendation: A Centralized Online Database of Cases that Recognized Well-Known Marks

The international trademark community look at the issue of listing of well-known marks differently. The Law Committee of the European Communities Trade Mark Association in its 2005 position paper on the creation of a special register for well-known trademarks has expressed its reservations.[77] However, Mexico, the former Yugoslav Republic of Macedonia, and the US proposed in 2005 to the Standing Committee on the Law of Trademarks, Industrial Designs and Geographical Indications of WIPO to continue its analysis and follow up on the issue of national registers of well-known marks,[78] which has not yet resulted in any conclusion to date. The Board of Directors of the International Trademark Association recommends in

76 The same can be said of other marks with stronger reputations, such as "marks with reputation" in the EU and "marks that have been established in trade," "marks making headway in the traffic," or "marks known in the country" in the German Trademark Act.

77 At http://www.ecta.org/com6_pp.php.

78 At https://www.wipo.int/edocs/mdocs/sct/en/sct_15/sct_15_2.pdf.

its 2005 resolution regarding well-known marks that countries electing to establish well-known mark registries design and operate them in a manner that affords legal certainty concerning rights in well-known marks and apply the principles of the WIPO Provisions for the protection of well-known marks.[79]

This author has recommended and continues to advocate that national IPOs of the WTO Members establish and maintain an online database of cases that recognize well-known marks. The database should have the following characteristics: non-misleading, all-inclusive and centralized, user-initiative, as well as informative and time-sensitive.

- Non-misleading: The database should not be named as a "Register of Well-Known Marks" or a "Database of Well-Known Marks." Such nomenclature leads to the misconception that listed marks was and still are well-known and that non-listed marks were and still are not well-known. It also abets the type of misuse by rightsholders that can be observed in China. Rather, "Database of Well-Known Marks Cases" would be a more appropriate title. In addition, database users should be reminded of the fact that many well-known marks remain unlisted simply because they have not been disputed.
- All-inclusive and centralized: The database should include all final decisions that provide recognition to well-known marks, whether made by an IPO (in rejection, opposition, and invalidation cases), by courts of all instances and competences, by the competition authority, or by the administrator of domain names. As a result, there should be no need to link with or look up other databases. The more inclusive the database, the more transparent will the recognizing organization's decisions and reasoning be. An all-inclusive and centralized database will also compel recognizing organizations to do a better job.
- User-initiative: The database should enable users to set their own search parameters and remind them that they need to assess case-by-case whether the listed marks are still well-known.
- Informative: The more informative the database, the less likely it is to be misused. Therefore, information such as the case context and key reasons why listed marks were recognized as well-known should be included. Users should be able to search the full text of every decision.
- Time-sensitive: Unlimited listing of cases that recognized well-known marks could mislead users by bringing back to life long-dead and forgotten marks. Therefore, the database should consider the time-sensitiveness of well-known marks recognition by limiting the time frame of collected cases, preferably not prior to the last five years of trademark protection. Five years should be appropriate even for today's fast-changing internet world.

79 At: http://www.inta.org/index.php?option=com_content&task=view&id=1383&Itemid=153&getcontent=3.

Part IV

FRANDly Licensing of SEPs

When the first industrial revolution took place in the 18th century (around 1760 to about 1820–1840), the development and adoption of industrial standards, de jure and de facto alike, became the key to human progress in technologies. The first industrial revolution led to the first globalization (between 1870 and 1914) which required technical standards to be harmonized across national borders. The ITU established in 1865 is probably the first international SSO to develop technical standards to interconnect telecom networks internationally.

Industrial standards are common goods in nature and initially did not incorporate any proprietary rights, such as IP. However, technologies evolve at breath-taking speed and more and more private SSOs composed of major industrial players started to take a leading role in the standardization of technologies. As a result, the incorporation of IPs, especially patents, into standards becomes inevitable. Once integrated into standards these patents become SEPs, which enable their patentees to enjoy extra market power that derives not from their own technical merits but from the network effects of a technical standard.

To reign in such market power thrown upon SEP patentees and to solve other challenges such as patent ambush and excessive royalty rates, an initiative was taken in the 1980s.[1] The American National Standards Institute (ANSI)[2] adopted in 1983 an IP policy which specified that a standard could not be approved until members had assured the association that they either did not have any patents reading on the standard or that any such patents would either not be asserted or offered

1 Layne-Farrar, A. (2013). A review of IPR policy revisions in the wake of antitrust actions. *8th International Conference on Standardization and Innovation in Information Technology* (p. 6). IEEE, at: https://www.researchgate.net/publication/271547732_A_review_of_IPR_policy_revisions_in_the_wake_of_antitrust_actions.

2 ANSI is a private, non-profit organization that administers and coordinates the US voluntary standards and conformity assessment system. Founded in 1918, the institute is also an umbrella organization to which many standards organizations belong. It works in close collaboration with stakeholders from industry and government to identify and develop standards- and conformance-based solutions to national and global priorities. See https://www.ansi.org/about/introduction.

DOI: 10.4324/9781003597766-12

on royalty free or RAND terms.[3] Other SSOs followed to set up FRAND licensing policy/practice that requires members to declare if their patents are essential and are willing to license them on FRAND terms before incorporating them into standards.

With the rise of the fourth industrial revolution, driven by IoT, 5G, autonomous vehicles, and AI, new ICT standards are ballooning, and so are the issues of (reverse and forward) compatibility and interconnectivity between standards. To smooth out the setting up, taking on and working of new standards, FRAND licensing of SEPs is of ever more critical importance.

"In a large sense, FRAND licensing works fairly well."[4] However, FRAND licensing of SEPs does not always happen as a matter of course. On many occasions, SEP patentees and implementers do disagree on the FRAND-compliant terms and conditions of SEP licensing, as there is an imbalance of negotiation power between both sides which have very different interest constellations. Disputes arise. Major economies have developed and applied divergent legal standards to solve them.

This part of the book dedicates two chapters to deal with related issues. Chapter 9 first deals with SSOs, SEPs, and discusses some important facets of FRAND licensing of SEPs, setting the stage for Chapter 10, which explores some solution mechanisms that would facilitate FRAND licensing of SEPs on a global scale.

3 Layne-Farrar, A. (2013). A review of IPR policy revisions in the wake of antitrust actions. In *8th International Conference on Standardization and Innovation in Information Technology* (p. 5). IEEE, at: https://www.researchgate.net/publication/271547732_A_review_of_IPR_policy_revisions_in_the_wake_of_antitrust_actions.

4 Merges, R. (2022). *American Patent Law—A Business and Economic History* (p. 426). Cambridge University Press.

9 SSOs, SEPs, and FRAND Licensing of SEPs

1. SSOs

There are quite a number of major SSOs, especially in the ICT sector. Some SSOs are legally recognized, for example, CEN (European Committee for Standardization), Cenelec (European Committee for Electrotechnical Standardization), and ETSI (European Telecommunications Standards Institute)[1] are officially recognized by Regulation (EU) No. 1025/2012 as providers of European standards.[2] The three European standardization organizations will send an annual report on the implementation of this regulation to the Commission.

Most SSOs are from grassroots. For example, SSOs with comprehensive coverage: ANSI, International Electrotechnical Commission (IEC), Institute of Electrical and Electronics Engineers (IEEE), Internet Engineering Taskforce (IETF), and Organization for the Advancement of Structured Information Standards (OASIS).

There are also SSOs with more specific and narrower purposes. For example, Advanced Television Systems Committee (ATSC), DVD Forum, BluRay Disc Association, Society of Motion Picture and Television Engineers (SMPTE), and VMEbus International Trade Association (VITA) are more limited to standards for storing digital content. Broadband Forum, Open Mobile Alliance (OMA), and Telecommunications Industry Association (TIA, registered in the US) standardize mobile communication. There are also SSOs which function as umbrella organizations of other SSOs, such as the 3rd Generation Partnership Project (3GPP).

Voluntary SSOs remain free to structure their membership rules and their internal organizational procedures as they wish. In many areas, SSOs have already taken over the role of nation-states in setting standards.

1 ETSI was set up in 1988 by the European Conference of Postal and Telecommunications Administrations in response to proposals from the EC. ETSI is registered as an association under French law. ETSI has special role in Europe, which includes supporting European regulations and legislation through the creation of Harmonised European Standards. See https://www.etsi.org/about.

2 CEN, CENELEC, and ETSI have been working with the EC since 1984 when a cooperation agreement was signed. See https://single-market-economy.ec.europa.eu/single-market/european-standards/key-players-european-standardisation_en.

DOI: 10.4324/9781003597766-13

2. Antitrust Scrutiny of SSOs

Collaborative standard setting, although capable of producing substantial benefits from many aspects, inherently give rise to antitrust risks as SSOs, by their nature, facilitate agreements among competitors. The collaborative standard-setting process replaces marketplace competition for selecting technology once one of the competing technologies has been chosen, and competition between technologies is generally diminished due to the high costs of switching to alternatives.[3] In the collaboration, there are risks of excluding alternative technologies due to either combined economic incentives of members to implement the chosen technology or abuse of market power gained through the standard. While collaboration among competitors is reasonably necessary to promote compatibility and interoperability, it also needs to be conducted with great care under the supervision of the antitrust law, lest it might reduce competition beyond what is necessary to achieve its benefits.[4]

Therefore, "any agreement on the part of SSO members is potentially subject to antitrust scrutiny as a contract, combination or conspiracy, in restraint of trade."[5] The results of SSOs' activities must correspond to the standardization needs and must be made in conformity with the laws.[6] Most importantly, SSOs should ensure that all persons wishing to use their standards must be given access to those standards; standards are available for use on FRAND terms but taking into account the circumstances of the use.[7] For some, "Good governance rules" for SSOs must be developed under competition law.[8]

2.1. The US

Early on, the FTC was conscious of the competition concerns related to SSOs. In December 1978, it initiated a rulemaking procedure to examine the extent of

3 Dubianshy, J. (2018). Competition, intellectual property rights and collaboratively set standards: Federal trade commission advocacy and enforcement. In Bharadwaj, A., Devaiah, V., & Gupta, I. (Eds.), *Complications and Quandaries in the ICT Sector Standard Essential Patents and Competition Issues* (pp. 105–139). Springer.

4 Melamed, D., & Shapiro, C. (2018). How antitrust law can make FRAND commitments more effective. *Yale Law Journal, 127,* 2129.

5 Cotter, T. (2009). Patent holdups, patent remedies, and antitrust responses. *Journal of Corporation Law, 34*, 1200.

6 Commission of the European Communities. (1992). *Intellectual Property Rights and Standardization* (COM (92) 445 final), 1.1.3–1.1.4.

7 Commission of the European Communities. (1992). *Intellectual Property Rights and Standardization* (COM(92) 445 final), 6.2.1.

8 Lundqvist, B. (2013). *Standardization under EU Competition Rules and US Antitrust Laws: The Rise and Limits of Self-Regulation* (p. 336). Edward Elgar.

possible FTC Act violations in standards development and certification. Its Bureau of Consumer Protection completed a report in 1983, finding:

> standards are developed by committees composed substantially of representatives of competing firms within the affected industry and others with clear commercial interests without procedural safeguards, particularly a substantive complaint handling process to check upon unreasonable standard decisions. Participants tended to promulgate standards that enhance their own competitive position or exclude competitors out of the market.[9]

The FTC has since taken on SSOs on several occasions.[10]

US courts have been sensitive to antitrust issues that may arise and have found antitrust liability in circumstances involving the manipulation of the standard-setting process[11] or the improper use of the resultant standard to gain a competitive edge over rivals, recognizing that collaboratively set standards can reduce competition and consumer choice and have the potential of prescribing the direction for market development.[12] Courts have focused on SSOs' internal policies that self-policed such misconduct and clarified that SSOs were obligated to provide safeguards to ensure competition envisioned by antitrust law. The US Supreme Court clearly established the principle that the SSO cannot validate the anticompetitive activities of its members by adopting rules that fail to provide safeguards sufficient to prevent the standard-setting process from being biased by members with economic interests, which must be no more restrictive of competition than reasonably necessary to enable achievement of the legitimate purpose of standard setting.[13]

The Congress felt that the threat of treble damages under antitrust law pressures SSOs to restrict their standard development activities at a great cost to the US and enacted the National Cooperative Research and Production Act of 1993 (NCRPA) and its amendment via the Standards Development Organization Advancement Act of 2004 (SDOAA). Both assesses the antitrust liability of the standard-setting

9 USFTC Bureau of Consumer Protection. (1983). *Standards and Certification: Final Staff Report* (pp. 333–334). Federal Trade Commission, Bureau of Consumer Protection.

10 Layne-Farrar, A. (2013). A review of IPR policy revisions in the wake of antitrust actions. In *8th International Conference on Standardization and Innovation in Information Technology* (pp. 2–3). IEEE, at: https://www.researchgate.net/publication/271547732_A_review_of_IPR_policy_revisions_in_the_wake_of_antitrust_actions.

11 For example, the US Supreme Court found that a scheme by a member company and an officer of the SSO to cause a competitor's product to be wrongfully deemed non-compliant with the standard violated both Sections 1 and 2 of the Sherman Act. See *American Society of Mechanical Engineers, Inc. v. Hydrolevel Corp.*, 456 US 556 (1982).

12 See USFTC Bureau of Consumer Protection. (1983). *Standards and Certification: Final Staff Report* (pp. 28, 34). Federal Trade Commission, Bureau of Consumer Protection; Gilbert, R. (1992). Symposium on compatibility: Incentives and market structure. *The Journal of Industrial Economics*, *40*, 1.

13 *Allied Tube v. Indian Head, Inc.*, 486 US 492 (1988), 509.

activity of an SSO under the rule of reason[14] and limits possible antitrust damages to actual as opposed to treble damages plus costs of suit, including reasonable attorney's fee.[15]

Thereafter, the CAFC recognizes that cooperation by competitors in standard-setting "can provide procompetitive benefits the market would not otherwise provide, by allowing a number of different firms to produce and market competing products compatible with a single standard." Therefore, the activities of a "standards development organization while engaged in a standards development activity" are subject to the rule of reason.[16]

2.2. The EU

The 2012 Regulation on European standardization[17] expressly confirms that European SSOs are subject to competition law to the extent that they can be considered an undertaking or an association of undertakings within the meaning of Articles 101 and 102 TFEU.[18] Consequently, the standard-setting agreements made by these SSOs can violate Articles 101 and 102 TFEU.

Overall speaking, the EC treats standardization agreements, in essence the FRANDly licensing of SEPs, the same way as it treats patent pools (see Section 3 of Chapter 7). It therefore recognizes that standardization agreements usually produce significant positive economic effects,[19] but points out that standardization can also be detrimental to competition through three main channels, namely reduction in price competition, foreclosure of innovative technologies, and exclusion of, or discrimination against, certain companies by prevention of effective access to the standard.[20] Standardization agreements which do not restrict competition by object must be analyzed in their legal and economic context with regard to their actual

14 15 USC 4302 provides that:

> In any action under the antitrust laws . . . the conduct of (1) any person in making or performing a contract to carry out a joint venture, or (2) a standards development organization while engaged in a standards development activity, shall not be deemed illegal per se; such conduct shall be judged on the basis of its reasonableness, taking into account all relevant factors affecting competition, including, but not limited to, effects on competition in properly defined, relevant research, development, product, process, and service markets.

15 15 USC 4303(a).

16 *Princo Corp. v. International Trade Commission*, 616 F.3d 1335–1336 (Fed. Cir. 2010, "Princo II").

17 Regulation (EU) No. 1025/2012 of the European Parliament and Council of October 25, 2012, on European standardization (Regulation on European standardization). The Regulation on European standardization was later amended by EU Regulation 2022/2480 (December 14, 2022) regarding decisions of European standardization organizations concerning European standards and European standardization deliverables. However, no amendment was made with regard to what was cited here.

18 Preamble (13), Regulation on European standardization.

19 EC, Guidelines on the applicability of Article 101 of the Treaty on the Functioning of the European Union to horizontal co-operation agreements (2023/C 259/01 "Horizontal Guidelines"), Paragraph 439.

20 EC, Horizontal Guidelines Paragraph 441. Lundqvist, B. (2013). *Standardization under EU Competition Rules and US Antitrust Laws: The Rise and Limits of Self-Regulation* (p. 198). Edward Elgar.

and likely effect on competition. In the absence of market power, a standardization agreement is not capable of producing restrictive effects on competition. Therefore, restrictive effects are most unlikely in a situation where there is effective competition between a number of voluntary standards.[21]

However, if standard development agreements create market power, they will, nevertheless, generally fall outside the scope of Article 101(1) when participation in standard development is unrestricted and the procedure for adopting the standard in question is transparent, and standardization agreements contain no obligation to comply with the standard and provide effective access to the standard on FRAND terms.[22] If a standardization agreement constitutes restriction of competition under Article 101(1) yet provides significant efficiency gains[23] that can be passed on to consumers and outweigh the restrictive effects on competition, it can still be exempted according to Article 101(3).[24]

In order to ensure effective access to the standard, the IPR policy should require participants wishing to have their IPR included in the standard to provide an irrevocable commitment in writing to offer to license their essential IPR to all third parties on FRAND terms.[25] However, in the enforcement of FRAND commitment, SSOs need to require good faith disclosure and ensure that the IP is bound by the commitment even after its transfer.[26]

The EC does not require the SSO to verify whether licensing terms of participants fulfill the FRAND commitment. Rather,

> Participants will have to assess for themselves whether the licensing terms and in particular the fees they charge fulfil the FRAND commitment. Therefore, when deciding whether to commit to FRAND for a particular IPR, participants will need to anticipate the implications of the FRAND commitment, notably on their ability to freely set the level of their fees.[27]

3. SEPs

3.1. Declaration

In the ICT sector, there is a large volume of declared SEPs which are low-value-per-patent.[28] A combination of factors is driving the number, such as the growing demand for new standards, fear of antitrust liability over undeclared

21 EC, Horizontal Guidelines Paragraph 448.
22 EC, Horizontal Guidelines Paragraphs 449 and 451.
23 EC, Horizontal Guidelines Paragraph 473.
24 EC, Horizontal Guidelines Paragraph 485.
25 EC, Horizontal Guidelines Paragraph 456.
26 EC, Horizontal Guidelines Paragraphs 457 and 458.
27 EC, Horizontal Guidelines Paragraph 459.
28 Merges, R. (2022). *American Patent Law—A Business and Economic History* (pp. 473–474). Cambridge University Press.

patents that are later incorporated into standards (therefore it is better to declare as many SEPs as possible and as early as possible), lack of essentiality check on declared SEPs (neither by SSOs nor by licensees),[29] and a strategic race to own industry-spanning essential patents.[30]

According to the 3GPP, the number of SEP holders for 3G and 4G has grown from two in 1994 to 130 in 2013, and the number of declared SEPs rose from fewer than 150 in 1994 to more than 150,000 in 2013.[31] As of 2020 around 95,000 patents had been declared essential for the 5G standard.[32]

The declaration of SEPs is sometimes accompanied by other declarations. For example, since 2007 VITA adopted an ex-ante royalty disclosure policy that asks its members to declare the maximum royalty rate for their patents with essential claims, as part of its SEP declaration. If a member fails to do so, it has to license its patents on a royalty-free basis.[33] The 2022 IEEE SA Standards Board Bylaws also mentions "At its sole option, the Submitter may provide with its Letter of Assurance any of the following: (i) a not-to-exceed license fee or rate commitment, (ii) a sample license agreement, or (iii) one or more material licensing terms."[34]

3.2. Licensing

There are at least two features in the licensing of SEPs.

Due to the large volume of SEPs licensing of individual patents based on individual licensing negotiation is simply not feasible. Rather, the licensing of SEPs

29 Even licensees will not verify the essentiality of declared SEPs, for two reasons: it is useless to challenge them, as those patents are already part of the standard, and verifying the essentiality of all SEPs would be simply infeasible due to prohibitive expenditure on time and resources and also possibly the lack of technical capability.

30 Ernst, D. (December 2016). *Standard-Essential Patents within Global Networks—An Emerging Economies Perspective*, at: https://ssrn.com/abstract=2873198.

31 Galetovic, A., & Gupta, K. (2017). *Royalty Stacking and Standard Essential Patents: Theory and Evidence from the World Mobile Wireless Industry*, at: https://ssrn.com/abstract=2790347.

32 *IPLytics—Fact Finding Study on Patents Declared to the 5G Standard.* (2020), at: https://www.iplytics.com/wp-content/uploads/2020/02/5G-patent-study_TU-Berlin_IPlytics-2020.pdf. This figure is cited by UKIPO, Consultation Outcome "Standard Essential Patents and Innovation: Summary of Responses to the Call for Views" (Updated July 5, 2023).

33 14.2.2 and 14.3 VITA Standards Organization (VSO) Policies and Procedures (July 2022, 3.1 Revision) require

> Each WG Member must declare the maximum royalty rate for all patent claims that the VITA Member Company they represent (or its Affiliates) owns or controls and that may become essential to implement the VSO Draft Proposed Standard. WG Members are encouraged to attach to the Declaration a draft licensing agreement for all patent claims essential to implement the VSO Draft Proposed Standard. If a WG Member fails to adequately and timely disclose, the VITA Member Company must license it to the extent it is essential to a VSO Draft Proposed Standard on a royalty free basis. However, according to Renata Hesse/Frances Marshall, in practice patentees usually declare a much higher royalty, which helped little to define FRAND; see Hesse, R., & Marshall, F. (2018). US antitrust aspects of FRAND disputes. In Contreras, J. (Ed.), *The Cambridge Handbook of Technical Standardization Law* (p. 269). Cambridge University Press.

34 6.2 of IEEE SA Standards Board 2022 Bylaws.

must be based on package licensing. The licensees or license-seekers can only either take the whole package or leave it. With a patent package deal in place, licensees could complain about having to pay for patents that they do not really need or use or that are no longer valid (some older patents in the portfolio will expire, notwithstanding that new ones will flow in). This leads to a point of conflict between SEP patentees and their licensees.

The second feature of SEP licensing is that it traditionally took place chiefly among ICT companies but is now often undertaken between ICT companies and firms in other industries, such as automotive. Divergent perspectives on licensing rates from across different industries are rising, "fostering unease over SEP-related negotiations and disputes."[35] This also makes the solution of disputes through cross-licensing more difficult.

4. The Qualcomm Whirlwind

Qualcomm holds thousands of FRAND-encumbered SEPs that comprise ETSI's 3G/UMTS and 4G/LTE cellular communication standards. Qualcomm is not only a world champion in holding SEPs in mobile communication, but also in carefully designed licensing practices which has caused a worldwide whirlwind. Basically, Qualcomm maintains a "no license, no chips" policy under which it will supply its baseband processors only on the condition that cell phone manufacturers agree to sign a license agreement for Qualcomm's SEPs at its preferred license terms. This tactic forces cell phone manufacturers to pay elevated royalties to Qualcomm. Despite its commitment to license its SEPs on FRAND terms, Qualcomm has consistently refused to license competing suppliers of baseband processors. Qualcomm realized that any competitor that won Apple's business would become stronger by working with Apple. Qualcomm also extracted at least one exclusive contract (from 2011 to 2016)[36] from the world's number one smartphone brand Apple in exchange for a rebate, foreclosing Qualcomm competitors' access to the most coveted buyer of high-end chips.

As a result, as the veteran of ICT industry Patrick Van de Wille, former chief communications officer at InterDigital (2012–2021) bluntly points out,

> SEP owners have turned to needless complexity to try to maintain an untenable status quo, while the other side hammers out a simple message: it's unfair. The status quo . . . is one where a single company, Qualcomm, manages to seize for itself more revenue than all other major licensors, combined, multiplied by two.[37]

35 JPO Standard Essential Patents Portal Site, at: https://www.jpo.go.jp/e/support/general/sep_portal/.

36 Apple later signed a six-year license agreement with Qualcomm (effective as of April 1, 2019, including a two-year option to extend, and a multiyear chipset supply agreement), at: https://www.apple.com/newsroom/2019/04/qualcomm-and-apple-agree-to-drop-all-litigation.

37 Van de Wille, P. (2023). *Why SEP Owners Have Lost the FRAND Debate*, at: https://www.managingip.com/article/2c108scnd804r4g1dscn4/opinion-why-sep-owners-have-lost-the-frand-debate.

The Qualcomm whirlwind is worth documenting as it showcases the difficulty to reach FRAND licensing of SEPs when the dominant SEP patentee refuses to. It also exposes the divergence between the US, where Qualcomm is headquartered, and other major economies.

4.1. In Asia

In 1990 Qualcomm caught the attention of the JFTC. The JFTC issued a cease-and-desist order against Qualcomm on September 30, 2009, relating to Qualcomm's unfair license agreements with Japanese manufacturers. Tokyo High Court stayed the enforcement of the order on February 12, 2010.[38] After years of proceedings, the JFTC reversed its ruling and revoked the cease-and-desist order against Qualcomm in 2019.[39]

Qualcomm has made a record in Taiwan by convincing the TFTC to settle with it out of court after first being condemned and heavily fined by the TFTC for abusing dominant market power via conducts described earlier, by playing on Taiwan's geopolitical needs of having more allies.[40]

Qualcomm was not less lucky with KFTC in South Korea and the PRC. The KFTC has found Qualcomm[41] engaged in the following anti-competitive conducts: discriminatory royalty, providing rebates and charging royalty for expired patents. As a result, the KFTC imposed a fine of approximately 260 billion Korean Won (about US $229 million) on Qualcomm. The KFTC also imposed the following corrective orders on Qualcomm: no charging of different royalties based on whether or not modem chips of competitors have been used; no providing of rebates conditional upon purchase of Qualcomm's modem chips or RF chips at levels that exclude competitors; and no demanding of unreasonable continued payment of royalties after the expiration or invalidation of patents (Qualcomm I). On appeal, the Seoul High Court in 2013 upheld the KFTC's decision and remedial orders for the most part. The Supreme Court reversed only the part against Qualcomm

38 For more see Suzuki, M. (2017). Enforcement of FRAND-encumbered SEPs. In Liu, K.-C. (Ed.), *Annotated Leading Patent Cases in Major Asian Economies* 241–261. City University of HK Press.

39 Freeman, M. (2019). After nearly a decade, Japan's antitrust regulator reverses ruling against Qualcomm. *San Diego Union-Tribune*, at: https://www.sandiegouniontribune.com/business/technology/sd-fi-qualcomm-japan-ruling-20190318-story.html.

40 The TFTC and courts in Taiwan were completely ignorant of the development of law on SEP licensing in other jurisdictions which requires that the remuneration for SEPs must be FRAND. As a result, the SEP license seeker in Taiwan, Princo, despite winning its antitrust case against Philips, the SEP owner, lost completely in the royalty payment dispute. For more see Liu, K.-C. (2020). Unprepared, unable and unwilling to deal with FRAND licensing of SEPs in Taiwan? In Liu, K.-C., & Hilty, R. (Eds.), *SEPs, SSOs and FRAND—Asian and Global Perspectives on Fostering Innovation in Interconnectivity* (pp. 173–190). Routledge.

41 For more see Kim, B. (2017). Anti-competitive licensing practice: Qualcomm's abuse of market dominance. In Liu, K.-C. (Ed.), *Annotated Leading Patent Cases in Major Asian Jurisdictions* (pp. 184–193). City University of HK Press.

pertaining to the offering of the RF chip rebates and remanded it to the lower court for further proceedings.[42]

Again in 2017, KFTC found Qualcomm in violation of its FRAND commitments and abuse of dominance due to SEPs in refusing to license mobile SEPs to willing licensees (competing model chipset makers), coercing handset makers to sign unfair license agreements by linking chipset supply with the license agreements, offering portfolio license only to handset makers, and forcing unilaterally decided licensing terms without undergoing a reasonable value assessment process. It imposed a 1.03 trillion Korean won (approximately US $927 million) fine on Qualcomm (Qualcomm II).[43]

The KFTC also ordered corrective measures on Qualcomm: (I) upon request by modem chipset companies, engage in good-faith negotiations for patent license agreements, without offering unjustifiable conditions, and if necessary submit to a determination of terms by an independent third party; (II) not to demand that handset companies execute and perform under patent license agreements as a precondition for purchasing modem chipsets; (III) not to demand unjustifiable conditions in Qualcomm's license agreements with handset companies, and upon request renegotiate existing patent license agreements; and (IV) to notify modem chipset companies and handset companies of the decision and order imposed on Qualcomm and report new or amended agreements to the KFTC.

Qualcomm appealed the KFTC's decision. On December 4, 2019, the Seoul High Court found that the KFTC's disposition of imposing an administrative fine in the amount of one trillion won on Qualcomm was lawful, but cancelled the KFTC's remedial orders described in (III) (solely insofar as they correspond thereto) and in (IV) previously cited, and dismissed the remainder of Qualcomm's action to cancel the KFTC's decision.[44] On April 13, 2023, the Supreme Court issued a decision upholding the Seoul High Court's decision. It held that Qualcomm used its dominance in the SEP license market and modem chipset market for each standard to mutually and organically link Conduct 1 (refusing to execute and limiting patent license agreements with competing modem chipmakers) and Conduct 2 (executing patent license agreements with handset manufacturers by linking modem chipset supply agreements with patent license agreements) and found that there was anticompetitive intent and effect.[45]

42 Kim, B. (2017). Anti-competitive licensing practice: Qualcomm's abuse of market dominance. In Liu, K.-C. (Ed.), *Annotated Leading Patent Cases in Major Asian Jurisdictions* (pp. 184–193). City University of HK Press.

43 Kim, B. (2017). Anti-competitive licensing practice: Qualcomm's abuse of market dominance. In Liu, K.-C. (Ed.), *Annotated Leading Patent Cases in Major Asian Jurisdictions* (pp. 184–193). City University of HK Press.

44 Seoul High Court Decision 2017 Nu 48 (decided on 4 December 2019), at: https://fair-standards.org/wp-content/uploads/2020/07/200722_Seoul-High-Court-2017Nu48-Final-Judgment_English-Translation.pdf

45 Lee, C., Kim, H., Choi, J.-H., & Choi, J. H. (2023). *Abuse of Dominance in South Korea*, at: https://www.lexology.com/library/detail.aspx?g=46cbf586-f0ea-4b75-96c8-21e9f73bf059

In the PRC, the then one of the three competition authorities, NDRC concluded in 2015 that Qualcomm had abused its dominant position in the wireless communication SEP licensing market and the baseband chip sale market in violation of China's Anti-Monopoly Law by (I) charging unfair high licensing fees (including charging for expired SEP, demanding free cross-licensing and using the wholesale prices of the whole device as royalty base), (II) tying-in non-SEP with SEP, and (III) demanding no-challenge clause (not to challenge the patent licensing agreements) in the sale of baseband chips. The NDRC ordered Qualcomm to cease the mentioned abusive use of market dominance. Given the severity, wider extent and longer duration of the abuse the NDRC imposed a fine of RMB ¥6.088 billion (approx. US $975 million), which is 8% of Qualcomm's revenue in 2013 in China.[46]

In addition, the NDRC agreed to Qualcomm's rectification plan. Therein Qualcomm agreed not pursue legal action to contest NDRC's findings and promised, in future licensing, it will (I) offer licenses to its current 3G and 4G essential Chinese patents separately from its other patents and provide patent lists during negotiation; (II) negotiate with license seekers in good faith and provide fair consideration if it seeks cross-licensing; (III) not condition the sale of baseband chips upon the buyer's signing a patent license agreement with unreasonable terms and agreeing not to challenge unreasonable terms in patent license agreements. For licenses of Qualcomm's 3G and 4G essential Chinese patents for branded devices sold for use in China, Qualcomm will charge royalties (I) of 5% for 3 G devices (including multimode 3G/4G devices) and 3.5% for 4G devices (including 3-mode LTE (Long Term Evolution)-TDD devices) that do not implement CDMA or WCDMA, (II) each case using a royalty base of 65% of the net selling prices of the device.[47]

In this conjuncture it is worth reflecting on whether the many concrete undertakings, commitments, and corrective measures that Qualcomm has made to the competition authorities in the PRC, Korea, and Taiwan have the potential of reaching beyond these economies and becoming binding on Qualcomm on a worldwide scale when they do licensing of SEPs in other economies. If SEP patentees are allowed to apply their undertakings to a certain national competition authority only to that particular jurisdiction and refuse to apply them elsewhere, it can hardly be "non-discriminatory." Therefore, Qualcomm should be expected to also apply these commitments in other economies with similar situation, unless it can justify the non-application.

The two specific commitments that Qualcomm has made have such potential: it shall not practice "No Patent License, No Chips" (not to condition the sale of baseband chips upon the buyer's signing a patent license agreement (PRC Qualcomm

46 NDRC, FaGaiBanJiaJianChuFa (2015), No. 1 (decided on February 9, 2015).

47 Qualcomm press release "Qualcomm and China's National Development and Reform Commission Reach Resolution" (February 9, 2015), at: https://investor.qualcomm.com/news-events/press-releases/detail/672/qualcomm-and-chinas-national-development-and-reform.

case and Korea Qualcomm II case) and no exclusive purchase deal with rebate with buyers of chips made with its SEPs (not to conclude any chip supply contract with its chip customers that conditions the provision of royalty rebate on the latter's agreement to exclusively purchase chips from Qualcomm, Korea Qualcomm II).[48]

4.2. The EU[49]

In 2018, the EC fined Qualcomm €997 million for abuse of dominant market position on the worldwide market for chipsets compatible with the LTE standard. The infringement lasted from February 2011 to September 2016. Qualcomm prevented rivals from competing in the market by making significant payments, billions of US dollars, to a key customer, Apple, on the condition it would not buy from rivals. Qualcomm illegally shut out rivals from the market for LTE baseband chipsets for over five years, thereby cementing its market dominance. These payments were not just reductions in price—they were exclusivity payments, so that Apple would exclusively use Qualcomm's baseband chipsets in all its iPhones and iPads.[50]

However, the first instance court of the EU, the General Court, annulled the decision, in its entirety, in 2022. The Court bases its conclusions on the finding of a number of procedural irregularities which affected Qualcomm's rights of defense, and an analysis of the anticompetitive effects of the incentive payments. It found the EC failed to provide an analysis to support the findings that the payments concerned had actually reduced Apple's incentives to switch to Qualcomm's competitors.[51] The EC did not appeal the decision. This might be because the General Court "went to great pains to examine and adjudicate on a large numbers of pleas each of which, on its own, would have justified annulling the Commission's decision."[52]

48 Kim, B. (2017). Anti-competitive licensing practice: Qualcomm's abuse of market dominance. In Liu, K.-C. (Ed.), *Annotated Leading Patent Cases in Major Asian Jurisdictions* (pp.184–193). City University of HK Press.

49 Some distinguishes European approach to SEP-related concerns into three phases: (I) A first phase (1980-2009) characterized by long-standing soft-touch approach of the EC vis-à-vis the standard-setting process. (II) A second phase (2009–14) dominated by competition law investigation into FRAND licensing, leading to a much more nuanced, articulated, and IPR-focused approach. (III) A third phase (2015-present), where CJEU and national courts decided on SEP disputes, and the EC initiated direct regulation of SEP. See Barazza, S. (2023). Standard essential patents and FRAND licensing: The evolution of the European approach. In Bosher, H., & Rosati, E. (Eds.), *Development and Directions in Intellectual Property Law* (pp. 494–495). Oxford University Press.

50 EC C (2018) 240 (decided on January 24, 2018).

51 Judgment of the General Court, Case T-235/18 (decided on June 15, 2022) –*Qualcomm v. Commission* (Qualcomm–exclusivity payment).

52 To prevail "in abuse of dominance cases is extremely rare: the present case appears to mark the first time in 20 years the Court has quashed at first instance a Commission abuse of dominance decision." See Rare EU Antitrust Victory for Qualcomm Before the EU General Court (2022), at: https://www.quinnemanuel.com/the-firm/our-notable-victories/rare-eu-antitrust-victory-for-qualcomm-before-the-eu-general-court/.

4.3. The US

The US, at long last, started to grapple with the issue of FRAND licensing of SEPs concerning Qualcomm, when the USFTC[53] and the tech giant Apple brought antitrust suits against Qualcomm on January 17 and 20, 2017, in the Northern District and Southern District Court of California, respectively.[54] Surprisingly, Apple and Qualcomm settled this dispute on April 16, 2019, which included a payment from Apple to Qualcomm, a six-year license agreement with a two-year option to extend, and a multiyear chipset supply agreement.[55]

However, the Northern District Court found in *ITC v. Qualcomm* that, among others, Qualcomm's pattern of refusing to provide licenses to competitors, although it has made FRAND commitment: MediaTek (2008), Project Dragonfly (2011), Samsung (2011), VIA, Intel (2004 and 2009), HiSilicon (2009), Broadcom, Texas Instruments, and LGE (2015). It concluded that Qualcomm had violated its antitrust duty to license its SEPs to rivals and decided in the FTC's favor.[56] However, the decision was unanimously reversed by the Ninth Circuit on August 11, 2020.[57]

5. Major Issues Surrounding FRAND Licensing of SEPs

5.1. Holdup or Holdout?[58]

In the context of licensing SEPs, it is probably fair to say that SEP patentees have a much stronger negotiation edge against license seekers, as the former is blessed

53 The USFTC charged Qualcomm with violating Section 5 of the FTC Act over the same set of licensing practices described. *The Federal Trade Commission v. Qualcomm Incorporated*, 5:17-cv-00220, Document 1, filed January 17, 2017.

54 Apple sought declarations with respect to several of Qualcomm's patents and alleged that Qualcomm breached certain agreements and violated federal antitrust laws. Apple also sought declaratory judgments of non-infringement by Apple of nine of Qualcomm's patents, or a declaration of royalties Apple must pay for the patents. Separately, Apple sought to enjoin Qualcomm from seeking excessive royalties from Apple and to disgorge royalties paid by Apple's contract manufacturers that the court finds were not FRAND. In addition, Apple claimed that Qualcomm has refused to deal with competitors in contravention of Qualcomm's agreements with applicable SSOs used its market position to impose contractual obligations on Apple that prevented Apple from challenging Qualcomm's licensing practices, tied the purchase of Qualcomm's CDMA-enabled and "premium" LTE-enabled chipsets to licensing certain of Qualcomm's patents, and required Apple to purchase baseband chipsets exclusively from Qualcomm as a condition of Qualcomm's payment to Apple of certain rebates, in violation of Section 2 of the Sherman Act. See case 3.17-cv-00108-GPC-NLS Document 1 filed January 20, 2017, 2.

55 At: https://www.apple.com/newsroom/2019/04/qualcomm-and-apple-agree-to-drop-all-litigation/.

56 *FTC v. Qualcomm Inc.*, 411 F.Supp. 3d 733 et al (N.D. Cal. 2019) (decided on May 21, 2019).

57 At: https://cdn.ca9.uscourts.gov/datastore/opinions/2020/08/11/19-16122.pdf.

58 According to Robert Merges, holdup is "to use of an ownership claim . . . to extract far more . . . than the single claim intrinsically merits," whereas holdout is the counterpart of holdup: "Patent owners try to maximize patent leverage; implementers try to string along patent owners." id., 428, 429; Justice Richard Arnold perceives holdup as patentee "treating the SEP as akin to a 'ransom strip' of land" and holdout as "an implementer being "able to implement a technical solution covered by an

with standards, that no one can afford to bypass, and their network luck-in effects and become "tigers with wings." Therefore, holdup by SEP patentees is more of a real concern than holdout by bad-faith users of SEPs. This is especially true of semiconductors, biotechnology, computer software, and the Internet, where patent thicket is a serious issue.[59]

The FRAND mechanism is basically to prevent the holdup by SEP patentees made possible only by SSO's adoption of their patents into the standards. In essence, FRAND commitment is a consideration provided by the SEP patentee in exchange for the inclusion of its patent in the standard during the standard-setting process. SEP patentees voluntarily limit their patent rights and royalties within FRAND terms because they expect their inventions will enjoy extra market power as a result of standard adoption. The FRAND commitment must be taken seriously, as binding and consequential. Only then can the holdup problem be avoided.

Of course, even SEP licensing is not without bad-faith users who are mostly small timers or SMEs, hard to detect, and costly to go after. These can only occupy small market shares, as they have to stay below the radar.

However, in the US, antitrust agencies seem to have a couple of changes of heart, swinging from holdup fear to holdout and again to holdup fear. At the height of curbing patent trolls, the FTC and USPTO jointly issued in 2013 Policy Statement on Remedies for Standard Essential Patents Subject to F/RAND Commitment.[60] According to the Statement, SEP patentee's application for injunction is against the public interest, unless the alleged infringer is unwilling or unable to conclude a licensing agreement on FRAND terms. However, since November 2017, the then US Assistant Attorney General of the DOJ Makan Delrahim has moved the DOJ in a direction that allows SEP owners more freedom to use the exclusionary potential of those patents. DOJ also has redirected its focus toward the conduct of licensees and the SSOs. On December 7, 2018, the USPTO withdrew its consent from the 2013 Joint DOJ-USPTO Statement. Eventually, the USPTO, the National Institute of Standards and Technology (NIST), and the DOJ jointly issued in December 2019 a Policy Statement on Remedies for Standard Essential Patents Subject to F/RAND Commitment. According to the Statement its predecessor, the 2013 Statement has been misinterpreted to suggest that a unique set of legal rules should be applied in disputes concerning SEPs subject to a F/RAND commitment and that injunctions and other exclusionary remedies should not be available in actions for infringement of SEPs. The Statement emphasized "a patent owner's F/RAND commitment is a

---

SEP without paying the reasonable market value for a licence (or perhaps anything at all)." Arnold, R. (2021). SEPs, FRAND and mandatory global arbitration. *GRUR*, 124.

59 In great details discussed Sapiro the vices of patent holdups, which can only be amplified by SEPs. See Shapiro, C.C. (2001). Navigating the patent thicket: cross-licenses, patent pools, and standard-setting. In Jaffe, A., Lerner, J., & Stern, S. (Eds.), *Innovation Policy and the Economy* (Vol. 1, pp. 119, 124–126). MIT Press.

60 2013 Policy Statement on Remedies for Standards-Essential Patents Subject to Voluntary F/RAND Commitments 1–10, at: https://www.justice.gov/sites/default/files/atr/legacy/2014/09/18/290994.pdf.

relevant factor in determining appropriate remedies, but needs not act as a bar to any particular remedy."[61]

With the change of the administration from Trump to Biden, the Statement was withdrawn on June 8, 2022, by the agencies, "after considering potential revisions to that statement." Before they make those revisions, "DOJ will review conduct by SEP holders or standards implementers on a case-by-case basis to determine if either party is engaging in practices that result in the anticompetitive use of market power or other abusive processes that harm competition."[62]

The German Federal Court of Justice once had been driven by fear for holdout and ruled in the 2009 "Orange Book Standard" case that the application of injunctive relief by dominant patentee could have violated Article 20 (prohibited conduct of undertakings with relative or superior market power) of the German Competition Act, provided however that (I) the defendant has made unconditional offer to sign the licensing agreement and (II) started paying royalties into an escrow account for the patentee or provided guarantee for royalty payment.[63]

The CJEU disagreed and ruled in *Huawei v. ZTE* that Article 102 TFEU must be interpreted as meaning that the proprietor of a SEP does not abuse its dominant position,

> by bringing an action for infringement seeking an injunction prohibiting the infringement of its patent or seeking the recall of products for the manufacture of which that patent has been used, as long as prior to bringing that action, the proprietor has, . . . after the alleged infringer has expressed its willingness to conclude a licensing agreement on FRAND terms, presented to that infringer a specific, written offer for a license on such terms, specifying, in particular, the royalty and the way in which it is to be calculated preventing holdup by the patentee.[64]

The CJEU's imposition of duty on the SEP patentee is obviously driven by the consideration that it can practice the holdup strategy to the detriment of license seekers. The *Huawei v. ZTE* decision led the BGH to modify its stance.

Over here in Asia, at least Chinese Guidelines on IPR Abuse is driven more by the concern of holdup by SEP patentees, as Article 27(2) provides that:

> SEP patentees who have dominant market power may exclude or restrict market competition by applying for injunctive relief. In determining whether competition is indeed excluded or restricted, following factors can be taken into consideration: the behavior of the negotiating parties and their genuine

61 2019 Policy Statement on Remedies for Standards-Essential Patents Subject to F/RAND Commitment, 4, at: https://www.justice.gov/atr/page/file/1228016/dl#.

62 Withdrawal of 2019 Policy Statement on Remedies for Standards-Essential Patents Subject to F/RAND Commitment, at: https://www.uspto.gov/sites/default/files/documents/SEP2019-Withdrawal.pdf.

63 German Federal Court of Justice KZR 39/06 (decided on May 6, 2009).

64 CJEU C170/13 (decided on July 16, 2015).

intention, relevant SEPs encumbered with what kind of promises, licensing terms and conditions offered by the negotiating parties, impacts of such injunctive relief on licensing negotiation, and impacts of such injunctive relief on downstream market competition and consumer interests.

5.2. FRANDly Negotiation

The FRAND license of SEPs is not just about the reasonableness of the substantive terms and conditions of the licensing agreements, FRAND now also refers to the process by which a license is negotiated, especially procedural good faith in negotiation, which can be called the FRANDly negotiation requirement. This requirement applies equally to SEP patentees and license seekers. It takes two to play ping pong, and wherever there is a "ping" from one party of the negotiation, there must be a corresponding "pong" from the other. Or as the German Federal Court of Justice has phrased it aptly:

> The willingness of the infringer to acquire a licensee, like the willingness of the patent proprietor to grant a license, must not be limited to a one-off expression of interest in licensing or the submission of a (counter)offer. Rather, both parties are required to contribute in a manner appropriate to the situation and in accordance with the principles of good faith so that an appropriate balance of the conflicting interests can be negotiated in the form of a license agreement on FRAND terms.[65]

Whether parties have acted FRANDly should be judged based on the situation of each case in light of the behavior of both sides in licensing negotiations. For example, the presence or absence of the presentation of the infringement and whether it designates the patent and specifies the way in which it has been infringed, the presence or absence of the offer for a license on the conditions and whether it specifies its base for calculation and the attitude in corresponding to the offers and whether prompt and reasonable counteroffers were made.[66]

5.2.1. On the Part of SEP Patentees

FRANDly SEP patentees must first and foremost make their patent information, including scope and duration, known or available, inform the implementers about the accused infringement, enter and conduct negotiation in good faith, including to enable the conclusion of a licensing deal by offering concrete base or framework for negotiation drawn from their past licensing experiences, and by reacting and

65 German Federal Court of Justice KZR 35/17 FRAND-defense II (*Sisvel v Haier* decided on November 24, 2020).

66 Similarly, Part 3(1)(i)(e) of Japanese IP Guidelines.

responding timely and concretely to inquiries and offers made by the implementers during the whole negotiation process.

In Germany, the Federal Court of Justice has set high requirements for dominant SEP patentees' FRANDly negotiation. It rules that dominant SEP patentees have special duties vis-a-vis willing license seekers. It opined that the claiming of a prohibitory injunction, recall and destruction of infringing goods does not abuse its market power by a patentee even if the infringer has not yet bindingly declared the readiness to conclude a license agreement according to certain appropriate conditions when the patentee is to blame for not trying sufficiently on its part to live up to the special responsibility associated with its market dominant position by enabling the principally willing infringer to conclude a license agreement.[67]

The German Federal Court of Justice further rules that dominant SEP patentees can derive special behavioral duties in particular from the following: the infringer, who has been made aware of the infringement, has unequivocally declared that it will seek a license on FRAND terms but was not or at least not immediately in the position to formulate the conditions that the patentee must grant under the observance of no discrimination and hampering. Such duties can oblige the patentee to clarify its license terms in detail so as to enable the willing license seeker to examine whether the demand by the license constitutes a misuse of the market dominant position.[68]

5.2.2. On the Part of Willing License Seekers

Although an implementer does not owe a FRAND obligation to the SSO, an implementer who wishes to take advantage of the patentee's FRAND obligation must themselves negotiate in a FRANDly manner to show they are willing to license seekers. In essence, willing license seekers must enter negotiation in good faith, be tentative to the notice and offers from SEP patentees and react and respond timely and concretely throughout the whole negotiation process. That said, a license seeker should not be considered as "unwilling" even if they intend to challenge (via litigation or arbitration) validity, essentiality or possible infringement of the SEP as long as they undertake licensing negotiations in good faith in light of the normal business practices.[69]

67 German Federal Court of Justice, KZR 36/17, 1 (decided on May 5, 2020).

68 German Federal Court of Justice, KZR 36/17, 1 (decided on May 5, 2020).

69 Japanese IP Guidelines (Part 3(1)(i)(e)) is of similar opinion. So is IEEE SA Standards Board 2022 Bylaws:

> The Submitter of an Accepted LOA who has committed to make available a license for one or more Essential Patent Claims agrees that it shall neither seek nor seek to enforce a Prohibitive Order based on such Essential Patent Claim(s) in a jurisdiction against an implementer who is willing to negotiate in good faith for a license. Seeking further information upon initial notice of infringement or choosing to litigate or arbitrate over any of the foregoing issues, however, does not by itself mean that a party so choosing is unwilling to negotiate in good faith.
>
> 6.2

In Germany, the license seekers are expected to unequivocally indicate their willingness to sign the licensing agreement with the SEP patentees. The Federal Court of Justice rules that:

> The proprietor of a SEP who brings a patent infringement action for a prohibitory injunction, recall and destruction does not abuse its market power if the infringer, who has been made aware of the infringement and the willingness to license, has not unequivocally indicated that it will seek a licensee on FRAND terms.[70]

In China, the Beijing IP Court found no FRANDly negotiation on the part of the license seeker Sony in the following situation and upheld the first-instance decision and injuncted Sony from continuing infringement of the SEP licensees: negotiation went from March 2009 to March 2015, but no agreement was reached. The plaintiff XXJ has provided a patent list on SEPs and licensing agreements and offered reasonable help to license seekers, based on which Sony should be able to tell whether its products infringed the SEPs at issue without asking XXJ to provide a claims comparison chart. XXJ was willing to provide such a chart under NDA, whereas Sony replied that it would not "conduct any commercial negotiation before comprehensive assessment of XXJ's patents and confirming their reasonable values." Repeatedly, in its reply Sony disputed that its existent or future products used WAPI patents, it saw no reason to acquire license from XXJ, without providing any explanations or suggestions on how to move negotiation forward. Even during litigation, Sony never offered concrete licensing terms, paid in escrow the licensing fee with the court it asserted or provided a guarantee that was not lower than the fee.[71]

5.3. FRANDly Terms and Conditions

The most controversial and the least understood component is what are FRAND-compliant terms and conditions, making this area of law uncertain. This might defeat the purpose of why SSOs have recognized SEPs.

5.3.1. To Bundle Non-SEPs with SEPs or Not?

The EC TTBER and Article 101 Guidelines (Point 235), Japanese IP Guidelines (Part 2(i)(b)), Korean IP Guidelines (p. 21), and the Taiwanese Tech Licensing Guidelines (Point 6(1)) are all very mindful of the risk that invalid patents may be included in the package, which would force licensees to pay higher royalties

70 German Federal Court of Justice KZR 35/17 FRAND-defense II (*Sisvel v Haier* decided on November 24, 2020).

71 Beijing IP Court, *Xian Xidian Jetong (XXJ) v. Sony Mobile (China)* 2015 JingZhiMinChu No. 1194 (decided on March 22, 2017).

and prevent innovation in the field covered by the invalid patents. Consequently, the practice of package licensing "non-essential" patents along with "essential" at one price will seem to be questionable in these jurisdictions, if not per se anticompetitive.

In practice, competition authorities in Korea (Qualcomm II case), the PRC (*NDRC v. Qualcomm*), Japan (Part 4(5)(iv) IP Guidelines), and Taiwan (6(3) Tech Licensing Guidelines) blacklist "the compelling of the licensee to purchase, accept or use patents or technical know-how that he does not need." In specific, these economies make it illegal per se to bundle SEPs with non-SEPs by SEP holders which have dominant market power. In India, Section 84(7)(c) of the Patent Act treats "coercive package licensing" as a ground for applying for compulsory license. If SEP patentees coerce to bundle SEPs with non-SEPs in India, it is highly likely that it will not be accepted by Indian courts and its competition commission.

In contrast, the courts in the US and the UK take it for granted. In the middle of the two groups of jurisdiction stands the German Federal Court of Justice, which takes a rule of reason approach.

The German lower courts were initially against such bundling,[72] then the Federal Court of Justice takes a more conditional or rule of reason approach. According to it, the offering of portfolio licenses does not violate competition law as long as (I) they do not oblige the licensee to pay for non-SEPs and (II) royalties are calculated so as not to disadvantage implementers seeking to offer products for a specific region only. Correspondingly, the patentee is not obliged to accept an implementer's offer to only license the patent(s) in suit. The Court states that worldwide SEP portfolio licenses are customary and efficient but it does not make it a condition of their FRANDliness that they correspond—in the words of the CJEU—to "recognised commercial practices in the field."[73]

5.3.2. Component License or End-Product License

In Asia, on the issue of charging royalties for SEPs based on the whole devices or the smallest saleable patent practicing unit (SSPPU), competition authorities in the PRC,[74] Korea and Taiwan do not require that the calculation of FRAND-compliant

72 The bundling of essential with non-essential patents within one licensing portfolio was not permitted by Düsseldorf Regional Court, March 31, 2016, 4a O 126/14, GRUR-RS 2016, 8040, Note 162—Saint Lawrence/Vodafone, March 31, 2016, 4a O 73/14, juris, Note 228 (BeckRS 2016, 131580, Note 167).

73 German Federal Court of Justice, KZR 36/17 (decided on May 5, 2020).

74 For example, Shenzhen Intermediate People's Court ruled in 2013 that InterDigital violated its FRAND obligations and the licensing rate paid by Huawei for InterDigital's SEPs should not exceed 0.019% of the actual sales prices of Huawei's wireless devices. In *Huawei v. Unwired Planet*, Nanjing Intermediate Court ruled in 2019 that Huawei needed to pay just one SEP owned by UP at the rate of 0.00225% (single mode) and 0.0018% (multiple modes) of the devices. Beijing IP Court and awarded XXJ economic damages RMB 8,629,173, based on multiple of RMB 1 per device that the plaintiff charged other licensees (2015 JingZhiMinChu No. 1194 (decided March 22, 2017). The IP Court under the Supreme People's Court regularly applied end-product licensing. One recent

royalties be based on SSPPU and allow royalties to be based on end-products.[75] In India, the New Delhi High Court took the view that the determination of royalty should be based on the sale price of the end product and not on the chipset.[76]

In Dolby v. Oppo and Vivo (2016), the New Delhi High Court adjudicated that Dolby's interim royalty should be fixed at Rs. 34 for every device manufactured, sold or imported before the final disposal of the case, and the Indian entities were permitted to continue manufacturing, selling and importing the products. Noteworthy is that Indian courts find nothing special about licensing of SEPs and granted injunction orders against SEP licensees as requested by SEP owners automatically.[77]

5.3.3. National Rates v. Global Rates

While some SEP patentees adopt national portfolio licenses, some adopt global portfolio licenses for all countries and all relevant patents in its portfolio. Which one of the two practices is more widely used in the industry is hard to tell. National courts are now faced with the issue whether to decide national or global rates. Courts in Japan, the PRC and India follow their counterparts in the US and UK and do not shy away from determining FRAND-compliant rates. However, *Unwired Planet v. Huawei* decided by the UK High Court is a watershed,[78] especially for courts in the PRC which have previously decided exclusively on national rates.

Noteworthy is that in the UK Unwired Planet case, Unwired Planet proposed in June 2015 to offer a worldwide SEP portfolio license, a UK SEP portfolio license (the UK portfolio consists of more patents than just the five SEPs in suit) and per-patent licenses for any SEPs the licensee chose. The royalties claimed for per-patent licenses or a UK portfolio were higher than the global rate on offer.[79]

---

example is (2022) ZuiGaoFaZhiMinZhong Nos. 907, 910, 911, 916, 917, and 918 (decided on December 12, 2023).

75 See Liu, K.-C., & Hilty, R. (Eds.). (2020). *SEPs, SSOs and FRAND—Asian and Global Perspectives on Fostering Innovation in Interconnectivity* (p. 10). Routledge.

76 In *Ericsson v. Intex* (2013), (I.A. No. 6735/2014 in CS(OS) No.1045/2014 pronounced on March 13, 2015, at: https://indiankanoon.org/doc/74163100/Paragraph 158). In *Dolby v. Oppo and Vivo* (2016). The New Delhi High Court adjudicated that Dolby's royalty should be fixed at Rs. 34 (later reduced to 20) for every device manufactured, sold, or imported as an interim royalty before the final disposal of the case. See Dhar, B., & Joseph, R. (2020). Chapter 12 Standard essential patents and FRAND licensing: A view from India. In Liu, K.-C., & Hilty, R. (Eds.), *SEPs, SSOs and FRAND—Asian and Global Perspectives on Fostering Innovation in Interconnectivity* (p. 268). Routledge.

77 See for example *Telefonaktiebolaget LM Ericsson (Publ) v. Mercury Electronics CS(OS)* 442/2013; *Tlefonaktiebolaget LM Ericsson (Publ) v. M/s Best IT World (India) Private Limited (iBall) CS (OS)* 2501/2015.

78 See *Unwired Planet International Ltd. v. Huawei Technologies Co.*, (2015) EWHC 2097 (Pat) (UK High Court, decided on July 21, 2015) (Huawei appealed against Birss J's orders. On October 23, 2018, the Court of Appeal handed down a judgment dismissing the appeal: [2018] EWCA Civ. 2344. The decision was upheld by the UK Supreme Court, [2020] UKSC 37(decided on August 26, 2020).

79 See *Unwired Planet International Ltd. v. Huawei Technologies Co.*, (2015) EWHC 2097 (Pat) (UK High Court, decided on July 21, 2015) (Huawei appealed against Birss J's orders. On October 23, 2018, the Court of Appeal handed down a judgment dismissing the appeal: [2018] EWCA Civ. 2344.

What Unwired Planet really wanted was a global license and would accept whatever rate and terms set by the court. However, Huawei engaged only on the terms of a UK portfolio license with Unwired Planet but did not engage on Unwired Planet's proposed terms of a global license.[80] Huawei contended that only a UK portfolio license would be FRAND and it would accept any royalty rate set by the court.[81] Huawei positively asked the court to set a UK-only rate.[82] However, the court decided global rates by concluding that:

> Unwired Planet's portfolio today is (and in 2014 it was) sufficiently large and has sufficiently wide geographical scope that a licensor and licensee acting reasonably and on a willing basis would agree on a worldwide licence. They would regard country by country licensing as madness. A worldwide licence would be far more efficient. It might well have different rates for different regions and for different standards but that is another matter. The employment of different rates would not lead the parties to abandon a worldwide licence and go for country by country licensing.[83]

The UK Supreme Court upheld the decision, but based on the consideration that "It is the contractual arrangement which ETSI has created in its IPR Policy which gives the court jurisdiction to determine a FRAND licence and which lies at the heart of these appeals."[84]

The decision was upheld by the UK Supreme Court, [2020] UKSC 37(decided on August 26, 2020), Paragraph 7.

80 See *Unwired Planet International Ltd. v. Huawei Technologies Co.*, (2015) EWHC 2097 (Pat) (UK High Court, decided on July 21, 2015) (Huawei appealed against Birss J's orders. On October 23, 2018, the Court of Appeal handed down a judgment dismissing the appeal: [2018] EWCA Civ. 2344. The decision was upheld by the UK Supreme Court, [2020] UKSC 37(decided on August 26, 2020), Paragraph 16.

81 See *Unwired Planet International Ltd. v. Huawei Technologies Co.*, (2015) EWHC 2097 (Pat) (UK High Court, decided on July 21, 2015) (Huawei appealed against Birss J's orders. On October 23, 2018, the Court of Appeal handed down a judgment dismissing the appeal: [2018] EWCA Civ. 2344. The decision was upheld by the UK Supreme Court, [2020] UKSC 37(decided on August 26, 2020), Paragraph 23.

82 See *Unwired Planet International Ltd. v. Huawei Technologies Co.*, (2015) EWHC 2097 (Pat) (UK High Court, decided on July 21, 2015) (Huawei appealed against Birss J's orders. On October 23, 2018, the Court of Appeal handed down a judgment dismissing the appeal: [2018] EWCA Civ. 2344. The decision was upheld by the UK Supreme Court, [2020] UKSC 37(decided on August 26, 2020), Paragraph 45.

83 See *Unwired Planet International Ltd. v. Huawei Technologies Co.*, (2015) EWHC 2097 (Pat) (UK High Court, decided on July 21, 2015) (Huawei appealed against Birss J's orders. On October 23, 2018, the Court of Appeal handed down a judgment dismissing the appeal: [2018] EWCA Civ. 2344. The decision was upheld by the UK Supreme Court, [2020] UKSC 37(decided on August 26, 2020), Paragraph 543.

84 [2020] UKSC 37(decided on August 26, 2020), Paragraph 58.

5.4. FRANDly Exercise of SEPs

5.4.1. Can FRAND-Incumbent SEP Patentees Injunct Against Willing License Seekers?

Asian courts are inclined to answer this question negatively. The IP High Court in Japan held that a SEP holder would abuse its patent right if it sought injunctions against a willing FRAND licensee. The Seoul Central District Court likewise ruled that a FRAND-committed SEP holder would have abused its right if it sought injunctive relief against a willing licensee who negotiates in good faith,[85] which is shared by the KFTC.[86] In India, the New Delhi High held in *Telefonaktiebolaget Lm Ericsson v. Competition Commission of India*[87] that "there is good ground to hold that seeking injunctive reliefs by an SEP holder in certain circumstances may amount to abuse of its dominant position"[88] and:

> Suffice to say that in certain cases, such threats (namely to file a complaint in the SEBI (Securities and Exchange Board of India)–added by the author) by a proprietor of a SEP, who is found to be in a dominant position, could be held to be an abuse of dominance.[89]

In China, the SPC issued "Interpretation on Certain Issues Related to Patent Infringement Disputes (2)", which does not support injunction application by SEP patentees who have intentionally breached their FRAND commitment:

> If during the negotiation of terms and conditions for the implementation of SEPs, SEP patentees intentionally breach their obligation derived from their FRAND commitment made in the standard setting process, which leads to failure in reaching patent licensing agreement, and the accused infringers have not obviously defaulted, courts generally shall not support patentees' claim for injunction against the implementation. (Article 24(2))[90]

85 Lee, J.-A., & Jong, S. J. (2020). Chapter 6. Asian perspectives. In Liu, K.-C., & Hilty, R. (Eds.), *SEPs, SSOs and FRAND—Asian and Global Perspectives on Fostering Innovation in Interconnectivity* (pp. 144–145). Routledge.

86 KFTC, IP Guidelines provides:

> However when an injunction is filed limitlessly, patent hold up . . . can occur. Thereby an act of filing an injunction against willing licensees by an SEP holder who promised to license its SEP on FRAND terms can be determined as a behavior that restricts competition in the relevant market as it exceeds the reasonable extent of exercise of patent right.

5B

87 Judgment delivered on March 30, 2016, W.P.(C) 464/2014 & CM Nos. 911/2014 & 915/2014.

88 Judgment delivered on March 30, 2016, W.P.(C) 464/2014 & CM Nos. 911/2014 & 915/2014, Paragraph 199.

89 Judgment delivered on March 30, 2016, W.P.(C) 464/2014 & CM Nos. 911/2014 & 915/2014, Paragraph 200.

90 SPC FaShi (2016) No.1 (issued on March 21, 2016).

Beijing IP Court has ruled that SEP patentees may not seek injunction against an implementer if neither negotiating party has defaulted, or while the SEP holder has defaulted and implementer has not during a good-faith negotiation.[91]

Courts in the US and the UK also tend not to grant injunctions for FRAND-incumbent SEP patentees against willing license seekers. In the 2012 *Apple v. Motorola* case, Justice Richard Posner (9th Circuit Judge) sat on Eastern District Court of Illinois and rejected the injunction application filed by Motorola against Apple:

> Motorola committed to license the '898 to anyone willing to pay a FRAND royalty and thus implicitly acknowledged that a royalty is adequate compensation for a license to use that patent. How could it do otherwise? How could it be permitted to enjoin Apple from using an invention that it contends Apple must use if it wants to make a cell phone with UMTS telecommunications capability —without which it would not be a cell phone.[92]

In the UK, the High Court ruled that

> The legal effect of the FRAND undertaking relating to a SEP is not that the implementer is already licensed. Its effect is that an implementer who makes an unqualified commitment to take a licence on FRAND terms (the wording can be settled by the court (or by an arbitrator)) cannot be the subject of a final injunction to restrain patent infringement. Whereas an implementer who refuses to take a licence on terms found by the court to be FRAND has chosen to have no licence, and so if they have been found to infringe a valid patent an injunction can be granted against them.[93]

5.4.2. To Continue to Pay Royalty for Expired Patents or Not

Competition authority in Korea (Qualcomm I),[94] the PRC (*NDRC v. Qualcomm*),[95] and Taiwan (Philips CD-R case) take the stance that once patents, whether SEPs or

91 Beijing IP Court, 2015 JingZhiMinChu No. 1194 (decided on March 22, 2017), p. 37.

92 *Apple, Inc. v. Motorola, Inc.*, 869 F.Supp. 2d 901, 914 (N.D. Ill. 2012) (decided on June 22, 2012).

93 [2017] EWHC 711 (Pat) (May 4, 2017). However, the UK High Court at the end did issue a final injunction against Huawei, for the following reasons: Unwired Planet has established that Huawei has infringed two valid patents, Huawei has not been prepared to take a license on the terms that Justice Birss found to be FRAND, and Unwired Planet were not in breach of competition law.

94 See Kim, B. (2017). Anti-competitive licensing practice: Qualcomm's abuse of market dominance. In Liu, K.-C. (Ed.), *Annotated Leading Patent Cases in Major Asian Jurisdictions* (p. 188). City University of HK Press.

95 Li, J., & Lin, X. (2017). Anti-monopoly case against Qualcomm's patent licensing practice. In Liu, K.-C. (Ed.), *Annotated Leading Patent Cases in Major Asian Jurisdiction* (p. 219). City University of HK Press.

non-SEPs, expire, the licensees should not be required to continue to pay a royalty for them. The NDRC has forcefully reasoned why this is so:

> Even as Qualcomm asserts that there is constant flowing of new patents into its patent portfolio, the total number of patents its patent portfolio increases. However, the number of patents in the portfolio does not necessarily reflect the value of those patents. Therefore, the Qualcomm's assertion that new patents could compensate expired patents could not be verified. Qualcomm did not provide assessment and notice on whether new patents are necessary for the licensees and of value. Nor did Qualcomm measure and annualize the change of value between expired and new patents. Qualcomm continues to charge the same amount of license fees for the patent portfolio over many years, based vaguely on that new patents are constantly rolling in to the patent portfolio. This actually blurred the subject matters of the patent license for licensees, made the licensees continue to pay royalty fee for expired SEPs.[96]

This might look too rigid. However, they mirror or resemble the "Nine No-Nos" that reigned in the US from 1970 to 1995,[97] especially "no mandatory package licenses" and "no royalty provisions not reasonably related to the licensee's sales." It took the US twenty-five years to transition to Antitrust Guidelines for the Licensing of Intellectual Property that looks at these issues from the perspective of the rule of reason. Then the Asian stance should be treated with equal understanding and tolerance, to allow Asian economies time to evolve according to their changing conditions and mindsets.

5.5. To Intervene from Competition Law or Not?

While major Asian jurisdictions and the EC have treated FRAND licensing of SEPs as an antitrust issue (supra Subsections 4.1 and 4.2), the German Federal Court of Justice has also tried quite a few cases of FRAND licensing of SEPs under antitrust law, as private enforcement of anti-monopoly law is common in Germany, including the challenge of IP licensing. For example, it held in the 2004 "Spundfass" (tight drum) case that the discriminatory refusal of a de facto SEP patentee to license undermines the competition freedom of others and therefore justifies the defense of no infringement.[98] Noteworthy is that the SPC in China reminds courts in its latest "SPC's Interpretation on Some Legal Issues Related to The Trial of Civil Monopoly Disputes" to take the initiative to look into the competition law aspects of cases, which were not initiated as civil monopoly disputes but were

96 NDRC, FaGaiBanJiaJianChuFa (2015), No. 1 (decided on February 9, 2015).
97 See Subsection 5.2.3 of Chapter 4.
98 BGH KZR40/02 (decided on July 13, 2004).

found by a court after hearing them as those cases. The court shall refer them to another court with jurisdiction if it does not have jurisdiction. (Article 7).[99]

In contrast, the US (supra Subsection 4.3) and the UK have thus far treated this as a pure contract issue. In the UK, Justice Birss ruled in *Unwired Planet v. Huawei* that it was not necessary to rely on competition law to enforce the FRAND undertaking. The boundaries of FRAND and competition law are not the same. A rate may be above the FRAND rate but not contrary to competition law. There is only one set of license terms which are FRAND in a given set of circumstances. Unwired Planet did not abuse their dominant position by issuing these proceedings for an injunction prematurely, by maintaining a claim for an injunction in these proceedings, by seeking to insist on a worldwide license, by attempting to impose unfair prices or by bundling SEPs and non-SEPs.[100]

99 SPC FaShi (2024) No. 6 (issued on June 24, 2024), effective on July 1, 2024.

100 *Unwired Planet International Ltd. v. Huawei Technologies Co.*, [2015] EWHC 2097 (Pat), Paragraphs 806(20–5), 807(17).

10 To Facilitate FRANDly Licensing of SEPs on a Global Scale

1. Introduction

The deficiencies in FRAND licensing of SEPs have not been effectively mitigated despite the increasing amount of litigation (and arbitration) over the past two decades. In 2016 the EC identified in its Communication on Standardisation Priorities for the Digital Single Market three main areas where the SEP licensing environment could be improved: the opaque nature of much information on SEPs; the unclear valuation of patented technologies involved in standards and the definition of FRAND; and uncertainty in the enforcement of SEPs. The EC further issued in 2017 its communication setting out the EU approach to SEPs to address the urgent need to set out key principles that would foster a balanced, smooth and predictable framework for SEP licensing. These key principles reflect two main objectives: incentivizing the development and inclusion of top technologies in standards by ensuring a fair and adequate return for these contributions and ensuring smooth and wide dissemination of standardized technologies on fair access conditions. Driven by SEP implementers in the EU, the EC came up in 2023 with its Proposal of a Regulation on SEPs (draft SEP Regulation).[1] The draft SEP Regulation seeks to enhance the transparency of FRAND licensing of SEPs and to speed up the setting of FRAND terms and conditions via an alternative dispute resolution mechanism.

The draft SEP Regulation vindicates my earlier advocacy on the need for a depository of FRAND-compliant terms and conditions, an essentiality check, and effective arbitration.[2] However, the Draft as it currently stands is insufficient to do the job properly. But it "signals one clear truth to the IP community: that the pro-SEP side has comprehensively lost the debate of ideas when it comes to defending the current mobile phone licensing regime."[3] The following sections describe

1 (EU)2017/1001 (27.4.2023 COM (2023) 232 final.

2 See Liu, K.-C., & Zhang, H. R. (2019). Propositions for regulated self-regulation of SSOs. In Liu, K.-C., & Hilty, R. (Eds.), *SEPs, SSOs and FRAND—Asian and Global Perspectives on Fostering Innovation in Interconnectivity* (pp. 379–397). Routledge.

3 Van de Wille, P. (former chief communications officer at InterDigital 2012–2021) (2023). *Why SEP Owners Have Lost the FRAND Debate,* at: https://www.managingip.com/article/2c108scnd804r4g1dscn4/opinion-why-sep-owners-have-lost-the-frand-debate.

DOI: 10.4324/9781003597766-14

the deficiencies of the current FRAND licensing framework for SEPs and then explore mechanisms that could help alleviate those deficiencies.

2. Deficiencies of Current FRAND Licensing Framework

Although there is some very limited advocacy in the US, where the most powerful SEP patentees originate, of no governmental intervention,[4] it is now beyond doubt that current FRAND licensing of SEPs has many deficiencies, such as excessive declaration of SEPs, unclear and vague FRAND-compliant terms, and an unseemly grab for jurisdiction between national courts of different countries.

2.1. Over Declaration of SEPs

Over the last thirty years, the cumulative number of declared SEPs by SEP patentees with various SSOs has increased drastically.[5] According to empirical research by IPlytics in 2016, over 200,000 SEPs had been declared with global major SSOs. However, patent pool licensing is a minor proportion; only 9% of declared SEPs are pooled. As a result, patent thickets are rife in the field of SEP licensing.[6] Implementers and product manufacturers need to obtain multiple licenses from multiple patentees, making the transaction costs for securing licenses for SEPs prohibitively high.[7]

Often the declared SEPs, voluminous as they are, are not technologically or commercially essential. Some industry insiders estimate that only 30% or less of declared SEPs are really needed for the implementation of a standard.[8] For

4 In 2016 David Kappos, the former director of the USPTO, warned that:

> the promise of a remarkable future brought about by the fourth industrial revolution is at risk. Governments and technology users are taking aim at patent-based innovation incentives associated with standards. The very same standards that have been such huge successes are being questioned as if the facts were precisely opposite of what they are.

He suggests that "We should comprehend, confront, and dispel key myths surrounding the drivers of innovation in the digital era: SEPs." See Kappos, D. *The *Real* Innovation Economy—Conclusion: Debunking Myths at the Intersection between Intellectual Property and Competition Laws*, at: https://www.ipnomics.net/p_16727. A rebuke to this advocacy, see Liu, K.-C. (2019). As a matter of standard for Asia and beyond? In In Liu, K.-C., & Hilty, R. (Eds.), *SEPs, SSOs and FRAND—Asian and Global Perspectives on Fostering Innovation in Interconnectivity* (pp. 21–23). Routledge.

5 Pentheroudakis, C., & Baron, J. (2017). *Licensing Terms of Standard Essential Patents: A Comprehensive Analysis of Cases* (p. 31). Publications Office of the European Union.

6 Shapiro, C. (2001). *Navigating the Patent Thicket: Cross Licenses, Patent Pools, and Standard-Setting*, at: https://ssrn.com/abstract=273550.

7 Pohlmann, T., & Blind, K. (2016). *Landscaping Study on Standard Essential Patents (SEPs)* (pp. 8, 53), at: http://ec.europa.eu/DocsRoom/documents/20741/attachments/1/translations/en/renditions/native.

8 Pohlmann, T., & Blind, K. (2016). *Landscaping Study on Standard Essential Patents (SEPs)* (pp. 8, 53), at: http://ec.europa.eu/DocsRoom/documents/20741/attachments/1/translations/en/renditions/native.

example, Fairfield Resources International, Inc., the Association of Radio Industries and Businesses of Japan, and the Telecommunications Technology Association of South Korea have found that there were only 529 genuine SEPs among the 1,889 declared SEP families within the 3GPP standards.[9] In the judgment in *Huawei v. Samsung*, it is stated that SEP assessment data from Thomson Reuters showed that out of 7,077 declared SEP families in 4G/LTE global standards, only 2,535 patents are really SEPs.[10]

2.2. *FRAND-Compliant Terms Unknown and Keep Changing*

2.2.1. *Terms Unknown Due to Confidentiality*

Under the influence of ANSI, ETSI, IEC and ITU, the FRAND policy has been the global practice for standards adopted by SSOs.[11] However, most SSOs have made no effort to clarify and their vague FRAND rules and have left enforcement efforts to others.[12] In practice, in SEP licensing the parties always first sign non-disclosure agreements (NDAs) before the commercial and technological negotiations start. For example, ETSI's IPR Guide points out that:

> It is recognized that NDAs may be used to protect the commercial interests of both potential licensor and potential licensee during an essential IPR licensing negotiation, and this general practice is not challenged. Nevertheless, ETSI expects its members (as well as non-ETSI members) to engage in an impartial and honest Essential IPR licensing negotiation process for FRAND terms and conditions.[13]

Therefore, requiring signing an NDA is widely regarded as justified when considering FRAND licensing.

9 See Tokyo IP High Court, 2013 (Ne) 10043 (decided on May 16, 2014), at: http://www.ip.courts.go.jp/eng/vcms_lf/25ne10043full.pdf, 132.

10 See *Huawei v. Samsung*, Shenzhen Intermediate People's Court (2016) Yue03MinChuZi No. 840 (decided on January 11, 2018), 161.

11 Contreras, J. (2018). Form and variation in FRAND and other standards licensing commitments. In Contreras, J. (Ed.), *The Cambridge Handbook of Technical Standardization Law* (p. 172). Cambridge University Press.

12 Halpern, M. (2021). *Arbitrating Standard Essential Patent Licensing Disputes* (p. 16) [doctoral dissertation]. Queen Mary University of London, London.

13 ETSI, §4.4 Guide on Intellectual Property Rights (adopted by Board #133 (June 10, 2021), at: https://www.etsi.org/images/files/IPR/etsi-guide-on-ipr.pdf, which is intended to help ETSI members and any other party involved in ETSI's standardization activities to understand and implement the ETSI IPR Policy. According to the public statement made by the ETSI, "The ETSI IPR Policy and the IPR Guide texts stand as independent documents in their own right." Available at: https://www.etsi.org/intellectual-property-rights.

In Germany, courts have held that the SEP holder has "justified confidentiality interests, for instance by entering into an NDA."[14] In the PRC, a refusal to sign an NDA is regarded as a sign of unwillingness to obtain a license, which could result in injunctive relief.[15]

In addition, courts tend to show great deference to SEP holders' alleged confidentiality interests. In the famous Unwired Planet case in the UK, the Patents Court held that:

> publication of the commercial licensing information in issue (subject to a few exceptions) would substantially weaken the position of various companies mentioned in the judgment, particularly as licensors but also as licensees. That interference with the competitive position of the telecommunications market is unwarranted.[16]

As a result, no one in the business of licensing SEPs is allowed to reveal, disclose, or discuss any terms and conditions of any particular SEP licensing agreement. This leads to comparable license terms relating to the same SEPs being completely hidden from market participants. No meaningful discussion of the FRAND terms can be conducted by reference to what others may have agreed, making the FRAND licensing of SEPs an empty promise.

2.2.2. Terms Keep Changing

IEEE, as one of the leading major SSOs, keeps changing its criteria for determining FRAND terms. In 2015, IEEE adopted a dramatically different patent policy, which was regarded as deviating from so-called "FRAND harmony."[17] The policy included the following elements: (1) a new definition of "reasonable rate" that significantly devalues SEPs through mandatory provision ("determination of such Reasonable Rates **should** include, but need not be limited to, the consideration of"): (a) limiting the value to be based on the value added to the smallest saleable compliant implementation, (b) requiring the value to reflect relative contribution by all other patent holders, and (c) excluding existing licenses covering use of the Essential Patent claim, where such licenses were obtained under the explicit or implicit threat of a prohibitive order (an interim or permanent injunction, exclusion

14 *Sisvel v. ZTE*, District Court Dusseldorf, 4a O 27/16, 13.07.2017; Dusseldorf Appeal Court decision, I-2 U23/179 (decided on July 18, 2017).

15 See *Iwncomm v. Sony*, Beijing High People's Court, (2017) JingMinZhongZi No. 454 (decided on March 28, 2018).

16 *Unwired Planet International Lt v. Huawei Technologies Co. Ltd (UK) Co. Ltd & Anor* (2017) EWHC 3083 (Pat) (decided on November 30, 2017).

17 Katznelson, R. (2015). *Perilous Deviations from FRAND Harmony—Operational Pitfalls of the 2015 IEEE Patent Policy*. 2015 IEEE 9th International Conference on Standardization and Innovation in Information Technology, at: http://ieeexplore.ieee.org/document/7535599/.

order, or similar adjudicative directive) as comparable licenses;[18] (2) prevention of SEP patentees from "seeking, or seeking to enforce, a Prohibitive Order except as provided in this policy";[19] and (3) good faith negotiation obligation without unreasonable delay.[20]

The IEEE 2015 patent policy drew criticism from SEP patentees for allegedly hurting their innovation incentives,[21] which resulted in a swing back of the pendulum by IEEE 2022 Bylaws, effective since 2023, in the direction of a more SEP-patentee-friendly position. For example, the mandatory considerations when determining Reasonable Rates have been changed to "optional." In addition, the value of SEPs is no longer limited to the value added to the smallest saleable compliant implementation but can include the SEP's contribution to "another appropriate value level of the Compliant Implementation."[22]

2.3. Jurisdiction Grab by National Courts

Different national courts solve SEP disputes independently, each in its own way and can develop conflicting legal standards. Traditionally, courts in different countries have followed the comity principle to allow the most suitable court to solve disputes that have functionally the same issues.

However, patentees and implementers pursue a forum shopping strategy to launch lawsuits in a jurisdiction that best fits or maximizes their commercial interests. To prevent other courts from getting in the way of their chosen ones, parties also may apply for an anti-suit injunction (ASI). An ASI is a means for SEP patentees to secure the forum of their choice by compelling their opponents to drop their litigation in other jurisdictions (which may be either their home turf or where the

18 IEEE-SA Standards Board 2015 Bylaws 6.1. This remains unchanged in IEEE-SA Standards Board 2022 Bylaws.

19 IEEE-SA Standards Board 2015 Bylaws 6.2 has provided:

> The Submitter of an Accepted LOA . . . agrees that it shall neither seek nor seek to enforce a Prohibitive Order based . . . in a jurisdiction unless the implementer fails to participate in, or to comply with the IEEE, the outcome of, an adjudication, . . . in that jurisdiction by one or more courts that have the authority to. This remains unchanged in IEEE-SA Standards Board 2022 Bylaws.

20 IEEE-SA Standards Board 2015 Bylaws 6.2 has provided

> The Submitter of an Accepted LOA . . . agrees that it shall neither seek nor seek to enforce a Prohibitive Order based . . . in a jurisdiction unless the implementer fails to participate in, or to comply with the IEEE, the outcome of, an adjudication, . . . in that jurisdiction by one or more courts that have the authority to.

This remains unchanged in IEEE-SA Standards Board 2022 Bylaws.

21 See Fair Standards Alliance & Hu, S. T. (2019). Stakeholders' views on policy concerns and regulatory framework for self-regulation by SSOs. In Liu, K.-C., & Hilty, R. (Eds.), *SEPs, SSOs and FRAND—Asian and Global Perspectives on Fostering Innovation in Interconnectivity* (pp. 361–378). Routledge.

22 IEEE-SA Standards Board 2022 Bylaws 6.2. See also Quinn, G. (2022). *IEEE Approves Pro-Patent Holder Policy Updates*, at: https://ipwatchdog.com/2022/09/30/ieee-approves-pro-patent-holder-policy-updates.

working of SEPs and sale of SEP-protected products is actually taking place) and instead having to litigate in the jurisdiction where such an injunction is issued. To counter an ASI, an anti-anti-suit injunction (AASI) may be applied for in certain countries.

As part of this trend, courts in multiple jurisdictions compete to grab jurisdiction by granting ASIs and AASIs to exclude foreign courts from trying important cases that may have profound ramifications for domestic legal and business communities.[23]

Since the *Microsoft v. Motorola* case in 2012 at the latest,[24] courts in the US have issued ASIs to prohibit litigants from initiating or continuing any parallel SEP-related litigation in other jurisdictions that would preempt the US court's jurisdiction.[25] In 2015, the Northern District Court of California granted InterDigital's motion to require Pegatron (a Taiwanese company which had filed a civil complaint with TIPCC, alleging that InterDigital had abused its market power by improperly setting, maintaining or changing the royalties) to dismiss its suit in Taiwan.[26] In 2017, the Southern District of California denied Qualcomm's request for an anti-suit injunction but in 2018 the Northern District Court of California issued an anti-enforcement injunction in *Huawei v. Samsung* to enjoin Huawei from enforcing an injunction on Chinese SEPs that had been granted by the Shenzhen Intermediate People's Court.[27]

The High Court in London also held ASI to be permissible in Conversant v. Huawei and ZTE in 2018.[28] In Germany the Munich Regional Court granted an AASI in *Continental v. Nokia*, the first time a German court had issued this type of measure, after finding that to start legal proceedings seeking an ASI in the US with the aim of halting an action in Germany was not compliant with German

23 Justice Richard Arnold describes this phenomenon as "jurisdictional battles." See Arnold, R. (2021). SEPs, FRAND and mandatory global arbitration. *GRUR, 70,* 123. For an analysis of the anti-comity nature of ASIs and AASIs see Tsang, K.F., & Lee, J.-A. (2022). The Ping-Pong Olympics of antisuit injunction in FRAND Litigation. *Michigan Technology Law Review, 28(2),* 317–320, at: SSRN: https://ssrn.com/abstract=3968645.

24 The US District Court for the Western District of Washington granted Microsoft an anti-suit injunction preventing Motorola from enforcing a potential German court injunction in a parallel patent infringement proceeding. See *Microsoft Corp. v. Motorola Inc.*, No. 10–01823-JLR (April 12, 2012) (Order).

25 In the US, under the framework set by the Ninth Circuit, any one of the four factors can justify an anti-suit injunction, including whether the foreign litigation would "(1) frustrate a policy of the forum issuing the injunction; (2) be vexatious or oppressive; (3) threaten the issuing court's in rem or quasi in rem jurisdiction; or (4) prejudice other equitable considerations." See *E. & J. Gallo Winery v. Andina Licores S.A.*, 446 F.3d 984, 990 (9th Cir. 2006).

26 InterDigital 2017 Annual Report, 32, at: http://www.snl.com/interactive/newlookandfeel/4103938/2017AnnualReportandNoticeof2018ASMandProxy%20Statement.pdf.

27 At: https://law.justia.com/cases/federal/district-courts/california/candce/3:2016cv02787/299039/ at 310.

28 In this case, an injunction would have been issued but for ZTE's pre-emptive amendment of its foreign claims, see *Conversant Wireless Licensing S.A.R.L. v. Huawei Techs. Co. Ltd. and ZTE Corp.*, (2018). EWHC 2549 (Ch) at 24 (decided on October 2, 2018).

law, and therefore should be enjoined.[29] A Paris Court decided in 2019 to issue an AASI requiring the SEP implementer Lenovo to withdraw its ASI action filed before the Northern District Court of California; this was upheld by the French Court of Appeal in 2020.[30]

Over here in Asia, the Supreme People's Court in Beijing issued its first-ever SEP-related injunction in the form of an anti-enforcement injunction (or, more precisely, an act preservation ruling) against Conversant in August 2020, prohibiting it from enforcing a decision rendered only two days earlier by the Dusseldorf district court in Germany.[31] The SPC's decision was likely a response to the joined decisions of the UK Supreme Court just two days earlier in *Unwired Planet v Huawei* and *Conversant v Huawei*.[32] Then the Wuhan Intermediate People's Court took the world by surprise when issuing in September 2020 a global ASI against InterDigital in its suit against Xiaomi (a Chinese company),[33] and by issuing another global anti-suit (excluding even other Chinese courts) and an anti-administrative complaint injunction in March 2021 against Ericsson (the Swedish company) in its suit against Samsung.[34]

Why is there such a jurisdiction grab among national courts?[35] Three reasons come to mind. One is the subtle feeling or suspicion that certain national courts act less than prudently in their case-handling and issuance of an injunction, act with legal chauvinism or with an unjustifiably long arm.[36]

The second reason is that certain courts have begun to compete to be the favored forum among parties by developing positions favorable to one particular party (patent holders versus product manufacturers). Jurisdictions renowned for setting lower global FRAND rates may attract cases from manufacturers seeking to

29 Munich Regional Court 21 O 9333/19 Order of July 11, 2019.

30 The dispute was between IPCom and Lenovo. Noteworthy is that the Court of Appeal overturned the order of the first instance court, prohibiting any further anti-suit motions which might be filed by Lenovo, on the basis that the mere possibility of a future application did not justify such an order, see https://www.taylorwessing.com/en/insights-and-events/insights/2020/06/ipcom-v-lenovo---court-of-appeal-of-paris.

31 SPC (2019) ZuiGaoFaZhiMingZhong Nos. 732,733,733–1 civil ruling (decided on August 20, 2020).

32 Arnold, R. (2022). The EU's WTO complaint against China can only be resolved by establishing legally enforceable global arbitration of SEP disputes. *Journal of Intellectual Property Law & Practice, 17(4)*, 329.

33 Wuhan Intermediate People's Court (2020) Er01ZhiMingChu 169–1 civil ruling (decided on September 23, 2020).

34 Wuhan Intermediate People's Court (2020) Er01ZhiMingChu 743 civil ruling ((decided on December 25, 2020).

35 Tsang, K.F., & Lee, J.-A. (2022). The Ping-Pong Olympics of antisuit injunction in FRAND litigation. *Michigan Technology Law Review, 28(2)*, 323–326, at SSRN: https://ssrn.com/abstract=3968645.

36 Justice Richard Arnold even pointed out "the perception in some quarters that the courts of Western nations which accept jurisdiction to settle global FRAND licences are exercising—or at least enabling patentees based in those nations to exercise—economic hegemony over implementers based in non-Western nations." See Arnold, R. (2021). SEPs, FRAND and mandatory global arbitration. *GRUR, 70*, 123.

challenge the rates offered by SEP patentees. India could be such a jurisdiction, and so might China.[37]

In the UK, the pro-patentee *Conversant v. Huawei and ZTE* decision by the Court of Appeal[38] has been seen as "likely to cement the UK's place as a jurisdiction of choice for SEP owners who are looking to obtain global FRAND determinations."[39] In the US, the Eastern District Court of Texas at one point in time attracted "roughly half of the annual portion of four thousand infringement suits filed each year" in the US by being quick and friendly to patentees.[40]

The third reason is that nowadays SEPs are increasingly becoming the object of trade policy: this "might lead to a vicious circle of conflicting judgments on the ground, follow-up ASIs, and thus considerable new inefficiencies in global licensing and enforcement of SEPs."[41] Judges, being human, are sometimes influenced by such trade policy issues.

In the following section, it is proposed that we reconcile conflicting legal standards across nations through persuasion or better argumentation.

3. To Reconcile Conflicting Legal Standards Through Persuasion

The conflicts between different legal standards can be solved not by preferring one set of standards to the other, but through empathy for the differences and an understanding as to where they are coming from and leading to, together with mutual respect for a nation-state's choice of path and standards that best suit its developmental needs. These differences need not be "harmonized," as they represent diverse values and perspectives. Dialogue and mutual persuasion are the only way towards reconciliation.

3.1. FRAND Commitment as a Contract with Third-Party Beneficiaries

3.1.1. Justification

Common law jurisdictions such as the US and England treat the FRAND commitment between a SEP patentee and an SSO as a contract with third-party beneficiaries. These third-party beneficiaries are not party to the contract itself, but they stand

37 Contreras, J. (2019). The new extraterritoriality: FRAND royalties, anti-suit injunctions and the global race to the bottom in disputes over standards-essential patents. *Boston University Journal of Science & Technology Law, 25(2)*, 251–290, at SSRN: https://ssrn.com/abstract=3339378.

38 (2019) EWCA Civ. 38 (decided on January 30, 2019).

39 Bristows LLP, *Conversant v. Huawei & ZTE*: Court of Appeal jurisdiction Judgment 3 (decided on January 30, 2019), at: https://www.bristows.com/news-and-publications/articles/the-unwired-planet-appeal-and-future-issues.

40 Merges, R. (2022). *American Patent Law—A Business and Economic History* (p. 450). Cambridge University Press.

41 Leistner, M. (2019). European experiences: EU and Germany. In Liu, K.-C., & Hilty, R. (Eds.), *SEPs, SSOs and FRAND—Asian and Global Perspectives on Fostering Innovation in Interconnectivity* (pp. 355–356). Routledge.

to realize a benefit once the contract is concluded, namely the signing of a licensing agreement with SEP patentees for the use of those SEPs. In other words, the third party who is a willing license seeker is entitled to enforce the contract between the SEP patentee and an SSO by asking the former to sign a FRAND-compliant licensing agreement with the license seeker.[42]

By contrast, although Article 328 of the German Civil Code recognizes the notion of a contract with third-party beneficiaries (Vertrag zugunsten Dritter), the legal practice does not allow at all a contract with third-party beneficiaries that is of a "property (*in rem*)" nature, but only one of an "obligation (*in personam*)" nature.[43] Patent licensing is considered to be a "property act"[44] that can universally exclude, with "property effects" as the patentee may exercise his patent right when it is infringed.

This arises because German legal practice follows the principle of certainty (Bestimmtheitsgrundsatz) which requires that an act of disposition which is of a "property" nature is only permissible when its scope is certain or at least sufficiently ascertainable. The FRAND commitment made by SEP patentees to SSOs is only a self-imposed unilateral obligation, not a contract between SEP patentees and SSOs with third-party beneficiaries.

However, the purpose of the principle of certainty is to protect a debtor's interests in being able to know the scope of the obligation towards third parties. Therefore, it prohibits contracts with third-party beneficiaries with property effect when the third parties are not certain or at least not sufficiently ascertainable. Obviously, this traditional view does not fit the intangible nature of patent rights. What is required of a patentee when they commit to issue a license to any willing third party (license seeker) is that they tolerate the latter's use of his patent rights in return for FRAND financial returns. The tolerance gives rise to no costs to the patentee. Therefore, the tolerance of use by one party is no different to the tolerance of use by one hundred or even unlimited parties and does not therefore impose an unforeseeable and unduly onerous burden on the patentee; the costs involved are the same, namely zero. The view of certain German scholars that the FRAND commitment by the SEP owner should qualify as a contract with third-party beneficiaries, based on the agreement between SEP patentees and the respective SSO, should be followed.[45]

42 *Microsoft Corp. v. Motorola, Inc.*, 696 F.3d 872 (9th Cir. 2012); *Apple Inc. v. Motorola, Inc.*, No. 2012–1548 (Fed. Cir. 2014). Section 1(3) Contracts (Rights of Third Parties) Act 1999 of the UK stipulates "The third party must be expressly identified in the contract by name, as a member of a class or as answering a particular description but need not be in existence when the contract is entered into."

43 MüKoBGB/P. Gottwald (2022) §328 Rd. 278 (9. Aufl. C.H. Beck).

44 Article 20 of the German Patent Act stipulates: "The patent shall lapse if 1. the proprietor of the patent surrenders it by written declaration to the German Patent and Trade Mark Office, or 2. the annual renewal fee or the difference is not paid in due time." Another "property act" in the patent realm is a "written surrender of patent."

45 See Hilty, R., & Slowinski, P. (2015). Standardessentielle Patente—Perspektiven außerhalb des Kartellrechts. *GRUR International*, 788.

German principles of contracts with third-party beneficiaries have been adopted in varying degrees by some Asian civil law jurisdictions. For example, Taiwan recognized this type of contract when it enacted its Civil Code in 1929.[46] Shang-Kuan Shi, probably the most influential commentator on both sides of the Taiwan Strait, has early on (in 1954) discussed it and its application in Germany and Japan, however without mentioning the principle of certainty in detail. He concludes that "the provisions on contract with their party beneficiaries could be applied to in rem contracts and their ensuing disposing contracts by analogy, provided that the assignment of property right is preceded by hand-over (for movables) or registration (for unmovable)."[47] The PRC recognizes for the first time such a contract type in its Civil Code of 2020.[48] However, the certainty principle is likely unknown to Japan, Korea, the PRC, and Taiwan.

In practice, courts in the PRC, Japan and Korea have not yet recognized FRAND commitments made by SEP patentees towards SSOs as contracts with third-party beneficiaries between SEP patentees and SSOs for the benefit of implementers, but instead, they are viewed as a mere willingness to grant a license to a third party. Those courts applied other legal principles such as fairness, good faith, no abuse of rights, and estoppel to deal with disputes between SEP patentees and license seekers related to or based on a FRAND commitment.[49]

Jurisdictions with a civil law tradition are advised to recognize FRAND commitments as contracts with third-party beneficiaries between SEP patentees and the SSOs to which the former have made their FRAND commitment. This would more effectively avoid holdups by SEP patentees, help the implementation of patents that are now part of standards and the proliferation of new products these patents are

46 Taiwan's Civil Code has three articles that deal with contract with third-party beneficiaries. The most relevant one provides:

> (1) When it is provided in a contract that an obligation shall be performed to a third party, the offeror may demand the debtor to perform the obligation to the third party, and such third party also has the right to demand performance direct from the debtor. (2) So long as the third party has not expressed his intent to take advantage of the contract specified in the preceding paragraph, the parties may modify the contract or revoke it. (3) If the third party expresses to either of the parties his intent not to take advantage of the contract, he is deemed to never have any right under the contract. Article 269

47 Shi, S.-K. (1954). *The General Theory of Obligation* (p. 594). Self publication.

48 Article 522(2) of PRC's Civil Code stipulates:

> Where it is provided by law or agreed by the parties that a third person may directly request the debtor to perform the obligation to him, and the third person does not explicitly reject it within a reasonable period of time, if the debtor fails to perform the obligation to the third person or the performance does not conform to the agreement, the third person may request the debtor to bear default liability. The defenses that the debtor has against the creditor may be asserted against the third person.

49 Lee, J.-A., & Jong, S.J. (2020). Asian perspectives. In Liu, K.-C., & Hilty, R. (Eds.), *SEPs, SSOs and FRAND—Asian and Global Perspectives on Fostering Innovation in Interconnectivity* (pp. 128–132). Springer.

meant to create. For such a contract to come to bear, there needs to be compelling reasons.

Only with a properly functioning legal construct of a "contract with third-party beneficiaries" will the utility of SEPs be maximized and the purpose of SSOs fulfilled.[50] Any contract, including those with third-party beneficiaries, needs ascertainable parties and terms and conditions. Here, we first need to determine who the willing third-party beneficiaries are. This should not be difficult (see Subsection 5.2 of Chapter 9). It should not be an obstacle to recognizing such a contract. Then the terms and conditions of licensing agreements between SEP patentees and implementers although not immediately available and need time to work out, but should be ascertainable under the FRAND framework, especially with the help of the suggested competence center to be set up by the designated major SSOs (see infra Section 5).

The FRAND commitment alone does not in itself form a licensing agreement between SEP patentees and SEP implementers. It bestows upon willing and good-faith license seekers immunity from being sued for patent infringement and injuncted, and a right to conclude a licensing agreement.[51]

3.1.2. Further Ramifications

A. NO INJUNCTIVE RELIEF AGAINST WILLING IMPLEMENTER

In 2015, IEEE changed its IPR policy and disallowed SEP holders who have made a FRAND commitment to file for injunctive relief against a willing implementer.[52] The IEEE SA Standards Board 2022 Bylaws amended that basic position with minor changes in wording. Now an SEP patentee: "shall neither seek nor seek to enforce a Prohibitive Order based on such Essential Patent Claim(s) in a jurisdiction against the implementer who is willing to negotiate in good faith." Rather than this unclear position, it is suggested that the 2015 IEEE stance that there shall be no injunctive relief against a willing implementer is preferable, or as Dan Burk has suggested, a patentee who wishes to enforce his patent rights disregarding FRAND terms should have a right to an injunction only if they pay the costs of the competitor who needs to adopt an alternative technology.[53]

50 Hilty, R., & Slowinski, P. (2015). Standardessentielle Patente—Perspektiven außerhalb des Kartellrechts. *GRUR International*, 788.

51 Hilty, R., & Slowinski, P. (2015). Standardessentielle Patente—Perspektiven außerhalb des Kartellrechts. *GRUR International*, 790–791.

52 IEEE SA Standards Board 2015 Bylaws 6.2.

53 See Burk, D. (2013). Intellectual property in the cathedral in access to information and knowledge—21st century challenges. In Beldiman, D. (Ed.), *Intellectual Property and Knowledge* 7. Edward Elgar Publishing.

The extreme imbalance of market power between SEP patentees and potential licensees leads to a high likelihood of daunting costs of holdup by SEP patentees. Patent/IP offices cannot take a laissez-faire approach but rather intervene to smooth the FRAND licensing of SEPs, by allowing after voluntary licensing negotiations have failed, the application of the compulsory license mechanism available in most national patent laws. Such intervention is conducive to the implementation of new technologies embodied in SEPs and to market competition, and ultimately to new momentum for inventive activity leading to SEPs.

To make such compulsory licensing work efficiently in the SEP context, SEP owners should be required to speed up the voluntary licensing negotiation process, as they are versed in the licensing businesses and have standardized operation procedures in place. Patent offices should therefore shorten the 'reasonable period' that would be allowed for the average compulsory license negotiation. In addition, use in the interim by potential licensees of SEPs should be allowed after paying the standard market rate, provided that the actual royalty will be later adjusted following a competent authority's decision.

Furthermore, there will be a plethora of SEP implementers and if compulsory licensing of SEPs has to be undertaken on a case-by-case basis as Article 31(a) of the TRIPS Agreement ("authorization of such use shall be considered on its individual merits") could be interpreted to require), this will cause unreasonable repetition costs. National patent laws can learn from the compulsory patent licensing regime of the UK which not only allows individual compulsory licenses but also a compulsory license as of right (see Subsection 3.2.3 of Chapter 5). That should mean that every license seeker who satisfies the conditions for a compulsory license that the patent office registers or designates on the patent registry may use the SEPs in question without going through an individual compulsory license process, provided they pay the designated royalty.

3.2. Not To Bundle Non-SEPs with SEPs

The two seemingly justifiable reasons for SEP owners to bundle non-SEPs with SEPs and license them together are the ease of portfolio management and the guarantee of comprehensive coverage for the licensees. However, "ease of portfolio management" is a highly dubious one, as SEPs are declared by their owners who clearly know that these SEPs are separated and different from non-SEPs. As regards the extent of coverage of any license agreement, it should be the choice of the license-seekers alone. If SEPs owners bundle non-SEPs with SEPs in their license they are misusing their position to impose non-SEPs on the licensees, leading to an issue of abuse of dominance as the licensees are compelled to accept. Consequently, it is legally and objectively unjustified to bundle SEPs with non-SEPs when licensing the SEPs.

The "unbundled" requirement of the US Telecommunications Act of 1996 could provide a supporting footnote to this argument. The law requires, that when an entity entering the market chooses to lease certain of an incumbent's network elements, the incumbent cannot refuse and has a duty to provide them on an "unbundled basis" on "just, reasonable, and nondiscriminatory" terms (see Subsection 4.1 of Chapter 3). In addition, mandatory package licensing has been listed in the US as one of the Nine No-Nos (sixth) (see Subsection 3.5.2 of Chapter 3).

The Proposals for Amendment of TRIPS by a group of European IP scholars also take a similar view and suggest elevating the present "Member *may* adopt" clause of Article 40(2) of TRIPS Agreement to

> Members *shall* adopt . . . appropriate to prevent or control such practices [competition-restraining IP licensing practices–added by author], which may include for example exclusive grant-back conditions, conditions preventing challenge to validity and coercive package licensing, in the light of the relevant laws and regulations of the Member concerned.[54]

3.3. To Issue Anti-Suit Injunction or Not?

An ASI allows a domestic court to restrain a party subject to its jurisdiction from proceeding in a foreign court in circumstances that are unjust. As a matter of principle, although the domestic court has the power to enjoin a party from proceeding with a suit in a foreign country, it is suggested the power should be used sparingly.

In the US at least, a three-part inquiry governs a district court's assessment of the propriety of an ASI.[55] First, the court must evaluate: "whether or not the parties and the issues are the same, and whether or not the first action is dispositive of the action to be enjoined."[56] Secondly, the court must assess "whether at least one of the so-called 'Unterweser factors' applies."[57] Thirdly, the court must inquire into whether the impact on comity is tolerable.[58]

In general, when asked to issue ASI or ASSI courts are advised to examine whether the domestic case and foreign cases are functionally the same. One convincing example of a correct determination of functional identity can be found in the California Southern District Court's rejection of Qualcomm's motion for an ASI to enjoin Apple from filing parallel lawsuits in other jurisdictions. Between January 23, 2017, and April 11, 2017, Apple filed a total of eleven lawsuits against Qualcomm and its subsidiaries in the UK, Japan, the PRC, and Taiwan. All but one of these lawsuits were filed before Qualcomm had answered Apple's original

54 Kur, A. (Ed.). (2011). *Intellectual Property Rights in a Fair World System* (pp. 507, 600). Edward Elgar Publishing. (The proposed rule is binding as to the goal to be achieved, but flexible on the national execution. The specifically mentioned clauses are not considered "per se" illegal. Competition authorities should focus more on the effects of clauses, rather on their formal character.)

55 *Microsoft v. Motorola*, 696 F.3d 872, 881 (9th Cir. 2012).

56 *Applied Med. Distrib. Corp. v. Surgical Co.*, 587 F.3d 909, 914 (9th Cir. 2009).

57 *Microsoft v. Motorola*, 696 F.3d 872, 881 (9th Cir. 2012).

58 *Microsoft v. Motorola*, 696 F.3d 872, 881 (9th Cir. 2012).

complaint in California. Qualcomm petitioned for an antisuit injunction, which was rejected.

> The record before the Court demonstrates that the boundaries of this dispute are not limited to the United States. Multiple sovereign states and bodies have posed legal challenges to Qualcomm's business model on the belief that Qualcomm's conduct in their respective jurisdictions has an adverse effect on competition in their territories. To issue an anti-suit injunction, therefore, would directly impede upon the ongoing efforts in the UK, the PRC, Japan, and Taiwan to assess the anticompetitive effects of Qualcomm's licensing and chip practices on their markets. Accordingly, the Court finds that the impact on comity is not tolerable and weighs against the issuance of an anti-suit injunction.[59]

If asked to issue an ASI or AASI that would exclude major Asian economies' jurisdictions, other non-Asian courts are advised to be cognizant of the fact that the former have set up specialized IP courts or chambers[60] to handle their heavy caseloads, which makes them experienced in rendering decisions that substantively solve SEP-related problems, as well as being time- and cost-effective.

3.4. Intervention by Competition/Antitrust Law

As mentioned in Section 4 of Chapter 9, major Asian jurisdictions have also treated FRAND licensing of SEP as an antitrust issue in parallel to its contractual issues, whereas the US has thus far treated it as purely contractual even though SSOs have long been subject to antitrust scrutiny. The need for intervention by antitrust law is evident, not least in Asian economies.

First off, SSOs often designate the country where they are established as the applicable jurisdiction and its law as the applicable law when FRAND-related controversies arise.[61] SSOs are mostly established in the US and France. Evidently, there is a risk that the patent (or market regulation) policy of other countries where SEP implementers are headquartered will be hollowed out as a result of applying only US and French law. National patent laws are thereby effectively rendered powerless due to the territoriality principle.

59 *Apple Inc. v. Qualcomm Inc. US District Court Southern District of California*, Case No. 3:17-cv-00108-GPC-MDD (decided on September 7, 2017) by Hon. Gonzalo P. Curiel.

60 Liu, K.-C. (2022). *IP Laws and Regimes in Major Asian Economies—Combing Through Thousand Threads of IP to Peace in Asia* (p. 4). Routledge.

61 For example, ETSI is registered in France and applies French law as the applicable law. Therefore, Seoul Central District Court, Korea and Tokyo IP High Court in 2013 (Ne) 10043 decision applied French Civil Code in the determination of the nature of FRAND commitment. Taiwan IP and Commercial Court applied Dutch law to determine the royalty and interest rate for delayed payment of royalty. See Liu, K.-C. (Ed.). (2017). *Annotated Leading Patent Cases in Major Asian Jurisdictions* (pp. 427–438). City University of HK Press.

In addition, there is a particularly high risk of patent holdup, a practice which is anti-competitive as it not only may "overcompensate patentees" but can lead to increased prices at the consumer level, the prevention of specific products entering the market entirely, and may "ultimately, undermine the standard-setting process."[62] Competition authorities should scrutinize FRAND licensing of SEP cases that impact their particular domestic market, especially when SEP licensees are forced to withdraw any antitrust lawsuits against SEP holders due to an arbitration clause. The usual arbitration tends to take a formalistic and purely contract law approach to the interpretation of a patent license agreement and ignore the dominant market power possessed by the SEP licensors and its possible abuse. Understandably, arbitrators often do not wish to upset these SEP patentees who are an important source of arbitrators' income by looking beyond the written contracts.[63]

4. To Rationalize the Calculation of FRAND-Compliant Rates

4.1. To Choose Reasonable Factors for Determining Reasonable Royalty

In the US, the *Georgia-Pacific* factors, with some modifications, are widely used by courts in their determination of a reasonable royalty, and FRAND-compliant rates.[64] The fifteen factors are used to simulate a hypothetical bilateral negotiation between parties,[65] and may be useful reference points for other jurisdictions in the determination of what is a reasonable royalty.

62 Halpern, M. (2021). *Arbitrating Standard Essential Patent Licensing Disputes* (p. 63) [doctoral dissertation], Queen Mary University of London.

63 For example, International Centre for Dispute Resolution (ICDR) issued a final award on April 17, 2013, in a proceeding InterDigital initiated to resolve a dispute surrounding its 2008 PLA with Pegatron and required Pegatron to pay Qualcomm $29.9 million, including $23.5 million for past patent royalties and $6.2 million in interest, and additional amounts for certain arbitration costs and expenses. ICDR further issued a final award on May 13, 2014, in a dispute between Arima and InterDigital regarding Arima's PLA and awarded InterDigital unpaid patent license fees of US $14.5 million plus US $9.1 million in interest and related fees and costs.

64 For example, *Microsoft v. Motorola*, 2013 WL 2111217 and In re Innovatio IP Ventures, LLC, 2013 US Dist. LEXIS 144061 (N.D. Ill. Sep. 27, 2013).

65 These factors are: 1. Royalties patentee receives for licensing the patent in suit. 2. Rates licensee pays for use of other patents comparable to the patent in suit. 3. Nature and scope of license in terms of exclusivity and territory/customer restrictions. 4. Licensor's established policy and marketing program to maintain patent monopoly by not licensing others to use the invention. 5. Commercial relationship between licensor and licensee, such as whether they are competitors or inventor and promoter. 6. Effect of selling the patented specialty in promoting sales of other products of the licensee; the existing value of the invention to the licensor as a generator of sales of his non-patented items; and the extent of such derivative or convoyed sales. 7. Duration of patent and term of license. 8. Established profitability of the products made under the patent, its commercial success and its current popularity. 9. Utility and advantages of patent property over old modes and devices. 10. The nature of the patented invention; the character of the commercial embodiment of it as owned and produced by the licensor; and the benefit of those who have used the invention. 11. The extent to which the infringer has made use of the invention and the value of such use. 12. The portion of profit or selling price customarily allowed for the use of the invention. 13. The portion of realizable

The important features of SEP licensing include the huge number of licensed patents, their non-exclusive nature, the equal treatment of licensees, and their ex-ante nature but exclude consideration of ex-post factors such as the effects of selling the patented specialty to promote sales of other products of the licensee, the established profitability of products made under the patent, the character of the commercial embodiment of the patented invention owned and produced by the licensor and the proportion of realizable profit attributable to the invention, etc. Therefore, Factors 3, 4, 5, 6, 8, 10, and 13 of the *Georgia Pacific* factors are to be largely ignored.

Specifically, as SEP owners are obliged to issue a license to anyone who is willing to pay FRAND-compliant royalty, Factor 4 should be excluded.[66] The licensing of SEPs can only be non-exclusive and no limitation on consumers and the area of sale should be allowed, so as to promote the standards contained in SEPs, this, therefore, excludes Factor 3. The commercial relationship between SEP owners and the licensees (Factor 5) should also be excluded, otherwise the issue of "non-discriminatory" would be extremely difficult to determine.[67]

Moreover, different from normal patent licensing negotiations which would consider many ex-post factors, the FRAND rates for licensing of SEPs can only be based on an ex-ante assessment of the SEPs and the alternative technologies, excluding the values ensuing after the adaptation of standards. To quote Mark Lemley and Carl Shapiro: "the reasonable royalty rate does not include the value attaching to the creation and adoption of the standard itself. To allow patentees to capture that value would undermine the goals of the FRAND commitment."[68] Consequently, Factors 6, 8, 10, and 13 are to be excluded from the consideration of reasonable royalty.

4.2. To Adopt the "Lump-Sum" or Aggregate Approach

When determining FRAND-compliant terms for numerous SEPs, a lump-sum/aggregate approach for all the SEPs involved would seem to be the only sensible method.[69] Otherwise, each patentee may be tempted to charge the monopoly

profit attributable to the invention as distinguished from non-patented elements, significant features or improvements added by the infringer, the manufacturing process or business risks. 14. Opinion testimony of qualified experts. 15. Outcome from hypothetical arm's length negotiation at the time infringement began. *Georgia-Pacific Corp. v. United States Plywood Corp.*, 318 F.Supp. 1116, 1119–2 (S.D.N.Y. 1970), modified and aff'd, 446 F.2d 295 (2d Cir.); *Unisplay, S.A. v. American Electronic Sign Co., Inc.*, 69 F.3d 512, 517 n.7 (Fed. Cir. 1995).

66 *Microsoft Corp. v. Motorola Inc.*, 696 F.3d 872 (9th Cir. 2012).

67 *Microsoft Corp. v. Motorola Inc*, (W.D. Wash. November 12, 2013), No. C10–1823JLR, Paragraph 102.

68 Lemley, M.A., & Shapiro, C. (2013). A simple approach to setting reasonable royalties for standard-essential patents. *Berkeley Technology Law Journal, 28*, 1148.

69 However, according to the JPO's "Guide to Licensing Negotiations Involving Standard Essential Patents" (issued in 2018 and revised in 2022), "These two approaches are not contradictory. Both approaches may be combined to calculate the rate so as to ensure a more reliable rate through

price, thereby creating royalty stacking and a "tragedy of the anti-commons." The approach of adding up every patent (counting-every-SEP) would ignore the technical merit of patents by valuing quantity over quality. The counting-every-SEP approach can furthermore lead to over-patenting (by, for example, fragmenting the patent claims in the original single patent into claims in several derived patents) and over-declaration of SEPs by patentees.

The lump-sum or aggregate approach should factor in all other relevant SEPs.[70] In other words, all relevant SEPs must be taken into consideration. To use the terminology of the EC draft SEP Regulation, a global aggregate royalty, the maximum amount of royalty for all SEPs, should be worked out.

Ideally, licensees should only pay one reasonable aggregate royalty for all the SEPs they require, and SEP owners would then share this royalty among themselves according to their respective technical contributions. This would greatly enhance the efficiency of FRAND licensing of SEPs and maintain the necessary incentives to invest in innovation.

It is noteworthy that the Tokyo IP High Court in *Apple v. Samsung* chose the aggregate cap of a 5% royalty. This decision was based on a consensus between the parties, Nokia's statement that "the industry-wide aggregate royalty rates for the IPRs for the WCDMA should not exceed 5%," and the market practices of the UMTS-related SEP owners as well as the WCDMA patent platform, a patent pool set up by the UMTS SEP owners.[71] The pool set a standard royalty rate of 0.1% per patent but specified that if an increase in the number of certified essential patents would result in the cumulative rate exceeding 5%, the royalty rate per patent would be adjusted so the cumulative rate does not exceed 5%.[72]

4.3. *To License at the Component Level*

To license SEPs at the end-product level not only affects the legal certainty of implementers of SEPs and end-product manufacturers but also increases

---

comparison of the results." (p. 49). The UK Justice Birss is of the opinion "A top-down approach can also be used in which the rate is set by determining the patentee's share of Relevant SEPs and applying that to the total aggregate royalty for a standard but this may be more useful as a crosscheck." "In assessing a FRAND rate counting patents is inevitable." See *Unwired Planet International Ltd. v. Huawei Technologies Co.*, [2015] EWHC 2097 (Pat) (UK High Court, decided on July 21, 2015) Paragraph 806(10) and (11). In other words, while adopting a bottom-up approach, the court double-checked whether royalty stacking has occurred with a top-down approach. This was supported also by the ruling of the UK Supreme Court in 2020. On the other hand, in *TCL v. Ericsson* case in 2017, the US Federal District Court, while adopting a top-down approach, double-checked it with a bottom-up approach.

70 Lemley, M.A., & Shapiro, C. (2013). A simple approach to setting reasonable royalties for standard-essential patents. *Berkeley Technology Law Journal, 28*, 1150–1151.

71 Tokyo IP High Court 2013 (Ne) 10043.

72 Nakamura, O., & Kerr, C.M. (2008). Current status of platformWCDMA and its joint patent licensing. *NTT Docomo Technical Journal, 10(3)*, 66, at: https://www.docomo.ne.jp/english/binary/pdf/corporate/technology/rd/technical_journal/bn/vol10_3/vol10_3_064en.pdf.

transaction costs and complicates the determination of FRAND-compliant rates. In the non-IoT industries, licensing at a component level has been the common IP licensing practice, while SEP holders often prefer to license their patents to end-product manufacturers.[73]

However, in Asia, competition authorities in the PRC, Korea, and Taiwan do not require that the calculation of FRAND-compliant royalties be based on the component level and have allowed royalties to be based on end-products. Likewise, the New Delhi High Court. Also, IEEE now makes the adoption of component-level royalties optional, after flipping its position in its 2022 Bylaws.[74]

The Max Planck Institute of Innovation and Competition in Munich is of the opinion that:

> SEP licensing at the component level is more conducive to a predictable and efficient licensing framework than licensing at end-product level. Both eliminating uncertainty as to the extent SEPs may be lawfully used and guaranteeing a level-playing field for those using them on different levels of the value chain constitute structural requirements of an innovation-oriented standardisation. None of them is adequately taken into account when SEPs are licensed to end-product manufacturers.[75]

73 See Drexl, J. et al. (2024). Position statement of the Max Planck Institute for Innovation and Competition of February 6, 2024, on the Commission's Proposal for a Regulation on Standard Essential Patents. *Max Planck Institute for Innovation & Competition Research Paper No. 24-03*, Paragraph 34, at: SSRN: https://ssrn.com/abstract=4719023.

74 IEEE first changed its IPR policy in 2015 and advocated the adoption of SSPPU. IEEE-SA Standards Board 2015 Bylaws 6.1 has prescribed "'Reasonable Rate' shall mean appropriate compensation to the patent holder for the practice of an Essential Patent Claim excluding the value, if any, resulting from the inclusion of that Essential Patent Claim's technology in the IEEE Standard. In addition, determination of such Reasonable Rates should include, but need not be limited to, the consideration of: "The value that the functionality of the claimed invention or inventive feature within the Essential Patent Claim contributes to the value of the relevant functionality of the smallest saleable Compliant Implementation that practices the Essential Patent Claim." However, IEEE-SA Standards Board 2022 Bylaws changed that position:

> "Reasonable Rate" shall mean appropriate compensation to the patent holder for the practice of an Essential Patent Claim excluding the value, if any, resulting from the inclusion of that Essential Patent Claim's technology in the IEEE Standard. Some optional considerations for determination of Reasonable Rates are: The value that the functionality of the claimed invention or inventive feature within the Essential Patent Claim contributes to the value of the relevant functionality of the smallest saleable Compliant implementation that practices the Essential Patent Claim or to another appropriate value level of the Compliant Implementation (underlined added by the author).

75 Drexl, J. et al. (2024). Position statement of the Max Planck Institute for Innovation and Competition of 6 February 2024 on the Commission's Proposal for a Regulation on Standard Essential Patents. *Max Planck Institute for Innovation & Competition Research Paper No. 24–03*, Paragraph 98, at: SSRN: https://ssrn.com/abstract=4719023. Similarly, Mark Lemley and Douglas Melamed advocated that changes in patent law are needed to ameliorate patent trolls, which included providing remedies for patent infringement commensurate with the actual scope of the invention and insisting on damages be calculated with the reference to the smallest saleable component that incorporated patented technology, not the whole product; otherwise, the patent holders can claim as reasonable

It is submitted that this approach is preferable, so that SEP patentees will not be over-compensated, and consumers not overcharged.

5. Designated Major SSOs to Set Up a Competence Center

Lawyers by their professional training are rarely well-tutored in and conversant with science and technology. They would usually be unaware that in the 3GPP standards "the major standards contributors—Nokia, Qualcomm, Ericsson and, recently through brute force, Huawei—all contribute roughly equally to the development of the standard."[76] It is hence very disturbing and discomforting to see how generalist courts, often divorced from business realities, in the US, the UK, and the PRC, presumptuously assess the technical contribution of some SEPs, determining the FRANDliness of some offers, calculating different global rates for the same set of SEPs, and pronouncing that "only one set of license terms could be FRAND."[77]

Courts and lawyers must look more for external help. The EC has decided to rely on EUIPO, which has hitherto been dealing exclusively with trademark and design registrations and ironically lacks the technical expertise to set up a competence center to facilitate FRAND licensing of SEPs.[78] There is also a risk of overlapping functions and unnecessary duplication of efforts between EUIPO and SSOs.[79] Therefore, the ETSI has expressed its concerns "that the creation of a second register in the EUIPO would only confuse and possibly disincentivize innovators to disclose their SEPs in Europe."[80] It is bewildering that the EC did not opt to ask one or more of the three European standard organizations, CEN, Cenelec, and especially ETSI, to establish a competence center. In a similar vein, WIPO in its Strategy on SEPs 2024–2026 envisions WIPO as a source of knowledge and data

royalties an excessive share of the value of the product that includes both the patented technology and other contributions made by the defendant. See Lemley, M., & Melamed, D. (2013). Missing the forest for the trolls. *Columbia Law Review, 113(8)*, 2176.

76 Van de Wille, P. (2023). *Why SEP Owners Have Lost the FRAND Debate*, at: https://www.managingip.com/article/2c108scnd804r4g1dscn4/opinion-why-sep-owners-have-lost-the-frand-debate.

77 Disturbing examples include the court's determination that:

> the Revised MNPA overstates the value of Unwired Planet's SEP portfolio. The HPA understates the value of that portfolio; the value R for the relative strength of Unwired Planet's portfolio as compared to Ericsson's for 4G is 7.69%; the values of R for 2G, 3G, and 4G range from 2.38% to 9.52%.

78 Deutsche Vereinigung für gewerblichen Rechtsschutz und Urheberrecht e.V. (2023). Stellungnahme der GRUR zu dem Vorschlag der Europäischen Kommission für eine Verordnung zu standard-essentiellen Patenten, 9–10 (COM (2023) 232) at https://www.grur.org/uploads/tx_gstatement/2023-08-08-GRUR-Stn_EU_KOM_Vorschlag_standard-essentiellen_Patenten_COM-2023–232.pdf

79 Leanza, S. (2023). *The EU Regulation on Standard Essential Patents: A Way to Fix What is Not Broken?* 16, at SSRN: https://ssrn.com/abstract=4683127.

80 See https://www.documentcloud.org/documents/23780757-dg-23-07_proposal-for-a-regulation-on-seps-etsi-views56.

on FRAND licensing of SEPs, and as a provider of services, which might include a voluntary essentiality check service using the pooled resources of IPOs.[81]

It is self-evident that SSOs are composed of players in the standard-setting process and could easily establish a committee with the most up-to-date professional knowledge about the standards in question, their major contributors, and respective contributions.[82] SSOs should take a more proactive role in facilitating the FRAND licensing of SEPs.[83] "It becomes imperative to assign an increasingly central role to standardization bodies in resolving FRAND disputes and determining the appropriate financial burden for standard implementers."[84]

It is therefore only logical that the major SSOs such as ETSI and IEEE, which have large volumes of SEPs and litigated cases concerning FRAND licensing of SEPs, would be suitable candidates to set up a competence center to bridge the differences between SEP owners and implementers.

In this regard, Matthias Leistner has advocated that SSOs should be required to establish adequate SEP licensing policies:

> the most promising way ahead would be to require the SSOs to take licensing practice into account from the very beginning and to include such considerations, including aspects of royalty stacking, in their policies and in the procedural framework for inclusion of new patents in certain standards.[85]

A competence center should be funded by SSOs, but operate independently, with experts from both the SEP patentee group and the implementer group, on

81 At https://www.wipo.int/edocs/pubdocs/en/wipo-pub-rn2024-12-en-wipo-strategy-on-standard-essential-patents-2024-2026.pdf.

82 Liu, K.-C., & Zhang, H.R. (2019). Propositions for regulated self-regulation of SSOs. In Liu, K.-C., & Hilty, R. (Eds.), *SEPs, SSOs and FRAND—Asian and Global Perspectives on Fostering Innovation in Interconnectivity* (pp. 390–395). Routledge.

83 In this regard, some suggest that SSOs adopt an exclusive forum selection clause in their policy to reduce undesirable transaction costs stemming from ASIs and subsequent legal actions.

> By including this clause in their IP policies or FRAND documents, SSO can designate the jurisdiction that is home to the law specified in the choice of law clause, which is the natural forum for that law. For example, since the IP policy of ETSI has already contained a choice law designating French law, the French court shall be designated as the court with exclusive jurisdiction to settle all FRAND related disputes.

See Tsang, K.F., & Lee, J.-A. (2022). The Ping-Pong Olympics of antisuit injunction in FRAND litigation. *Michigan Technology Law Review, 28(2),* 371–372, at SSRN: https://ssrn.com/abstract=3968645. However, the prospect of having French courts to have exclusive jurisdiction over cases of this nature can be terrifying as they are least experienced and least accessible and transparent to the outside world.

84 Leanza, S. (2023). *The EU Regulation on Standard Essential Patents: A Way to Fix What Is Not Broken?* (p. 23), at: SSRN: https://ssrn.com/abstract=4683127.

85 Leistner, M. (2019). European experiences: EU and Germany. In Liu, K.-C., & Hilty, R. (Eds.), *SEPs, SSOs and FRAND—Asian and Global Perspectives on Fostering Innovation in Interconnectivity* (pp. 353–354). Routledge.

either an ad hoc or term basis. Once the center is up and running, other minor SSOs could procure services from it.

A successful example that supports this suggestion is the International Patent Evaluation Consortium (IPEC) comprised of patent attorneys and lawyers from various countries formed under the PlatformWCDMA for joint patent licensing. The IPEC evaluates and certifies essential WCDMA patents worldwide and the evaluation fees are paid by the applicants for inclusion in the standard. Patent evaluation is performed independently of PlatformWCDMA. Certified patents are published on the 3G Licensing Ltd. website.[86]

The competence center created by the designated major SSOs could provide at least three core services: an essentiality check, a depository of FRAND-compliant rates, and a FRAND arbitration service. This is also in line with the suggested governance principles for patent pools in Subsections 8.2 and 8.3 of Chapter 7.

5.1. Essentiality Check

The declaration of its patents as SEPs and the inclusion of those patents in a standard can strengthen exponentially the bargaining power of a patent owner and even lead to a dominant market position, which is not, in fact, due to the technological merits of those patents. Therefore, the essentiality of the declared SEPs should not be left unchecked as is currently the case. Conducting an essentiality check would increase transparency with regard to whether the disputed patent is essential to the standard and would facilitate and underpin licensing negotiations conducted by any other parties.

Some national and regional IPOs have decided to intervene. The JPO decided in 2018 to issue an advisory opinion based on Article 71(1) of the Japanese Patent Act[87] on the essentiality of SEPs in dispute and promulgated the "Manual of 'Hantei' (Advisory Opinion) for Essentiality Check" for practitioners on March 28, 2018, (last revision June 26, 2019). The provision of such checks commenced on April 1, 2018. The EC decided in the draft SEP Regulation to task the competence center under EUIPO to conduct SEP essentiality checks.[88]

86 Nakamura, O., & Kerr, C.M. (2008). Current status of PlatformWCDMA and its joint patent licensing. *NTT Docomo Technical Journal, 10(3)*, 66, at: https://www.docomo.ne.jp/english/binary/pdf/corporate/technology/rd/technical_journal/bn/vol10_3/vol10_3_064en.pdf.

87 JPO Standard Essential Patents Portal Site at: https://www.jpo.go.jp/e/support/general/sep_portal. Article 71(1) of Japanese Patent Act provides "A request may be made to the Patent Office for its advisory opinion on the technical scope of a patented invention."

88 According to the draft SEP Regulation, broad scope of information on SEPs will be made available through the competence center (SEP register and SEP database) by requiring SEP holders, patent pools, and competent courts of members to submit the said information and requiring SEP holders to notify standards with SEPs and aggregate royalties and to register SEPs. A SEP that is not registered within the time-limit may not be enforced in relation to the implementation of the standard in a competent court of a Member State, from the stipulated time-limit until its registration in the register (Article 24(1)). The competence center will conduct essentiality checks of SEPs by evaluators based on annual sampling or voluntary proposals by SEP holders or implementers of up to 100 registered

However, a competence center under the designated major SSOs run by experts from both sides of the industry, SEP patentees and implementers, would be the most suitable agency to check on the essentiality of declared SEPs. The essentiality check could be done either ex-ante before the patented invention is included in the standard or ex-post after inclusion, upon request from SEP patentees or implementers. If it establishes a lack of essentiality of some SEPs, then its decision must by default be disclosed to enhance transparency.[89]

Once the essentiality check mechanism is in operation, patentees would be more prudent in making SEP declarations. In turn, this would reduce the overclaiming of SEPs. By doing so, there would be no need for the ex-post essentiality checks based on annual sampling of up to 100 SEPs envisioned by the EC draft SEP Regulation.

5.2. FRAND-Compliant Rates Depository

In order to ascertain whether the royalties that SEP owners are charging are FRAND, comparable licenses are of high referential value.[90] However, as a result of the wide use of NDAs, prior license information is seldom disclosed. Parties must negotiate based on their own, sometimes limited, licensing experience and information asymmetry is often a serious issue. A transparent and competitive licensing market hardly exists, and this is a breeding ground for abusive conduct.[91] The EC has therefore rightly pointed out that:

> As there is no common repository for such expertise, work and research may be unnecessarily duplicated at serious cost to the parties involved. More accessible FRAND-related information could increase predictability for

SEPs from different patent families, which result can be challenged by peer evaluation or appeal before the Boards of Appeal of the EUIPO (Article 29). The evaluator shall issue his reasoned opinion to the competence center within six months from its appointment (Article 31(5)). The result of the essentiality check conducted and the reasoned opinion of the evaluator or the final reasoned opinion of the peer evaluator is non-binding but may be used as evidence before stakeholders, patent pools, public authorities, courts, or arbitrators. However, where shall evaluators and conciliators come from if not from SSOs? Are there enough evaluators and conciliators to meet many deadlines? These problems can hardly be mitigated by cooperating with the EPO and WIPO as the German Association for the Protection of Intellectual Property opines, as both do not have the manpower to deal with the work demand of the Regulation.

89 Liu, K.-C. (2023). Guaranteeing the right to fair trial in IP-related arbitration—in Germany perhaps? and elsewhere? *International Review of Industrial Property and Competition Law*, *54(8)*, 17.

90 See, for example, *US: Microsoft Corp. v. Motorola, Inc.*, No. C10–1823JLR, 2013 WL 2111217; Germany: Saint Lawrence v Vodafone, Dusseldorf District Court, 4a O 73/14, March 31, 2016; *UK: Unwired Planet v. Huawei Judgment* ([2017] EWHC 2988 (Pat)); *PRC: Huawei v. InterDigital, Guangdong Higher People's Court*, (2013) Yue Gao Fa Min San Zhong Zi 305 (decided on October 16, 2013).

91 For example, in its SEPs portfolio licensing agreement, Qualcomm prohibits its licensees from reselling acquired chips to its competitor, which is covered by the NDA. See Liu, K.-C. (2019). As a matter of standard for Asia and beyond? In Liu, K.-C., & Hilty, R. (Eds.), *SEPs, SSOs and FRAND—Asian and Global Perspectives on Fostering Innovation in Interconnectivity* (pp. 5–60). Routledge.

businesses such as IoT players, facilitate the licensing process in general and provide support and benchmarks in dispute settlement.[92]

Major SSOs should ask SEP patentees to deposit at the competence center details of their charged FRAND-compliant royalty rates for the same SEPs and even for different SEPs. The competence center should treat confidentially the commercially sensitive details of deposited royalty rates as parties often allege that they are trade secrets, and not unnecessarily compromise their secrecy. The competence entre could compile the collected information and classify it according to international patent classifications, after anonymization as the German Arbitration Panel according to the German Act on Employees' Patents has done.[93] The information could be provided to interested parties and help the voluntary negotiation and determination of FRAND terms for licensing of SEPs.

5.3. FRAND Arbitration Service

Arbitration generally has many advantages over litigation in court and has become more popular in IP disputes.[94] The EC draft SEP Regulation provides a structured procedure for the determination of the FRAND terms and conditions of a SEP license. Parties to SEP licensing negotiations shall initiate a FRAND determination process prior to any court proceedings, a determination which is without prejudice to the possibility of either party requesting the competent court of a Member State to issue a provisional injunction of a financial nature against the alleged infringer (Article 35). The duration of the FRAND determination process is limited to nine months. The conciliator must put forward reasoned proposals for a determination of FRAND terms and conditions, mediate among parties in establishing a global aggregate royalty, and provide a non-binding opinion on an aggregate royalty.

However, usual arbitration procedures are not suitable for solving FRAND licensing of SEPs, even if they follow the more balanced "FRAND ADR Case Management Guidelines" suggested by the Munich IP Dispute Resolution Forum in 2018.[95]

First and foremost, bound by a strict requirement of confidentiality, to a very large extent arbitrators are just as clueless as the parties, as no one can assert that

92 EC, 2.4. Com/2017/0712 Setting out the EU approach to Standard Essential Patents.

93 See Subsection 4.6.2 of Chapter 4.

94 Liu, K.-C. (2023). Guaranteeing the right to fair trial in IP-related arbitration—in Germany perhaps? AND Elsewhere? *International Review of Industrial Property and Competition Law*, *54*(8), 3–4.

95 The FRAND ADR Case Management Guidelines (at https://www.ipdr-forum.org/wp-content/uploads/2020/06/frand-guidelines_helvetica_rz6_klein_online.pdf) reminds that ideal candidates for arbitrators "would have specific expertise in the field of standardization and related competition law issues." (Paragraph 52). It further suggests that "public policy considerations have to be balanced with confidentiality as an established ADR-principle" (p. 9) and "at least the methods and principles adopted by the parties and the arbitral tribunal in the determination of FRAND terms and conditions should be made public" (p. 12).

he/she has seen any FRAND-compliant rates until and unless they have access to at least two comparable rates for similar situations. This is very rare, if not non-existent. Secondly, arbitration is usually on a case-by-case basis and operates behind closed doors. Therefore, even if one panel gets the FRAND terms right, by some stroke of luck, the next panel will start from scratch and may just as easily get it wrong. Thirdly, the normal arbitration tends to take a formalistic and pure contract law approach to the interpretation of a SEP license and ignores the dominant market power possessed by SEP licensors and its possible abuse.

Instead of the standard arbitration, it is suggested here that SSOs provide arbitration services to SEP owners and implementers. However, up to now, SSOs have largely refrained from determining FRAND-compliant terms for two reasons: technical experts are not in a good position to decide on licensing terms, and SSOs fear antitrust violations for possible price fixing. However, these are not valid reasons for SSOs not to help determine FRAND terms, but instead are reasons for SSOs to do the determination conscientiously.

To elaborate on this suggestion: The competence center to be set up under the designated major SSOs (as suggested earlier) would have a rich database to provide such a service as it would become the depository for FRAND-compliant terms and conditions and performance of essentiality checks. The competence center's coverage would be global just as are the SSOs. It could provide a one-stop global clearance for both SEP patentees and implementers and avoid multiple arbitration cases and the resultant royalty stacking.[96]

For arbitrating FRAND licensing of SEPs, the composition and working methods of the competence center could learn from the Arbitration Panel in the German Patent and Trademark Office, which resolves disputes between employees and employers over the reasonable compensation for employees' inventions derived in the course of employment, in arbitrating FRAND licensing of SEPs. The employee invention Arbitration Panel is composed of a legally trained chair and two assessors who have special experience in the technical field to which the invention is related. In practice, the assessors normally come from the legal or patent departments of big companies in the relevant fields and have good knowledge of common license rates through their own companies' licensing practices.

The competence center could further learn from the Arbitration Panel's practice of periodically publishing Licensing Rates for Technical Inventions, as licensing is a common practice in all industrial fields and anonymized licensing rates are collectable data. The competence center could also consult other collections of licensing rates on the market that are more comprehensive than just for compensating

96 There has been a proposal of limiting the options for institutional arbitration of SEP licensing disputes to only one institution—the World Intellectual Property Organization, based on the proclaimed success of the UDRP (Uniform Domain-Name Dispute-Resolution Policy) as a gamechanger in resolving trademark-based domain name disputes. See Halpern, M. (2021). *Arbitrating Standard Essential Patent Licensing Disputes* (p. 231) [doctoral dissertation]. Queen Mary University of London. However, the WIPO is far more distant than major SSOs from FRAND license of SEPs.

employees' inventions.[97] From these collected license rates the competence center would get a good picture of how much reasonable compensation should be for a specific FRAND licensing of SEPs.

In summary, this form of cross-border arbitration has all the advantages of the global mandatory arbitration model that has been envisioned and promoted by Lord Justice Arnold of the English Court of Appeal.[98]

6. Antitrust Intervention When SSOs' Self-Regulation has Failed

If the designated major SSOs fail to take the initiative to set up and maintain an independent competence center to provide the three services previously mentioned, then competition authorities should intervene to enforce the regulated self-regulation of SSOs policy.[99] Competition authorities can impose fines or corrective measures,[100] and punish violations such as anti-competitive cartels or abuses of market dominance.[101]

The rationale behind this suggestion is that although SSOs are cartels composed of their members, the SSOs' agreement and IP policy to incorporate the proprietary patents of their members into the standards is exceptionally exempted from cartel and abuse of dominance prohibitions if and only if SEPs are indeed licensed out on FRAND-terms as all members have committed to. If FRAND licensing of SEPs does not work out as promised, and as a result standards and SEP implementers are

97 Gross, M., & Strunk, G. (2021). *Liznezgebühren* (5. Aufl.), 1–821. Recht und Wirtschaft.

98

> First, it would enable the core issue of the terms of a FRAND licence to be directly addressed without the need for complex and expensive preliminary litigation over issues of patent infringement/essentiality and validity. Secondly, it would avoid the need for a multiplicity of patent infringement actions in multiple territories. Thirdly, it would avoid the need for a race to the court and battles over jurisdiction. Fourthly, it would enable FRAND terms for the whole world to be determined by one tribunal, avoiding the risk of inconsistent decisions. Fifthly, it would enable the use of a multinational arbitral tribunal which could have specialist expertise and command the confidence of both patentees and implementers, and of all nations.
>
> See Arnold, R. (2021). SEPs, FRAND and mandatory global arbitration. *GRUR, 70*, 127

99 There have already been reform suggestions that urge competition agencies either to dictate policy rules for SSOs or at least define guidelines that SSOs would be (strongly) encouraged to follow, see Layne-Farrar, A. (2013). *A Review of IPR Policy Revisions in the Wake of Antitrust Actions* (p. 1), at: https://www.researchgate.net/publication/271547732_A_review_of_IPR_policy_revisions_in_the_wake_of_antitrust_actions.

100 Matthias Leistner has similarly suggested that "If reasonable approaches are not achieved upon the initiative of the SSOs, further initiatives for incentivizing and regulating respective self-regulation of the SSOs should be contemplated," for example, "competition law exemptions could be made dependent on the SSO's adoption of respective policies." Leistner, M. (2019). European experiences: EU and Germany. In Liu, K.-C., & Hilty, R. (Eds.), *SEPs, SSOs and FRAND—Asian and Global Perspectives on Fostering Innovation in Interconnectivity* (p. 354). Routledge.

101 Some already argue that some of the procompetitive assumptions for patent pools are no longer true when applied to FRAND licensing of SEPs, as SEP pools have lessened efficiency-enhancing effects, see Jurata, J., & Luken, E.N. (2021). Glory days: Do the anticompetitive risks of standards-essential patent pools outweigh their procompetitive benefits? *San Diego Law Review, 58*(2), 417, 430–452, at: SSRN: https://ssrn.com/abstract=3622615.

overburdened with cross-border litigation or other dispute resolution procedures, and national courts have lost appropriate regard for the international comity principle, SEP patentees can be viewed as using FRAND commitment as an illegitimate means of luring implementers into the game for an unjustified kill.

Ultimately competition authorities could disallow SSOs from incorporating proprietary patents into their standards as the whole purpose of the FRAND commitment is to assure SSOs that patentees will not abuse their extraordinary market power that results from the SSOs' incorporation of their patents into standards that are hard for others to bypass by refusing to deal, including any de facto refusal by asking non-FRAND terms. Such a commitment is a formal promise between the parties and should be treated seriously, as refusal to license SEPs or refusal to license SEPs FRANDly, means SSOs should de-incorporate these SEPs from the standards. Otherwise, there may be an illegitimate collusion between SSOs and SEP patentees to deceive implementers into a situation of patent holdup. It is incumbent on SSOs to which SEP patentees have made their FRAND license commitments to better evaluate the sincerity of such commitments and decide whether to again incorporate the committers' other patents into future standards based on their previous track record on signing or not signing FRAND-compliant licensing agreement with willing license seekers.

7. Conclusion

The FRAND licensing of SEPs is far from being a commercial or legal reality, despite so many litigated cases the world over. There are serious deficiencies in the current FRAND framework. The "de-risk" maneuver by many US-led economies and their rebuilding of global supply chains based not on economic efficiency but perceived national security concerns is fragmenting the globalization that brought peace and prosperity over the last forty years and provided the foundation stone for the global FRAND licensing of SEPs. To reconcile conflicts between different legal standards has become more and more challenging, and without new initiatives may become impossible.

The private sector, especially major SSOs, should now take the initiative to take charge of the process of patching up the many lacunae created by geopolitical fears. A competence center under the designated major SSOs' umbrella should function as an independent and professional mechanism between SEP patentees and implementers. Such a center would smooth FRAND licensing of SEPs through conducting essentiality checks, be the depository of information on FRAND-compliant rates and provide arbitration services to resolve disputes related to FRAND licensing of SEPs. Otherwise, intervention by competition authorities will become a must to ban or curtail SEPs and require SSOs to only include non-proprietary technologies into their standards.

Part V

The Exercise of Trademark Rights

Trademark rights are becoming rights in gross and enjoy extensive and enhanced protection, including statutory (even punitive) damages and criminal sanctions, in many jurisdictions. Therefore, the exercise of trademark rights intersects with competition law in a variety of ways throughout many economies, ranging from the protectable functions of a trademark, "use" or "non-use" of others' trademarks in keyword advertisement by search engines, the contracting out of limitations to trademark rights, and the exhaustion of trademark rights. However, given its word limits, this volume in this Part will only point out the contention between brand owners and the dealers of their secondhand products and work toward its solution by introducing new dimensions into the trademark equilibrium, such as corporate social responsibility and the circular economy.

DOI: 10.4324/9781003597766-15

11 Balancing Secondhand Branded Goods Markets With Brand Owners via Corporate Social Responsibility

1. Introduction

Secondhand markets have been around for a long time. Many people buy their first bikes, motorcycles, watches, or cars secondhand. Secondhand markets recycle usable products, exploit limited resources to the fullest, and are therefore an institution of sustainability and circular economy,[1] although some are the creation of marketing gimmicks.[2] With the hype of luxury brands and luxury economy,[3] less pricy and more accessible secondhand branded goods become sought-after, as they embody the continued glamour and quality of brands, and could even become desirable vintage pieces for collectors and auction houses.[4] "Pre-owned luxury is now a real and deeply rooted trend, especially among younger customers."[5] Secondhand markets

1 Secondhand goods are not necessarily used products but have been pre-owned by others. For example, Rolex produces annually about one million pieces of watches (Rolex does not release any business data. However, according to https://millenarywatches.com/how-many-watches-rolex-make/. Rolex manufactures between 800,000 and one million watches per year. Another statistic estimates that Rolex produced 1.05 million watches in 2021, see https://www.thewatchmuse.com/blog/a-rolex-case-study, which can be sold to only a limited number of regular customers. These customers can gain significant profit by immediately reselling the just-bought and unused watches in original packages at higher prices than the original ones to satisfy insatiable demand, leading to pre-owned but unused secondhand Rolex watches.

2 Ty, the manufacturer of Beanie Babies (which Ty copyrights as "soft sculptures"), deliberately creates a shortage of each Beanie Baby by charging a very low price and not producing enough copies to clear the market at that price. As a result, a secondary market is created. The secondary market gives widespread publicity to Beanie Babies, so much so that some Beanie Babies were selling for thousands of dollars. See Landes, W., & Posner, R. (2003). *The Economic Structure of Intellectual Property Law* (p. 121). Harvard University Press.

3 See generally Sun, H., Beebe, B., & Sunder, M. (Eds.). (2015). *The Luxury Economy and Intellectual Property—Critical Reflections*. Oxford University Press.

4 See for example The Investment Value of Hermès, at: https://baghunter.com/blogs/news/investment-value-of-hermes.

5 The statement by the chairman and CEO of Kering François-Henri Pinault, see Guilbault, L. (2021). *Kering Bets on First-mover Advantage with Resale*, at: https://www.voguebusiness.com/companies/kering-bets-on-first-mover-advantage-with-resale.

DOI: 10.4324/9781003597766-16

for branded goods with sophisticated value chains mushroom, attracting echelons of customers the world over and generating staggering commercial values.[6]

The resale of secondhand goods takes many forms, from resale of the products as they have been sold, to resale of products with alterations and refurbishment, to upcycling in fashion and jewelry that use secondhand branded products as raw materials for new creations. This chapter deals only with the first form of resale, as the other two have different legal issues that have been competently analyzed by Annette Kur and Martin Senftleben, two leading trademark experts.[7]

Secondhand markets for branded goods have long been plagued by counterfeits which sometimes can be extremely hard to distinguish from genuine ones. To respond, brand owners go to great lengths and expenses to curb and battle counterfeits, such as authorizing only their own boutiques and those third-party retailers who are specifically approved by them after a careful review process, designating points-of-sale, assigning every product a designated number, setting up internal record system chronicling every phase in the production cycle, and manufacture in select authorized factories on a "to order" basis and provide their factories with only enough supplies to make the specific number of products that have been ordered.

As a standard practice, brand owners do not train any third-party units or reveal any internal information to them. Nor do they authorize or certify any third-party units' authentication ability. Therefore, in trademark infringement suits brought by brand owners against resellers of their secondhand products, courts often find themselves in a predicament, namely, where and how to find the most trustworthy experts or institutions other than the brand owners to authenticate branded products. If at the end of the day, it will always be the brand holders to have the final say on the (un)authenticity of their secondhand products, wouldn't there be moral hazards for them to act in a self-serving way, such as to proclaim that the disputed products were fakes even if they were genuine but only parallel imported or resold?[8] Wouldn't that kind of behavior amount to unfair or anti-competitive acts by brand owners? Do we need new institutions to deal with these issues?

This chapter is dedicated to clarifying and solving at least some of the previously mentioned questions. It will first examine case law found in Taiwan and the US that touches upon these issues; secondly, reflect on many of the associated problems exhibited by this case law. Thirdly, this chapter will then argue for the need to set

6 According to Tamerler, J. (2021). Everything isn't Gucci: Trademark law and the secondhand luxury goods market. R*euters*, at: https://www.reuters.com/legal/legalindustry/everything-isnt-gucci-trademark-law-secondhand-luxury-goods-market-2021-06-18/. In 2019 secondhand luxury resale grew 25 times faster than retail and what is now a $28 billion secondhand apparel market and will more than double to an astonishing $64 billion by 2024.

7 Kur, A. (2021). 'As Good as New'—Sale of repaired or refurbished goods: commendable practice or trade mark infringement? *GRUR International, 70(3)*, 228–236; Senftleben, M. (2023). *Fashion Upcycling and Trademark Infringement–A Circular Economy/Freedom of the Arts Approach*, at: SSRN: https://ssrn.com/abstract=4470873.

8 It is a known fact that brand owners are generally opposed to parallel import as it would lead to intra-brand competition and reduce their profits.

up an independent third-party mechanism to mitigate between brand owners and resellers. Fourthly, it then introduces a new paradigm of corporate social responsibility (CSR) to better balance the interests of resellers of secondhand branded products and brand owners. Fifthly, it ends with a conclusion that also points out the prospect of CSR for other IP areas.

2. Secondhand Markets for Branded Goods in Trouble

There is limited case law in Taiwan and the US, at least to the knowledge of this author, that handles controversies between brand owners and resellers of secondhand branded goods. No similar cases can be found in the European Union (EU), including Germany, and China.[9]

2.1. Case Law in Taiwan

In Taiwan, the resale of secondhand branded goods is quite popular. However, the resale market has been limited to small businesses run by individuals. French luxury brands Hermes and Louis Vuitton (LV) have brought some unnerving civil and criminal cases against individual resellers of their secondhand products.

2.1.1. The Civil and Criminal Cases Hermes Brought Over Four Bags in 2008

A certain Ms. Lee was a former employee of Hermes Boutique at the Regent Hotel in Taipei for over one year and a half. Several years after she left the boutique, she was criminally charged by Hermes with trademark infringement for selling three fake Birkin bags and one fake Haut Acourroies bag (two from France and another two from Italy) via two secondhand shops of branded goods as genuine ones at prices of NT $220,000 (about US $7,000), NT $230,000, NT $800,000, and NT $800,000, respectively.[10] After the criminal case was finalized, Ms. Lee was sentenced to six months imprisonment under a three-year probation, Hermes brought a civil suit against Ms. Lee and asked for an astronomical amount of damages, NT $1 billion 25 million (about US $30 million).

In determining the damages, the Taiwan IP and Commercial Court (TIPCC) first derived the unit retail price of a fake bag by adding up the total sale prices of the

9 China's SPC in its Regulations on the Application of Law to Adjudicate Online Consumer Disputes Fa-Shi (2022) No. 8 (effective on March 15, 2022) does touch upon "online trading platforms for secondhand products," but only to confirm courts' support for consumers' demand that sellers bear the responsibility of a business operator when consumers suffered damages from products purchased from "online trading platforms for secondhand products," if courts could ascertain that the sellers are conducting commercial activities after an overall assessment of the nature, source, quantity, prices, frequency of sales by the sellers, and of the facts if there were other sales channels and income.

10 TIPCC 2008 Xing-Zi-Shang-Yi No.3 criminal decision (decided on October 27, 2008).

four bags and then averaging them.[11] The TIPCC then decided that 500 times[12] of the average price (NT $512,500) was a just number after weighing that the defendant engaged in infringement (passing fake bags off as genuine ones at high prices) for about six months, the loss suffered by the plaintiff and the gains by the defendant. It ruled that Ms. Lee must pay NT $256,250,000 (about US $8,541,000) damages to Hermes.[13]

2.1.2. The Civil Case LV Brought Over Four Bags in 2017[14]

Ten years later, LV sued two secondhand dealers for selling four counterfeit LV bags online. The primary question for the case was whether those bags were genuine or indeed counterfeit. Appraisers were called in to solve this question. The single bench judge in its capacity as the first instance court approved of the two appraisers' ability and granted the applications filed by the parties to recruit them as experts.

The defendant retained someone who has worked for an online secondhand shop "Milan Station" in Hong Kong specializing in the trade of pre-used bags,[15] and has received authentication training to tell fakes from genuine ones while working for Milan Station between 2004 and 2014. The appraiser was running a shop of her own when the case was initiated, trading 30–60 secondhand bags in a month. LV appointed its IP manager as an appraiser who has been sent to the LV factory every year to receive authentication training for five years.[16]

However, the two appraisers came to completely opposite conclusions, with LV's appraiser denying and the defendant's affirming the genuineness of the bags.

11 NT220,000 + NT230,000 + NT800,000 + NT800,000 = NT $2,050,000 ÷ 4 = NT $512,500.

12 Taiwan's Trademark Act has adopted the statutory damages for trademark infringement between the amount not fewer than 500 times and not more than 1,500 times the unit retail price of the infringing goods in 1985. The lower limit of 500 was repealed in 2012 for its possibility of disproportionate overcompensation. See Liu, K.-C. (2022). *IP Laws and Regimes in Major Asian Economies—Combing Through Thousand Threads of IP to Peace in Asia* (pp. 128–129). Routledge.

13 TIPCC 2008 Chong-Fu-Min-Zi 1 (decided on March 26, 2009). The decision is to be criticized for several reasons. First, since this is a civil decision based on the prior criminal decision, it should be bound by the factual determination of the latter. Therefore, after the criminal decision found that "the percentage of fake bags among the genuine bags that the defendant has sold is only small," the civil decision should not have insinuated otherwise by stating that:

> the sale of counterfeit goods often took place via abnormal commercial channels, the defendant remained silent about the sales volume, the infringed were unable to calculate or prove actual loss, not to mention that the infringer would speed up dumping the counterfeits with any and all means, causing the infringed more harm.

Second, according to the criminal decision, the total amount of bags sold by Ms. Lee was around thirty, the number of 500 times is simply too large to be anywhere close to the number of lost sales of the genuine bags.

14 TIPCC 2016 Min-Shang-Su-Zi 49 (decided on 30 November 2017).

15 At: https://www.milanstation.shop.

16 TIPCC 2016 Min-Shang-Su-Zi 49, 10.

The court found that both appraisals contained to a certain extent subjective feelings or descriptions that were hard to verify and could not be checked by others. Upon further inquiry by the court, LV's appraiser refused to provide the criteria for genuine goods and the concrete deviation of the fakes from genuine ones based on trade secretion protection.[17]

The court was faced with a dilemma, namely, to decide which appraisal is more credible than the other. Eventually, it gave the credit to LV's appraiser due to the following reasons: Authentication necessarily involves knowledge of the anti-counterfeiting measures LV applied to products. It is then natural that the appraiser authorized by the trademark owner has a more complete and comprehensive understanding than the one appointed by the defendant. The defendant's appraiser admitted that neither he/she nor their trainer had received training from LV. LV's appraiser asserted that their appraisal would not affect their salary, which was not disputed by the defendant. This showed the independence and trustworthiness of the assessment of LV's appraiser.[18] The decision awarded LV NT $600,000 in damages, which was about 20.07 times the highest price among the four bags, instead of the average price of the four bags, namely NT $29,000.[19] The decision was not appealed and became final.

2.1.3. A Criminal Case Involving LV and a Secondhand LV Bag in 2020

The complainant bought a pre-owned LV bag at a price of NT $56,000 (where a genuine one cost NT $62,500) from the defendants via Shopee.tw. They immediately returned the bag as they thought it was a fake. The complainant got a speedy full refund via the refund mechanism provided by the Shopee platform, yet still filed a criminal complaint against the two resellers. The bag was certified by LV as fake and the two defendants were indicted by a public prosecutor.

A bench of three judges at Taoyuan District Court found the defendants guilty and sentenced them to one year and four months imprisonment without probation. The sentence was clearly too harsh as no consumer harm was caused and none of the defendants had a prior criminal record. However, it was based on a typical consideration by courts of "the relationship between the defendants and the complainant, the fact that the defendants did not reach mediation or settlement with LV or the complainant, nor compensate LV's loss." To get a lenient sentence on appeal the defendants must appease the complainant and the LV to show a mended "relationship" and good "attitude."[20] From this legal necessity misconduct can arise.

17 TIPCC 2016 Min-Shang-Su-Zi 49, 11.

18 TIPCC 2016 Min-Shang-Su-Zi 49, 11.

19 TIPCC 2016 Min-Shang-Su-Zi 49, 16.

20 Article 57 of Taiwan's Criminal Code stipulates:

> Sentencing shall base on the liability of the offender and take into account all the circumstances, and special attention shall be given to the following items: 7. Relationship between the offender and the victim. 10. The offender's attitude after committing the offense.

The defendants did manage to "settle" with LV, but not without a handsome price: payment of NT $50,000 as damages, a public apology published in a newspaper, and an undertaking not to commit.[21] However, the defendants failed to settle with the complainant as the latter asked for NT $800,000 in damages. This is clear evidence of criminal trademark cases being abused to blackmail resellers of second-hand branded goods. At the end, the TIPCC in its capacity as appellate court reduced the criminal sentence to one year and one month, with probation of two and three years, after taking into consideration the mentioned effort made by the defendants.[22] The defendants have been embroiled in a criminal ordeal for three and a half years for reselling but refunding an alleged fake LV bag.

2.1.4. The Criminal Case LV Brought Over One Wallet in 2022[23]

In a 2022 decision, the Taiwan Supreme Court revoked the criminal decision by the TIPCC which found the defendant guilty of fraudulent gaining of money via the internet sale of one fake LV wallet for NT $3,000 and condemned the defendant to one-year imprisonment without probation. The Supreme Court remanded the case back to the TIPCC to reexamine the defense raised by the defendant:

> He has acquired the confiscated wallet as a secondhand product from online website Brandear in Japan at the price of NTI, 795. Brandear has not provided document that authenticated it as genuine, but bar code which showed that Brandear has examined the wallet. He has indicated in the description that the wallet was antiquated and of lesser quality, his purchase price was reasonable . . . and he started the bid from one NT dollar.

The Supreme Court then asked the TIPCC to thoroughly investigate the interior canvas, the materials, specification, quality, and craftsmanship of the overall sewing, etc. to clarify whether the seized wallet was a secondhand wallet of LV. The Supreme Court challenged the appraisal report presented by LV, based on which the previous decision was made, as having only conclusion, and lacking explanation about the method and information of the appraisal and how the appraiser has applied his expertise to come to the conclusion that the wallet was a fake.[24]

The apex court's refusal to blindly accept the appraisal report prepared by brand owners while they are the complainant of a criminal case is a glaring contrast to some lower court decisions[25] and might be pointing a new direction for the future.

21 It begs the question; what damages LV has actually suffered from a fully refunded sale of an alleged fake LV bag.

22 TIPCC 110 Xing-Zhi-Shang-Su-Zi 26 (decided on October 21, 2021).

23 Taiwan Supreme Court 2022 Tai-Shang-Zi 1271 criminal decision (decided on April 14, 2022)

24 Taiwan Supreme Court 2022 Tai-Shang-Zi 1127 criminal decision, two to three.

25 Such as TIPCC 2019 Xin-Shang-Yi-Zi 16 criminal decision (decided on June 27, 2019).

2.2. *Case Law in the US*

The resale of secondhand branded goods is a high-flying business with much sophistication and a larger scale.[26] Corporatized resellers are striving to innovate the market by authenticating the secondhand products they handle and screening out fakes. However, sometimes they are still sued by brand owners. Chanel, an active litigant to protect its well-known marks, also in the US, sued two resellers of its secondhand goods in 2018 in the US District Court, S.D. New York for trademark infringement, counterfeiting, and false advertising.[27] The first case was against The RealReal, and the second case was against What Goes Around Comes Around ("WGACA"). Chanel does not sell secondhand or vintage Chanel goods and declares that "only Chanel itself can know what is genuine Chanel."

2.2.1. *Chanel Inc. v. RealReal Inc.*

The RealReal is a company specializing in secondhand luxury consignment. It takes possession of goods and guarantees that what it sells is authentic. The RealReal represents itself as "the world's largest online marketplace for authenticated, consigned luxury goods." The RealReal states that it has developed the most rigorous authentication process in the marketplace and that it is the only resale company in the world that authenticates every single item sold. The RealReal further represents that there is no other resale company doing more to remove fakes from the market every day and put counterfeiters out of business, that its dedicated Quality Control team provides an additional layer of control to help prevent fakes from being sold on its site, and that its team works diligently and is constantly innovating to ensure it keeps fraudulent products off the market.[28] The RealReal assures that every member of its authentication team, including its copywriters, receives thorough training on all categories of products they authenticate.[29]

CHANEL brought action against The RealReal for trademark infringement and counterfeiting, among other things. The RealReal filed a motion to dismiss, which was partially denied in March 2020, as the judge found Chanel's claim may proceed on a direct infringement.[30]

26 Some resale companies even went public on the stock market. For example, on June 28, 2019, The RealReal went public on Nasdaq under the symbol REAL and raised $300 million during its IPO, see https://en.wikipedia.org/wiki/The_RealReal.

27 In addition, Chanel also wages trademark infringement and counterfeiting lawsuit against sellers of upcycled jewelry using Chanel's authentic buttons, see Chanel Wages New Trademark Lawsuit Aimed at Upcycled Jewelry, at: https://www.thefashionlaw.com/chanel-wages-new-trademark-lawsuit-aimed-at-upcycled-jewelry/ (June 27, 2023—By TFL); *Chanel, Inc. v. Vintage to Vogue Designs, LLC, et al.*, 3:23-cv-01397 (N.D. Tex.).

28 449 F.Supp. 3d 430 (S.D. N.Y. 2020).

29 449 F.Supp. 3d 432 (S.D.N.Y. 2020).

30 It found Chanel has adequately averred that The RealReal marketed and sold counterfeit Chanel products and that The RealReal's own customers have complained about receiving counterfeit

In its counterclaims, The RealReal brought up the antitrust or monopolization issue, claiming that Chanel, faced with a new threat to the core of its business model of a limited supply and few access points for consumers, has waged an aggressive campaign of exclusionary and anticompetitive conduct–including repeated interference with The RealReal's business relationships—in an effort to monopolize the market. The case was then in suspension in favor of mediation since April 2021.[31]

> After several mediation sessions, the parties were unable to reach a resolution, and the stay was lifted in November 2021. Chanel then sought a partial stay of discovery on the Company's counterclaims and unclean hands defense while Chanel's motion to dismiss and strike those claims are pending, and on 10 March 2022, the Court granted Chanel's request. The parties continue to engage in fact discovery regarding Chanel's counterfeiting and false advertising claims against the Company. Fact discovery is currently scheduled to be completed by August 15, 2023, and all depositions of fact witnesses will be completed by no later than 15 July 2023.[32]

2.2.2. *Chanel, Inc. v. WGACA, LLC*[33]

WGACA is a reseller like The RealReal and has sold, or offered for sale, secondhand Chanel products via its website, in its retail stores, at trunk shows or pop-up shops, and through e-commerce platforms. WGACA purchases goods from individuals and international whole-sellers, without asking for documentation of how they obtained title to the goods. WGACA guarantees the authenticity of all products sold and employs a team of in-house experts to authenticate all goods before they are sold. However, WGACA does not disclose that these in-house experts have never worked for or been trained by Chanel. WGACA does not keep written records of the authentication process for the individual items but does maintain a database of the fact that the authentication process was conducted. It also, since 2017, stopped publicizing on its website the Chanel Serial number of goods it has available for sale.

Chanel sued WGACA for trademark infringement and a false association between Chanel and WGACA. The case ended with a summary judgment in response to the parties' motion.

The summary judgment found WGACA liable for trademark infringement in its sales of point-of-sale items which are not products or for sale or authorized by

merchandise. These facts were sufficient to plausibly allege that The RealReal directly infringed Chanel's trademark. 449 F.Supp. 3d 441–442 (S.D.N.Y. 2020).

31 The court issued on April 5, 2021, an order approving the parties' joint stipulation to stay the case in favor of mediation. *Joint Stipulation & Ord., Chanel, Inc. v. The RealReal, Inc.*, 449 F.Supp. 3d 422, No. 1:18-CV-10626 (S.D.N.Y. 2020).

32 The RealReal's 2023 Annual Report, 29–30, at: https://investor.therealreal.com/static-files/3e7e27ed-8921-4578-8efd-6c36b0019ce5.

33 LLC, 2022 WL 902931, No. 18 Civ. 2253 (LLS) (S.D.N.Y. March 28, 2022).

Chanel for their initial sale and therefore cannot be considered genuine as a matter of law.[34] The decision also found trademark infringement by WGACA in eleven non-genuine Chanel handbags sold as having been authorized for sale by Chanel's Renato Corti factory in Italy and with serial numbers stolen from the Renato Corti factory before being assigned to any bag.[35] The decision further found trademark infringement by WGACA in one Chanel-branded handbag with a pirated serial number (its characteristics differ materially from the product authorized by Chanel for sale).[36]

3. Some Reflections

3.1. Trademark Bullying by Brand Owners

Trademark laws from industrialized and newly industrialized economies nowadays foresee an arsenal of comprehensive remedies of both civil and criminal nature at the disposal of trademark owners. This allows them to exercise trademark rights in a disproportionally harsh manner, a trademark bully tactic some brand owners indulge in, such as suing alleged infringers indiscriminately with criminal charges for insignificant amounts of "fake" goods (e.g., over one wallet in the 2022 LV criminal case in Taiwan), thereby unnecessarily oppressing and tarnishing them with state criminal power. Trademark bullying is when brand owners ask the alleged infringing individuals to pay an astronomical number of damages (in the 2007 Hermes case in Taiwan Hermes asked for an insane amount of US $30 million in damages). Trademark bullying happens when the infringement suit targets resellers who work diligently to innovate and improve the secondhand market, which would benefit the brand owners as well, if not even more.[37]

In jurisdictions where criminal prosecution actually plays a leading role in dealing with trademark infringement, the previously mentioned perils would be further amplified. People can easily game the criminal system for personal profits and stymie secondhand markets for branded goods, as the 2020 criminal case involving LV and a secondhand LV bag manifests.

34 LLC, 2022 WL 902931, No. 18 Civ. 2253 (LLS) (S.D.N.Y. March 28, 2022), 40.

35 LLC, 2022 WL 902931, No. 18 Civ. 2253 (LLS) (S.D.N.Y. March 28, 2022), 41.

36 LLC, 2022 WL 902931, No. 18 Civ. 2253 (LLS) (S.D.N.Y. March 28, 2022), 46. On February 8, 2024, a New York jury unanimously ruled in favor of Chanel in their lawsuit against WCAGA and awarded Chanel $4 million in statutory damages, see https://www.lexology.com/library/detail.aspx?g=a22db135-43c3-46dc-b201-9a671f622860.

37 Hulme, K. (2018). *Intellectual Property vs Corporate Social Responsibility*, at: https://www.burnesspaull.com/insights-and-events/news/how-does-the-use-of-intellectual-property-rights-fit-with-corporate-social-responsibility.

3.2. Brand Owners Pushing the Envelope of Their Rights

If powerful brand owners eventually prevail in their trademark infringement cases against resellers of secondhand products, as LV and Hermes have in Taiwan, would mean at least two dangers. One is that a new resale authentication right would be created for brand owners without any statutory law foundation.[38] Brand owners could have absolute control over the secondhand market for branded goods, as their trademark rights never really exhaust, and

> luxury secondhand goods are stuck being sold in a manner that rewards lack of oversight because it is the only way to escape inevitable liability, while at the same time, selling platforms controlling products are not given the opportunity to improve the secondhand industry.[39]

The other danger, at least in the US trademark context and those others who follow the US model, is that "luxury brands are pushing the bounds of trademark law into the very territory the Lanham Act drafters feared, namely antitrust territory . . . by conferring durationally limitless, exclusive rights to enforce one's mark" that harms competition at the expense of consumers.[40]

3.3. Unfair and Anti-Competitive Concerns

Generally, expansive trademark protection can have a negative impact on freedom of competition.[41] Many brand owners have strong market power and financial resources to conduct unfair and anti-competitive acts against resellers of their secondhand products, such as using their dominance to deny the resellers advertising and retail relationships including with other luxury retailers, denigrate secondary

38 Baumgarten, B. (2021). One too many sticks for the trademark bundle? The unintended consequences of luxury brands' push for a post-first sale authentication right. *Loyola of Los Angeles Entertainment Law Review*, *42(2)*, 11, 156–157.

39 Tamerler, J. (2022). The Ship of Theseus: The Lanham Act, Chanel, and the secondhand luxury goods market. *Fordham Intellectual Property, Media and Entertainment Law*, *32*, 470.

40 Tamerler, J. (2022). THE ship of Theseus: The Lanham Act, Chanel, and the secondhand luxury goods market. *Fordham Intellectual Property, Media and Entertainment Law*, *32*, 469. The Lanham Act of 1946 was met with resistance from the DOJ which was of the opinion that trademarks were monopolies, benefited only big enterprises, and were often used to violate antitrust law. As a compromise, Congress authorized the USFTC to apply with the USPTO to cancel undeserving registered trademarks (generic, functional, fraudulently obtained, misrepresentative, etc.) to keep as much as possible an open space to later trademark applicants and registrants (15 USC §1064 (Cancellation of registration)). The general attitude towards trademarks before 1946 was mistrust, derived from the anti-business sentiments of the Great Depression in the 1930s. See Leaffer, M. (2006). Sixty years of the Lanham Act: The decline and demise of monopoly phobia. In Hansen, H. (Ed.), *US Intellectual Property Law and Policy* (pp. 111–113). Edward Elgar Publishing.

41 See Senftleben, M. et al. (2014). Recommendation on measures to safeguard freedom of expression and undistorted competition in EU trade mark law. *European Intellectual Property Review*, *2015*, 341.

resellers as "likely fake," misrepresent that only brand owners can authenticate their products, and treat resellers unequally by not suing the luxury reseller in which brand owners hold a significant investment and have a business relationship.[42]

Additionally, the development of secondhand markets for branded goods hinges on the resellers' ability to tell genuine from fake ones, which depends to a large extent on the help of brand owners. This renders brand owners superior market power in relation to small- and medium-sized (SME) resellers who can also become competitors of brand owners as brand owners enter the secondhand market themselves. If brand owners refuse to provide authentication-related help with reasonable remuneration, it can be unfair competition. If this refusal to help with reasonable remuneration is conducted to drive out any form of intra-brand competition, including resale of secondhand products to maximize profits, then there is a serious issue of abuse of superior market power in relation to SME competitors, and even an issue of monopolization, attempt to monopolize, and abuse of monopolistic power.[43]

4. The Need of an Independent Third-Party Mechanism

The cases in Taiwan and the US also get us thinking about whether there is a need to establish an independent and neutral third-party mechanism that can bridge between brand owners and resellers of their secondhand products by checking but without publicly disclosing the alleged trade secrets of brand owners and authenticating secondhand branded products? If the answer is yes, based on what legal foundation can we conceptualize and realize that mechanism? The following will answer the first question affirmatively (4.1) and overcome its legal hurdle (4.2). Section 5 will provide the legal foundation.

4.1. The Justification

As pointed out by TIPCC in the civil decision over the case that LV brought in 2017,

> after knowing the context of the problem, we realize why the organization and personnel of authentication work cannot be narrowly viewed just as a matter of commercial freedom of trademark owners, but rather a public issue which concerns the public that might trade in secondhand trademarked

42 According to the legal representative of The RealReal, at: https://www.paulweiss.com/practices/litigation/antitrust/news/new-york-judge-greenlights-the-realreal-s-antitrust-counterclaims-in-high-stakes-lawsuit-by-chanel?id=39456.

43 According to Kerley's, it is possible under CJEU's decision (*Sirena Srl v. Eda Srl (40/70)* [1971] E.C.R. 69 at [16]) that a particularly well-known trademark might be in a dominant position via having such a powerful goodwill that others could not effectively compete. In such a case the marked product might constitute a relevant market in its own right. See Mellor, J., Llewelyn, D., Moody-Stuart KC, T., Keeling, D., Berkeley, I., & Chantrielle, A. (2023). *Kerly's Law of Trade Marks and Trade Names* (17th ed.), 19–015. Sweet & Maxwell.

> goods . . . and must to certain extent be interlinked with and influence the right-maintaining litigation of trademark owners. . . . Trademark owners virtually dominate the life and death of the secondhand market, which contradicts to some degree the exhaustion principle.

There are both legal and economic justifications for an independent third-party mechanism that in turn will help courts solve disputes equitably.

4.1.1. Legal Justification

Since brand owners do not train, authorize, or certify any third-party units with regard to authentication of their secondhand products, both courts and the defendants can hardly verify/falsify the appraisal reports by the appraisers. "Thus, appraisers appointed by trademark owners become almost the unchallengeable deciders of fake/genuine goods and of the results of litigation. However, paradoxically, these trademark owners themselves are one party of litigation."[44]

In addition, sometimes brand owners set up internal record systems and quality control mechanisms that are intractable for outsiders (courts and the defendants) but could influence the (un)authenticity of disputed products and the outcome of court cases. As Judge Louis Stanton pointed out in *Chanel, Inc. v. WGACA, LLC*:

> the present record describing Chanel's internal system is fissured and needs to be smoothed out by the fact finder. Chanel itself offers contradicting explanations of how its internal system would record the authorization for sale of a bag that went directly from the factory quality control processes and into the market rather than first passing through a distribution center. WGACA also calls into question the reliability of Chanel's record system: Despite these yearly reviews and despite the six month normal turnaround for the manufacture of a bag, a number of allotted serial numbers going back to the early 1990's were never entered into the ORLI system as having gone through the QC review, but were not identified as "missing" until, in some cases, nearly 20 years later.[45]

If courts continue to decide in favor of brand owners who are comfortably hiding behind the pretense of trade secrets, it would be a blatant violation of due process of law or procedural fairness. Therefore, this author sees the need for such a mechanism existent and justified in the context of secondhand markets for branded products.

4.1.2. Economic Justification

In the making of brands and during their life cycle, brand owners owe their patrons, customers, and fans fiduciary duties, as brands are the result of their patronage over

44 TIPCC 2016 Min-Shang-Su-Zi 49, 12.
45 LLC, 2022 WL 902931, No. 18 Civ. 2253 (LLS) (S.D.N.Y. March 28, 2022), 33.

the years, not the other way around. Such fiduciary duties include helping to maintain a transparent, trustworthy, and functional secondhand market where patrons, existent and prospective alike, can resell and source pre-owned products.

On top of that, brand owners stand to profit directly from smooth-functioning secondhand markets where the resale and source of their branded products are made easy. The ease of resale in turn triggers a bigger appetite for buying new pieces of branded products in the firsthand market.

Perceiving this virtuous circle between the secondhand and firsthand markets, some brand owners have already brought resale in-house, for example, in October 2020, Gucci launched its own online consignment shop with The RealReal, selling both its own archival and pre-worn pieces sourced from Gucci itself.[46] Some brand owners partner with resellers, for example, century-old watch retailer Bucherer became Rolex's official partner in selling the brand's certified pre-owned timepieces.[47]

Above all, healthy secondhand markets for branded products can make a significant contribution to the most needed circularity of the human economy and society.

4.2. Overcoming the Legal Hurdle of Trade Secret Protection

The one seemingly insoluble hurdle lying ahead for the establishment of such an independent third-party mechanism is the trade secret protection defense of brand owners, as they would refuse, understandably, to share with any outsiders their trade secrets in authenticating goods they manufactured. However, there should be appropriate distribution of the burden of proof between brand owners and resellers, "taking into account the equal importance of trade mark protection on the one hand and freedom of expression and freedom of competition on the other." Trade secret protection should not be the absolute hurdle.

Similarly, in the context of FRAND licensing of SEPs, the draft SEP Regulation of the European Commission sees too much trade secret protection hindering FRAND licensing of SEPs and seeks to make available detailed information on SEPs and existing FRAND terms and conditions to facilitate licensing negotiations.[48] Among other things, this Regulation stipulates that:

> 1. Persons involved in alternative dispute resolution proceedings concerning SEPs in force in a Member State shall disclose to the competence centre within 6 months from the termination of the procedure the standards and the implementations concerned, the methodology used for the calculation of FRAND terms and conditions, information on the name of the parties, and on

46 See https://cpp-luxury.com/gucci-launches-online-shop-with-consignment-site-the-realreal/.

47 See www.voguebusiness.com/companies/the-hard-luxury-resale-race-heats-up. Kering (luxury conglomerate that owns Gucci and Saint Laurent) now has a 5% stake in Vestiaire Collective (online resale shop for secondhand luxury bags), see Laure Guilbault, Kering bets on first-mover advantage with resale, at: https://www.voguebusiness.com/companies/kering-bets-on-first-mover-advantage-with-resale.

48 EC. (2023). Proposal for a Regulation of the European Parliament and of the Council on standard essential patents and amending Regulation (EU) 2017/1001 Brussels, 27.4.2023, COM 232 Final.

> specific licensing rates determined. 2. No confidential information shall be disclosed by the competence centre without the prior consent of the affected party.
>
> Article 11 Information on FRAND determinations

For more see Chapter 7.

In the context of auditing of algorithms, it would also require certain disclosure of proprietary algorithms to an independent third-party mechanism described previously (see Chapter 10). Trade secrets must not be limitlessly protected.

5. Finding the Legal Foundation for such a Mechanism

Current trademark law regime as we know it does not provide a solid legal foundation for the establishment of such an independent third-party mechanism. The widely adopted "no abuse of trademark rights" principle could arguably be used to deal with assertive and powerful brand owners, provided that it is stretched to the extreme, which is not easily possible in many jurisdictions. Furthermore, from this negative principle can hardly an independent and neutral third-party mechanism be derived. It takes a positive principle, such as CSR.

The application of competition law, including anti-unfair competition law and anti-monopoly law, and their resultant remedies, mostly composed of one-off orders of cease-and-desist, monetary punishment, and breaking up (mergers), are unsuitable to mandate and maintain such a mechanism that is meant to operate over the long haul.

In the following, I will argue that CSR could be the legal foundation for such a mechanism.

5.1. CSR in General

The 1953 seminal book "Social Responsibilities of Businessmen" by Howard Bowen marks the beginning of the modern-day discussion on CSR.[49] Over time, the essential meaning of CSR is that business entities not only have obligations towards their shareholders in endless pursuit of maximizing private profits but also toward their employees, suppliers, and society in enriching their well-being and welfare as well, so that they can prosper together in a sustainable way and share fruits more evenly.[50] The more powerful, successful, and resourceful business entities are, the more socially accountable they should be held. The more socially accountable businesses are, the more profitable they will be, as they will be able

49 Bowen, H. (2013). *Social Responsibilities of the Businessman* (pp. 1–298). University of Iowa Press. JSTOR, at: https://doi.org/10.2307/j.ctt20q1w8f.

50 Iqbal, T. (2021). *The Enlightened Shareholder Value Principle and Corporate Social Responsibility–A Theoretical and Qualitative Analysis* (p. 5). Routledge.

to attract and retain desired employees, enhance reputation, and superior financial performance.

Beginning from an altruistic stance, the social perception and demand for CSR has in the meantime solidified and become part of the general business and legal establishment, as the following laws show:

> Started from 2005, Chinese Company Law stipulates that a company, when engaging in business activities, shall abide by laws and administrative regulations, observe social moralities and business ethics, act in good faith, accept the supervision of the Government and the general public, and **undertake social responsibilities** (Article 5(1)). China further generalizes in its Civil Code of 2020 that profit-driven juristic persons shall abide by commercial ethics, maintain transaction security, accept governmental and societal oversight, and undertake social responsibilities when conducting operation activities. (Article 86)

Indian Company Act, 2013 takes another step forward and demands that every sizable company (having a net worth of rupees five hundred crore or more, or turnover of rupees one thousand crore or more or a net profit of rupees five crore or more) shall constitute a CSR Committee under the Board which shall ensure that the company spends, in every financial year, at least two percent of its average net profits made during the three immediately preceding financial years in pursuit of its CSR policy (Section 135(1) and (5)).

In Taiwan, the Financial Supervisory Commission started to provide banks with good CSR with preferential treatment in their efforts to acquire other financial institutions in 2108. The Regulations Governing Investments in Other Enterprises by Commercial Banks ("Regulations") require a commercial bank, which in its initial investment in other financial holding companies, banks, insurance companies and securities firms, excluding pure online banks, to obtain more than 10% of the shares with voting rights or paid-in capital of these institutions and to provide required documents (Article 5(2)), in order to facilitate consolidation of financial institutions by providing commercial banks the opportunity to first obtain shares of other financial institutions and later to negotiate merger and consolidation. However, the Regulations exempt banks from such an obligation if they meet the conditions of good corporate social responsibility, among others (such as sufficient capital, good management capability, global expansion capability) (Article 5(2) proviso).[51]

In the EU, the Commission adopted "A renewed EU strategy 2011–14 for Corporate Social Responsibility" in 2011, which was followed by Directive 2013/34/EU with regard to disclosure of non-financial and diversity information by certain large undertakings and groups, formally institutionalizing CSR. Directive

51 Namely the board meeting minutes of the invested institutions with the resolution of no objection, and a signed agreement or contract with the insiders and related parties of the invested institutions to acquire more than 25% of the shares to be sold.

2013/34/EU was replaced by the Corporate Sustainability Reporting Directive, effective January 5, 2023, which modernizes and strengthens the rules about the social and environmental information that a broader set of large companies, as well as listed SMEs (approximately 50,000 companies in total), are required to report on sustainability.[52]

For sure, CSR is poised to permeate into other specific areas of law, as societal and legal expectations of CSR will grow under the pressing and popular call of environment, social and governance (ESG) principles of the United Nations.[53]

5.2. Discussion of CSR in the Context of IP

The CSR principle was first discussed in the context of IP probably around 2005. The initial tone was tentative, altruistic, and not legal:

> there is scope for a more **altruistic approach** to have real impact, by IP owning corporations taking steps which they are not required to take, sharing IP, making new use of available tools, and not arguing for the boundaries of infringement to be further extended, or those of defences and exceptions limited.[54]

Only recently people started sporadically talking about "Intellectual Property versus Corporate Social Responsibility."[55] No consensus within the IP community has emerged that would adopt CSR into the IP family.[56] That said, the influential International Association for the Advancement of Teaching and Research in Intellectual Property (ATRIP) has started an encouraging development to explore the need and means to enhance the circularity of IP regimes.[57]

52 See https://finance.ec.europa.eu/capital-markets-union-and-financial-markets/company-reporting-and-auditing/company-reporting/corporate-sustainability-reporting_en.

53 UN and Swiss Federal Department of Foreign Affairs. (2005). *Who Cares Wins, Connecting Financial Markets to a Changing World—Recommendations by the Financial Industry to Better Integrate Environmental, Social and Governance Issues in Analysis, Asset Management and Securities Brokerage*. Financial Sector Initiative, at: https://www.unepfi.org/fileadmin/events/2004/stocks/who_cares_wins_global_compact_2004.pdf.

54 Brown, A. (2005). Socially responsible intellectual property: A solution? *Script-ed, 2(4)*, 498.

55 Hulme, K. (2018). *Intellectual Property vs Corporate Social Responsibility*, at: https://www.burnesspaull.com/insights-and-events/news/how-does-the-use-of-intellectual-property-rights-fit-with-corporate-social-responsibility.

56 However, Haochen Sun passionately advocates sweeping social responsibilities for tech companies, the responsibility to reciprocate, the responsibility to play a positive role, and the responsibility to confront injustices created by technological development, which might have significant impact on IP landscape. See Sun, H. (2022). *Technology and the Public Interest*, 121 et al. Cambridge University Press.

57 ATRIP 41st Conference (9–12 July 2023 in Tokyo) has a panel dedicated to IP, Sustainability and Environmental Law in which "Closing the Loop on Circular Economy: The Overlooked Role of IP" was discussed among other topics.

5.3. The Need to Reach Beyond Trademark Law

Although consensus on the adoption of CSR into IP is lacking, the current trend in the trademark field unequivocally recognizes the need to reach or look beyond trademark turf. In this conjuncture, it is worthwhile to refer back to the two insightful articles that deal with the other two forms of resale of secondhand products, namely products with alteration and refurbishment and upcycling, by Annette Kur and Martin Senftleben respectively. Kur's paper on the sale of repaired or refurbished goods discussed whether the concurrent use of the brand's mark and the repairers/refurbishers would infringe the former's trademark and came to a finding of no trademark infringement within the trademark regime provided that, by additional labeling or accompanying product information, it is clarified that, how and by whom the original product has been transformed.[58] This is clearly not a pure trademark or trademark-internal view but was imbued with a good portion of unfair competition law thinking, as she points out that "the evaluation gradually **shifts** from a pure trade mark law analysis **towards an unfair competition-informed approach**."[59]

Senftleben's paper on fashion upcycling and trademark infringement concludes that although "In the EU, the referential use defence seems capable of offering a robust basis for upcycling,"

> In order to fully develop this defence, however, it is important to go beyond circular economy arguments and include lines of reasoning that consider the particular importance of the message that is conveyed with the sale of upcycled products: the urgent need **for a change of production and consumption patterns**.[60]

It did not find pure trademark argument sufficient and advocated a pattern change in production and consumption. What has this change to do with solving the trademark issues related to upcycling, if the trademark regime under his understanding is not already driven by CSR thinking or something similar?

5.4. Introducing CSR into Trademark Law

The introduction of CSR into trademark law needs no legislative intervention, as CSR is now perceived as one of the fundamental legal principles that underpin our human society, just like the principle of proportionality. Courts could usher in CSR

58 Kur, A. (2021). 'As Good as New'—Sale of repaired or refurbished goods: Commendable practice or trade mark infringement? *GRUR International, 70(3)*, 234. For this Kur coined the term "combined use."

59 Kur, A. (2021). 'As Good as New'—Sale of repaired or refurbished goods: Commendable practice or trade mark infringement? *GRUR International, 70(3)*, 236.

60 Senftleben, M. (2023). *Fashion Upcycling and Trademark Infringement—A Circular Economy/Freedom of the Arts Approach* (p. 1), at: SSRN: https://ssrn.com/abstract=4470873.

when trying litigated cases by rendering disadvantageous or unfavorable procedural rulings and substantive decisions, if parties, resellers of secondhand branded products and brand owners alike, fail to comply with what CSR expected of them.

5.4.1. CSR Expected of Resellers

First and foremost, CSR would require resellers to educate and inform their customers that authentication is at best an educated estimate, not an exact science.[61] Therefore, resellers are expected not to guarantee 100% authenticity of products that flow through their channels, so as not to mislead and disappoint consumers and upset brand owners. That said, resellers should provide appropriate channels for the public to hold them accountable, such as a full refund in case of authenticity dispute.

In addition, given that there are currently no third-party authenticators to outsource authentication to, resellers are expected to develop authentication processes and employ trained experts that are commensurate with resellers' business scale and financial capacity. SME resellers could meet this expectation by forming cooperation to conduct joint authentication.

Collectively resellers are also expected to develop industry-wide standards for best practices, including appropriate documentation of the sources of goods, sale/buy prices, the identity of traders, notification mechanism against counterfeits and liability for fake goods.

5.4.2. CSR Expected of Brand Owners

The CSR principle would initially expect brand owners to safeguard the independence and trustworthiness of the internal authentication reports they submitted to courts as evidenced by assuring the appraisers of "independent promotion, performance assessment, and continuous tracking of the correctness of appraisement, which must be subject to external scrutiny."[62] If the brand owner plaintiff continues to assert absolute protection of its trade secret and completely shield its authenticity appraisement from external scrutiny, then "it would be certain that the plaintiff

61 In this regard, Fashionphile has made an exemplary statement:

> Our specialists who have been trained for hours in Chanel inspect the colour and shape of all hardware, and follow the brand guides that we update on a regular basis to reflect the latest seasonal additions. Overall, they check for tarnishing, chipping, streaking, any ripple effects, or a rough finish, as well as incorrect engravings and screws that are inconsistent with Chanel standards.

See https://blog.fashionphile.com/chanel-serial-codes-decoded/. Fashionphile also provides Chenel Authentication Guide: Serial Codes, Decoded to educate consumers.

62 Z.-H. Cai (the judge who decided the 2017 LV case in Taiwan), The Survival Struggle of Secondhand Market for Branded Goods (in Chinese), Commercial Times (published in Taiwan), April 29, 2020.

should be awarded a losing verdict if the defendant successfully denies the independence and trustworthiness of the appraiser appointed by the plaintiff."[63]

If brand owners continue to resort to courts in similar cases, then CSR would further expect brand owners to proactively support independent third-party authentication and accreditation bodies, to lessen the workload of courts and speed up the solution of disputes. Brand owners are expected to share with these neutral third parties qualitative and quantitative standards governing the authentication of their products, as these standards are even more lacking in the luxury world than in the art world.[64] In return, these neutral third parties should treat this information as confidential material.[65] Of course, this support will have to be compensated with reasonable remuneration. With the fulfillment of this expected CSR, we can create a trustworthy secondhand market environment where people can buy and/or sell branded goods with confidence.

6. Conclusion

The introduction of the CSR paradigm into the trademark regime is targeted at setting up of an independent third-party mechanism to balance the interests of resellers of secondhand branded goods and the protection of brand owners who have deep pockets to misuse the trademark regime. In the future, the CSR principle could be further applied and developed by courts, which are receivers and conveyors of societal perceptions of CSR,[66] as an overarching principle to calibrate, soften or relax the rigid exclusivity of trademark rights.[67] More importantly, the CSR prerogative can keep trademark law abreast of the call of our time, maintaining the sustainability of our blue planet. What has happened in the trademark field with regard to CSR could well inspire other IP realms, such as patent,[68] design and copyright law, and provide lessons learned.

63 The obiter dictum of the 2017 LV decision by the TIPCC which rejected the defendant's assertion that LV abused its right or acted against the principle of good faith in exercising its trademark right.

64 Baumgarten, B. A. (2022). One too many sticks for the trademark bundle? *Loyola of Los Angeles Entertainment Law Review, 42*, 145.

65 Baumgarten, B. A. (2022). One too many sticks for the trademark bundle? *Loyola of Los Angeles Entertainment Law Review, 42*, 166.

66 Dan Burk and Mark Lemley also think in the context of patent, "it is the courts, not Congress or the PTO, that are best positioned" to tailor "the unitary patent rules on a case-by-case basis to the needs of different industries," see Burk, D., & Lemley, M. (2009). The patent crisis and how courts can solve it. *Stanford Public Law Working Paper No. 1349950*, 5, at SSRN: https://ssrn.com/abstract=1349950.

67 However, some still cling to the monopolies, both demand-side and supply-side, of trademark rights even in the digital age, see Griffiths, A. (2017). Trademark monopolies in the digital age. *Intellectual Property Quarterly, 27*, 123–151.

68 Thomas Cotter and Chung-Lun Shen discussed convincingly "Destruction, Proportionality, and Sustainability: A Law-and-Economics Analysis" in the realm of patent law during the 41st ATRIP Conference. So did Yusuke Tachibana's report "IP and Competition Law and Environmental Law: Focusing on the 'Right to Repair.'"

The Reports of the Appellate Body of the World Trade Organization (WTO) over the dispute between Philip Morris Asia Limited (HK) and Australia could be a herald of such a development. The Reports considered that Article 8 of the TRIPS Agreement offers "useful contextual guidance for the interpretation of the term 'unjustifiably' in Article 20."[69] The Panel noted that:

> the principles reflected in Article 8.1[70] express the intention of the drafters of the TRIPS Agreement to preserve the ability for WTO Members to pursue **certain legitimate societal interests**, at the same time as it confirms their recognition that certain measures adopted by WTO Members for such purposes **may have an impact on IP rights**, and requires that such measures be 'consistent with the provisions of the [TRIPS] Agreement.'[71]

69 Article 20 of the TRIPS Agreement stipulates:

> The use of a trademark in the course of trade shall not be unjustifiably encumbered by special requirements, such as use with another trademark, use in a special form or use in a manner detrimental to its capability to distinguish the goods or services of one undertaking from those of other undertakings.

70 Article 8.1 of the TRIPS Agreement stipulates:

> Members may, in formulating or amending their laws and regulations, adopt measures necessary to protect public health and nutrition, and to promote the public interest in sectors of vital importance to their socio-economic and technological development, provided that such measures are consistent with the provisions of this Agreement.

71 WT/DS435/AB/R (June 9, 2020), 202.

Part VI

Data, Algorithms, IP, and Competition

"While human beings have used various instruments and technologies to create and innovate, they themselves have been the main driving force of creativity and innovation. AI puts that into question, raising numerous challenges to the existing intellectual property regime."[1] However, this volume only aims at clarifying some of the issues related to data that train AI machine learning and algorithms that decide AI decision-making. With the insight so gained, we would be better poised to solve the fundamental and controversial conundrum of whether existing human-centric IP regimes based on promoting incentives and avoiding disincentives may no longer be relevant or "even positively detrimental" especially when generative AI comes into play.

1 Lee, J.-A., Hilty, R. M., & Liu, K.-C. (2021). Roadmap to artificial intelligence and intellectual property. In Lee, J.-A., Hilty, R. M., & Liu, K.-C. (Eds.), *Artificial Intelligence and Intellectual Property* (p. 1). Oxford University Press.

DOI: 10.4324/9781003597766-17

12 Data and Algorithms for the Data-Driven Economy[1]

1. Introduction

With the ubiquitous take-up of digital technology and digitization of products, services, and business processes, we find ourselves in a data-driven economy which has data and algorithms as its two pillars. Data, and especially big data, generated and collected by netizens and smart machines (devices) connected via the internet of things (IoT) are essential raw materials for new products or services, business models and competition. As another even more important pillar of the data-driven economy, algorithms decide the collection, compilation, analysis of data and shape the final function of artificial intelligence (AI).

Controversies are on the rise about the protection of and access to data, algorithms being biased or even designed to distort competition and harm consumers. How can we best regulate data and algorithms to boost the data-driven economy? How can we overcome the intellectual property (IP) hurdles, copyright and trade secret in particular, of data and algorithms that might hinder the data-driven economy?[2]

This chapter will first focus on data by discussing its typology (identifying three types of data), protection, access, and use. The second focal point of this chapter deals with algorithms and proposes six principles for auditing algorithms. It advocates the need for a global governance mechanism consisting of a new treaty, run by a council, and implemented by a professional bureau.

1 This chapter is based on my article "Regulatory Issues of Data and Algorithms for The Data-Driven Economy," 72 GRUR-(Gewerblicher Rechtshutz und Urheberrecht) International: Journal of European and International IP Law) Int. No. 9 (2023), 853–863.

2 The question of whether algorithm-driven market interactions challenge traditional economic models of competition law such as explicit and tacit collusion has been negatively answered by some arguing that there are strong theoretical and practical reasons for believing that pricing algorithms will lead to widespread collusion without human involvement. See Veljanovski, C. (2022). Pricing algorithms as collusive devices. *International Review of Intellectual Property and Competition Law, 53(4)*, 604–622. However, new competition regulation for algorithms must be developed. See Picht, P.G., & Freund, B. (2018). Competition (law) in the era of algorithms. *MPI Research Paper No. 18–10*, at: https://ssrn.com/abstract=3180550.

DOI: 10.4324/9781003597766-18

2. Data

As vital as data are for the data-driven economy, there is no generally accepted definition of data in the legal world due to its diverse nature. The widely read and referenced Max Planck Institute for Innovation and Competition's (MPI) Position Statement on Data Ownership and Access to Data (Position Statement on Data) does not provide a definition of data.[3] The EU adopts a clear definition of "data" in its Regulation 2022/868 on European data governance and amending Regulation 2018/1724 (Data Governance Act, May 30, 2022): "data" means any digital representation of acts, facts or information and any compilation of such acts, facts or information, including in the form of sound, visual or audio-visual recording (Article 2, No.1). This squarely pinpoints the characteristic of what is being transmitted via the internet and IoT, namely the digitized acts, facts, or information, and could be a suitable working definition.

2.1. Determining the Type of Data We are Talking About as the First Step

The diversity of data and the situations in which data are collected and exploited demand a nuanced approach to data. We have to be mindful of what kind of data we are talking about and dealing with. Our approach to data is necessarily one of typology, which is not clear-cut dissection; rather it has core content with some flexible and amorphous rims and allows certain variations.[4] Different types of "data can be subject to fundamentally different conditions, whether in terms of collection, processing, function, or downstream uses,"[5] and could face different legal issues. Differentiated legal judgments should be worked out for different types of data.

There are two basic categories of data, personal or purely technical or factual data.[6] This chapter does not touch upon personal data, as it is more about privacy, a topic beyond its theme. This chapter does see three types of data under the "data of purely technical or factual nature" according to the level of copyright or neighbouring protection in a descending order. Sometimes, efforts will have to be made to draw the line between the three types of data, sometimes there will be overlap.

3 Drexl, J. et al. *Data Ownership and Access to Data (2016)—Position Statement of the Max Planck Institute for Innovation and Competition of 16 August 2016 on the Current European Debate MPI Position Statement on Data*, paragraphs 2 and 8, at: https//ssrn.com/abstract=2833165.

4 Marradi, A. (1990). Classification, typology, taxonomy. *Quality & Quantity*, *24*, 129.

5 Hilty, R. (2018). Big data: Ownership and use in the digital age. In Seuba, X., Geiger, C., & Pénin, J. (Eds.), *Intellectual Property and Digital Trade in the Age of Artificial Intelligence and Big Data* (pp. 90, 91). CEIPI-ICTSD.

6 In the context of discussing ownership of data, Reto Hilty identifies three types of data mainly according to the connection with and closeness to natural persons. The three types are "data of purely technical or factual nature" (e.g., machine data), "person-related data" (data that involve a "reference" or "connection" to individual people such as personal data and consumer behavior data), and data not directly "attributed" to an individual person but can easily produce the relation to a person ("personenbeziehbar" data), Hilty, R. (2018). Big data: Ownership and use in the digital age. In Seuba, X., Geiger, C., & Pénin, J. (Eds.), *Intellectual Property and Digital Trade in the Age of Artificial Intelligence and Big Data* (pp. 90, 91). CEIPI-ICTSD.

The first type of data is copyright-protected data that clearly satisfy the requirements of copyright (originality and personal characteristics) under national copyright regimes. The second type is data specifically generated to achieve a certain goal or purpose, such as the training materials tailor-made for machine learning (ML), which however are not necessarily protected under national copyright law. If they are not, then they still could deserve some protection against trade secrets (secrecy, commercial value due to its secrecy, and reasonable steps taken to protect the secrecy), misappropriation, and unfair competition in appropriate cases. The third type is big data generated by netizens and smart devices (such as smartphones, grids, etc.) around the clock and the globe, interconnected via the internet and IoT, and collected and used by platforms large and small. The thriving e-commerce via APPs on smartphones has generated the most number of big data. Big data by its nature is furthest away from copyright protection as will be elaborated later.

2.2. *The Protection of Data*

Copyright-protected data by its very nature already enjoys the legal protection of copyright and does not warrant further investigation at this juncture. In the following, the discussion will focus on data specifically generated for achieving a certain goal or purpose and big data.

2.2.1. *Data Specifically Generated to Achieve a Certain Goal*

In order to achieve a certain goal or purpose, such as supervised ML, labeled data (or a training dataset, training data) are needed.[7] Data labeling is a contribution of data generators as they collect data from various sources, select and organize data, improve their relevance, and adjust data into a machine-readable format. The accumulation and consolidation (agglomeration, organization, selection, and processing) of data require intellectual and professional creation. Therefore, certain labeled data for achieving a certain goal or purpose could qualify as works worthy of copyright protection as compilation, depending on national law.[8] Once they do, they will ascend to the first data type and be dealt with accordingly.

In many cases, data augmentation is a common strategy for handling data scarcity. It works by synthesizing new data from existing training data, with the objective of improving the performance of the downstream model. In the field of self-driving area, industry leaders like Google have been relying on simulations to

7 For more see So, A.M.-C. (2019). Technical elements of machine learning for intellectual property law. In Lee, J.-A., Hilty, R.M., & Liu, K.-C. (Eds.), *Artificial Intelligence and Intellectual Property* (pp. 11–27). Oxford University Press.

8 Article 10(2) of TRIPS:

> 2. Compilations of data or other material, whether in machine readable or other form, which by reason of the selection or arrangement of their contents constitute intellectual creations shall be protected as such. Such protection, which shall not extend to the data or material itself, shall be without prejudice to any copyright subsisting in the data or material itself.

create millions of hours of synthetic driving data to train their algorithms.[9] A thus synthesized data corpus is in essence the result of the operation of a certain algorithm or data augmentation method,[10] similar to data generated from copyrighted software, and therefore does not deserve copyright protection.[11] However, such a synthesized data corpus, when satisfying all the necessary requirements, can be subject to trade secret protection.

2.2.2. Big Data

Big data are characterized by 4Vs, namely "volume, veracity, velocity, and variety" as their technical features: data with huge size (volume), rapid change or updating for data collection and analysis (veracity and velocity), and various data sources, which include internet browsers, social media sites, apps, cameras, cars, and a host of other data-collection tools (variety).[12]

The 4Vs feature of big data renders it as aggregate human legacy than private goods, and therefore does and could not enjoy ownership rights.[13] Neither is there a need or justification for creating exclusive copyright rights or property rights in big data nor for applying any sui generis right of database to big data (such as the EU).[14]

9 Dilmegani, C. (2024). *What Is Synthetic Data? Use Cases & Benefits in 2024*, at: https://blog.aimultiple.com/synthetic-data/#benefits; Golson, J. (2016). Google's self-driving cars rack up three million simulated miles every day. *The Verge*, at: https://www.theverge.com/2016/2/1/10892020/google-self-driving-simulator-3-million-miles.

10 The Q&A on Technical Aspects of Artificial Intelligence: An Understanding from an Intellectual Property Law Perspective, prepared by the MPI reminds us that:

> A distinction should be made between the direct output of a model and the potential practical applications of this output . . . from an intellectual property law perspective, distinct legal issues can arise with regard to direct outputs and their applications of an ML model.

11 Daniel Gervais seems to have a similar reservation: "the question whether machine-created productions can qualify as copyright works is either still open or resolved in favour of a need for human authorship." See Gervais, D. (2019). Exploring the interfaces between big data and intellectual property law. *Journal of Intellectual Property Information Technology and Electronic Commerce Law (JIPITEC)*, *22*, Paragraph 28.

12 Rubinfeld, D., & Gal, M.S. (2017). Access barriers to big data. *Arizona Law Review, 59*, 345–347.

13 Ding, W.J., & Chen, L. (2022). Regulating the use of big data: Justifications, perspectives and the Chinese way forward. *Computer Law & Security Review*, *46*, 1.

14 The Position Statement on Data, although it does not specifically mention that it is dealing with the legal treatment of big data, could well be applied to big data, see Paragraphs 9–11 (individual data), 25 (customer data), 3, 5, 39 (personal data), 13, 34, 39 (raw data), and 12 and 37 (big data) of the Position Statement on Data. It does not see any need or justification for creating exclusive rights in big data (Paragraphs 4–8. In fact, the Position Statement on Data mentions big data twice in addition to "individual data," "customer data," "personal data," "raw data," and "data set" when discussing specific issues) or for applying the sui generis right of database in the EU to big data (see Paragraphs 9–11). The experiences of legal ownership protection of databases have shown that there are more negative effects, such as interference with the freedom to conduct a business and competition and impeding the development of downstream data markets, than positive effects, see Hilty, R. (2018). Big data: Ownership and use in the digital age. In Seuba, X., Geiger, C., & Pénin, J. (Eds.), *Intellectual Property and Digital Trade in the Age of Artificial Intelligence and Big Data* (p. 90). CEIPI-ICTSD.

This is exactly the understanding of the Chinese government[15] and the legislative principle taken by the EU Data Act, a sector-specific regulation to enhance access to data. Recital 6 of the EU Data Act states "a general approach to assigning access and usage rights on data is preferable to awarding exclusive rights of access and use."

Indeed, statistics show that data markets keep growing rapidly without the blessing of an exclusivity right. The global big data market is forecasted to grow to US $103 billion by 2027, more than double its expected market size in 2018. With a share of 45%, the software segment would become the largest big data market segment by 2027.[16]

To sum up, the issue of "protection" of big data should not be addressed in the sense or direction of giving proprietary entitlement over big data to any entity, which has some control over part of it, given its diverse nature and source. Rather, we must ensure that big data, from both private and public sectors, are not prevented from forming, accumulating, and flowing freely. The protection is to allow big data to snowball as the single most valuable capital of society for economic and technological innovation.

2.3. Access to and Use of Data

If all players can access and use data freely, it is then easily conceivable that more and better products and services would be provided more quickly and cheaply to consumers. However, there are legal mechanisms and obstacles that control or prevent data collection and mining or raise the costs thereof.

2.3.1. Copyright-Protected Data

The 2022 Position Statement of the MPI on the draft Data Act (Position Statement on Data Act) points out:[17]

> Data—in the form of digitized pictures, music, films etc—may enjoy copyright protection. In such cases, copyright law—not just the sui generis database right—could create obstacles to the exercise of data access and use rights . . . (and) hinder interoperability.

15 According to *Opinions on Constructing Infrastructure for Data to Better Unleash the Function of Data*, at: https://www.gov.cn/zhengce/2022-12/21/content_5732906.htm, issued by the State Council of the PRC on December 19, 2022, the right to hold data, the right to process and exploit data, and the right to manage digital products, rather than property rights, shall be established.

16 See https://www.statista.com/statistics/254266/global-big-data-market-forecast/.

17 Drexl, J. et al. (2022). *Position Statement of the Max Planck Institute for Innovation and Competition of 25 May 2022 on the Commission's Proposal of 23 February 2022 for a Regulation on Harmonised Rules on Fair Access to and Use of Data (Data Act), (9)*, at: https//ssrn.com/abstract=2833165.

A. DATA FROM THE PRIVATE SECTOR

The most used tool for large-scale accessing and using copyright-protected data is through text and data mining (TDM), which is the technological analysis of materials for patterns, trends, and uses other than their intended purpose. It requires "copying" and could need copyright owners' prior permission. However, to get copyright owners' individualized permission for TDM would be "an insurmountable obstacle" that will slow down the data-driven economy.

That said, the necessary copying, digitization, and processing during TDM could be seen from a different lens, as it does not "use" the works in the traditional sense that is for personal enjoyment, appreciation, comprehension, or inspiration (non-expressive use), and would therefore not affect the economic utilization of those works (non-consumptive use or non-market-encroaching use). TDM therefore could be argued as not constituting copyright infringement.[18] Furthermore, the widespread use of TDM has unlimited potential benefits for the global data-driven economy, just to name a few: creating tools for education and research, fostering innovation and collaboration, boosting open science, addressing grand challenges (climate changes and global epidemics),[19] and could justifiably enjoy exemptions from copyright liability.

In the US, the use of copyrighted text during TDM even for commercial purposes could be permitted under the widely permissive fair use doctrine so long it is transformative and does not serve as a substitute to the original work but enhances information-gathering techniques and serves a new purpose.[20] However, such a generous fair use approach is hard for any other country to follow. Therefore, major jurisdictions have introduced specific clauses to exempt TDM from copyright infringement.

For example, the UK adopted in 2014 a clause which provides that copying for "computational analysis" by a person who has legal access to the work is not copyright infringement, and in a contract which purports to prevent or restrict the making of such copies, that term is unenforceable.[21] However, the exemption is

18 Sag, M. (2012). Orphan works as grist for the data mill. *Berkeley Technology Law Journal, 27(3)*, 1502, 1523, 1544; Google. (2018). *Copyright in the Digital Age—An Economic Assessment of Fair Use in New Zealand* (p. 25). Deloitte Access Economics, 2018, at: https://www2.deloitte.com/content/dam/Deloitte/nz/Documents/Economics/dae-nz-copyright-fair-use-final.pdf. See also Sobel, B. (2021). A taxonomy of training data: Disentangling the mismatched rights, remedies, and rationales for restricting machine learning. In Lee, J.-A., Hilty, R.M., & Liu, K.-C. (Eds.), *Artificial Intelligence and Intellectual Property* (pp. 221–244). Oxford University Press.

19 See International Federation of Library Associations and Institutions. (2015). *The Hague Declaration on Knowledge Discovery in the Digital Age*, at: https://www.ifla.org/publications/node/91863; United Nations Industrial Development Organization. (2018). *World Statistics on Mining and Utilities*. UNIDO, at: https://www.unido.org/resources/publications/cross-cutting-services/world-statistics-mining-and-utilities.

20 *Kelly v. Arriba-Soft*, 336 F.3d 811 (9th Cir. 2003); *Authors Guild v. Google*, 770 F.Supp. 2d 666 (S.D.N.Y. 2011); *Authors Guild v. HathiTrust*, 755 F.3d 87 (2d Cir. 2014). *Google LLC v. Oracle America, Inc.*, 593 US ___ (2021).

21 Section 29A(1) and (5) of the Copyright Designs and Patents Act 1988 prohibits copyright holders from making reservations: copyright owners cannot prevent or restrict copying for text and data analysis for non-commercial research through contracts.

limited to research for a non-commercial purpose, and thus far remains untested by case law.[22]

The EU adopted in 2019 the Directive on Copyright and Related Rights in the Digital Single Market (Copyright Directive) and introduced two clauses which narrowly allow TDM. (I) If TDM is done by research organizations and cultural heritage institutions and of works or other subject matter to which they have lawful access (Article 3(1)), it must be for the purposes of scientific research. (II) If TDM is done generally by all those who enjoy lawful access to underlying mined materials, and reproductions and extractions can only be made when the use of works and other subject matter has not been expressly reserved by their rightsholders in an appropriate manner, such as machine-readable means in the case of content made publicly available online (Article 4(1) and (3)). Copyright holders can decide to opt out or contract out TDM, which would make TDM virtually impossible.

Japan first provided the exception of recording works in information analysis by computer for both commercial and non-commercial purposes in 2009, which was criticized for its vague and outdated rules.[23] In 2018, Japan amended the Copyright Act (effective since 2019) and introduced broadly termed clauses exempting related activities in data mining and analysis. The amendment allows users to exploit a work, in any way and to the extent considered necessary, in any of the following cases, or in any other case in which it is not a person's purpose to personally enjoy or cause another person to enjoy the thoughts or sentiments expressed in that work; provided, however, that this does not apply if the action would unreasonably prejudice the interests of the copyright owner in light of the nature or purpose of the work or the circumstances of its exploitation:

(i) if it is done for use in testing to develop or put into practical use technology that is connected with the recording of sounds or visuals of a work or other such exploitation;
(ii) if it is done for use in data analysis (meaning the extraction, comparison, classification, or other statistical analysis of the constituent language, sounds, images, or other elemental data from a large number of works or a large volume of other such data);
(iii) if it is exploited in the course of computer data processing or otherwise exploited in a way that does not involve what is expressed in the work being perceived by the human senses (for works of computer programming, such exploitation excludes the execution of the work on a computer), beyond as set forth in the preceding two items (Article 30–4).[24]

22 See Rosati, E. (2019). Copyright as an obstacle or an enabler? A European perspective on text and data mining and its role in the development of AI creativity. *Asia Pacific Law Review, 27(2)*, 198–217.

23 European Alliance for Research Excellence. (2018). *Japan Amends Its Copyright Legislation to Meet Future Demands in AI and Big Data*, at: http://eare.eu/japan-amends-tdm-exception-copyright.

24 Some criticize that the formulation of Articles 30–4, although underpinned by a strategic innovation policy goal, is conceptually wrong, theoretically flawed, and normatively unambitious, see

Clearly, Japan's broad TDM exemption to copyright provides more freedom compared to the UK and the EU. This chapter would argue that the Japanese approach should be preferred by other jurisdictions to facilitate more access to and use of copyright-protected data.

In this context, it is desirable to introduce some compensation mechanism for holders of mined copyrighted works, after all, miners or their machines benefit from TDM of others' works. It would be fairer than the free "fair use." This would be equal to establishing a statutory license of others' works for the TDM purpose, where there is no need for prior good-faith negotiation but a need to provide reasonable compensation to be determined by the copyright office or its likes. Such a license would not violate the three-step test as the third step "may be met by compensating right holders."[25]

B. DATA FROM THE PUBLIC-SECTOR

A large part of copyright-protected data comes from the public sector, including public-funded education and R&D institutions, public utilities, government agencies, etc. As a result, the importance of having open access to those data cannot be emphasized enough. Huge amounts of public-sector data if made open could be used to facilitate the development of the data-driven economy.

The EU promulgated Directive 2019/1024 on open data and the re-use of public sector information (June 20, 2019), requiring its members to ensure that documents to which this Directive applies and that documents on which libraries, including university libraries, museums, and archives hold IPRs and documents held by public undertakings, are re-usable for commercial or non-commercial purposes (Article 3). After the transposition date of this Directive (17 July, 2021), the EU follows up with the Data Governance Act in 2022 to lay down conditions for the re-use, within the Union, of protected data held by public sector bodies. It prohibits exclusive agreements pertaining to the re-use of such data (Article 4), conditions for re-use shall be non-discriminatory, transparent, proportionate, and objectively justified with regard to the categories of data and the purposes of re-use and the nature of the data for which re-use is allowed (Article 5), and any fees charged for re-use shall be transparent, non-discriminatory, proportionate and objectively justified and shall not restrict competition (Article 6), Member States shall ensure that all relevant information concerning the application of Articles 5 and 6 is available and easily accessible through a single information point (Article 8), among other things.

Margon, T., & Kretchmer, M. (2022). A deeper look into the EU text and data mining exceptions: Harmonisation, data ownership, and the future of technology. *GRUR International, 71(8)*, 685–701.

25 See Gervais, D. (2019). Exploring the interfaces between big data and intellectual property law. *Journal of Intellectual Property Information Technology and Electronic Commerce Law (JIPITEC), 22,* Paragraph 61. See also He, T.X. (2021). Copyright exceptions reform and AI data analysis in China: A modest proposal. In Lee, J.-A., Hilty, R.M., & Liu, K.-C. (Eds.), *Artificial Intelligence and Intellectual Property* (pp. 196–220). Oxford University Press.

However, the EU's approach to public-sector data is still limited by its fee-paying thinking. In this regard, the Council of the OECD has made bolder suggestions in its 2008 Recommendation on Enhanced Access and More Effective Use of Public Sector Information (PSI). In addition to openness, access, and transparent conditions for re-use, quality control (to ensure methodical data collection and curation practices to enhance quality), and safeguarding the integrity of PSI, it also prescribes other means to achieving effective use of PSI: exercising copyright in ways that facilitate re-use, for example, waiving copyright and creating mechanisms that facilitate waiving of copyright and use of orphan works, pricing PSI transparently and consistently within and across different public sector organizations if PSI is not provided free of charge. It further suggests the setting up of redress mechanisms, facilitating public-private partnerships, and furthering international access and use.

National states could realize the widest possible cross-border re-uses of public-sector data by following the OECD suggestions. In particular, waiving copyright or creating mechanisms that facilitate the waiving of copyright will definitely simplify and ease the access to and use of copyright-protected data from the public sector.

2.3.2. Data Specifically Generated for Achieving a Certain Goal

Data specifically generated for achieving a certain goal or purpose that is not copyright-protected could also be subject to TDM by others. Understandably, holders of this type of data would take reasonable measures to prevent access to their data and to protect their secrecy. This would exclude any access, through TDM or not. Interested parties will have to start voluntary licensing negotiations for TDM activities on a case-by-case basis. This again will slow down the data-driven economy. Legal regimes must then be prepared for the eventuality of failed negotiations, especially when such data are of critical importance for market competition. Statutory licensing of such data shall be installed as discussed in 2.3.1.A.

2.3.3. Big Data

Access to and use of big data is necessary for market entry, effective competition, and improving social welfare. Therefore, it would be desirable to provide ready access to big data, allowing every market player to achieve compatibility, technical upgrades, and the creation of new products and services. However, both national states and private firms set up a host of barriers to the collection, storage, synthesis, analysis, flow, and use of big data.

A. GOVERNMENT BARRIERS

Divergent national laws on the flow of personal and non-personal data, including cross-border transfer, are the most prominent government barriers to the access and use of big data. According to the United Nations Conference on Trade and Development (UNCTAD), 137 out of 194 countries have put in place legislation to secure the protection of data and privacy.[26] As stated, the following discussion will mainly target national regulations on non-personal data. Many countries have enacted laws and regulations to exert various forms of control over storage, cross-border transfer, and localization of non-personal data. According to a study by the Information Technology and Innovation Foundation (ITIF) in 2021, the number of data-localization measures in force around the world has more than doubled between 2017 (35 countries had implemented 67 restrictions) and 2021 (62 countries have imposed 144 restrictions).[27] Some nations base their decisions on the mistaken notion that it will mitigate cybersecurity concerns; others do so out of purely mercantilist reasons.

Basically, strict cross-border data transfer rules such as data localization,[28] threaten to impede the utilities of big data, as they increase costs and add complexity to the collection and maintenance of data, and reduce the size of

26 See https://unctad.org/page/data-protection-and-privacy-legislation-worldwide.

27 Cory, N., & Dascoli, L. (2021). *How Barriers to Cross-Border Data Flows Are Spreading Globally, What They Cost, and How to Address Them*. Information Technology & Innovation Foundation, at: https://itif.orng/publications/2021/07/19/how-barriers-cross-border-data-flows-are-spreading-globally-what-they-cost.

28 The US has proposed or enacted a few data localization requirements, most of which focus on public procurement. For example, the Internal Revenue Service issued publication 1075–Tax Information Security Guidelines For Federal, State, and Local Agencies and the Department of Defense require all cloud-computing service providers that work for the department to store data domestically. Domestic data storage requirements are sometimes a requirement for other federal public procurement contracts but are not an explicit government-wide policy. See ITIF, Cross-Border Data Flows: Where Are the Barriers, and What Do They Cost? Internationally, the US supports the elimination of barriers to data flow as much as possible. It actively promotes free cross-border data transfer through bilateral and multilateral free trade agreements (FTA). For example, Article 15.8 of the 2012 US-Korea FTA provides that "Recognizing the importance of the free flow of information in facilitating trade, and acknowledging the importance of protecting personal information, the Parties shall endeavor to refrain from imposing or maintaining unnecessary barriers to electronic information flows across borders." The EU Regulation 2018/1807 on a Framework for the Free Flow of Non-Personal Data (effective since May 2019) prohibits members from imposing data localization requirements unless data localization restrictions are justified on the grounds of public security in compliance with the principle of proportionality (Article 4(1)). China's Cybersecurity Law requires that personal information and important data collected and produced by critical information infrastructure operators (those whose business relates to public communications and information services, energy, transport, water conservancy, finance, public services, and e-government affairs, etc.) be stored within China, and if it is indeed necessary to provide such information and data to overseas parties due to business requirements, security assessment shall be conducted by the national cyberspace administration (Article 37) which may refuse to issue security assessment and disallow the outflow of data. The Cyberspace Administration of China (CAC) issued in 2022 "Regulations on Assessing the Security of Transferring Data out of the Country." It requires select data processors, which satisfy one of the following criteria, to undergo data security assessment with the CAC through the provincial cyberspace department: 1. They are delivering important data out of the country; 2. They are critical information infrastructure operators or data processors that process personal information of more than one million people; 3. They have delivered accumulatively personal data of 100,000 people or sensitive personal data of 10,000 people since January 1 of the previous year; 4. As required by national cybersecurity department (Article 4). It defines important data as those once falsified, damaged, leaked, illegally acquired or used, national security, economic operation, social stability, public health and security might be endangered (Article 19). National

potential datasets supply, eroding the informational value that can be gained by cross-jurisdictional studies.[29]

B. PRIVATE BARRIERS

Private companies also use a variety of barriers, such as exclusive dealing, pricing and conditioning access, to hinder or even disable users' direct or indirect access via third parties to and use of big data, to which they have contributed.[30] In addition, as the Japan Fair Trade Commission in its Report of the Study Group on Data and Competition Policy (2017) warns unjust data hoarding by monopolistic or oligopolistic enterprises may be an issue under the Antimonopoly Act, namely refusal to admit access to big data which are essential to competitors' business and for which it is technically or economically difficult for competitors and/or customers to obtain substitutable data, without justifiable grounds.[31]

However, antitrust law in most cases is not suitable to address the issue of access to and use of big data, as it provides only time-consuming, case-specific, ex-post measures, and cannot keep abreast with the fast-developing data market. More effective would be ex-ante regulations.[32] In line with the considerations, the EC Data Act puts forward a set of rules on access to and use of data. Article 3(1) prescribes that "Products shall be designed and manufactured, and related services shall be provided, in such a manner that data generated by their use are, by default, easily, securely and, where relevant and appropriate, directly accessible to the user." In addition,

> The user should be free to use the data for any lawful purpose. This includes providing the data the user has received exercising the right under this Regulation to a third party offering an aftermarket service that may be in competition with a service provided by the data holder, or to instruct the data holder to do so. The data holder should ensure that the data made available to the third party is as accurate, complete, reliable, relevant and up-to-date as the data holder itself may be able or entitled to access from the use of the product

---

cybersecurity department may refuse to issue security assessment and disallow the outflow of data, which can be appealed to the department, however whose decision is final (Article 13).

29 See UNCTAD. (2016). *Data Protection Regulations and International Data Flows: Implications for Trade and Development*; Chander, A., & Lj, U. (2015). Data nationalism. *Emory Law Journal, 64*, 677, 730. For a more comprehensive analysis of these concerns, see Lee, J.-A. (2018). Hacking into China's cybersecurity law. *Wake Forest Law Review, 53*, 57, 78–87.

30 Rubinfeld, D., & Gal, M.S. (2017). Access barriers to big data. *Arizona Law Review, 59*, 362–363.

31 Japan Fair Trade Commission Competition Policy Research Center. (2017). *Report of Study Group on Data and Competition Policy*, at: https://www.jftc.go.jp/en/pressreleases/yearly-2017/June/170606.html.

32 However, the Position Statement on Data (Paragraphs 32–38) opines only sector-specific regulations might be required, if at all. Also, Hilty, R. (2018). Big data: Ownership and use in the digital age. In Seuba, X., Geiger, C., & Pénin, J. (Eds.), *Intellectual Property and Digital Trade in the Age of Artificial Intelligence and Big Data* (p. 92). CEIPI-ICTSD.

> or related service. Any trade secrets or intellectual property rights should be respected in handling the data.
>
> Recital 28

Therefore Article 4(1) requests:

> 1. Where data cannot be directly accessed by the user from the product, the data holder shall make available to the user the data generated by its use of a product or related service without undue delay, free of charge and, where applicable, continuously and in real-time. This shall be done on the basis of a simple request through electronic means where technically feasible.

Article 5(1) further imposes "the obligation on the data holder to make data available to users and third parties nominated by the users in certain circumstances":

> Upon request by a user, or by a party acting on behalf of a user, the data holder shall make available the data generated by the use of a product or related service to a third party, without undue delay, free of charge to the user, of the same quality as is available to the data holder and, where applicable, continuously and in real-time

and "Where a data holder is obliged to make data available to a data recipient under Article 5. . . it shall do so under fair, reasonable and non-discriminatory terms and in a transparent manner (Article 8(1))."[33]

With regard to big data holders' unjust data hoarding, one possible regulation is a rule requiring them to make big data they control widely available at a FRAND price when the sharing of data is socially beneficial. A potentially instructive model might be FRAND licensing requirements that are central to the operation of SEPs (de facto compulsory license of big data).[34]

"It is feared that the competitive advantage of big data holders as the initial trade secret holder stemming from the discretion to authorize access to, acquisition and use of a trade secret would be diminished."[35] However, FRAND license of big data held by private parties for the purpose of TDM will only happen with reasonable remuneration, which if properly determined could be close to the market value of data and would not necessarily diminish the competitive advantage of the initial big data holders. Besides, they can also benefit from the FRAND license regime to enhance their access to others' data.

33 Rubinfeld, D., & Gal, M. S. (2017). Access barriers to big data. *Arizona Law Review, 59*, 373.
34 Rubinfeld, D., & Gal, M.S. (2017). Access barriers to big data. *Arizona Law Review, 59*, 373.
35 (286) Position Statement on Data Act.

3. Algorithms

According to the German Bundeskartellamt and the French Competition Authority, an algorithm can be broadly understood as "a sequence of simple and/or well-defined operations that should be performed in an exact order to carry out a certain task or class of tasks or to solve a certain problem or class of problems."[36] Algorithms decide how software, computers, and AI work as well as how data are being collected and exploited. Algorithms can make decisions on online trading (search, pricing, and terms and conditions), reputation, financing, develop patterns humans cannot detect, help consumers make decisions and promote their welfare, etc.

However, algorithms do not provide information about their internal decision-making process and are often described as a black box.[37]

3.1. Algorithm as a One-Way Mirror

Former CEO of Google Eric Schmidt told a scary story in 2010 of how this one-way mirror works:

> With your permission you give us more information about you, about your friends, and we can improve the quality of our searches, we don't need you to type at all. We know where you are. We know where you've been. We can more or less know what you're thinking about.[38]

Algorithms take in data about us and convert it into risk calculations, paid rankings, and personalized recommendations that may have vitally important consequences for us, and yet are immune from scrutiny.[39] Facebook and WeChat decide who we are, Amazon and Jingdong (JD.com) decide what we want, Google and Baidu[40] decide what we think, all because of algorithms, and we know nothing about them.[41] If we cannot deal with the opacity and complexity they now possess, then deception, overpricing, and fraud will continue to flourish.[42]

36 German Bundeskartellamt and French Competition Authority. (2019). Algorithms and competition. *Working Paper*, 3, at: https://www.autoritedelaconcurrence.fr/sites/default/files/algorithms-and-competition.pdf.

37 See Wachter, S., Mittelstadt, B., & Russell, C. (2018). Counterfactual explanations without opening the black box: Automated decisions and the GDPR. *Harvard Journal of Law & Technology, 31(2)*, 3, at: SSRN: https://ssrn.com/abstract=3063289.

38 See https://www.theatlantic.com/technology/archive/2010/10/googles-ceo-the-laws-are-written-by-lobbyists/63908.

39 Pasquale, F. (2015). *The Black Box Society—Secret Algorithms That Control Money and Information* (p. 4). Harvard University Press.

40 Baidu, a notorious internet giant in China, has 60.87% market share in the Chinese search engine industry (http://gs.statcounter.com/search-engine-market-share/all/china (as of December 2022)) and has long been suspected of self-serving Baidu's eco-system, and yet no investigation has ever been launched against it.

41 Dyson, G. (2012). *Turing's Cathedral: The Origins of the Digital Universe* (p. 308). Pantheon.

42 Pasquale, F. (2015). *The Black Box Society—Secret Algorithms That Control Money and Information* (p. 15). Harvard University Press.

3.2. Challenges Algorithms Pose

Algorithms, being a one-way mirror, are posing challenges to the data-driven economy.

For one thing, individual users and consumers are overwhelmed by algorithms, their unassisted self-help can be of limited use due to knowledge disadvantages,[43] and the self-regulation by tech giants and major platforms alone has often proven to be futile. If not correctly designed, algorithms may collect and process data beyond the original purpose for which the data is collected and used for violating the established principle that data should only be collected for named and specific purposes.[44] This is a common practice by internet companies, which may benefit consumers to an extent but also bring harm to them. Take personalized online shopping or targeted online marketing as an example. Admittedly, it reduces the bewildering options for consumers and saves them time and effort to locate what best meets their demand. However, it also shapes consumers' preferences, subjects them to a monotonous consumption pattern especially when they are willing to buy something outside their past choices, and makes first-degree price discrimination against consumers to maximize profits.[45]

For another, it is extremely difficult for individuals and even countries to verify whether globally applied algorithms are as bias-free and competition-neutral as they alleged. In addition, nowadays, tech giants and governments only preach, accept, and practice open AI, responsible AI, trustworthy AI, explainable AI, etc.,[46] but are less forthcoming about informing the public about their algorithms, not to mention the auditing of their algorithms. However, algorithms decide the purposes for which data are collected, analyzed, and used, and therefore the right and wrong of AI. Any discussion about regulating AI would not be complete without discussing algorithms and their auditing.

The previously-mentioned challenges enlighten abundantly clear the necessity of auditing algorithms. Then the next burning question lying ahead is how to conduct the auditing, especially in a cross-border context.

43 See Wagner, G., & Eidenmüller, H. (2018). Down by algorithms? Siphoning rents, exploiting biases and shaping preferences: regulating the dark side of personalized transactions. *University of Chicago Law Review*, *86*, 589.

44 Article 5(1)(b) of the GDPR provides that "Personal data shall be: (b) collected for specified, explicit and legitimate purposes and not further processed in a manner that is incompatible with those purposes . . . ('purpose limitation')."

45 First-degree price discrimination, alternatively known as perfect price discrimination, occurs when a firm charges a different price for every unit consumed. The firm is able to charge the maximum possible price for each unit based on consumers' individual preferences and reservation prices to capture all available consumer surplus for itself. First-degree discrimination was once rare in practice but has become a daily reality thanks to big data and big algorithm. See https://www.economicsonline.co.uk/Business_economics/Price_discrimination.html.

46 Such as the Executive Order on the Safe, Secure, and Trustworthy Development and Use of Artificial Intelligence issued by US President Joe Biden on October 30, 2023.

3.3. Six Principles for Auditing Algorithms[47]

"Algorithm auditing is the research and practice of assessing, mitigating, and assuring an algorithm's safety, legality, and ethics,"[48] which would require the right mixture of direct and indirect regulations through architecture, norms, market, and the law.[49] It is to "foresee that a new industry is emerging, Auditing and Assurance of Data and Algorithms, with the remit to professionalize and industrialize AI, ML and associated algorithms."[50] I put forward six fundamental principles for auditing algorithms.

3.3.1. Choosing the Right Objects (Objectives) of Audit

Any algorithmic audit must have its main emphasis or objectives. In this regard, the Beijing Internet Court has elaborated:

> Fundamentally, algorithms are designs based on the self-values of the designer under the guidance of social values, and therefore cannot be completely excluded from the influence of subjective elements. In practice, there could be algorithmic bias and discrimination. In order to reasonably evaluate algorithms, we need to comprehensively consider the **purposes of algorithms and the process and results of implementing** these algorithms. To objectively and accurately evaluate the application of the algorithms of the disputed software, and also to avoid unjustified suppression by judiciary decisions of the R&D on the application of algorithms, we need to distinguish between the general commercial purpose, the design of rules and the design of algorithms.[51]

To put it more concretely, the following four could reasonably be the right objects (objectives) of algorithmic auditing:

- Performance and Robustness: algorithms should be safe and secure, not vulnerable to tampering or compromising of the data they are trained on. Systems

47 German Bundeskartellamt and French Competition Authority. (2019). *Algorithms and Competition*, at: https://www.autoritedelaconcurrence.fr/sites/default/files/algorithms-and-competition.pdf.

48 Koshiyama, A. et al. (2021). Towards algorithm auditing: A survey on managing legal, ethical and technological risks of AI, 2. *ML and Associated Algorithms*, at: SSRN: https://ssrn.com/abstract=3778998 or http://dx.doi.org/10.2139/ssrn.3778998. This paper has some twenty stakeholders ranging from those working on policy and regulation, to industry practitioners and developers.

49 See Lee, J.-A. (2022). Algorithmic bias and the new Chicago school. *Law, Innovation and Technology, 14(1)*, 95–112, at: https://doi.org/10.1080/17579961.2022.2047520.

50 Koshiyama, A. et al. (2021). Towards algorithm auditing: A survey on managing legal, ethical and technological risks of AI, 26. *ML and Associated Algorithms*, at: SSRN: https://ssrn.com/abstract=3778998 or http://dx.doi.org/10.2139/ssrn.3778998.

51 Beijing Internet Court (2020) Jing Min Chu No. 9526 (decided in 2021). The appeal against this decision was later dropped.

should neither cause nor exacerbate harm or otherwise adversely affect human beings. This entails the protection of human dignity as well as mental and physical integrity.

- Bias and Discrimination: algorithms should avoid unfair treatment of individuals or groups. To diagnose and mitigate bias in decision-making, we first need to differentiate between Individual and Group level fairness.
- Interpretability and Explainability: algorithms should provide decisions or suggestions that can be understood by their users, developers, and regulators.
- Algorithm Privacy: algorithms should be trained to follow data minimization principles as well as adopt privacy-enhancing techniques to mitigate personal or critical data leakage.[52]

These four objects are not independent of each other—they overlap and interact. For example, debias procedures will affect the model performance, global and local interpretation, and, potentially, data minimization aspects.[53]

3.3.2. *Imposing An Asymmetric Audit Obligation*

We are quickly evolving from the "big data" wave to "big algo" wave. Soon there will be "billions" of algorithms making decisions with minimal human intervention.[54] Therefore, it is imperative that algorithm-auditing be targeted at players with significant market power, just like the WTO Reference Paper of 1996: the negotiating group on basic telecommunications targets a "major supplier" which is a supplier which has the ability to materially affect the terms of participation (having regard to price and supply) in the relevant market for basic telecommunications services as a result of control over essential facilities or use of its position in the market.[55]

In conformity with this asymmetric regulation, the 2022 EU Regulation on contestable and fair markets in the digital sector and amending Directives (EU) 2019/1937 and (EU) 2020/1828 (Digital Markets Act, DMA) and Regulation on a Single Market For Digital Services and amending Directive 2000/31/EC (Digital Services Act, DSA) impose independent audit obligation only on designated

52 Koshiyama, A. et al. (2021). Towards algorithm auditing: A survey on managing legal, ethical and technological risks of AI, 8–11. *ML and Associated Algorithms*, at: SSRN: https://ssrn.com/abstract=3778998 or http://dx.doi.org/10.2139/ssrn.3778998.

53 Koshiyama, A. et al. (2021). Towards algorithm auditing: A survey on managing legal, ethical and technological risks of AI, 12. *ML and Associated Algorithms*, at: SSRN: https://ssrn.com/abstract=3778998 or http://dx.doi.org/10.2139/ssrn.3778998.

54 Koshiyama, A. et al. (2021). Towards algorithm auditing: A survey on managing legal, ethical and technological risks of AI, 1–2. *ML and Associated Algorithms*, at: SSRN: https://ssrn.com/abstract=3778998 or http://dx.doi.org/10.2139/ssrn.3778998.

55 See Chou, Y.T., & Liu, K.-C. (2006). The paradoxical impact of asymmetric regulation in Taiwan's telecommunications industry. *Telecommunications Policy, 30*, 171–182.

gatekeepers and very large online platforms (VLOP) and very large online search engines (VLOSE).[56]

Article 15(1) and (3) of the DMA mandates that within six months after its designation as a gatekeeper, it shall submit to the EC an independently audited description of any techniques for profiling of consumers that the gatekeeper applies to or across its core platform services listed in the designation decision. The gatekeeper shall make publicly available an overview of the audited description and update that description and that overview at least annually. Article 15(2) empowers the EC to adopt an implementing act to develop the methodology and procedure of the audit, which is yet to happen.

Article 37(1) of the DSA mandates a similar obligation of independent auditing, asking designated VLOPs and VLOSEs to conduct, at their own expense and at least once a year, independent audits to assess compliance with the obligations set out in Chapter III of DSA and any commitments undertaken pursuant to the codes of conduct and the crisis protocols.

3.3.3. *Resting Duty to Disclose and Explain with Deployer and Operator of the Algorithm*

It should be incumbent on the deployer and operator of algorithms to disclose what kinds of algorithms they are using and the design logic, parameters, and system of algorithms, as they are best in the know. In the Google case,[57] it took the EC years of investigation to find that Google used at least two dedicated algorithms (only one has been disclosed Panda, with the other anonymized), as opposed to normal generic ones,[58] to identify and demote competing comparison-shopping services in Google's general search results.[59] Had Google been subject to the duty to disclose and explain, the case would have been dealt with much faster.

Article 40 of the DSA now provides that for the purposes of providing access to data that are necessary to monitor and assess compliance with the DSA, providers of VLOPs or of VLOSEs shall, at the request of the Commission, etc., explain

56 On April 23, 2023, the EC designated 17 VLOPs and two VLOSEs that reach at least 45 million monthly active users based on the user data that they had to publish by February 17, 2023. The 17 VLOPS include Alibaba AliExpress, Amazon Store, Apple AppStore, Booking.com, Facebook, Google Play, Google Maps, Google Shopping, Instagram, LinkedIn, Pinterest, Snapchat, TikTok, Twitter (now X), Wikipedia, YouTube, and Zalando. The two VLOSEs are Bing and Google Search.

57 On June 27, 2017 the EC concluded that Google abused its dominance in the general internet search market in 13 members of EEA by positioning and displaying more favorably on its general search results pages its own comparison shopping service, and caused harm to its competitors, such as TripAdvisor and Expedia. The EC imposed the highest-ever fine of Euro 2.42 billion on Google.

58 The function of generic algorithms can be summarized as follows: in response to the user query in Google's general search engine, generic search algorithms are used to rank web pages, including those of competing comparison shopping services. These algorithms include the PageRank algorithm. Google also applies a variety of adjustment mechanisms to the results of the PageRank algorithm "to improve the user experience." See Case AT 39740, Para. 345.

59 See Case AT 39740, Para. 359.

the design, the logic, the functioning, and the testing of their algorithmic systems. Similarly, one decision rendered by the Beijing Internet Court is of the opinion that the deployer and operator of the involved algorithms are obliged to disclose the principles, mechanisms, and application procedures of the algorithms.[60]

3.3.4. Audit Should Abide by the Proportionality Principle

There are seven levels of access that an auditor can have of a system. It ranges from the highest level "White-box" where all the details encompassing the model are disclosed to the lowest level to "Process-access" where only indirect observation of a system can be made.[61] Tech giants and major platforms are zealously guarding their "secret sauce"—the complex algorithms. Google is an example in point.[62] Therefore, the proportionality principle should then be called for. It requires that if auditing can achieve algorithmic accountability by looking at the external inputs and outputs of a decision process, rather than at the inner workings,[63] then auditing should not start from the highest level of access and demand the direct disclosure of source code. Sometimes doing so, as suggested by Kroll et al., is neither necessary nor sufficient for algorithmic accountability. Moreover, it may cause the creation of "gaming" strategies, which can subvert the algorithm's efficiency and fairness. In the Google Shopping case, the EC did not examine Google's algorithms per se. Instead, the EC collected and analyzed contemporary documents of Google and its competitors: 5.2 terabytes (TB = 1024 GB) of data, including 1.7 billion actual searches with Google.[64]

3.3.5. Audit Must be Done Independently and Professionally

Who could be the trusted auditors of algorithms?[65] Given the daunting number of auditing, it is justified to empower/mandate a neutral, independent, and professional third-party organization to provide an auditing service. So requires Article 37(3) of the DSA that audits shall be performed by organizations that are independent of, do not have any conflicts of interest with providers of VLOPs or VLOSEs, have proven expertise in the area of risk management, technical competence, and

60 Beijing Internet Court (2021) Jing Min Chu No. 30475(decided in 2022). The decision was not appealed.

61 Koshiyama, A. et al. (2021). Towards algorithm auditing: a survey on managing legal, ethical and technological risks of AI, 4. *ML and Associated Algorithms*, at: SSRN: https://ssrn.com/abstract=3778998 or http://dx.doi.org/10.2139/ssrn.3778998.

62 Pasquale, F. (2015). *The Black Box Society—Secret Algorithms That Control Money and Information* (p. 13). Harvard University Press.

63 Kroll, J.A. et al. (2017). Accountable algorithms. *University of Pennsylvania Law Review, 165*, 633, 654.

64 See Sections 7.2 and 7.3 of Case AT 39740—Google Search (Shopping).

65 Pasquale, F. (2015). *The Black Box Society—Secret Algorithms That Control Money and Information* (p. 141). Harvard University Press.

capabilities, and have proven objectivity and professional ethics, based in particular on adherence to codes of practice or appropriate standards.

Auditors,

> should comply with core independence requirements for prohibited non-auditing services, firm rotation, and non-contingent fees, in order to perform their tasks in an adequate and trustworthy manner. If their independence and technical competence is not beyond doubt, they should resign or abstain from the audit engagement.[66]

The audit report should be substantiated, in order to give a meaningful account of the activities undertaken and the conclusions reached. It should help inform, and where appropriate suggest improvements.[67]

3.3.6. Audit Should Demand Reasonable Level of Care from Deployer and Operator of Algorithms

Algorithmic technologies are still being developed and relevant norms of the trade are yet to mature. We should encourage algorithmic innovation by setting a reasonable level of care to be demanded from deployers and operators of algorithms. Any auditing should be pursued with the goal of not stifling innovation and not offsetting the beneficial effects of algorithms for businesses, consumers, and society as a whole.[68]

These same considerations were also expressed by the Beijing Internet Court:

> Algorithms have unavoidable defects. However, their deployer should fulfil the level of care that corresponds to the risks of the algorithms involved. . . . The defendant has fulfilled the duty of providing care corresponding to the risks of the algorithm and taken reasonable precautionary measures to prevent infringement, therefore has no subjective culpa, and did not commit an infringement, although there has been systemic misjudgement caused by technical constrains.[69]

3.4. The Oversight Over the Auditing of Algorithms

The competent authority must have the power to oversee the actual auditing of algorithms, by investigating the audit reports and imposing fines and penalties on

66 Recital (92) of the DSA.

67 Recital (93) of the DSA.

68 See Wagner, G., & Eidenmüller, H. (2018). Down by algorithms? Siphoning rents, exploiting biases and shaping preferences—the dark side of personalized transactions. *University of Chicago Law Review, Forthcoming; Oxford Legal Studies Research Paper No. 20/2018*, 2, at SSRN: https://ssrn.com/abstract=3160276 or http://dx.doi.org/10.2139/ssrn.3160276.

69 Beijing Internet Court (2021) Jing Min Chu No. 30475 (decided in 2022).

non-compliance.[70] Following a fine for non-compliance, the competent authority should take extra care to ensure that non-compliance be remedied in a timely and satisfactory way. Article 75(2) of the DSA therefore prescribes that the infringer shall draw up and communicate, within a reasonable period specified in the authority's decision an action plan setting out the necessary measures which are sufficient to end or remedy the infringement. Those measures shall include a commitment to perform an independent audit and shall specify the identity of the auditors, as well as the methodology, timing, and follow-up of the audit.

4. International Governance on Algorithms and Their Auditing

Any national and unilateral approach towards algorithmic auditing would be ill-advised, as algorithms of major market players could mean the national competitiveness and treasure of the country where they are headquartered. Therefore, the international community must establish an international governance mechanism on algorithms and their auditing, which could consist of a treaty-council-bureau trilogy. The EU and China could lead the initiative.

4.1. The World Algorithm Treaty

An e-commerce initiative was launched at the eleventh WTO Ministerial Conference in Buenos Aires on December 13, 2017, which was co-convened by Japan, Singapore, and Australia. Following the informal meeting of Ministers on the WTO's e-commerce initiative on January 25, 2019, 76 WTO Members, including the EU, US, and China (changing its conservative stance on this issue at the last minute[71]), representing over 90% of global trade issued a Joint Statement on Electronic Commerce. The Joint Statement confirms Members' intention to commence WTO negotiations on trade-related aspects of electronic commerce and seek to achieve a high standard outcome that builds on existing WTO agreements and frameworks with the participation of as many WTO Members as possible.[72]

The e-commerce initiative has witnessed the consolidation of text proposals in areas including cross-border data flows, data localization, source code, electronic transactions frameworks, cybersecurity, and electronic invoicing, as well

70 According to Article 73(1) and (2) of the DSA, the EC can impose fines not exceeding 6% of the infringer's total worldwide annual turnover in the preceding financial year where it finds that the provider, intentionally or negligently violates the DSA; the EC can impose fines not exceeding 1% of the infringer's total annual income or worldwide turnover in the preceding financial year, where they intentionally or negligently supply incorrect, incomplete, or misleading information, etc.

71 Baschuk, B., & Donnan, S. (2019). China to join talks on $25 trillion e-commerce market at last minute. *Bloomberg*, at: https://www.bloomberg.com/news/articles/2019-01-25/china-is-said-to-join-global-e-commerce-talks-at-last-minute.

72 WTO Joint Statement on Electronic Commerce (WT/L/1056).

as advanced discussions on market access.[73] However, no concrete agreement has been reached at the 12th Ministerial Conference held in 2022.

Given the ever-stronger unilateralism exhibited by the US, the prospect of a successful WTO e-commerce agreement is bleak. To create new hope and opportunity for international governance principles and framework for algorithms and their auditing, the world needs new narratives and momentum, a new World Algorithm Treaty (WAT) with its own council and international bureau separated from the WTO, might do the job.

Such a new world governance can only be established if the three leading data-driven economies, the EU, the US, and China can agree on the rules (I) for the exploitation of data, and (II) for auditing algorithms that decide the collection and use of data. It would be naïve to think that this would be easily feasible under the current geopolitical circumstances. However, China driven by its world-leading data-related industries and the EU eager to amplify its Brussel effects as a world leader in setting standards for the data-driven economy, in addition to their shared civil law tradition of constantly codifying rules, China[74] and the EU are actively

73 WTO Joint Statement Initiative on E-commerce Statement by Ministers of Australia. (December 2021). Japan and Singapore, at: https://www.wto.org/english/news_e/news21_e/ji_ecom_minister_statement_e.pdf.

74 The "Guiding Opinions on Strengthening the Comprehensive Governance over Algorithms Applied in the Internet and Information Services" promulgated by the CAC, etc. (effective on September 17, 2021) is probably the first-ever government document on the issue of algorithmic governance among leading ICT countries and deserves our attention. It set the basic principles of algorithm governance: to establish multi-stakeholder security and governance mechanism over algorithms, to promote security management based on classification and grouping of algorithms, to effectively identify algorithms that have high risks, and to protect the IPRs for algorithms. According to the Opinions, China strives to establish within three years or so a comprehensive governance over algorithms that has sound governance mechanisms for algorithmic safety, an oversight system for algorithmic safety, and a well-regulated algorithmic eco-system. The focal points of the three pillars are summarized as follows: **(I) Sound governance mechanisms for algorithmic safety.** China will strengthen the regulatory governance by striving to perfect the policy and regulation of governance over algorithmic safety, to speed up the promulgation of regulations for algorithms, to specify the addressees, scope, requirements, and legal liabilities of algorithmic regulation, to set standards and guidance. China is to optimize the structure of algorithmic governance that would lead to coregulation by multi-stakeholders with governmental scrutiny and oversight, duty-fulfilling enterprises, industrial self-regulation, and societal monitoring. China will impose more duties on enterprises requiring them to establish liability systems for algorithmic safety, ethical review of technologies, and institutions in charge of managing algorithmic safety. **(II) Oversight system for algorithmic safety**. China will try to effectively monitor algorithmic risks by conducting daily monitoring, providing early warnings about hidden hazards of not complying with laws and regulations, unfairness, and unjust resulting from the application of algorithms, and identifying algorithmic safety-related problems. China will actively roll out a safety assessment of algorithms by setting up professional teams, studying the mechanisms and principles of algorithms, assessing the defects and loopholes of algorithms, and proposing targeted counter-measures. China will orderly usher in the registration of algorithms and set up classification and grouping for algorithms. **(III) Well-regulated algorithmic eco-system.** China will set up correct directions for algorithms, which include promoting the core values of socialism, insisting on correct political direction, public opinion orientation, and value orientation. China will work on the openness and transparency of algorithms by urging enterprises to

exploring relevant regimes that are of international ramifications, there is still a beacon of hope if China can show its good faith to the rest of the world by lifting the ban on the US tech giants and major platforms (Google, Facebook, YouTube, X (formerly Twitter), etc.) which are at the same time world's biggest collectors, generators and exploiters of data and deployers and operators of dominant algorithms. China further needs to win the EU's trust[75] by promoting shared values. Only then will the EU broker between China and the US.

4.2. The World Algorithms Council

The World Algorithms Council (WAC), which will be in charge of the administration of the WAT, should be a public-private partnership with multi-stakeholders, especially algorithm giants, following the International Telecommunication Union (ITU)[76] model with 193 Member States as well as some 900 companies, universities, and international and regional organizations.

The first step for the WAC to take would probably be to set up standards for classifying algorithms by varying levels of regulatory scrutiny based on the complexity of the algorithms. In that regard, it is worth considering the setting up of common parameters that would include "public values" and "public interests" in the design of algorithms to keep the operation of algorithms honest.

Then the WAC needs to establish guidance for auditing to ensure that algorithms are developed with adequate neutrality (free of biases and competitive distortion) and margins of safety. The WAC is further to establish satisfactory measures of predictability and explainability, and finally to distribute liability for harm among coders, implementers, distributors, and end-users.[77]

---

timely, reasonably, and effectively disclose the basic principles of algorithms, to adequately explain the results of algorithms, to provide smooth venues for filing complaints, etc.

75 In 2020, the EC announced "A European strategy for data." According to this strategy, "The vision of a common European data space implies an open, but assertive approach to international data flows, based on European values . . . . Building upon the strength of the Single Market's regulatory environment, the EU has a strong interest in leading and supporting international cooperation with regard to data, shaping global standards and creating an environment in which economic and technological development can thrive, in full compliance with EU law . . . The Commission is convinced that international cooperation must be based on an approach that promotes the EU's fundamental values, including protection of privacy. The EU must ensure, therefore, that any access to EU citizen's personal data and European commercially sensitive data is in compliance with its values and legislative framework. In that context, transfers and sharing of data between **trusted countries** should be promoted."

76 The ITU is a treaty organization founded under the aegis of the United Nations, and one of its responsibilities is to develop telecom standards to ensure networks and technologies seamlessly interconnect; see https://www.itu.int/en/about/Pages/default.aspx.

77 See generally Tutt, A. (2017). An FDA for algorithms. *Administrative Law Review, 69*, 83, 107–109.

4.3. The World Algorithms Bureau

The WAC needs to set up its actual algorithmic auditing agency, the World Algorithms Bureau (WAB), which is in line with the call of Samuel Altman, CEO of OpenAI that makes ChatGTP, for coordinated international regulation of generative AI, such as International Atomic Energy Agency.[78] The WAB should be an organization of experts who reflect and represent common and special interests. This is probably the only conceivable way of building a globally trustworthy and consistent algorithm auditing mechanism. The determinations of the WAB can be relied upon by national competent authorities in their law enforcement activities.

If internet/tech giants and dominant platforms, etc. fail to cooperate fully with the WAB for auditing purposes, the WAB should be empowered to monitor dominant algorithms, alert the public of possible dangers associated with major algorithms, advise the public to avoid such algorithms, blacklist their deployers and/or operators, issue corrective orders, and even impose fines.

5. Conclusion

This chapter is written out of the concerns of how to boost a vibrant and sustainable data-driven economy. It hopes to facilitate a comprehensive understanding of different and possible approaches to regulating access to and use of data and auditing algorithms. It proposes six principles for auditing algorithms, some of which have already been put into practice. It even daydreams of a new global governance framework for regulating data and auditing algorithms. Even if this dream is not within the reach of our immediate future, depending on how we collectively work on it, it might nevertheless revitalize or resurrect the e-commerce initiative of the WTO. Anyway, further study and action must follow up.

78 See https://edition.cnn.com/2023/06/09/tech/korea-altman-chatgpt-ai-regulation-intl-hnk/index.html.

Index

Made in the USA
Las Vegas, NV
19 September 2026

8ebab3c2-e83c-420f-9918-10074a6a4369R02